GO BACK TO WHERE YOU CAME FROM

GO BACK TO WHERE YOU CAME FROM

THE BACKLASH AGAINST IMMIGRATION
AND THE FATE OF WESTERN DEMOCRACY

SASHA POLAKOW-SURANSKY

NATION
BOOKS
New York

Nation Books
116 East 16th Street, 8th Floor
New York, NY 10003
www.publicaffairsbooks.com/nation-books
@NationBooks

Printed in the United States of America

First Edition: October 2017

Published by Nation Books, an imprint of Perseus Books, LLC,
a subsidiary of Hachette Book Group, Inc.
Nation Books is a co-publishing venture of the Nation Institute and Perseus Books.

The Hachette Speakers Bureau provides a wide range of authors for
speaking events. To find out more, go to www.hachettespeakersbureau.com
or call (866) 376-6591.

The publisher is not responsible for websites (or their content) that are not owned by the publisher.

Print book interior design by Jack Lenzo

Library of Congress Cataloging-in-Publication Data
Names: Polakow-Suransky, Sasha, 1979– author.
Title: Go back to where you came from : the backlash against immigration and the fate
    of western democracy / Sasha Polakow-Suransky.
Description: First edition. | New York : Nation Books, [2017] | Includes bibliographical
    references and index.
Identifiers: LCCN 2017021269| ISBN 9781568585925 (HC) | ISBN 9781568585932 (EB)
Subjects: LCSH: Europe--Emigration and immigration--Public opinion. | United
    States--Emigration and immigration--Public opinion. | Europe--Emigration and
    immigration--Government policy. | United States--Emigration and immigration-
    -Government policy. | Populism--Europe. | Populism--United States. | Identity
    politics--Europe. | Identity politics--United States. | Europe--Politics and
    government--21st century. | United States--Politics and government--21st century.
Classification: LCC JV7590 .P625 2017 | DDC 304.8/4--dc23
LC record available at https://lccn.loc.gov/2017021269

ISBNs: 978-1-56858-592-5 (hardcover), 978-1-56858-593-2 (ebook)

LSC-C

10 9 8 7 6 5 4 3 2 1

In memory of Ton Beekman,
who showed me the splendor and squalor of Europe

Contents

Section IV
THE NEW NORMAL

Introduction

The Threat Within

THE FRENCH SOCCER STAR PATRICE EVRA HAD JUST PASSED THE BALL across midfield when the first blast shook the Stade de France, a few miles north of Paris, at 9:20 p.m. on November 13, 2015. It was the seventeenth minute of a match between France's national soccer team and Germany's. After a moment of confusion, the crowd cheered, thinking they were hearing fireworks, and the referees allowed the teams to play on.

At 9:25, a team of gunmen mowed down a group of diners at a small Cambodian restaurant in Paris's trendy tenth arrondissement and in a bar across the street. A few minutes later, at 9:30, a second blast shook the Stade de France. President François Hollande took an urgent phone call from his seat at the stadium. The blasts were not fireworks, it turned out, but suicide bombs. Hollande's aides realized a major assault on Paris was under way, and he was soon whisked away to safety.

For the next ten minutes, the attackers left a trail of carnage and dozens of dead as they moved toward the Place de la République, attacking another bar and a restaurant, before one bomber detonated his suicide vest at the Comptoir Voltaire restaurant.

At 9:40, the deadliest of the attacks hit the Bataclan, a popular concert hall where the Eagles of Death Metal were playing to a sold-out crowd of 1,500. For two hours before the shooting began, a group of men sat in a small VW Polo a few hundred meters from the venue. One man recalls seeing them trying to park and went to tell them they'd get a ticket. The men gave him a cold look and didn't roll down the window. "They were wearing jackets," he told journalists, and seemed to be overweight and having trouble turning the steering wheel. "They had a lost look to them, as if they were drugged."[1] Only later did the man realize they looked bundled up because they had been wearing suicide vests.

When the gunmen in the car entered the concert hall, they fired indiscriminately. Most of the crowd fled for the exits, but dozens were shot. A pregnant woman dangled from a window ledge; some played dead for hours on the floor. It was not until after midnight that police stormed the building and killed the attackers. By then, eighty-nine people were dead. Hollande declared the attacks "a horror" on national television and imposed France's first nationwide state of emergency since the height of the Algerian war in 1961.

The shedding of blood in cosmopolitan Paris was met with shock and anger, coming just a few months after terrorists massacred twelve people at the offices of the French satirical magazine *Charlie Hebdo*. In France, a new intellectual undercurrent had already begun to paint Muslims as a fundamental threat to the republic, and the arguments only became more strident after the November 2015 attacks.

Michel Houellebecq's satirical novel *Submission*, which was featured on the cover of *Charlie Hebdo* the week of the massacre, became a best seller.[2] It depicts a France governed by the Muslim Brotherhood after the Socialist Party and center right choose to back it in the 2022 election rather than allow the Front National's leader, Marine Le Pen, to come to power. In Houellebecq's darkly comic dystopia, Parisian women are veiled and the Sorbonne is run by Saudi sheikhs.

The novel appeared in 2015, at a moment when the French intellectual firmament was already saturated with paeans to tradition and warnings of cultural decline. It was released soon after Alain Finkielkraut, one of France's most prominent philosophers, published *L'identité malheureuse* (The Unhappy Identity), which laments a country where those of solid French stock no longer feel at home among halal butchers and Arabic-speaking neighbors.[3] Once a man of the left, Finkielkraut now argues that a fundamental clash of civilizations is destroying French culture. The TV journalist Éric Zemmour published *Le suicide français* (The French Suicide), a common man's companion to Finkielkraut, with fewer philosophical references and more diatribes against the French national soccer team. It argues that the political correctness of the 1968 generation, on issues ranging from immigration to the European Union, has destroyed France.[4] He sold five hundred thousand copies. Both men who so vehemently defend the purity of French national identity happen to be the Jewish sons of parents from abroad (one born to Polish Holocaust survivors, the other to Algerian Jews).[5]

Elsewhere, authors with roots on the left have shaken up national debates: the German banker and Social Democratic Party member Thilo Sarrazin became a best-selling author with *Deutschland schafft sich ab* (Germany Abolishes Itself), a book that foresees the dumbing down of Germany and a loss of competitiveness as Muslim immigrants become a greater share of the population.[6]

All these writers presented the idea of a relentless Islamic tsunami engulfing Europe culturally and demographically, an idea popularized during the 1990s by Bat Ye'or, whose books conjured visions of a dark era of Muslim tyranny.[7] Her fear of "Eurabia" was so acute that she happily championed the arguments of Serbian nationalists during the Bosnian war, warning of the "gradual Muslim penetration of Europe" and attending conferences organized by the inner circle of Radovan Karadžić, who was later convicted of war crimes.[8] Her views spread to a mainstream audience through the best-selling polemics of Bruce Bawer, an American literary critic and gay rights advocate living in Europe who became a leading voice on the anti-Muslim right.

The idea of Islam conquering Europe has become a trope on both sides of the Atlantic, gaining traction with a new generation of politicians like Geert Wilders and Marine Le Pen, and directly inspiring violent killers like Anders Behring Breivik in Norway. In July 2011, Breivik bombed a government building in Oslo, then disguised himself as a policeman and shot down seventy-seven people, mostly children, at a Social Democratic Party summer camp. Bawer responded to that bloodbath by lamenting the fact that Breivik had dealt "a heavy blow to an urgent cause."[9] He later went on to brand Europeans who welcomed Muslim immigration as Quislings, after the Norwegian Nazi collaborator, effectively likening liberals to traitors who let Hitler conquer their homelands.[10]

For many of those denouncing the presence of Islam in Europe, there is an intellectual forefather. Jean Raspail is ninety-two. His phone number is blocked, and he rarely receives visitors at his small apartment decorated with books and memorabilia from his travels. These days, the new right hails him as a prophet.

Raspail's apocalyptic 1973 novel, *The Camp of the Saints*, envisioned boats full of "scraggy branches, brown and black" and "fleshless Gandhi-arms" descending on France's shores. Raspail writes of "an anthill slashed open" and an "endless cascade of human flesh. Every one of the boats, teeming, gushing with bodies, like a tub brimming over. Yes, the Third World had started to overflow its banks, and the West was its sewer."[11] Although Raspail's imagined invaders were not Muslims (they were poor Hindus), the image of the brown masses descending upon the West has been conveniently appropriated by the anti-Muslim right to satisfy current political tastes. As hundreds of thousands of migrants and refugees arrived in Europe from the Middle East and Africa in September 2015, French presidential candidate Marine Le Pen warned that Europe was being flooded with foreigners and urged her Twitter followers to read Raspail.[12]

The Camp of the Saints is a slow-burning account of a disaster foretold. Countries around the world look the other way as a massive fleet carrying hundreds of thousands of refugees approaches Europe. In the novel, the arrival of eight hundred thousand boat people causes a clash between the supposed true defenders of French civilization and the radicals, intellectuals, and hippies who naively welcome the newcomers.

"Already they saw it their mission to guide the flock's first steps on Western soil," Raspail writes contemptuously of the welcoming left. "One would empty out all our hospital beds so that cholera-ridden and leprous wretches could sprawl between their clean white sheets. Another would cram our brightest, cheeriest nurseries full of monster children." He was particularly afraid of miscegenation: "Another would preach unlimited sex, in the name of the one, single race of the future."[13]

His hero, an aging white professor, kills a dreadlocked hippie who tries to commandeer his hillside home to welcome the refugees. The book's chief villain is the smart, suave, mixed-race editor of a prominent left-wing Paris newspaper ("North African by blood, with an elegant crop of kinky hair and swarthy skin—doubtless passed down from a certain black harem slavegirl"). He celebrates the refugees in his columns and earns Raspail's ire as the "concoctor in chief of the poisonous slops poured piping hot each Monday into the feeble, comatose brains of the six hundred thousand readers of his weekly rag, served up in its fancy sauces."[14]

When the boats finally reach France, Raspail describes the landing as a "peaceful assault on the Western World."[15] His hatred barely disguised, he warns his readers, "The monster is here. He's aground off our shores, but he's still full of life. And everywhere, the same plea to throw your doors open, to take him in. Even from the Pope," he wrote in 1973, imagining a Francis-like pontiff, and deriding him as "that feeble voice of the sick Christian world." The book's heroes are those that shoot down refugees or fire on the boats at sea. "Listen to me. For Heaven's sake," Raspail's narrator pleads with his readers: "Shut your doors! Shut them tight, if it's not too late!"[16]

As the question of immigration has come to dominate political debate in wealthy democracies, the arrival of large numbers of asylum seekers has generally been cast one of two ways: far-right nationalists denounce each new wave of immigration as an alien invasion that must be stopped, while many on the progressive left insist that there's no problem. Both views are wrong.

In most societies, rapid immigration is bound to provoke a xenophobic reaction, especially when newcomers compete with locals for jobs, housing, and welfare benefits. Likewise, terrorist attacks tend to pit security concerns against basic liberties and test the resilience of democratic institutions.

When the two occur at the same time—and the terrorists belong to the same ethnic or religious group as the new immigrants—the combination of fear and xenophobia can be a dangerous and destructive force. Fear of fundamentalist Islam (which poses a genuine security threat) and animosity toward refugees (who generally do not) have been conflated in a way that allows populist far-right leaders across the world to seize upon ISIS attacks as a pretext to shut their doors to desperate refugees who are themselves fleeing ISIS.

As these fears have spread, anti-immigrant parties are no longer confined to the political margins. From France and Holland to Germany and Denmark, they are growing quickly, and their rhetoric has seeped into mainstream discourse. In all these countries, the trajectory has been similar. At first, immigrants were strangers and largely ignored. As unemployment rose and it became clear that guest workers planned to stay rather than return home, they came to be seen as competitors for work and welfare. But then came the 9/11 attacks, which put fear of Islamist violence at the center of the immigration debate in Europe and beyond. Suddenly, immigrants were not merely strangers or outcasts competing for jobs and benefits; they were potential terrorists who threatened the social order. In the wake of terrorist attacks in Europe, the debate over immigration and integration has morphed into a full-fledged culture war against what is perceived to be an immutable civilizational enemy that is fundamentally incompatible with Western democratic values. That view has led to a moral panic, and a series of voices have emerged to spread it. Anti-immigration rhetoric and nativist policies are increasingly becoming the new normal in liberal democracies in Europe and beyond—from the United States to Australia—where foreigners, especially Muslims, are seen as usurpers and blamed for society's ills.

Far-right leaders are correct that immigration creates problems; what they miss is that *they* are the primary problem.

The greatest threat to liberal democracies does not come from immigrants and refugees but from the backlash against them by those on the inside who exploit fear of outsiders to chip away at the values and institutions that make our societies liberal. By attempting to deal with the challenges of immigration by publicly denouncing judges, casting aside constitutional protections of minority groups, and stripping some citizens of their nationality, many of the world's most advanced democracies are effectively hitting the self-destruct button rather than take on new passengers.

When I began writing this book in 2015, I thought that none of this would happen tomorrow, and perhaps not even in the next decade, but that the political culture of many tolerant and progressive countries was already moving gradually in a dangerous direction—often with Russian encouragement. I was far too sanguine. Since that time, the Netherlands has passed a law authorizing the government to strip dual nationals of their Dutch citizenship if they are deemed a security threat.[17] A slew of French cities rushed to ban modest swimsuits on the grounds that they were an expression of Islamist radicalism. And in the United States, President Donald Trump attempted to bar immigrants and legal residents with green cards from entering the country and openly attacked the federal judges who halted his order, arguing in his daily Twitter storms that "bad people" are streaming in and that the courts will be to blame if terrorists attack America. Trump's comments are an explicit assault on the separation of powers at the core of American democracy.[18]

Modern liberal democracies have two crucial characteristics: they seek to reflect the will of the majority through elections and to protect the rights of minorities by enshrining them in constitutions and establishing independent judiciaries to check the power of popularly elected leaders.[19] As anti-immigrant parties become more prominent, they are privileging the former and trying to argue that the latter is irrelevant or, worse, anti-democratic. They are democrats only insofar as they believe in majoritarianism. They have no time for constitutional niceties that contradict the supposed will of the people.[20] It does not matter that some of the institutions they deride are foundational pillars of the American or French republic; courts and constitutions are dismissed as undemocratic for not reflecting the political zeitgeist and the current whims of the masses. According to their crudely democratic and profoundly illiberal logic, a passing wave of anti-Islamic sentiment, strongly felt by the majority, should take precedence over more than two hundred years of history.[21]

Rather than accept the easy mantra that liberal democracy is the world's greatest form of government and will therefore inevitably prevail, this book seeks to ask difficult questions about what happens if it does not. Just as authoritarian state capitalism is today seen as a viable, and even desirable, alternative model of governance from Russia to China to the Persian Gulf, an eroded form of democracy—one that is less liberal and less inclusive—could one day supplant the constitutional order that currently prevails in Western countries that are viewed by the outside world as progressive and tolerant but are now struggling to cope with an influx of migrants and refugees.

Indeed, if nativist populist parties continue to rise in popularity while terrorism remains an ever-present threat, they will eventually seek to curtail and trample the rights of immigrants and minorities. When that happens, constitutional democracies that are presumed to be stable and secure will be at risk of decay as populist demands for tough border policies and security trump commitments to protect civil liberties and minority rights, transforming countries that we once thought of as icons of liberalism into democracies only in name.

THE POLITICIANS AT THE VANGUARD OF TODAY'S ANTI-IMMIGRANT movement are far savvier than their predecessors. In Europe, Hitler cast a long shadow over politics for decades, making it difficult for viable leaders to emerge on the far right of the political spectrum. Today's anti-immigrant politicians have therefore gone to great pains to distance themselves from past populists with a penchant for scapegoating minorities and foreigners. They and their intellectual enablers warn that the presence of large numbers of Muslims poses a dire threat to European civilization, but they are adamant that there is no comparison between hostility to Muslims today and the anti-Semitism of the past. Jews never killed anyone, they claim; their transgressions were simply in the imagination of anti-Semites.[22] They forget the consequences of another violent act that shook Paris in November 1938, nearly seventy-seven years to the day before the carnage at the Bataclan.

In the summer of 1936, the fifteen-year-old Herschel Grynszpan left his hometown of Hanover, where his Jewishness was making it impossible to find work. First, he went to Belgium. Headed south, he then stowed away on a streetcar filled with factory laborers commuting to work across the border and made his way illegally into France, where he stayed with an aunt and uncle in Paris.[23] At a time when Poland was stripping its Jewish citizens of their nationality and the Nazi government was preparing to remove Jews from Germany, Grynszpan was caught in between.[24] Although he was born in Germany, he did not hold German citizenship, thanks to German law's emphasis on blood descent; his family was Polish. As Hitler cemented his hold on power, this legal distinction became deadly.

Two years later, on November 3, 1938, Grynszpan received a letter from his sister. "On Thursday evening rumors circulated that all Polish Jews had been expelled from the city. But we didn't believe it," she wrote. Then the Gestapo came to their door, and a police van took them away. "Each of us had an extradition order pressed into his hand," his sister told him. "They didn't permit us to return home anymore."[25]

In the newspapers, Grynszpan had already read of rampant disease and suicide attempts among the Jews deported to the Polish border; he knew his parents and sister were among them. When his uncle refused to send money to the family, Herschel was furious. He left the house and checked into a cheap hotel near Paris's Gare de l'Est. The next morning, Monday, November 7, he bought a gun from a nearby shop and took the Metro to the German embassy near the Quai d'Orsay. He told the security officers at the gate that he wished to apply for a visa and requested to see a diplomat once inside.[26]

Grynszpan was led to an office and closed the door behind him. With the price tag still hanging from the gun, he calmly fired five shots at Ernst vom Rath, the twenty-nine-year-old German consular official on duty. Three of the bullets missed; two struck Rath in the abdomen. Grynszpan showed no remorse. "From the moment I read my sister's postcard on Thursday," he told his French interrogators, "I decided to kill a member of the embassy."[27]

His victim did not die immediately, and Adolf Hitler and his propagandists put the attack and the dying man's struggle to immediate use. Hitler granted Rath a diplomatic promotion and sent his personal doctor to Paris to treat him. Joseph Goebbels immediately instructed Germany's pliant press to ensure that the assassination "completely dominate the front page."[28] The headlines blared: JEWISH MURDER ATTEMPT IN PARIS—MEMBER OF THE GERMAN EMBASSY CRITICALLY WOUNDED BY SHOTS—THE MURDERING KNAVE A 17-YEAR-OLD JEW. Another hinted of what was to come: THE SHOTS IN PARIS WILL NOT GO UNPUNISHED![29] Not even the führer's private physician could save him. Rath succumbed to his injuries on the evening of November 9 and quickly became a Nazi martyr.

When the news reached him, Hitler was in Munich, celebrating the anniversary of the 1923 Beer Hall Putsch, when he had tried and failed to overthrow the Bavarian government and landed himself in prison, where he dictated the text of *Mein Kampf* to his cellmate Rudolf Hess.

Hitler made it clear that no restraints should be placed on the "outraged people" of the Third Reich in retaliating for the Paris attack. "For once," Goebbels wrote in his personal diary, "the Jews should feel the rage of the people."[30]

Crowds had gathered at Munich's Old Town Hall to celebrate the putsch anniversary, and Goebbels knew how to stir their emotions. By then, the papers had dutifully trumpeted news of the shooting. "Ernst vom Rath was a good German, a loyal servant of the Reich, working for the good of our people in our embassy in Paris," Goebbels intoned. "Do I need to tell you the race of the dirty swine who perpetrated this foul deed?" he continued. "A Jew! Tonight he lies in jail in Paris, claiming that he acted on his own, that he had no instigators of this awful deed behind him."[31]

In the minds of Nazi propagandists, Grynszpan could not possibly be an isolated criminal; he had to be part of a larger plot. The Nazis' goal was to assign collective blame for the shooting and thereby legitimize collective punishment. "Comrades, we cannot allow this attack by international Jewry to go unchallenged!" Goebbels exclaimed. "Our people must be told, and their answer must be ruthless," he declared. "Together we must plan what is to be our answer to Jewish murder and the threat of international Jewry to our glorious German Reich!"[32]

What followed would come to be known as Kristallnacht. Later that night, Goebbels sent directives to the police and party officials, ordering spontaneous acts of violence. Synagogues were to be burned, Jewish shops vandalized, and all Jews with weapons disarmed and shot if they resisted.[33] Kristallnacht was a dramatic break with previous policy and a wake-up call to world leaders who had assumed Hitler was not a serious threat; it was the first instance of mass state-directed violence against Jews.[34] Even the graffiti to be plastered on Jewish property was prescribed: "Revenge for the murder of vom Rath!"[35]

At the time, most Jews saw Grynszpan as the direct cause of their misfortune and deeply resented him. The World Jewish Congress denounced the assassination, and Jewish writers sought to disown Grynszpan. With hindsight, many now regard him as a forgotten hero and valiant exemplar of Jewish resistance.[36]

On a moral level, there is no comparison between Grynszpan's act and the gratuitous violence of the Bataclan massacre in Paris, but there are parallels between the reactions that followed each attack. Regardless of whether the perpetrators were Jewish or Muslim, opportunistic politicians sought to capitalize on public anger. Both incidents were used to mobilize support for ostracizing, expelling, or stripping rights from an entire group due to the acts of a few of its members, or even to justify outright violence against them.

There has been no state-sponsored violence against Muslims in Western Europe, but the language used by populist politicians to target a group and all its members, from labeling North African minorities "scum" to calling for "de-Islamization," has a not-so-distant precedent. As World War II ended, there were a few prominent thinkers who foresaw that, despite the horrors of the Holocaust, a new backlash against another minority could one day arise. Not surprisingly, those who predicted that this danger might one day return were German Jews who survived the war.

DECADES BEFORE THE SWISS TOWN OF DAVOS BECAME A DESTINATION for global elites to mingle at exclusive parties and earnestly discuss the fate of the world, it was better known for hosting a debate that marked a decisive rupture in European thought. In 1929, Ernst Cassirer, an assimilated Jew and one of Germany's most prominent philosophers, squared off against Martin Heidegger, the rising star of German philosophy. Cassirer, a lonely defender of the Weimar Republic, argued for the continuing relevance of Enlightenment reason, whereas Heidegger advanced the revolutionary idea that all humans were "thrown" into the stream of history, unable to escape it or change its course. Four years later, in 1933, Heidegger was appointed head of the University of Freiburg, declared his support for Hitler, and joined the Nazi Party. Cassirer fled to England, then Sweden, and finally to the United States. He died in April 1945, three weeks before the Nazis surrendered. Before his death, Cassirer wrote, "the new philosophy did enfeeble and slowly undermine the forces that could have resisted the modern political myths" that gave rise to Nazi dictatorship. As a defender of Weimar Germany's doomed liberal constitutional government, he was skeptical of thinking that abandoned the quest for "objective and universally valid truth." In his view, "such philosophy renounces its own fundamental theoretical and ethical ideals. It can be used, then, as a pliable instrument in the hands of the political leaders."[37]

Cassirer had been a defender of the Weimar Republic's constitution several years before it collapsed into fascist tyranny. Even at a moment when the Nazis had won only 2 percent of the national vote, he knew all was not well in Weimar Germany and was at pains to prove that liberal democracy was not an un-German import. Constitutionalism was "by no means an alien presence in the whole of German intellectual history, let alone an intruder from beyond," Cassirer declared in a speech at the University of Hamburg.[38] Instead, he maintained, it was rooted in German philosophy and idealism.[39] As the next years tragically proved, Hitler and Goebbels managed to seduce most Germans with a very different set of authentically German political ideas.

In Cassirer's view, it was the propagation of what he called political myth—the carefully crafted sense of a collective destiny and duty—that transformed a constitutional democracy into a genocidal state in the span of a few years. "Germany's whole social and economic system was threatened with complete collapse," he recalled. "The normal resources seemed to have been exhausted," paving the way for a dramatic rupture.[40]

In times of peace, an orderly rational society "seems to be safe against all attacks." But in politics, Cassirer warned, "we are always living on volcanic soil." The eruption comes if a society's collective wish is frustrated—when, as he wrote, "all hopes of fulfilling this desire, in an ordinary and normal way, have failed." A society's fears and desires then become embodied in a strong and all-powerful leader. And at such a moment, Cassirer warned, "the former social bonds—law, justice and constitutions—are declared to be without any value." All that matters is the power of the leader and the myth he propagates.[41] It was a danger, in Cassirer's view, that could strike even in a modern democratic state. Rather than assume that democracy was stable, he insisted, citizens should "always be prepared for violent concussions that may shake our cultural world and our social order to its very foundations."[42]

The risk remained because the force of political myth is never truly vanquished. "It is always there, lurking in the dark and waiting for its hour and opportunity," Cassirer wrote. He foresaw the rise of spin doctors, who would play a central role in the manipulation of news. "The new political myths do not grow up freely. . . . They are artificial things fabricated by very skilful and cunning artisans," he argued. The molding of public opinion, he predicted, would become much more important than any army's arsenal. It was not the military rearmament of Germany that had laid the foundations for Nazism, he maintained. That was merely "the necessary consequence of the mental rearmament brought about by the political myths."[43]

The *Myth of the State* was the last book Cassirer ever wrote, and it was published posthumously. He was not optimistic despite his exile in the United States. "We are always threatened with a sudden relapse into the old chaos," he warned. "We are building high and proud edifices; but we forget to make their foundations secure." The Nazi myths were dismissed by many Jews and intellectuals as "so fantastic and ludicrous that we could hardly be prevailed upon to take them seriously," he recalled. "We should not commit the same error a second time."[44]

By the early 1990s, the threat of a relapse into chaos and Cassirer's dark warnings had almost completely disappeared from political debate. The Berlin Wall had fallen, the Soviet Union was a thing of the past, and despite the gathering clouds of war in the Balkans, where nationalist leaders were propagating the sort of myths of racial superiority that would once again bring genocide to European soil, there was giddy talk of a "peace dividend."

But the idea of "the end of history"—the popular idea that liberal democracy had definitively triumphed over communism after the Cold War—was always a fantasy. Since 1989, the world has seen state-sponsored mass murder in Bosnia and Rwanda and the resurgence of authoritarian powers. Indeed, the prevailing model of governance that exists in most Western European countries today was never inevitable, and its long-term survival is by no means guaranteed.[45]

Nor was democracy a guarantee of liberalism, as so many reflexively assumed. In 1997, long before he was a household name on CNN, Fareed Zakaria wrote an essay entitled "The Rise of Illiberal Democracy." The reflexive American assumption that democracies are necessarily liberal, with independent institutions and political freedoms, was wrong, he argued. "Today the two strands of liberal democracy, interwoven in the Western political fabric, are coming apart in the rest of the world. Democracy is flourishing; constitutional liberalism is not," he warned.[46]

Twenty years later, Zakaria's fear—at the time focused on countries like India and Venezuela—is coming to pass in the West as well. In his book on the topic, *The Future of Freedom,* Zakaria pointed out that the great political philosophers had foreseen the clash as early as the eighteenth century. Immanuel Kant, the intellectual forefather of those who adhere today to the theory that democratic governments are more peaceful, was never a fan of democracies. Kant thought they risked becoming tyrannical. Likewise, James Madison and Alexis de Tocqueville worried about the tyranny of the majority. Populist leaders, they knew then, have no time for courts or parliaments that check their power.

Democratization is not an unqualified good; it can go badly wrong if the majority's preference happens to be aggression. After all, there are many countries where most voters might favor systematic killing or expulsion of disliked neighbors or ethnic minorities. For Zakaria, it was liberalism, not democracy, that kept the peace.[47]

For democracy to remain on track in turbulent conditions, Zakaria insisted, the institutional "guardrails" must be strong. If they were not, a state could veer catastrophically off course. To survive, democracies would have to bind themselves to the mast, as Odysseus did when sailing past the beguiling songs of the sirens, constraining themselves from the temptation to overreach or self-destruct.[48]

"Constitutional liberalism is about the limitation of power; democracy is about its accumulation and use," Zakaria wrote.[49] At a moment when President Trump is openly questioning the legitimacy of federal judges appointed by Republican presidents and French mayors are seeking to ban religious Muslims from public beaches due to their choice of swimwear, it is a lesson worth recalling. "The institutions and attitudes that have preserved liberal democratic capitalism in the West were built over centuries," Zakaria argued. "They are being destroyed in decades. Once torn down they will not be so easy to repair."[50]

FIVE YEARS AFTER ZAKARIA'S ESSAY ON ILLIBERAL DEMOCRACY FIRST appeared, Jean-Marie Le Pen stunned all of Europe by defeating the Socialist candidate, Lionel Jospin, and advancing to the final round of the 2002 French presidential election. Terrified by the prospect of a far-right victory, the French left—including Communists, Greens, and Socialists—threw their support behind the incumbent president, Jacques Chirac, a pillar of the center-right establishment who had served as mayor of Paris for eighteen years before becoming president in 1995. This electoral strategy effectively isolated Le Pen's Front National (FN), depicting it as a cancerous force in the French body politic.

Two weeks later, on May 5, Chirac won the election with an astronomical 82 percent of the vote, trouncing Le Pen by the biggest margin in a French presidential election since 1848. Raucous celebrations spilled into the streets of Paris. "We have gone through a time of serious anxiety for the country. But tonight, France has reaffirmed its attachment to the values of the republic," Chirac declared in his victory speech. Then, speaking to the joyous crowds in the Place de la République, he lauded them for rejecting "intolerance and demagoguery."[51]

But May 2002 was not, in fact, a moment of triumph. Rather, it was the dying gasp of an old order in which the fate of European nations was controlled by large establishment parties.

Jean-Marie Le Pen was an easy target for the left and for establishment figures such as Chirac. He was a political provocateur who appealed as much to anti-Semites and homophobes as to voters upset about immigration and drew his support largely from the most reactionary elements of the old Catholic right. He was a familiar villain, and his ideology represented an archaic France, a defeated past. Moreover, he did not seriously aim for power and never really came close to acquiring it; his role was to be a rabble-rouser and to inject his ideas into the national debate.

In 2017, Europe's new far right is different. From Denmark to the Netherlands to Germany, a new wave of right-wing parties has emerged over the past decade and a half, and they are casting a much wider net than Jean-Marie Le Pen ever attempted to. And by deftly appealing to fear, nostalgia, and resentment of elites, they are rapidly broadening their base.

Unlike her incendiary father, Marine Le Pen ran a disciplined political operation during the 2017 presidential campaign and has proven that her party can win half of the vote or more in regions from the Côte d'Azur in the south, where she took 49 percent, to Pas-de-Calais in the north, where she won a 52 percent majority. She and her Danish and Dutch counterparts are not—as some on the left would like to believe—unreconstructed fascists or inconsequential extremists with fringe ideas lacking popular appeal.

These parties have steadily chipped away at the establishment's hold on power by pursuing a new and devastatingly effective electoral strategy. They have shed some of the right's most unsavory baggage, distancing themselves from skinheads, neo-Nazis, and homophobes. And they have deftly co-opted the causes, policies, and rhetoric of their opponents, seeking to outflank the left by blending a nativist economic policy—more welfare, but only for *us*—and tough anti-immigration and border security measures. By painting themselves as the protectors of social benefits that are threatened by an influx of freeloading migrants, they appeal to both economic anxiety and fear of terrorism.

The new populists have also effectively claimed the progressive causes of the left—from gay rights to women's equality and protecting Jews from anti-Semitism—as their own, by depicting Muslim immigrants as the primary threat to all three groups. The result is that liberal Democrats have begun to denounce Islam in the name of defending Enlightenment values, giving birth to a new form of far-right politics dressed up in progressive garb.[52] As fear of Islam has spread, with the populist right's encouragement, these parties have presented themselves as the only true defenders of Western identity and Western liberties—the last bulwark protecting a besieged Judeo-Christian civilization from the barbarians at the gates.

They have steadily filled an electoral vacuum left open by social democratic and center-right parties, who ignored festering resentment for years, opting for moral purity and political correctness rather than engaging with their own voters' growing anger over immigration—some of it legitimate, some of it bigoted. When it was already too late to prevent an exodus of angry working-class voters, establishment parties began to adopt the rhetoric of populist xenophobes, pushing the entire political spectrum to the right.

Brexit and Donald Trump's victory were just the beginning—and Marine Le Pen's defeat does not signal a turning of the tide. The new far right, from Europe to the United States and beyond, is poised to transform the political landscape of Western democracies, either by winning elections or simply by pulling a besieged political center so far in its direction that its ideas become the new normal.

To best understand how we reached this point, we must go back to the moment when Muslim immigrants first began to arrive.

SECTION I

FROM STRANGERS TO OUTCASTS

1

The Guests Who Overstayed

THE DUTCH COLONIZED THE WORLD'S LARGEST MUSLIM NATION FOR centuries. Their control of Indonesia was a brutal affair. Soldiers sang, "Wipe out that vermin, humiliate their nation / Plant in them the Dutch tricolour that brings civilization." A future prime minister, Hendrikus Colijn, serving as an officer in Indonesia during the late nineteenth century, wrote to his wife: "I've had to gather together 9 women and 3 children, who begged for mercy, and have them shot dead there and then. It was unpleasant work but there was no other way. The soldiers relished spearing them with their bayonets."[1]

When the Dutch finally left in 1949, they evacuated their local allies, the indigenous group known as the Moluccans. Just as the French evacuated the Algerian "harkis," who had collaborated with the French army, along with the pied-noir settler population, the Dutch brought the Moluccans north. "They had no choice, since the Indonesians would not let the 'traitors' go home," explains the Dutch-born historian Ian Buruma. But the Moluccans weren't interested in staying in the Netherlands. They were promised a swift return, which never happened; the Indonesians didn't want any traitors coming home. Instead, they were warehoused in the country's darkest corners, like the former Nazi transit camp of Westerbork, where thousands of Dutch Jews had been held just ten years earlier, before being sent east to the gas chambers.[2]

With labor shortages in key industries, the Dutch government— like Germany's—began to import large numbers of guest workers in the 1960s, most of them from Turkey and Morocco. Back then, it was not a left-wing position to support immigration. It was the free-market right that wanted open borders and pushed for the postwar guest worker scheme; unions and Social Democrats were hesitant, arguing the country should only do this if its own workers did not suffer.

The guest workers of that era were a boon for business; they did jobs the Dutch didn't want and accepted low wages. But no one anticipated the consequences down the line. The economic benefits started to look less desirable once it became clear they might not go back. Eventually, they were entitled to certain rights and developed expectations. The only alternative to granting equal social rights was to withhold citizenship based on birth.[3]

Some countries, like Germany, left guest workers' families in legal limbo for many years, barring the domestic-born children of immigrants from gaining nationality, thanks to citizenship laws based on blood descent.[4] But the idea of differential rights clashed with fundamental postwar European values. Hitler had tried to build a world based on racial hierarchy. After the war, the idea of excluding racial or religious groups was anathema to everything postwar Europe stood for. And when this modern notion of citizenship ran up against the unexpected presence of migrants, the default was to include rather than exclude foreigners.[5] It was one thing to restrict entry at the border; it was something else to deny people access to citizenship once admitted.[6]

All modern states distinguish between members and nonmembers. They are closed to outsiders on some level, and the legal consequences of that closure are significant, making citizenship a valuable asset for insiders and a coveted goal for foreigners. No one thinks to question, for instance, the fact that legal foreign residents cannot vote in national elections in most countries.[7]

The dilemmas posed by guest workers in Western Europe touched Britain, too. When large numbers of workers from the former colonies showed up after World War II, it was completely unforeseen. As citizens of the Commonwealth, millions of people across the former empire had the right to come to Britain; when the House of Commons debated citizenship laws in 1948, hardly anyone thought these erstwhile imperial subjects would take up the offer. When they did come, Jamaicans were shocked to see whites doing hard manual labor. Others immigrated due to specific local circumstances. When Pakistan built the Mangla Dam in the early 1960s, it displaced huge numbers of people; many of them went to work in the textile factories of northern England. Today, most of Britain's Pakistani population can trace its roots to the Mirpur district near the dam. It was not planned; the arrival of Britain's minority population occurred largely "in a fit of absence of mind."[8]

In France, the arrival of huge numbers of Algerians was directly related to war. Technically, the Algerians who moved to France before 1962 were not even immigrants, though that term is frequently used today to describe them and their children. Algeria was considered an integral part of France throughout the nineteenth century. When France finally granted Algeria independence after a bloody war, those who had enjoyed a special status in mainland France were, overnight, transformed into foreigners.[9]

When Holland's guest workers started to arrive in the 1960s, no one expected them to stay, let alone one day share the rights Dutch citizens enjoyed. When the economy took a downturn during the 1973 oil crisis, they could not simply be evicted. After all, Holland wasn't like today's Persian Gulf states, where most of the population is foreign and enjoys no citizenship rights at all.[10] Those small authoritarian monarchies can just kick people out; liberal democracies can't. And as more people remained, it became more difficult to reverse.

Soon, their wives and children joined them, at a time when many of the men were out of work. "Their stay was supposed to have been temporary, to clean out oil tankers, work in steel factories, sweep the streets," wrote historian Ian Buruma.[11] Gradually, immigrants moved into working-class areas, and white flight followed. It was only a matter of time before the issue exploded as both the number of immigrants and their demands for a place in society increased.

FOR CRITICS OF EUROPEAN IMMIGRATION POLICY, LIKE THE AMERICAN journalist Christopher Caldwell, the move toward inclusion was a fatal error. Even worse was that it might be the result of postcolonial guilt.[12]

It's an argument that was first articulated by the French philosopher Pascal Bruckner in his trenchant attack on white liberal guilt, *Tears of the White Man: Compassion as Contempt*. For Bruckner, the leftist ideas that were once subversive had become a "new conformism."[13] Europe was still behaving like an imperial power, he argued, but had become "messianic in a minor key. . . . Our superiority complex has taken refuge in the perpetual avowal of our sins."[14] But while some on the left looked the other way out of conformist solidarity with the third world, others were seething.

The increasingly hostile reaction to these "strangers" in the European capitals of the 1980s and 1990s was not a new phenomenon. The same had occurred a century before. The *London Evening Standard* warned of "vast foreign areas" and "Jewish anarchist gangs" in the nineteenth century; even Jack the Ripper was assumed to be a Jewish criminal.[15] In the United States, Catholic immigrants aroused intense hatred and violent backlash against "papists." Indeed, anti-Catholicism was a driving force behind the rebirth of the Ku Klux Klan in 1915; apart from engaging in violent terrorism, the KKK's primary policy goal was restricting non-Protestant immigration.

State legislatures in Arkansas, Florida, and Georgia passed "convent inspection laws" allowing the search of Catholic Church property on the grounds that young women were being enslaved as nuns and weapons for an imagined Catholic uprising might be stored there. (Americans fighting for women's suffrage were often virulently anti-Catholic, a position that prefigured the stance of today's anti-Islamic feminists.)[16] In 1921, a Klansman shot the Irish-born priest James Coyle on his doorstep in Birmingham, Alabama.[17]

Anti-Semitism was equally rife. By 1939, Hitler had conquered much of Central Europe, and Jewish refugees were fleeing to any country that would take them. That year, Congress rejected a bill that would have admitted twenty thousand German Jewish children, and public opinion polls showed that 83 percent of Americans were against relaxing immigration restrictions, and more than 60 percent opposed admitting Jewish children fleeing Europe.[18]

As late as 1950, mainstream writers in the United States were, like the suffragists, warning of the dangers posed by Catholics.[19] Paul Blanshard, the author of *American Freedom and Catholic Power,* was praised in left-wing magazines like the *Nation* and the *New Republic* as he warned of a group incapable of being integrated due to its "undemocratic system of alien control" and adherence to an ideology rooted in "medieval authoritarianism." Ten years before the election of John F. Kennedy banished anti-Catholic hatred into obscurity, liberal magazines were earnestly praising a xenophobic writer, viewing him as "a committed liberal who saw in the conservatism of the new immigrant neighborhoods a set of grave threats to the foundations of liberalism."[20]

Irish nationalists were also frequently denounced as supporters of terrorist groups across the Atlantic. As the Canadian journalist Douglas

Saunders writes, "The public tended to see Irish political violence not as a matter of politics or nationality but simply as an extension of the immigrants' religion"[21]—a refrain that is heard again today.[22]

WHEN THE JOBS THAT HAD DRAWN GUEST WORKERS TO HOLLAND BEGAN to disappear after the 1973 oil crisis, foreigners suddenly accounted for three times as many claims as native Dutch. But it was frowned upon to criticize these skewed numbers. As the Dutch welfare state frayed and expectations rose, the safety net no longer worked so well.[23]

By the 1980s, Holland was suddenly receiving a stream of newcomers who had no familiarity with the country's peculiar and unique customs—from never closing one's curtains during the day to cycling everywhere—that sometimes baffle even Brits and Germans. Sexual freedom and respect for gay rights were even more foreign to those from conservative cultures. The Dutch were being forced to explain something that was reflexively understood by natives and that they valued because it was implicit. Many were nostalgic for the days when everyone looked the same and knew what to say and do.[24]

By the end of the decade, the terms of debate on the left and the demands made by minorities had begun to shift, too. For decades, immigrants and their children had been focused on demanding equality. "What preoccupied them was not the desire to be treated differently but the fact that they *were* treated differently,"[25] argues the British writer Kenan Malik.

The Iranian government's fatwa against Salman Rushdie in 1989 was a turning point for the left. It was the moment when identity politics, under the banner of antiracism, replaced a commitment to individual liberties on the political left; religious fundamentalists threatening a writer with death no longer activated leftist passions. Rushdie himself was once a leading voice in these antiracism campaigns. He told a TV audience in 1982, "Four hundred years of conquest and looting . . . this stain has seeped into every part of the culture, the language and daily life. . . . British thought, British society has never been cleansed of the filth of imperialism. It's still there, breeding lice and vermin."[26]

But for antiracist activists, there seemed to be few results. Years of protests had "done little to dislodge skinheads from the streets, to prevent deportations, or to lessen the pain of beatings in police cells," writes

Malik. "Much of that anger, bitterness and bravado was looking for a new home." Radical Islamic organizations had a ready pool to draw on at a time when radicals were becoming disillusioned with the left. Meanwhile, the left was abandoning its commitment to universal values and embracing multiculturalism by focusing on people as members of communities rather than as fellow citizens.[27] And that meant, for an angry young rebel without a cause, that Islamist fundamentalism was very appealing. Malik's friend Hassan went from fighting off skinheads in the early 1980s to joining a radical Islamist group at the end of the decade.

In France, the shift was similar. In 1983, young Frenchmen and women of North African background marched all the way from Lyon to Paris. It was known as the March of the Beurs, a colloquial name for North African Arabs. The movement demanded an end to police brutality and hate crimes and aimed to counter the anti-immigrant vitriol of Jean-Marie Le Pen's Front National, which was just beginning to emerge as a political force. But that movement quickly faded. In some ways, it was co-opted by the Socialist Party, stripping it of its antiestablishment street cred. Mostly, however, argues the American writer Paul Berman, "the new movement was defeated by a newer movement, which competed for support in the immigrant neighborhoods." Islamists in Lyon were claiming they were the "true and authentic tribune of the poor and the downtrodden." In the worldview of the radical left, they seemed to be a true expression of proletarian resistance. "And, in a spirit of Marxist solidarity, the Trotskyists reached out," writes Berman.[28] Even the trade unions were using Islamic rhetoric in their strikes.[29]

On the other side of the political spectrum, a new intellectual force was taking shape, centered around the secretive Club de l'Horloge, the *Figaro* newspaper, and a group of conservative intellectuals, among them the *Figaro* columnist Alain de Benoist. It was known as GRECE, a French acronym alluding to ancient Greece, which stands for Research and Study Group for European Civilization. The left's reaction to this new intellectual branch of the right was largely to ignore it. By refusing to engage with their arguments or denouncing them as fascists, the left let the new right's vanguard evolve in the shadows. But these figures made an indelible impact on the ideology of the FN and the French right more broadly. Ideas like exclusive national preference in allocating social benefits started in those circles in the mid-1980s and remain an integral part of the FN's platform today.[30]

AHMED MARCOUCH GREW UP IN RURAL MOROCCO WITHOUT HIS FATHER, who had gone to Europe as a guest worker. He came to Holland in 1979, when he was ten, speaking neither Arabic nor Dutch, from a village with no electricity, water, schools, or buses. The journey from the Rif mountains was, for him, like being in "a time machine."[31]

The flight from Morocco to Holland is less than three hours, but for a ten-year-old it was "not only 3,000 kilometers" but also "100 years into the future" in terms of clothes and ideas. The family had to travel miles to find halal meat or staples of Moroccan cooking, like olive oil. Ahmed was one of fifteen children. When he arrived, he lived with his father and several siblings in a one-room apartment—with a curtain as a separator—in Amsterdam's east. He soon realized that his father couldn't fully function in Dutch society and needed his help.

He and his siblings respected their father as an authority figure, but the role reversal was jarring. "After a few years, you see that your father . . . doesn't know anything about the society," he recalls. It was up to the kids to translate. "My father asked me to read for him—the letters from the government." At the time, Marcouch was twelve and had less than two years of education in any language.[32]

At first, he wanted to be a carpenter. Then he got a job in a paper factory and in 1992 became a police officer in one of the rougher parts of the city. In 2010, he became a member of parliament for the Labor Party, with an office larger than the apartment he first lived in.[33]

Holland is famed as a tolerant society, largely owing to its decriminalization of soft drugs and prostitution and its generally permissive attitude toward everything from premarital sex to gay marriage. But in recent years, the overwhelming political force in society has been fear. And fear and tolerance never go together.

According to Marcouch, many of those supporting Geert Wilders's far-right Party for Freedom (Partij voor de Vrijheid, or PVV), were once Labor Party voters. Moreover, he says, they come from the very neighborhoods that families like his own moved into in the 1980s. Like the East Enders who left London for Essex in the 1980s and 1990s and became the backbone of the UK Independence Party (UKIP) in outer London and contributed to the impressively strong showing for the "Leave" camp during the Brexit referendum, those who left the eastern and western fringes of Amsterdam and moved to outlying areas that are now strongly pro-PVV feel something has been taken from them and that the neighborhoods they once called home are no longer recognizable. "They moved on without moving on," says Marcouch. For those who stayed behind, the feeling was "this is not my neighborhood anymore. I can't recognize my neighborhood. I can't talk with my neighbors. Their foods smell."[34]

It is similar to the refrain heard in old working-class areas of London. Michael Collins was a child growing up in the gritty South London neighborhood of Walworth when the conservative politician Enoch Powell gave an infamous speech in 1968. "Whole areas, towns and parts of towns across England will be occupied by sections of the immigrant and immigrant-descended population," warned Powell. Britain was, he argued, "a nation busily engaged in heaping up its own funeral pyre."

He compared complaints of discrimination from the left to those who tried to blind the country to the peril of Nazi Germany. For Powell, it was not immigrants who were suffering but white Englishmen. "The discrimination and the deprivation, the sense of alarm and of resentment, lies not with the immigrant population but with those among whom they have come and are still coming," he declared. "As I look ahead, I am filled with foreboding; like the Roman, I seem to see 'the River Tiber foaming with much blood.'"[35]

Collins recalls the murmurs of "Enoch was right" whispered throughout his neighborhood in the late 1960s. "We knew he looked like the kind of stranger we shouldn't take sweets from," but his message appealed to the working classes of South London. Even if the population of London was only 3 percent nonwhite at the time (and 2 percent nationally), Powell managed to build a following. There was fear of foreigners taking their jobs. "Somewhere between the bombs stopping, the bulldozers starting, and kids being warned about strangers, 'the coloureds' had become a talking point," Collins recalled.[36] The extent of Powell's support became clear when Tory leader Edward Heath fired him. Dockworkers, porters, factory hands, and members of the transport unions protested on his behalf. It wasn't necessarily an endorsement of his vitriolic speeches or even agreement with his views but a defense of his right to speak his mind.

The public debate became so polarized, Collins argues, that all fears about immigration and diversity were summarily waved off as illegitimate racism or worse. Something deeper was happening, too, according to Collins, that was reshaping the identity of people like his own family. "Many of the urban white working class saw themselves more as part of an ethnic group united by colour and culture, than as a class united by their work."[37]

By the 1980s, like in Marcouch's corner of Amsterdam, a mass exodus had begun. Some were called "Thatcher's Children"; "Essex Man" became shorthand for a new breed of Tory voter who was nouveau riche rather than middle class. And like the East Enders who moved to Essex, Collins's neighbors fled London for places like Bexley and Eltham. But they did not entirely leave their old lives or identities behind, living "like ex-pats, attempting to recreate aspects of the old neighbourhood within their new environment."[38] Their nouveau riche tastes for interior decoration and loud bling clothing became the object of mockery from those higher up the class ladder. But one day, they would exact their political revenge.

2

When Integration Fails

IN 1992, SOON AFTER AYAAN HIRSI ALI ARRIVED IN HOLLAND AND requested asylum, she bought a huge pink-and-purple carpet. Hirsi Ali, who is today better known as a crusading anti-Islamic feminist who for years lived under police protection, was then a Somali refugee who had fled an arranged marriage by disappearing during an airport layover in Germany and crossing the border to Holland. When she received a large check from the Dutch government to cover expenses after being granted asylum, she and a fellow Somali who shared an apartment immediately went to a local shop and spent it all on an exorbitantly priced garish carpet to cover every inch of floor in their new state-subsidized home. Her Dutch friends were appalled; for Hirsi Ali, at the time not accustomed to saving money or budgeting for essential expenses, it seemed an entirely reasonable thing to do.[1]

Eight years later, as Hirsi Ali was laying the groundwork for her own political career, the issues of immigration and integration—and how to deal with people unfamiliar with Dutch norms and behaviors on matters ranging from floor coverings to feminism—were thrust to the forefront of the country's political debate.

In early 2000, Paul Scheffer, a curly-haired Dutch intellectual seen as part of the left-leaning intelligentsia, rocked the country's political establishment. His article "The Multicultural Drama,"[2] published in the prestigious *NRC Handelsblad,* lashed out at those who assumed that everything would work out fine. "Many live with the misconception that the integration of ethnic minorities will have approximately the same course as the peaceful conciliation of religious groups in the Netherlands," he wrote. This, he argued, "reveals a boundless faith in elites." He likened this blind faith to those misguided Dutch who had favored neutrality on the eve of World War II; his article brought the immigration debate firmly onto the turf of the Dutch Labor Party.[3]

Whole generations, he insisted, had "been written off under the guise of tolerance," and the current policy of "limited integration increases inequality and contributes to a sense of alienation in society." What was needed instead was "a departure from the cosmopolitan illusion in which many wallow."[4]

What made his article so powerful was that its author wasn't regarded as a right-winger like the few politicians who had made noises about immigration and were quickly dismissed as racists or worse. Scheffer was a card-carrying member of the Labor Party, something that both outraged the left and forced them to listen.[5] His article was the first salvo in a debate that has dominated Dutch politics ever since.

For Scheffer, ostensibly progressive social policy was constraining the potential of refugees by taking people who are by nature and necessity innovative and transforming them into passive members of society. "The subsidized isolation of all those migrant families has turned out to be an obstacle to them, to their children and to society as a whole," he argued elsewhere. "The entrepreneurial instincts of those who left their home countries to earn money abroad is stifled by a society that attempts to protect people against every conceivable risk." They weren't, in his view, coming to Europe for benefit tourism, as some right-wingers like to argue. Instead, they were getting caught in the safety net after they arrived.[6]

Before Scheffer's article, and even after it was released, it was frowned upon to voice such critical views. But the establishment's failure to talk about it openly infuriated those who lived in the neighborhoods suddenly dominated by immigrants. They resented their politicians and felt they had never been consulted. Many of them came from the very neighborhoods that families like that of Dutch Labor Party politician Ahmed Marcouch moved into in the 1980s as white flight began. The poor Dutch families who couldn't afford to go stayed behind. Their message to the Labor Party was "You ignored us. You let it happen," says Marcouch.[7]

Labor's stance left a political vacuum, and those who felt no one spoke for them would soon find their political messiah in the unlikeliest of characters—a flamboyant gay Catholic professor who had no patience for political correctness.[8]

PIM FORTUYN'S TIME IN THE LIMELIGHT WAS SHORT, BUT IT WAS transformative. He was a former Communist and an openly gay man who boasted of sleeping with Muslim immigrants in Holland while calling for a ban on Muslim immigration—an electrifying figure in a country known for its staid politics.

Before founding his own party, Fortuyn had tried to join an establishment center-right party, the People's Party for Freedom and Democracy (VVD). The party's leader at the time, Frits Bolkestein, had been one of the first figures to speak critically about immigration in the early 1990s. He remembers Fortuyn as a talented but inflammatory politician. "He had a thoroughly theatrical personality, and that played in his favor," Bolkestein, now in his eighties, told me in his book-lined office overlooking the canals of Amsterdam. "I didn't want him to be in my parliamentary group, so I cold-shouldered him. . . . He would have acted as a fragmentation bomb."[9]

Fortuyn took his explosive rhetoric elsewhere and formed his own party. By fashioning a new type of far-right politics in progressive garb, he redirected the entire national debate in a way that has endured.

Fortuyn pushed the right toward a form of conservatism that could work in a country with progressive views toward homosexuality, prostitution, premarital sex, and other issues that are anathema to family-values conservatives in the United States. Fortuyn proved that the winning argument for the European far right was not an American-style appeal to conservative religious values but the claim that it was protecting women, gays, and secularism from backward Muslims.[10] The Netherlands was a perfect laboratory for this new strategy because, unlike France, it did not have a strong contingent of religious traditionalists opposed to women's liberation and gay rights. The new right had to hone its message for this audience. Right-wing intellectuals realized their mistake and followed Fortuyn's example. Almost overnight, they seemed to switch from being opposed to gay rights to favoring them.

It was Fortuyn who blazed the trail for the new generation of far-right leaders across Europe. He may not have intended to be a pioneer, but his brand of plainspoken political incorrectness and his depiction of Islamic culture as a backward and reactionary threat to the hard-won progressive values of Western Europe would provide a potent template for a modernized far right. His ideological inheritors in Dutch politics, as well as the revamped Front National in France, the Dansk Folkeparti (Danish People's Party, or DPP), and Germany's Alternative für Deutschland (AfD) have all emulated Fortuyn in their own ways.

Fortuyn had begun his political life on the far left. He was active in Communist groups and later tried to join the Labor Party. But it was his homosexuality, which he wore on his sleeve, that pushed him to the right. Fortuyn was a regular customer at Rotterdam's edgy gay clubs, where anonymous sex was common. He had always felt safe in Holland, but that changed.

One of the clubs, called Boundless, was attacked by immigrant youths, who smashed its windows. When a journalist asked him about his views on Islam in February 2002, he replied, "I have no desire . . . to have to go through the emancipation of women and homosexuals all over again." Moreover, there were not many countries where someone as openly gay as he was could succeed in politics. "I take pride in that," he said. "And I'd like to keep it that way."[11]

ON MAY 6, 2002, ONE DAY AFTER REVELERS FILLED THE STREETS OF Paris to celebrate Jacques Chirac's victory over Jean-Marie Le Pen, Fortuyn was gunned down by a radical animal rights activist as he emerged from a radio interview. His assassin later claimed that he had killed Fortuyn to stop him from using Muslims as "scapegoats."[12] In national elections nine days later, Fortuyn's eponymous party, the Pim Fortuyn List, became the second largest in the Netherlands with 17 percent of the vote. Bolkestein believes that Fortuyn's premature death may have made his ideas and his influence eternal in the way that a long, bruising political career never could have.[13]

After the assassination, an up-and-coming politician named Geert Wilders attempted to fill Fortuyn's shoes. Wilders started out working as a young staffer for Bolkestein in the VVD's party offices, where he focused on social affairs. "I had very little to do with him," says Bolkestein, but, he adds, "We were all happy with him." Wilders then served as a member of parliament for the VVD for several years until he began to clash with its leaders over a platform favoring Turkish accession to the European Union. By then, Bolkestein had stepped down as leader to become an EU commissioner in Brussels. Wilders soon left the party and started his own.

Speaking of his old understudy, Bolkestein is disdainful but not dismissive. "He has two arrows" in his quiver, says the former party leader. "The first arrow is indeed xenophobic," but the second is the same thing as the left: "To protect the workingman, which really should have been done by the Labor Party."

But as Labor moved away from its old base toward a more culturally liberal constituency, many of its voters started to look elsewhere. "They made a fatal mistake and really continue to make that mistake," Bolkestein says of his old political rivals, with a tinge of satisfaction. Faced with "the choice between the foreign-born and the labor classes, they chose the foreign-born . . . and they've paid for it dearly."[14] In March 2017, in a calamitous election result, 80 percent of Labor's MPs, including Marcouch, lost their seats, leaving a party that had once been the country's largest with just 9 of parliament's 150 seats.

Bolkestein himself has undergone a strange evolution in the eyes of the Dutch public, one that mirrors the shift experienced by the society as a whole. The left used to hate him and see him as "a fearmonger, even a racist."[15] Indeed, Bolkestein himself admits that he was appealing to voters who felt no one would say out loud what they were saying behind closed doors. "I said then, in the pub and the church, this is what people think. I gave voice to that," he told me.[16] Or, as he once put it more bluntly, "One must never underestimate the degree of hatred that Dutch people feel for Moroccan and Turkish immigrants. My political success is based on the fact that I was willing to listen to such people."[17]

And like in France, where many of the 1968 generation's brightest intellectual lights have veered right, Dutch leftists began to swing right out of antireligious fervor and defense of what they saw as liberal values under attack from Muslims. Though Bolkestein has long since left the political arena, his ideas have become a rallying cry for people who once hated him.[18] This is owing largely to another gruesome killing.

THE FILMMAKER THEO VAN GOGH WAS CYCLING ALONG ONE OF Amsterdam's perfectly maintained bike lanes on a gray morning wearing his customary uniform of suspenders and a T-shirt. It was a typical Dutch scene. Then Mohammed Bouyeri, a twenty-six-year-old Dutch-Moroccan man, approached Van Gogh and shot him. As the filmmaker tried to escape, Bouyeri fired again and again. He then produced a machete and cut the dead man's throat before stabbing a letter into Van Gogh's chest with a knife.

Witnesses later told journalists the greatest shock was that "the killer was so calm"—he kicked the corpse before casually walking away from the crime scene.[19] A shoot-out with police soon ensued, and Bouyeri took a bullet to the leg and was arrested. His goal was martyrdom, as the letter left on Van Gogh's body attested, in verse: "Drenched in blood these are my final words / Pierced by bullets / As I had hoped."[20]

But the core message left on the dead man's body was not directed at the victim; it was addressed to Ayaan Hirsi Ali, who had, since her arrival in the Netherlands, publicly renounced Islam, become a member of parliament for Bolkestein's VVD party, and collaborated with Van Gogh on his film *Submission,* which featured Koranic verses etched on the bare bodies of women. "With your attacks you have not only turned your back on the Truth, but you are also marching along the ranks of the soldiers of evil," the blood-soaked letter told Hirsi Ali. "This letter is God willing an attempt to stop your evil and silence you forever," he continued in a mix of Dutch and Arabic. "Islam has withstood many enemies and persecutions throughout History." Pressure would only fan "the flames of belief," he continued. "Your intellectual terrorism will not prevent this, on the contrary, it will hasten this. Islam will be victorious through the blood of the martyrs. They will spread its light in every dark corner of this earth and it will drive evil with the sword if necessary back into its dark hole."[21]

Hirsi Ali was immediately placed in hiding and whisked away to a secure air base, where she slept in the barracks.[22] She was soon given bodyguards by the Dutch government, who continued to accompany her years later after she had moved to the United States.

HOLLAND HAD LONG BEEN MOCKED BY GERMAN INTELLECTUALS AS A boring place where everything of consequence happened fifty years later.[23] That has changed. Since the 1960s, it has become a country where great cultural shifts happened first, from assisted suicide to permissive prostitution laws. Being known as a progressive trailblazer among everyone from gay couples to pot-smoking students had its consequences, though.

The 9/11 attacks, the murders of Fortuyn and Van Gogh, the threats to Hirsi Ali, and the rise of extremist Islam among Dutch-born children called everything into question and changed the way the left viewed

Islam.[24] It was a Salman Rushdie moment, a wake-up call, for many in Holland. And their anger erupted in the form of a powerful and profound sense of disappointment.

Now it wasn't only new right activists who were pushing back against the consensus on immigration; there were also many disappointed progressives—the people who saw the victories of the 1960s and 1970s as major battles that had been won, making sexual freedom, women's liberation, and gay rights an unquestioned part of Dutch society. For a generation that believed its wars against the church were won, suddenly there was a regression; those old victories seem tenuous.

At the same time, political views that were once radical, even revolutionary, had become quotidian. Feminism, gay rights, antiracism, and environmentalism were once the animating forces of left-wing activism; now they are in many cases state policy. "Idealism has been bureaucratized," argues the journalist Bas Heijne. "And when the establishment enforces universalism, you react against it." Heijne is a columnist for the *NRC Handelsblad,* the highbrow paper where Scheffer's bombshell article appeared. He splits his time between Holland and Paris, where I met him in a busy café. In his view, the Dutch left's abandonment of its core ideas helped speed the rise of the populist right. The Labor Party gave up on its message of solidarity, and a new ethic of being only responsible for oneself took over. With more and more immigrants, that quickly developed into a "why should I pay for you?" mentality. Terrorist attacks perpetrated by Muslims have only made matters worse.

"When the illusion disappears, it goes completely in the other direction," argues Heijne. "There is a sense that 'we are welcoming, and then they do this,'" he adds. The Dutch "have been terribly let down in their good intentions."[25]

PART OF HOLLAND'S INTEGRATION DILEMMA IS THAT IT WAS PREOCCUPIED with other things when immigrants first began arriving in the '60s and '70s. "Dutch society was not prepared because they were changing themselves," says Marcouch, the former Labor MP. Welcoming culturally distant foreigners in the midst of a national upheaval over feminism, gay rights, environmentalism, and religion wasn't a priority. The new immigrants were invisible guest workers, and no one gave them much thought. Meanwhile, the Moroccans saw sexual liberation, drugs, and prostitution. The reaction from the men was "We don't want our wives and daughters to become like that," which often resulted in girls being kept out of school.[26]

As the debate became more polarized after 9/11, religious observance suddenly became politically loaded. Teenage girls were telling teachers they couldn't shake hands and that they had to fast and pray while other Dutch kids were out drinking and having sex. Orthodox religious observance runs against everything that Dutch youth culture promotes.

The Dutch government assumed that the model it had used to successfully assimilate its own religious minorities throughout history would solve the problem. Separate schools and sports clubs are something the Dutch had tried; they called it *pillarization*, a system of viewing different religious groups as separate entities or pillars within the society, each with its own community leadership.

Pillarization (*verzuiling* in Dutch) was, after all, regarded as a success in integrating a large Catholic population that had long been marginalized as second-class citizens. Pillarization classified society according to its groups. As Ian Buruma describes it, "From the cabinet minister down to the lowest manual worker, everyone was part of one of the pillars that held up the edifice of Dutch society, and all the real or potential conflicts between the pillars were negotiated by the gentlemen who stood at their pinnacles." To many people, especially Christian Democrats, this seemed the obvious way to integrate Muslims.[27]

It was multiculturalism by another name and a strategy rooted in Dutch history. But, as the historian Han Entzinger has written, the model that had functioned so well before failed in integrating the country's new ethnic minorities.[28] They did not have their own established and recognized leaders, like the Dutch Jews or Catholics—and any attempt to graft past social engineering projects onto new phenomena is generally laden with pitfalls. For Paul Scheffer, the analogy simply didn't work. Muslims from abroad were fundamentally different from Dutch Catholics, he argued. "There was no prospect of a Muslim community as an organized or unified presence for the simple reason that the history of the guest workers that produces this migration was a community without elites."[29]

The one group that seemed to have a somewhat easier time was the Surinamese, who came from Holland's Latin American colony. They had a "colonial bonus," argues the University of Amsterdam historian Leo Lucassen. They already had been socialized in the culture of a country they had never seen. Equally important, he argues, was "the front-stage message" framed by the government that these people "are like us and that they belong." For Turks and Moroccans, neither of these factors applied. They didn't speak the language or have a cultural affinity with the Netherlands.[30]

Willem Schinkel, a sociologist at Erasmus University in Rotterdam, doesn't believe Holland has ever had any true interest in admitting foreigners to the national club. His office on the upper floors overlooks the once bombed-out and rebuilt city that is home to Europe's largest port. Rotterdam is Holland's largest and most diverse city, and the only one governed by an ethnic minority mayor, Ahmed Aboutaleb, who moved to the Netherlands from Morocco when he was fifteen. It is also the place that produced Pim Fortuyn and the brand of politics that still dominates Dutch debates.

Schinkel insists that the multiculturalism debate in Holland is based on fiction: the country has never had genuine multiculturalism. Instead, he argues, integration in Holland is about policing the borders of Dutchness to avoid welcoming outsiders into Dutch society. Integration places a huge burden on the individual to assimilate and become part of society while asking little of the larger society. When integration of immigrants fails, however, the responsibility is placed on the religious or ethnic community they come from. "It's two things at the same time. A person may not be well integrated, and we also know that the responsibility or the cause of this lies in his or her culture, which gets to be identified with a particular group or community assumed to exist as some sort of cohesive whole."[31] The larger community then suffers a sort of collective punishment from society, ostracized for producing terrorists like Bouyeri or for not criticizing them sufficiently.

Schinkel is highly critical of Scheffer for taking integration and turning it into a bogeyman for the country's ills. It was a red herring, he insists. The architects of the early integration policies believed that people would need their cultural identity to give them strength while they assimilated and would eventually shed it.

Integration became such a central issue in political debates after 2001 that all nuances were forgotten. "We've had difficulty defining Dutchness in ethnic terms partly because there was never any need to do so.

The Dutch colonial effort was an effort to keep the other outside," he says. When foreigners and ex-colonial subjects started to show up inside the country, there was a need to define and police the boundaries. The only way to define what Dutch society is, is to "constantly monitor and identify what does not belong to it," argues Schinkel. And this, he insists, is the "social function of the concept of integration, is to keep alive a reservoir of people identifiable as not part of society."[32]

After the murder of Theo van Gogh, there was a debate over how people failed to stop his killer, Mohammed Bouyeri. Many thought he appeared to be "well integrated." As a matter of public opinion, it quickly became a consensus "that as soon as he murdered a person, he wasn't well integrated after all," says Schinkel. But the same standard wouldn't have been applied to an ethnic Dutch murderer; indeed, integration, or lack thereof, was never discussed after Fortuyn was shot by a white Dutchman who professed extremist views about animal rights.

Once upon a time, getting a Dutch passport was considered the final stop on the road to successful integration. Now, Schinkel says, there has been a shift "from a focus on formal citizenship to what I call moral citizenship." No longer is a passport the end of the road; it's just the beginning. "Then begins the real moral work, the cultural work of integration." This shift, he insists, is evidence that newly naturalized Dutch are still being "monitored in terms of their not belonging to society" on the grounds that "you don't have the correct cultural outlook to be a true Dutch citizen."[33]

The Dutch values and habits that immigrants are expected to adopt are no longer merely wearing wood clogs, eating Gouda cheese, and having windows without curtains. A DVD used as part of a state integration effort with pictures of topless women on Dutch beaches and kissing gay couples sends the message that "'This is Holland,' a country of progressive people, and who takes issue with this should stay away."[34]

The problem, of course, is that for a liberal democracy to attempt to enforce liberal beliefs is a violation of its liberalism. A state can forbid and punish behaviors, but it cannot tell people what to think. Just as a liberal state tolerates those who hold fascist and anarchist views, it must tolerate those with Orthodox religious convictions. They are free to believe in white supremacy, the evils of government, or the sin of abortion so long as they don't violate any laws by acting on those beliefs.

Schinkel points out that if the metric for integration is the frequency of contacts with people of other ethnic groups, then "the ethnic Dutch are the least well integrated." Data is collected with the goal of feeding policy makers, and policy makers don't worry about how often a member of the Dutch Reformed Church meets Surinamese or Turks. "They're not measured!" exclaims Schinkel. They are just seen as the baseline, a control group. "The surveys only target those people who are a priori considered to be not a part of society, and then, the only question is the degree to which they are not." It is not just a matter of interaction with other races and religions, he argues. "If you were to actually measure the religiosity of the ethnic Dutch, if you were to incorporate their views on gender equality and homosexuality . . . and speak of the entire population in terms of integration, you would have a very small society, really."[35] Many of them are also outside the assumed norms of gay-loving, feminist, tolerant Holland's self-image.

THERE HAS BEEN ANOTHER MAJOR OBSTACLE TO GENUINE INTEGRATION, one that can be encapsulated in a single word. The Dutch use the word *allochtoon* to refer to those who are foreign or look it.[36] It is a ubiquitous term applied to anyone who does not look to be "native Dutch" and is deeply resented by almost every nonwhite Dutch person I've met. The official definition is someone with one or more parents born abroad, but it is never applied to someone with a German or Australian parent. Its use is interchangeable with *black* or *brown*. It is a term, the Dutch-Turkish writer Zihni Özdil argues, that creates a second class of citizens, stripping them of their Dutchness. Özdil once asked a national TV audience why, if *allochtoon* is neutral and nonracial, it is never applied to the former queen Beatrix, whose father was from Germany. Within minutes, he received death threats.

Özdil recently wrote a book called *Netherlands, My Fatherland*, intentionally borrowing one of the far right's slogans for his title. Holland is often praised for its tolerance and seen as an exemplar for other nations, but Özdil sees things differently. He believes that Holland's vaunted tolerance is really a form of condescension, an attitude that says, "You're not equal to me, I really don't like you, but I'm going to tolerate you." Protestants treated Catholics and Jews as second-class citizens for centuries, he points out. "They were tolerated, they were allowed to practice their religion as long as it's behind closed doors."[37]

Paul Schnabel, a senator for the centrist D66 party and the government's former social policy guru, has some experience with being a member of a Dutch religious minority. He grew up Catholic with a mother who was half-Indonesian. Looking back, he says, "You could say nasty things about Catholics you could never say about Jews in this country." Even the royal family, he says, didn't fully accept them as equals rather than outsiders loyal to the pope. It took the Second World War and their role in the resistance before the queen "would accept that they were also real Dutch citizens. It took a long time." Ironically, he adds, "Now we have a queen who is a Catholic and nobody is bothering anymore."[38]

It's harder for Muslims who aren't royalty. "I don't want to be tolerated in my own country, I want equality!" Özdil exclaims. "If you really hate me, but you have the respect to say it to my face, that's equality," he insists. "Diversity doesn't necessarily mean nice things. That's part of citizenship." But these debates have to take place without one group of citizens telling another, "You should get the fuck out."

Özdil has some experience in this regard. He writes columns about health care for the *NRC Handelsblad*. "Literally 80 percent of the responses I get from readers are, 'Oh, as if health care is better in Turkey. Go back if you don't like it,'" he tells me. Despite his Dutch passport and elite platform, readers still refuse to see him as Dutch. "The idea that someone with my looks and my name is writing about Dutch health care," he says, is unimaginable to some of his readers.[39]

Özdil reserves a special ire for a gentle white-bearded man named Rinus Penninx. Penninx is a leading scholar of immigration history in Holland; he also helped shape early Dutch integration policies in the 1980s. Özdil begins one of the chapters in his book with the following quotation: "Our policy is a policy that accepts that there are differences between people and you have to recognize these differences. Differences should be celebrated."

It is a line from Hendrik Verwoerd, one of the architects of apartheid in South Africa and the chief proponent of the policy of separate development—the idea that groups should live apart from one another, which, in practice, meant separate and unequal facilities, education, and citizenship rights. Özdil juxtaposes the quote with one from Penninx. "Every society consists of many groups that are different. Integration should concern itself with the way groups are situated in the society, so that it functions properly."[40]

To Özdil, this is an echo of apartheid, an idea that had its roots in Dutch Calvinist thought. He believes that Penninx's vision, well-meaning as it was, was to essentially adopt Verwoerd's logic: "Don't impose yourself on the other if the other doesn't want this. It's wrong." The idea of separate enclaves, living equally, is a fallacy. The legal doctrine of "separate but equal" that reigned for decades in the United States was rarely equal. Nor were South Africa's nominally independent homelands, built in the name of separate development.

"This is what Dutch liberals still do not want to face: the dynamics of power," he writes. Claiming that it's fine for Turks to live in their own enclave because rural Dutch whites do, too, "completely ignores the reality that white groups are not seen by society as 'the other' or 'un-Dutch.'"[41] By allowing minority enclaves and Turkish or Moroccan schools, he argues, Penninx is "pleading for Apartheid without realizing it."

ÖZDIL'S NEMESIS, PENNINX, HARDLY SEEMS LIKE AN ADVOCATE OF apartheid. He is friendly and soft-spoken, and his foot-long beard makes him look more like Santa Claus.

For the past four decades, Penninx has studied Turkish migration patterns and the regions the guest workers originally came from. Back in 1983, when Holland's national unemployment rate was 13 percent, the rate for Turkish workers was more than 40 percent. "They were there, and their jobs had gone," he told me over coffee in the small town of Gouda, famous for its cheese. "All these factories were closed down. . . . There was no alternative for them."[42]

It was at this point that the government realized that many would stay and would somehow have to be integrated. The goal was to give them "a proper place in Dutch society," which meant education, housing, and health care. "That went together with accepting their religion and worldview and culture, as far as we did not contradict Dutch values," he adds. Penninx was intimately involved in formulating these policies, and he still maintains that many of them were successful.

He points to data between the 1980s and the 1990s and comparisons of parents and their children. He cites companies like Corendon Airlines, a low-cost carrier founded by Turkish immigrants. But politically, integration was a failure. Figures like Scheffer cemented that consensus view. They argued that Holland had created parallel societies and had not done enough to "protect our own national culture." The discussion of integration also shifted away from groups to individual immigrants.

The view that immigrants needed to be better integrated into the social fabric, as Penninx describes it, "led to a redefinition of these policies in which the target groups were not groups anymore, but were individuals. It also meant that organizations of these groups were not important anymore." Policy was now at the personal level—something that liberals see as essential but multiculturalists focused on group rights deplore.

Penninx has thought deeply about what integration means. He divides the process into three stages: language, aesthetic sense, and normative values. Most migrants are very quick with the first stage because they need the language to succeed. The second involves tastes in food, art, and music, which is more difficult. "These things do not change very much in an adult's life. They eat the same kind of things because they like it," says Penninx. The same goes for music and art. Finally, there is the normative dimension: "You have to learn the distinction between good and evil. Which is different in different societies." Such views do not change easily. "Not with natives and not with migrants," he insists.

Penninx does not defend certain brutal practices in immigrant communities, but he does see trying to stop them with policy as futile. Public debate has branded all Muslim immigrants as guilty of being patriarchal, vengeful, and practitioners of genital cutting. "And of course, they hate homos," he adds. Immigrants are depicted as violating norms that many natives never adhered to in the first place. After all, there are a lot of white Dutch natives who do not accept homosexuality and some who even attack gays. They should be treated the same as migrants who commit similar crimes. If not, it amounts to discrimination, he argues. It is the distinction between those deemed to have an integration problem and those for whom that thought would never arise.

The exception, and the blind spot, of course, is that while many native Dutch might be vicious homophobes and have antiquated views on gender relations, there is not widespread genital cutting in rural Friesland, and there is among certain Somali immigrants. So should the government enforce any norms? I ask. The government must regulate society according to several basic norms, Penninx replies, "but don't have the illusion," he argues, that there's one specific group—immigrants—that you can resocialize.

To him, that smacks of old policies toward the poor. "They had the wrong ideas about how to raise children. They had the wrong ideas about alcoholism. . . . We had governmental programs where we put these people in resocialization camps." Penninx worries that such social engineering leads to dangerous places. What next? he asks. "You forbid these people to have children?" The government needs to ensure norms aren't violated, but he insists it cannot take preemptive action. Just as with fighting alcohol abuse, the government runs campaigns, but compliance is up to the individual.

Penninx even designed his own civic integration course in the 1990s and isn't opposed to the principle—it's the idea of making norms mandatory that riles him. "That's not how it works," he insists. If it doesn't work for native Dutch alcoholics or prisoners, why should it work for immigrants? He is adamant that there is a way to signal to people which rules must be obeyed without stigmatizing them. "What I'm protesting against is that you make this kind of policy so specifically for immigrants" while ignoring natives who violate the same norms.

Somalis know the norms about genital cutting, he insists. They have been in the country for twenty-five years now. And he thinks that there are more effective ways to prevent female genital mutilation than giving people integration courses. Public health institutions could take the lead. "They know what the problem is. . . . If you build it into the education of midwives, of people who are near to this, if you look at this as a health thing, then you're in a much better position to change."

In the end, he believes, one must "bet on the good intentions of both sides, knowing that there will be clashes, at some point, and being prepared for those clashes."[43]

Scheffer agrees that those clashes are the country's best hope for progress—but he has no time for cultural relativism. *Diversity* has become a buzzword, but it is "a completely empty word because it embraces everything and means nothing," he argues. His dismissal is a critique of those who place equal value on all ideas and identities. People with extremist beliefs could be regarded as a form of diversity; so could illiterates. "Not everything that is different has a value," he insists.

Scheffer claims that teachers, doctors, and police are embarrassed to confront newcomers with basic Dutch norms. "In biology class, it's become difficult to talk about evolution. It's become difficult during literature class to talk about Oscar Wilde, because he is a 'perverse' writer. Now, if you're going to scrap all the perverse writers from your curriculum, it will be a very short history of literature," he quips. "During sexual education, students come with the books and all the illustrations the parents have torn from the book. During swimming class, it's become very difficult to send children to mixed swimming class. So what do you do then?" he asks.

What typically happens is schools strive to accommodate demands and avoid conflict. "I think we should do the opposite," says Scheffer. It is confrontation, debate, and the resolution of conflicts like these that ultimately makes integration work.[44]

Özdil doesn't accept that the state should steer clear of criticizing certain minority groups' behaviors, as Penninx argues. Nor does he believe that things will simply work out if conflicts run their course. He is adamant that the state must punish certain behaviors. He insists that Dutch officialdom has no idea what they are encouraging and permitting under the guise of allowing groups to practice their own cultures. As far as he is concerned, the government needs to stop "facilitating, stimulating, funding apartheid."[45]

He is particularly worried about Islamic schools—some of them run by Turkish religious figures. People might say kids are performing better than in regular schools, so there's no problem. But there is. Özdil mentions marketing materials of a Turkish Islamic school featuring photos of a young boy reading a book in Turkish called *The Blood of Our Martyrs*, written by someone Özdil considers an "anti-Semitic, religious fundamentalist." To him, it is unacceptable that Dutch kids are reading those books in schools receiving government funding.

He has also taken heat from the right, who still can't accept him staking a claim to Dutch citizenship that is equal to theirs. When he invokes American-style concepts like unity in diversity, they bristle. "You want to demolish our *eigenheid*," they tell him—using a word that means *uniqueness* but sounds more like *nativeness* coming from them.[46]

It's not a surprising view, his fellow *NRC* columnist, the veteran journalist Bas Heijne, contends, so long as "being Dutch is like becoming part of a club." And for many young Dutch Turks and Dutch Moroccans, there hasn't been a sense of acceptance. Increasingly, the Dutch see these communities as closing themselves off and not wanting to "join us." Some have tried—he mentions that large numbers of Dutch Moroccan men try to join the police and the army but often drop out.[47]

Even Ayaan Hirsi Ali has been harmed by this sort of reflexive exclusion. Hirsi Ali spent time as a parliamentarian in the 1990s before she left the country. Her anti-Islamist credentials did not stop her from being hounded and almost kicked out of government when it emerged that some of the information on her asylum application had been false. Likewise, Khadija Arib, a Dutch Moroccan MP who holds dual citizenship because Morocco doesn't allow its subjects to renounce nationality, was hounded by Wilders when she was elected Speaker of parliament. She was not seen as a real Dutch citizen, says Penninx. "Even if you have this political career" and have been elected to high office, "you're not taken seriously."[48]

Özdil hopes that a genuine debate about citizenship will happen soon so that his belonging, and that of tens of thousands like him, will no longer be questioned. The risk, of course, is that the Dutch may then start blaming actual foreigners and not just those whom they perceive to be foreign. "My hope is that if citizenship isn't up for debate anymore, we will be one step ahead," he told me in early 2016, a year before he was elected to the Dutch parliament. "Otherwise, I'm really afraid. I'm keeping my Turkish passport. You never know," he says. "We know European history."[49]

3

The Nativist Nanny State

As the sun rose on a cold morning in October 1943, fourteen-year-old Bent Melchior, adrift in the Baltic Sea with eighteen other people, knew something was wrong.

On October 1, the German occupying authorities had ordered the arrest of Denmark's Jewish population. As word reached the Jews of Copenhagen that the Nazis were poised to raid their homes, families packed and fled the city. They paid huge sums to smugglers to secure passage to Sweden by circuitous routes less likely to be discovered by the Germans. Melchior's family was advised to head south to the island of Falster, several hours from Copenhagen and a roundabout way of getting to Sweden, which is just a few miles by sea from the capital. Melchior found himself on a fishing boat with an inexperienced captain. "He had never been out where he couldn't see land, so he didn't know how to navigate," he recalls. People were becoming seasick and retching. Passengers kept imagining they saw land only to find it was clouds. "After about seven to eight hours, there was land and there was a lighthouse," Melchior remembers. But the captain, not wanting to moor in the middle of the night, insisted on waiting until dawn.

Freezing and afraid, Melchior prayed that someone at the distant lighthouse would spot them. "But they didn't see us. So, we waited and waited until it started to become light hoping to see the sun rise over Swedish shores to the east," recalls Melchior. But when the sun came, it did not rise where it should have.

"Even I as a fourteen-year-old knew a few facts," says Melchior, namely, "that Sweden is east of Denmark and that the sun rises in the east." Looking out from the boat at dawn, Melchior was terrified to see the sun rising over open water. The poorly navigated vessel had veered off course and was now inadvertently heading back toward the southern tip of Denmark, which was firmly under Nazi occupation. "Had they seen us and God heard my prayer," says Melchior, "we would have been in the hands of the Germans."

As day broke and the captain realized his error, he turned around. The boat was low on fuel when it finally approached the southern Swedish coast. By coincidence, a six-year-old boy saw it far out at sea, and his father, a fisherman, came to fetch them. They reached land at 1:00 p.m. after eighteen hours at sea. Melchior still visits the boy, now eighty, who lives in the same house where they made landfall that morning.

Seven decades after his dramatic escape, Melchior has become something of a celebrity among Danish Muslims—an odd role for a rabbi who volunteered to serve in Israel's War of Independence in 1948. He returned to Copenhagen after the war and became a teacher and then, in 1969, the country's chief rabbi. In the early 1990s, when a group of Palestinians sought refuge in a Danish church after fleeing Lebanon, there was a debate about whether to allow them to stay. The Danish press and other nongovernmental organizations (NGOs) were shocked when Melchior, in the name of the Jewish community, argued they should remain.

Melchior's own background has colored his approach. He has spoken out for refugees "because I have been a refugee myself," he says. "He starts at the bottom, and that feeling has never left me." The rabbi has taken a keen interest in what Denmark's current government is doing, including running Arabic-language ads in Middle Eastern newspapers with the aim of discouraging anyone from seeking asylum by warning they won't get welfare benefits or be able to bring their families. "They are trying to send a message to refugees that Denmark is not a good place for them. Stay away," says Melchior.

What the policy makers posting discouraging ads in Middle Eastern newspapers have failed to see, says the rabbi, is that it tarnishes Denmark's international reputation. Saving most of the country's Jews in 1943 has been part of that good name, he believes. "They lost it in a few months in 2015."

In January 2016, just three months after the refugee crisis peaked, Denmark passed the so-called jewelry law, which stipulated that any valuables worth more than $1,500 would be confiscated from arriving refugees to fund the cost of accommodating them. Editorial pages and columnists across the world lined up to condemn the law; political cartoonists went further, likening Danish leaders to Nazis confiscating Jews' valuables.

The press and the far-right Danish People's Party have tried to portray those who make it to Europe as well-off and not in need of asylum—a suggestion that makes Melchior's skin crawl.

"People do not leave their homes without reason," he insists. "What would they find with the refugees? Do they come here with big fortunes?" he exclaims. The rabbi bristles at the suggestion that refugees are rich, because they sell everything they own and flee with some money in their pockets to pay smugglers and cover expenses wherever they end up. Denmark is always hailed for saving its Jews; it is often forgotten that the refugees of 1943 paid fishermen a fortune to ferry them across to Sweden. Melchior recalls that the amount paid for his passage alone was equivalent to nearly a year's rent for a six-room apartment. "It was money we never had seen," he told me.

"Denmark is not a poor country, for God's sake," says the rabbi. "We are rich people. There's food for everybody here, and even if we get a few tens of thousands more people, there will still be food for everybody."[1]

DENMARK, LIKE HOLLAND, HAS BEEN TRANSFORMED BY DEBATES OVER immigration and integration since the early 1990s, when Rabbi Melchior defended the right of Palestinian refugees sheltered in a Danish church to stay in the country. By the mid-1990s, many Danes were grumbling about the media's refusal to cover crimes committed by immigrants. To critics, the left's refusal to confront the dark side of immigration made it complicit in a spiral of silence. And in this growing public discontent, the editors of *Ekstra Bladet*, a popular daily tabloid newspaper, saw an opportunity. The paper swiftly produced an avalanche of reporting on refugee abuse of the welfare system, including a print and television series called *The Foreigners*, which featured a Somali man with two wives and eleven children who received upward of $75,000 per year in welfare benefits. The newspaper's accompanying editorials recommended that the government lower welfare payments for refugees to provide them with incentives to work. This media onslaught immediately captured the public's attention, and it held special appeal for working-class voters, who saw refugees as competitors for both jobs and benefits.[2]

The Scandinavian welfare system has always been premised on solidarity, with everyone paying their fair share and receiving what the state deems they deserve; as countries like Denmark have become more diverse, some of the trust sustaining it has broken down. There has been some abuse of the system by immigrants, some by natives, and a sizable dose of tabloid fearmongering depicting immigrants as cheaters and leeches sucking the system dry, but the larger issue is the growing unwillingness of the native wealthy to subsidize those seen as the foreign poor.

Defense of generous social benefits and openness to immigration have, since the 1960s, been staples of left-wing politics in Europe and the United States. In the 1980s and 1990s, scholars and journalists, many of them Social Democrats, began to warn that there was an inherent tension between large-scale immigration and a generous welfare state. After all, as numbers grew, expensive social programs would not be able to keep up, they argued. There was both a risk of overburdening and bankrupting the system and creating resentment of new beneficiaries if people no longer supported spending their tax dollars on people they didn't identify or empathize with. If high earners don't see poor immigrants as "themselves minus good fortune," the system collapses.[3]

Scholars like Harvard's Robert Putnam, famous for the book *Bowling Alone,* sparked an uproar in academic circles by arguing that more diverse communities have lower levels of trust.[4] It is no coincidence, he argued, that the United States has never had a comprehensive cradle-to-grave welfare state like Denmark's. The political support for state redistribution of resources to people seen as different and undeserving, often on racist grounds, simply wasn't there.

In countries like Denmark, which were until a few decades ago remarkably homogeneous, there was greater public willingness to fund a welfare state that aided the socially similar poor. After Putnam's article, the issue took on a life of its own. In response to a series of critics arguing that increasing immigration and promoting multiculturalism jeopardized the sense of solidarity needed to sustain a generous welfare state, the academics Keith Banting and Will Kymlicka assembled a team of scholars and devoted an entire volume to addressing the question empirically.

The authors worried whether declining support for welfare policies might lead to the rise of free-market parties opposed to redistribution. Their stated fear was the "Americanization" of generous European systems and the risk of "right-wing populist parties that combine anti-immigrant nativism with attacks on the welfare state."[5] But they were, for the most part, asking the wrong question: the risk wasn't the collapse of the welfare state but a nativist defense of it.

Although most writers at that time dismissed the risk posed by distrust or resentment of new neighbors, some recognized that while the overall minority share of the population didn't seem to erode support for welfare, rapid changes in the number of new immigrants did. They worried that some voters who had always supported the left's redistributionist policies might abandon the left if it didn't make a visible effort to control immigration.[6]

Even some of the most enthusiastic proponents of state-led multiculturalism acknowledged the challenge. Sustaining the welfare state wasn't so much of a problem in places with large but stable immigrant populations; it was in places where the immigrant share of the population was rapidly increasing that the cracks started to show. The book's critical conclusion warned that European Social Democrats should "begin to worry about potential future trade-offs" between diversity and redistribution.[7] By that point, it was already too late.

THE POPULIST RIGHT DID NOT COME OUT OF NOWHERE. IT RECOGNIZED an underserved niche in the political market of the 1990s, seized the opportunity, and has never let go. At the same time, the focus of activism on the left shifted dramatically from economic equality to identity, weakening the appeal of parties arguing for redistribution.[8] As the Social Democratic Parties across Scandinavia and Labor Parties in Holland and Britain moved away from their traditional blue-collar base and sought to attract voters from the growing educated middle class, their focus and core values shifted. Once upon a time, working-class interests drove political debate; now they have "become spectators in electoral battles for the educated middle-class vote," as Matthew Goodwin and Robert Ford argue in their book, *Revolt on the Right*.[9]

It's a pattern that has repeated itself in countless countries. By deftly dividing society into two groups—the pure people and the corrupt elite—populists have attracted those who usually don't bother to vote and lured others away from the traditional left.[10] There is a sense—whether right or wrong—among these forgotten voters that newcomers have not paid their way, becoming free riders.[11] As their views on immigration were dismissed as racist or simply ignored, their loyalties to the political left faded.[12]

The motivations of voters who abandon establishment parties for the far right are complex. Some are racist xenophobes who resent immigration and are nostalgic for an imagined past when their countries supposedly had no problems. But many are "reluctant radicals" who have grown increasingly angry at state institutions that they see as elitist and undemocratic.[13] These voters resent the establishment parties because they have failed to address basic issues like rising housing costs, fraying public services, unemployment, and cuts to welfare benefits.

When the only politicians who show any interest in their grievances are on the far right, the consequence is the rise of anti-immigrant populism. New arrivals present an easy target for blame, and far-right parties have masterfully manipulated economic anxieties by offering to both shore up the welfare state and stop the flow of immigrants.

For years, it was assumed that the far right in Europe would stick to an antisocialist economic platform. In 1995, a famous academic study of the far right aimed to define a formula for success for right-wing populist parties in Europe.[14] At a time when these parties had barely made a dent in parliaments, the authors, Herbert Kitschelt and Anthony McGann, concluded that in order to win, parties would need to combine commitment to free-market principles with a platform that criticized diversity and multiculturalism.

But they did anticipate a possible alternative model for success; they called it "welfare chauvinism," a strain of politics that can emerge in societies where contributors to a generous welfare system no longer see themselves as being in the same boat as some of those reaping the benefits of the welfare system. Likening the welfare state to a club, they argued that welfare chauvinism could lead to calls for exclusion or expulsion in order "to preserve national club goods."[15] Certain voters might become hostile to immigrants because they are themselves the existing beneficiaries of a welfare state, and they fear a broader backlash against the welfare system—or its financial collapse—if immigration rates increase. These welfare chauvinist voters are distinct from run-of-the-mill racists who don't care about welfare cuts and simply hate all foreigners.

If new right parties pursued this course, they predicted, they would move to the left economically, arguing for protection of the welfare state and increased social benefits—but for natives alone. Their platforms would combine hostility to immigrants, a strong sense of nationalism and patriotism, and the redistributionist politics commonly associated with the left. The authors concluded that welfare chauvinism might work well as a political strategy in poorer societies or places with strong ethnic divisions but was unlikely to succeed in advanced capitalist democracies unless, they conceded, there was a major economic catastrophe.[16]

The theory emerged in the heady end-of-history days of the mid-1990s when, apart from a genocidal war in the former Yugoslavia, Europe seemed headed for an era of prosperity and peace. But 9/11, the 2008 financial crisis, terrorist attacks on European soil, and the most recent influx of refugees changed the equation, unleashing a fear of Muslim immigrants at a time of economic uncertainty. Although the authors underplayed the relevance of their own theory, it has profound implications for European politics today.

Gradually, the theoretical fears that worried academics took concrete political form. Rather than combining nativist immigration policy with free-market economic policies, which seemed to be the trend on the European right in the 1970s and 1980s, the new right did something different, dealing an even more devastating blow to the left. The so-called populist right gradually became more socialist than the socialists on economic policy and made a direct appeal to the working class.

In small wealthy nations like Denmark and Holland, populist parties have succeeded in portraying the welfare state as the exclusive property of native-born citizens, a hard-earned jackpot to be protected from the grasping hands of undeserving new arrivals. In Denmark, the DPP siphons votes away from the left on a platform of reducing immigration and safeguarding Denmark's welfare benefits for native-born Danes. The same is true in France.

The theory of welfare chauvinism explains why so many former Social Democrats in Scandinavia and Holland and former Communists in France have gravitated to the populist right. Historically, they have been the beneficiaries of a generous state. Now, feeling abandoned by the left and Labor Parties that ostensibly represent their interests but instead support open immigration policies, they are terrified that their "club goods" are threatened by newcomers.

Kitschelt and McGann's 1995 book included a small graph plotting party ideologies along a continuum of socialist and capitalist economic policies on the one hand and authoritarian and libertarian politics on the other and predicting where the political battles in Europe were likely to take place.[17] Left empty was the space where socialist economic policy and authoritarian ideology converged. This is precisely the terrain that the new right has now occupied.

Maureen Eger and Sarah Valdez, two sociologists working in Sweden, have researched the evolution of far-right party platforms between 1970 and 2015; their findings are striking. In the past three decades, the DPP has moved steadily in the direction of welfare chauvinism, combining left-wing economic policy and a strongly authoritarian nationalist message against immigration. Today's DPP, which is now the second-biggest party in parliament, has come a long way from 1973, when the Danish right was led by Mogens Glistrup, a man who boasted he had paid zero income tax and ran on a strict antitax platform. (He eventually spent a few years in jail for tax evasion.) Since that time, new leaders have made immigration the central issue and moved to the left in their support for a robust welfare state.[18]

By treating the new European populists in the same way as the older free-market incarnation of the radical right, many analysts are missing the point. Parties that oppose immigration and defend the welfare state are fundamentally different from those that oppose both.[19]

In the 1970s and 1980s, the far right was preoccupied with libertarian economics and American-style conservatism; it was not an electorally successful formula in most countries. Then, in the mid-1990s, Eger and Valdez argue, "the radical right ceased to be economically right-wing."[20]

And that is when it began to win.

DENMARK'S RIGHTWARD SHIFT ON IMMIGRATION BEGAN WITH A CASE that centered on the family reunification rights of Tamil refugees who had come to Denmark from Sri Lanka. The conservative government's attempts to cast doubts on some refugee claims and restrict the entrance of family members ended in scandal, bringing down the government in

1993. In the scandal's wake, none of the political parties wanted to touch the refugee issue.

The way that Danes viewed the question of refugees and immigration was also beginning to change. In the 1980s, it was considered a moral question, says Arne Hardis, a journalist at the highbrow conservative weekly paper *Weekendavisen,* who has been following the immigration debate for thirty years. But in the 1990s, it became a political question. Critics were once asked what was wrong with their conscience; the emergence of real social tensions in the working-class areas in and around Copenhagen forced it onto the political agenda. "It's totally logical that if there's a political problem and no political party wants to take it up then a new one is going to arise," insists Hardis.[21] And so the Danish People's Party was born.[22]

The DPP arrived on the scene in 1995 and, with laser-like precision, they homed in on a certain type of voter they believed they could turn. They did not have access to Facebook microtargeting or data mining to determine political persuasions the way that Donald Trump's campaign did, allowing them to focus on white working-class voters who had traditionally voted for Democrats but seemed ripe for conversion. But the DPP in the mid-1990s did have an immigration policy that held great appeal for Social Democratic voters in areas where "the balance was going the wrong way."[23]

Søren Espersen, the DPP's deputy leader and the architect of many of its policies, points to the same moment. There was a time, he claims, when the Social Democrats at the local level looked to the DPP as potential allies on city councils. A mayor called him in the late 1990s, pleading for the DPP to run someone. It was the last day to register new candidates. "In those days, we had to persuade people to run," Espersen recalls wistfully. "Now we can't control them anymore."

He sent canvassers to gather signatures and talked a candidate into running. The last-minute DPP candidate ended up gaining enough votes for four seats, even if the party had only run one person. "It's ironic," says Espersen, looking back on the early days. Now, he believes, the DPP has become an open threat to the Social Democrats—and to conservative parties, too—though they have come for different reasons. Old-school conservatives and nationalists come for "God, King, and Country," he explains. The ex–Social Democrats come for what they believe their own party no longer offers them.[24]

The DPP leveraged the immigration issue to siphon away voters from the Social Democrats' traditional base, positioning itself early on a key issue that has come to define Danish politics. Danes pay high taxes and in return get excellent education and health care for free as well as benefits when sick or out of work. As the number of welfare-dependent immigrants grew, often because the state found it easier to give them a check and an apartment than train them for a job, resentment grew, too. There is a widespread fear that more people will come to the country and claim benefits and the "the bread will be buttered more thinly."[25]

The DPP responded by very effectively combining anti-immigrant rhetoric with a strong pro-welfare message that stresses quality health benefits and good care for the elderly. Espersen doesn't think the ex–Social Democrats are going back. "When one of those takes the step to vote for us, it is a very, very huge step he is taking," he says of voters who supported the Social Democrats all their lives. "And why should he go back? I mean to come over this first hurdle of voting for us, then he's done it."[26]

Hardis gives some Social Democrats credit for foresight. After all, it was mayors from the areas surrounding Copenhagen who were among the first to mention that immigration might have a downside and—even worse from a political perspective—threaten the Social Democrats' dominance of Danish politics and their comfortable hold on the working-class vote. As Hardis puts it, "It was their voters who were starting to live next to these new immigrants. It was their welfare state that was threatened."[27]

One of those places was the small satellite town of Herlev about ten miles west of central Copenhagen. The town's forty-two-year-old mayor, Thomas Gyldal Petersen, was a child in Herlev in the 1980s when the previous generation of mayors issued their warning, only to be ignored by the party elites. Now they are listening to him. Petersen has lived in Herlev all his life and is adamant that controlling immigration numbers is the only way to reverse the Social Democrats' political misfortunes and to stop communities like his from turning into ghettos with high unemployment. But many on the left argue that the party has moved too far to the right in order to keep its base on board, and that its harsher rhetoric about immigration is helping to normalize the DPP's views.

The road that led a center-left party to support legislation like the 2016 jewelry law has been long and tortuous, but the trajectory has been clear. The Social Democrats first began to lose their strongholds around the major cities in the 1990s, with many of their votes going to the DPP. The reason integration efforts have failed, Petersen argues, is because policy could not keep up with the influx. "We put a stronger and stronger effort into the integration work," he says, "but the challenge just got bigger and bigger."

He doesn't apologize for the tougher laws that outraged so many in Denmark and abroad. And even though he regards himself as a man of the left—he spent several years working as a lobbyist for the metalworkers' union—he is convinced that advocates of open borders have made matters worse and opened a door for the DPP. "The left wing in Denmark who are advocating for free immigration, they don't understand that with free immigration we are letting down the people who live here, and mainly the poor, the people without opportunities, we are hurting them."

He blames the left for failing to grasp that Denmark and the Social Democrats aren't in the same position they were in during the 1980s. "They believe that we have disappointed, we have abandoned our beautiful history," he says. "The problem is that what they look at as our beautiful history is actually a very small period in the '80s."[28]

THE BIGGEST SHOCK TO THE SOCIAL DEMOCRATS CAME IN 2001; IT WAS the first time that immigration was used as a wedge issue to determine an election. As the outgoing Social Democratic prime minister Poul Nyrup Rasmussen told me in 2002, a few months after his defeat, "They took a part of our rhetoric and tried to sell it as a new package to the people, and with some success, one may say."[29] The center-right coalition came to power but only because of the DPP's strong showing. Meanwhile, the left's focus became how to "stop the bleeding," says Petersen.[30]

Since that time, the DPP has dominated on the immigration issue and taken many voters with them. According to Morten Bødskov, a former justice minister and leading Social Democrat, they are caught between an electorate moving right, toward the DPP, and left-wing supporters who detest the party's harder line on immigration and flee to the far-left parties.[31]

The DPP has won virtually every debate relating to immigration: they succeeded in limiting numbers of immigrants, they have won the debate on Islam, and they were the first to say that freedom of movement within the EU would be a problem—which the 2015 refugee crisis seemed to confirm. Their analysis has in many ways become the default position in Danish politics. Thomas Gammeltoft-Hansen, a refugee expert at Lund University in Sweden and no fan of the far right, agrees: the DPP's vision crafted fifteen years ago "has swept the continent. They've conquered the mainstream." A large part of that success, he argues, is because "the far right has an instrument the left doesn't have: fear."[32]

Mayor Petersen doesn't buy into the DPP's rhetoric of stopping all immigration. "We have to take refugees to Denmark in a number that we can help," he tells me. "Every person that comes to Denmark, alone or with his family, should have the opportunity to make the best of themselves in this welfare society," he says. There is, however, a risk when the numbers reach a certain level.[33]

The key is a demographic balance. As soon as a school or housing project becomes majority immigrant, or for that matter majority unemployed, problems start to arise, he argues. He blames his own party's leadership in past decades. "Mayors in the '80s, they were warning, 'Something is going wrong. You have to change.'" But the party leadership "shut their eyes," he says. "If the balance tips, the welfare society cannot hold together and cannot be the support for everyone that it should be."

Such balance may only help so much. Aydin Soei, a Danish sociologist and the son of immigrants from Iran, believes there is a larger blind spot in the Danish government's thinking, one that those who have never experienced the state's famously generous social policies (or its troubled integration programs) from the receiving end fail to see. "Sometimes you forget that it's not only about how people are spread out; it's also because you didn't use people's resources," he says.[34]

Soei was born to Communist parents in Iran in 1982. He grew up on the working-class fringes of Copenhagen in the 1980s, not far from Mayor Petersen. Only a few years separate the two men. Petersen's town is a place where Soei spent some time as a teenager. "When I went into the middle of Herlev, that was in '97/'98, and the DPP was just rising," recalls Soei. He thought that he would try to make a good impression on old white people. "I had the prejudice that the ones who voted DPP are the elderly, and elderly women," he explains with a laugh. "So as a kid, I went up to them and I asked them in a really polite manner, 'Excuse me, can you tell me what time it is?' even though I knew what time it was," using the antiquated formal "you" that these days is reserved for the queen. "I thought then they'd be able to see that all young men with immigrant background aren't criminals—because that was the big debate at that point," he says.

But at home, there was a crisis. Soei has seen the disastrous consequences of joblessness up close. "A lot of my parents' generation ended up just on permanent social welfare. And the ones who had education, it was outdated," he remembers. "That's really a big tragedy" that has been passed on to children who have grown up with bitter parents who feel their skills weren't valued or recognized.

Soei's mother had a bachelor's degree in physics from the Soviet Union. "It would probably have been recognized from day one in the US, but not in Denmark. They wouldn't even translate her papers," he recalls angrily. His mother had to start from square one, but she managed. His dad did not.[35] Soei's father went from being a prestigious figure in a political movement in Iran to a nobody in Denmark. He became depressive and violent. Soei's recent book, *Forsoning* (Reconciliation), tells the story of his dad's descent into crime and his eventual expulsion from Denmark after murdering the father of one of Soei's classmates.[36]

Soei doesn't seek to excuse the crime, but he believes that if both his parents had been able to work, things might have turned out differently. "I don't buy the argument that you can just take the past, copy it till today one-to-one," he says. The way Denmark handled refugees and immigrants, especially in the 1980s, was a failure, he insists.

The reason, says Soei, is that the state treated all these people the same way as the chronically unemployed rather than seeing them as highly motivated job seekers with existing skills. After all, refugees are nothing like the long-term unemployed. They have weaknesses that chronically unemployed natives don't have (lack of language skills and cultural savoir faire), and they have strengths that many chronically unemployed workers lack (high levels of motivation, grit, and a desperate desire to work, earn, and rebuild). Given these strengths, Soei thinks that the welfare state's approach has been particularly disastrous: "To have a generation of children who grow up with parents who lack self-respect because of their social position" and then the kids "don't get the resources and the cultural capital" that comes through working. "It's the best way of learning the language, getting a network."[37]

For Rabbi Melchior, as for Soei, work is a crucial part of the equation if integration is to succeed. Arriving in a new country with no recognition of your qualifications is discouraging for anyone but devastating for some. His own father could work when they fled to Sweden in 1943 because there were so many Danish Jewish refugees in the country; they needed a religious leader. But not everyone was so lucky. If refugees could work, he believes, "it would change everything." Danes would see "these people are not a danger for you. They're kind people. They do their job. They work their hours." Keeping them inactive, especially when they don't want to be, is a recipe for disaster.[38]

It has become clear that framing immigration as a moral question no longer works politically, and it won't alter the political trends. "You can't as a political party in Denmark today say that you don't care how many Syrians or Afghans or Eritreans or Iraqis come to Denmark. You can't!" exclaims the conservative journalist Arne Hardis. "Even the left is saying the amount matters but what can we do—but they acknowledge that it's a problem." He believes that the Social Democrats' tougher stance may finally be paying off and stanching the bleeding of votes. The party, he says, "might be coming out of the woods," and after being "plagued night and day for thirty years," they seem to be holding their numbers in the polls despite the ongoing refugee crisis in Europe.[39] The former justice minister Bødskov is confident that the worst has passed. "I think we have lost what we can. I don't think we can lose much more," he says of the party's 26 percent showing in the 2015 election.[40]

Sixteen years after the shock of 2001, a quick glance at the political map of Denmark reveals inroads as impressive as the Republican Party's sweep of the reliably Democratic upper Midwest. Mayor Petersen logs on to his computer and pulls up Denmark's election atlas, like the granular county-by-county results published after elections in the United States. Their maps also have red and blue for the Social Democrats and the center-right Venstre Party, and now there's yellow, a relatively new color representing the DPP.

Pointing at a sea of yellow in rural areas of the country with few foreigners, Petersen explains, "The reason here is not about immigration politics," it's about jobs, especially manufacturing jobs that no longer exist or have moved abroad. "They feel like they're isolated from the growth in the country. They're disappointed. They're angry," he told me in April 2016 before the Republican primaries had concluded. "Like people who are following Donald Trump, actually."[41]

Section II

FROM OUTCASTS TO TERRORISTS

4

The Danish Cartoon Crisis and
the Limits of Free Speech

IN 2005, THE EDITORS AT *Jyllands-Posten*, DENMARK'S LARGEST NEWS-paper, were troubled by what they saw as a rising tide of self-censorship in the media, publishing, and popular culture. So Flemming Rose, the editor of the culture section at the time, invited a group of well-known Danish cartoonists to draw the Prophet Muhammad. The initial response was underwhelming, but within a few months—through a combination of diplomatic pressure from Islamic countries, a dismissive response to their complaints from the Danish government, and a concerted campaign by local imams—the cartoons had become a sensation and a scandal.

Those who were offended boycotted Danish dairy products. In Iraq and Pakistan, there were violent protests outside Danish embassies. In Beirut and Damascus, the Danish missions were set on fire. Saudi Arabia withdrew its ambassador, and Danish flags were burned in the West Bank.[1] The cartoon controversy had a long afterlife, and not just at the French weekly *Charlie Hebdo*, where their reprinting was cited as grounds for murder ten years later.

Rose, the editor who commissioned the infamous Muhammad cartoons, is not—as some critics have suggested—a raving Islamophobe or a card-carrying member of the Danish People's Party. He is a free-speech absolutist whose thinking has much more to do with his experience as a foreign correspondent in the Soviet Union, where he saw how totalitarian states muzzled dissidents and human rights activists by sending them to Siberia or worse. Moreover, Rose fervently believes in newspapers' capacity for heroism and social transformation.

As Rose relates in his book *The Tyranny of Silence,* his own family was saved from crushing poverty, homelessness, and separation thanks to the efforts of a crusading journalist, Rachel Bæklund, and an editor, Victor Andreasen. Rose's father had walked out on the family when he was very young, throwing their lives into disarray; when their mother couldn't find a permanent place to live, he and his brother were put in foster care. Bæklund interviewed Rose's mother, with him and his brother in tow, at Copenhagen's central station. The editor, Andreasen, splashed the story on the front page of Denmark's leading tabloid under the headline ARE YOU SLEEPING WELL, MR. HOUSING MINISTER? on September 2, 1963, with a prominent photo of Rose over the caption, "Mommy, when can we have somewhere to live?"[2] He was five years old.

At university, Rose studied Russian language and literature and later spent sixteen years as a foreign correspondent in Moscow, where he got to know many legendary Soviet dissidents and human rights activists. He eventually married a Russian, whose father was a committed Stalinist, and covered the fall of communism for the Danish press in the early 1990s. The experience was formative. Censorship was rife, and those who dared to stand up to the state were sent to labor camps or exiled. Like other academics and American writers, such as Richard Pipes and his son, Daniel, whose frame of reference was Soviet totalitarianism, Rose found in modern political Islam a similar demand to toe the line and a propensity for violence against those who dared to insult the party or the state.

The model is of course not fully transferable, and Denmark's small Muslim community cannot be compared to the Soviet state apparatus. The dissidents who produced underground samizdat newsletters and documented the Kremlin's human rights violations were up against a behemoth. When Rose and *Jyllands-Posten* took on the local Muslim clergy, they were up against a small minority. But on the ideological level, there were some similarities; both groups viewed criticism of their deities, whether sacred or secular, as off limits and legitimately punishable by violence.

Rose's more compelling Russian parallel is the recent spate of censorship in Russian art galleries, following precisely the same logic; Russian Orthodox Christians, once a marginalized group in the Communist era, now have the full backing of the Kremlin. When, in 2003, cutting-edge curators and atheist artists dared to display artwork that might anger religious Christians—a painting featuring Christ in front of the Coca-Cola logo, as well as a church built from empty vodka bottles—enraged Orthodox activists slashed the works and defaced them with spray paint. All six vandals were let off; a judge explained that they were shocked and their vandalism was an understandable reaction to profane images.[3] The same has occurred with Hindu fundamentalists in India and Sikhs opposed to a theater production in London.

As Rose argues, in all these cases, "the perpetrators were transformed into victims, victims into perpetrators."[4] The argument really comes down to a distinction between words and deeds. And by giving in to demands for censorship, whether from angry Muslims or the Russian Orthodox Church, the concept of tolerance is turned on its head, placing the burden on the speaker rather than the listener. No longer are citizens in a diverse society expected to tolerate unsavory views, reluctantly accepting what they disapprove of; the speaker is expected to "keep quiet and refrain from saying things that others may dislike." The result is that offended parties are considered victims while the offenders, like Rose, "are exposed to death threats, physical assault and sometimes even murder."[5] In addition to excusing violence, this twisted concept of tolerance takes away all human agency.

As the British intellectual Kenan Malik writes in his book on the Rushdie crisis, "Between words and deeds stands a human being, with a mind of his own, an ability to judge between right and wrong and a responsibility to face up to his own actions. It is not the words themselves that cause things to happen. . . . Words have consequences only if we choose to make them consequential."[6]

For Malik, the greatest sin of the outside world during the cartoon controversy was to afford the Danish imams who fanned the flames of the crisis by distributing the published images (as well as some other ones that had nothing to do with *Jyllands-Posten*) the honor of being "spokesmen for Danish Muslims." Coverage of the anti-cartoon protests seemed to confer a similar status on the Egyptian, Saudi, and Iranian governments despite the fact that many of Europe's Muslims are refugees from those same countries and would likely object to those officials speaking on their behalf.[7] Malik decries the many Western liberals who dismissed Muslim Danes like parliamentarian Naser Khader as an inauthentic Muslim because he did not take offense and protest the cartoons the way other Muslims did. "In liberal eyes . . . to be a real Muslim is to find the cartoons offensive. Once Muslim authenticity is so defined then only a figure like Abu Laban [one of the hard-line imams] can be seen as a true Muslim voice."[8]

The same problem has plagued Britain's multicultural policies. As Malik argues, the government has "treated minority communities as homogeneous wholes, ignoring conflicts within those communities. . . . They have empowered not minority communities but so-called community leaders who owe their influence largely to the relationship they possess with the state."[9] During the Rushdie controversy, this dynamic played out on a worldwide stage, and the objective of the Muslim community's self-appointed "leaders" was not, as Malik puts it, to "protect Muslim communities from unconscionable attack from anti-Muslim bigots" but to "assert their right to be the true voice of Islam" by silencing or sidelining their more moderate or radical critics within the community. And, in his estimation, these illiberal voices promoting violence against Rushdie in the late 1980s, like those fomenting anti-Danish sentiment in 2006, "succeeded at least in part because secular liberals embraced them," turning them into the authentic representatives of a supposedly monolithic Muslim community.[10]

For certain people who had once identified with the left, the hypocrisy was too much. The British writer Nick Cohen demanded to know why the liberal left was defending fundamentalist Islamists who clashed with everything they stood for. "Why will students hear a leftish post-modern theorist defend the exploitation of women in traditional cultures but not a crusty conservative don?"[11] And why on earth were supposed antifascists downplaying the crimes of the late twentieth century's preeminent genocidal leader, Slobodan Milošević, questioning the existence of Serb concentration camps, and denouncing Bill Clinton and Madeleine Albright for bombing Serbia as Noam Chomsky and some of his followers did? In Cohen's view, the academic left had fled from anything resembling universal values and retreated into a relativist cocoon that didn't differentiate between the Clinton administration and Milošević's murderous regime.

The leftist intelligentsia saw American imperialism as the only true enemy and couldn't imagine any other. As Cohen argued, "Writer after writer was incapable of grasping that people with brown skins were as capable as people with white skins were of forming a fascistic movement and murdering and oppressing others," a stance on display once again in the wake of the cartoon crisis, when there was great reluctance to condemn the offended even when they turned to violence.[12] The initial earthquake occasioned by the publication of the cartoons has had many aftershocks.

THE ELDERLY DANISH CARTOONIST KURT WESTERGAARD, FAMOUS AND reviled for penning the image of the Prophet Muhammad with a bomb in his turban, was at home on New Year's Day 2010 watching *The Wizard of Oz* with his five-year-old granddaughter. He had left the girl alone in front of the TV to go to the bathroom when he heard shattering glass. An ax-wielding man had smashed through the garden door, screaming "I'll kill you!" as he chased the seventy-four-year-old Westergaard through the house. The cartoonist ran back to his bathroom, a designated safe room, and locked the door, leaving the terrified five-year-old, who had a broken leg, lying in a cast on the couch.[13]

Westergaard's house outside the city of Aarhus was already a fortress with CCTV security cameras, bulletproof windows, and a panic button designed to bring police within two minutes. Since 2007, when the first credible death threats against him were confirmed by Denmark's intelligence service, Westergaard and his wife had been shuttled from hotel to hotel and eventually secret apartments when certain hotels refused to house him due to the security risks. His wife, Gitte, was told to leave her job at a local kindergarten until the mayor and the press intervened to reinstate her. We "lived in 10 different safe houses and drove 10 different cars,"[14] he told a reporter. In the end, it was the safe room that saved his life.

The decision to leave his granddaughter alone rather than confront the attacker was harrowing, but security officials had told him that terrorists would target him, not his family, because in their view it was he who had offended Islam. They were right.

The attacker, a twenty-eight-year-old Somali man, had taken a train from Copenhagen to Aarhus with an ax and a knife in his bag, hailed a cab to Westergaard's street, and jumped over a fence into the garden. He completely ignored the five-year-old and instead hacked at the reinforced bathroom door, screaming at Westergaard. When the police arrived, he ran from the house and hurled an ax at one of the officers. They shot him in the leg and arm.[15] The man was charged with terrorism and two counts of attempted murder and sentenced to ten years in prison.[16]

The Danish cartoon controversy matters because it accelerated the country's political shift toward the right. Danes who had never contemplated voting for the DPP now saw their embassies on fire, a seventy-four-year-old compatriot nearly murdered in his own home because of a drawing, and death threats against some of their best-known journalists. Suddenly, the DPP's platform was making sense.

They had warned that Muslims were extremists in waiting; now those warnings seemed to be coming true. The image that graced the cover of the DPP's 2001 campaign book, *Denmark's Future: Your Country, Your Vote,* featured angry bearded Muslims protesting aggressively, now a daily occurrence.[17] Politicians like Naser Khader, himself a Muslim and a refugee who came to Denmark as a child from Syria, drifted to the right of the political spectrum. Khader founded a group called Democratic Muslims and promptly received a death threat from one of the anti-cartoon imams.

Khader was once considered a man of the left, but his own politics have gradually moved to the right along with the country's. The Mohammed cartoon crisis was a turning point for him. He has been attacked as an Uncle Tom by Islamic fundamentalists and criticized by those on the left for not taking offense at the cartoons, as "authentic Muslims" apparently should. "I left the Radikale Venstre because I felt I was homeless politically," he says, referring to his former party. "The cartoon crisis made me change my political platform," he says, dismissing his former political home as a hotbed of cultural relativism. His old party advocated dialogue with Islamists; Khader disagreed, arguing, "Sometimes you have to be very, very hard" on extremists. He complains about most Danes' "naivety and superficial knowledge" of Islam and the Middle East. "It's very frustrating when people don't understand the DNA of this ideology," he told me.

Islamists tend to speak in a language that average Danes don't understand unless they have some background in theology or the politics of the Arab world. "You need people that understand Islam and the Koran," Khader argues. "If you don't understand the history of Islam and their language, it's very difficult" to make sense of the extremist groups' ideologies and aims. He doesn't think the far right has any special claim on such understanding; they have simply been more effective at mobilizing around the issue.

The DPP is not "more clever . . . or more expert on Islam than others. They don't know anything about it!" he exclaims. But they were willing to speak about problems that voters were worried about while establishment parties looked the other way. They "succeed because you have a collective denial. . . . Now the other parties have woken up."

To illustrate his point, he mentions a recent sermon by a well-known fundamentalist imam about whether Islam should dialogue with its enemies. As Khader recalls it, the imam asked, "Do you remember what Islam's army did with God's enemy at the Battle at Uhud?" The reference would be lost on most Danes, but not Khader. It is, he notes, a reference to a battle where Islamic soldiers massacred two Jewish tribes. Then, Khader recounts, the imam declared: "We should not dialogue with the enemy of God. We should trick them as we did in Uhud." He is adamant that religious leaders like this have no place in the country.[18]

In 2008, the same week that street riots were raging in Copenhagen in response to a police brutality case, seventeen publications decided to reprint the controversial cartoons in a show of solidarity with other newspapers being pressured in the courts in various countries.

The reappearance of the cartoons helped the riots evolve from a metropolitan Copenhagen event into a nationwide protest. The media, by portraying the riots as a mass phenomenon at a time when many people, including potential rioters, were glued to their TVs, played their part in spreading them. As one of the young men who participated told the sociologist Aydin Soei, "It's not like young people here were calling around all over the country asking people to set things on fire. The media were our spin doctors."[19]

Soei developed the concept of countercitizenship, or *modborgerskab*, a play on the Danish word for citizenship (*medborgerskab*), transforming a word that literally suggests living-with-ness into one that connotes a condition of living against or in opposition. The key causes of countercitizenship, he argues, are low education, low expectations, and the stigmatization that comes from living in areas that are constantly discussed as problems in public debates. Young Europeans from immigrant backgrounds are beginning to define themselves in opposition to society as countercitizens. In his view, the riots that rocked the Paris suburbs in 2005 and Copenhagen's immigrant neighborhoods in 2008 stem from accumulated lack of opportunities and recognition.[20]

Denmark's riots started after police accosted and beat a sixty-year-old disabled Muslim man in the largely immigrant area of Nørrebro. The man was a respected and well-known fixture in the community. The police initially denied the incident completely, blaming it on "boredom during the winter holidays," and later the officers were acquitted of any wrongdoing.[21]

As police moved in on the neighborhood, the media coverage was full of military metaphors about "pincer movements" while reporters dutifully parroted the government's line. Young men in the area described journalists going past to snap a quick photo and then driving on without stopping "as if we were in a zoo."[22]

Media accounts often use the shorthand "of foreign background" to describe criminals. When a white Danish man named Rasmus was found guilty of a murder in the center of Copenhagen's tourist district, the press incredulously described him as "not the typical image of a killer" and "not looking like a cold-blooded murderer." Indeed, he "came from good circumstances and went to a top private school."

The fact is that, in Denmark, those who look like twenty-year-old Rasmus usually walk free while people named Omar or Abas regularly get targeted for searches. Yet it has been a major debate in parliament whether young men who are not yet citizens but who have little connection to their parents' homeland can be expelled as a measure to prevent crime. That's because, Soei argues, "Middle Eastern ethnicity and violent crime are two phenomena that have become linked together in the media."[23]

First-generation women have done better, with many finding jobs in the service sector, but their brothers are suffering in a job market where stereotypically unskilled male jobs have largely disappeared. For those without education, unemployment is around 40 percent. As Soei argues, "unskilled men risk ending up at the bottom of society with lesser opportunities for creating a good life for themselves and winning recognition from their fellow citizens."[24]

Although the situation has improved somewhat in the last decade, there has been a corresponding spike in perceptions of discrimination, and not just among angry young men. On the contrary, Soei contends, "it is the best-educated citizens of immigrant background that feel themselves most discriminated against in Danish society"—people who feel that they "have earned the right to be recognized as fully equal citizens" but are still treated as outsiders.[25]

ONE OF THE KEY FIGURES IN CHARGE OF RESPONDING TO SECURITY threats at the time of the 2008 riots was Jakob Scharf. Denmark has, like France and Belgium, also had its intelligence failures. Before the attack that killed a guard outside Copenhagen's synagogue in February 2015, the Danish intelligence agency had contacted the prisons to ask about potential radicalization. According to Scharf, who led the agency from 2007 to 2013, one of the lapses occurred because the prisons didn't take warnings seriously, setting aside the reports they had received.

There's always a risk, he says, that when sifting through massive amounts of information, analysts will miss something. Quickly evolving technology also presents a challenge that makes it difficult for intelligence agencies to keep up. Nor does having people in the right place always prevent an attack. When the attacker struck at the Copenhagen synagogue, there were armed police present, and he still managed to shoot someone. Since then there have been armed police outside Jewish community buildings 24-7. "That's an extremely expensive way to create security. Does it change anything?" he asks. If the same attacker, deterred by police, decides to attack the shopping mall across the street, has the security actually helped?

For Scharf, the more important battleground is in the neighborhoods where young men susceptible to radicalization live. Some communities have been successful in rooting out terrorist elements; others have not. The key is a strong and secure sense of belonging. "If we want to mobilize local communities . . . we need to make sure that they do see themselves as being part of society in general and not being someone in opposition to the rest of society." And the tenor of the current debate in Denmark is doing the opposite. As in Holland, the default national identity is still seen as synonymous with being white and ethnically Danish.

Scharf has mixed feelings about Denmark's fierce debate. "On one hand, the debate lets off some steam" because those on the far right don't "feel the need to resort to violence," as they might in a more restricted society, he argues matter-of-factly and as someone who has dealt with threats from neo-Nazis as well as Islamic fundamentalists. "In other countries, they feel they can't talk about it at all," which sometimes leads to far-right militancy like the Norwegian killer Breivik's massacre. Scharf is not against the give-and-take of politics, but he objects to "the way of communicating" that has come to characterize Danish debates on immigration.[26]

Echoing Soei and some of his angry young sources, Scharf argues that the prevalent message in media and online is: if you're Muslim, you're not really part of this society.

The DPP's deputy leader, Søren Espersen, is having none of it. He completely rejects the argument that the tone of political debate and his own party's campaigns might drive extremism. If that were the case, argues Espersen, "there wouldn't be any of them in Pakistan, would there? Or Afghanistan or Yemen or Saudi Arabia. This has got nothing to do with what we do or say or the tone or anything, or bad integration," he insists. "It is simply these taught religious ways that make this possible. And it is the same all over, whether you put money into integration or you don't."

The Scandinavian nations, he argues, have invested more than anyone in integration, mentioning consultants and police-community dialogue groups. "It made no difference. The situation is the same in France, in Germany, in Austria and wherever." He doesn't seem concerned that money and effort may have been invested in bad ideas or the wrong programs.

Espersen also has no interest in the American melting pot model and British-style multiculturalism, arguing that enclaves, whether in Brooklyn or Bradford, are a disaster. "In America, you shut your eyes and don't want to hear about it. Take Jewish Williamsburg. They live their own life. Everything is within these borders. They go to work and come out and work here, and then go back again. Nobody knows what's happening," he argues. Christianity isn't immune, he concedes. Some fundamentalist groups in America are "absolutely mad" and no one pays attention "until they start killing each other."

He doesn't want "parallel states" in Denmark and he blames Muslim communities for failing to tackle the extremism in their midst. Instead, he complains, it's Christians who end up leading the fight. "They don't do a thing. Maybe out of fear," he adds.

As Espersen sees it, you must "publicly announce that you put the Danish constitution over your religious laws." And if that means taking kippas away from Jews or turbans from Sikhs in public buildings, so be it. "If that's the law of the land, then you abide. It works in France, and I think it's a good idea." He thinks it will help young Muslim women become free. The veil is anathema to Danish values, he believes. "To those young girls, especially in the Muslim society, it is a pressure. I see them with head scarves all the way down to five- or six-year-old girls." Here his feminist streak emerges, and it becomes clear how appealing the DPP's rhetoric could be for a traditional European feminist who deplores religious oppression of women. "Some of the best Muslim girls are very, very clever. They go in and take the highest educations and become doctors and lawyers and have high degrees and then they get married to their cousin and just stay home and make babies," Espersen laments.[27]

What he misses is that counterterrorism requires allies, and if those potential allies are angry and alienated or feel scapegoated by the larger society, they may be discouraged from helping. A paper published by Scharf's company, CERTA, and the foundation TrygFonden concluded that local communities, including moderate imams, are vital in fighting extremism and that feelings of marginalization can be manipulated to fuel radicalization.[28]

The findings focus on building strong, resilient communities that can detect and root out extremists. But the solution has a great deal to do with inclusion and a sense of belonging and investment in the larger society.

"One of the strongest identities we have in Western countries as individuals will be through the work we do," says Scharf.[29] If asylum seekers, or young men of immigrant background, are excluded from work life, how do they form a Danish identity? "I think that is the basic problem," he adds. "Where do they belong?" For the unemployed, religious extremist groups provide a strong, ready-made identity and a sense of camaraderie and belonging.

When a community is invested in the larger society and feels part of it, rather than a ghetto apart, locals can often be far more effective intelligence gatherers than any law enforcement agency. He mentions a network of Somali women in Funen, an island in central Denmark, where there have been problems with radicalization and extremism. These mothers are much more effective, he says, than the police's antiradicalization unit. "Instead of putting the ghetto label on a certain area," he says, they should be asking, "Where are the resources? What kind of local interests can we support?"

He believes the model could be hugely helpful in parts of France and Belgium. Instead of hoping that problems "will remain in these areas and will not slip into the rest of society," says Scharf, they should be engaging locals who "could be calling the parents, talking to neighbors, saying, 'Do you know what is going on?'" But making those communities feel they have a stake in society is a prerequisite to getting their cooperation.

In France and Belgium, the sense of exclusion is arguably even stronger. There are lots of young second- or third-generation immigrants who live on society's margins. Because of the rigid secularism in France, it is easier for radical groups to point to perceived injustices and recruit disillusioned young men. Citing the prohibition against veils in public schools is an easy way to inflame an already angry young person. In Britain, a country where police officers are permitted to wear turbans and no one stops a woman in full niqab walking down the street, the pitch must be different. It's harder to point to something in the UK that explicitly targets Muslims, Scharf says, so recruiters choose another injustice—blaming Britain for military interventions in Afghanistan and Iraq.

It's not just Muslims, he says; there are potential future Breiviks among the right- and left-wing extremists, too. What interests him is, who are these people becoming radicalized? What are the catalyzing issues? What makes radicalization succeed, and what is the process that draws them to extremism? Their profiles are quite similar; the reason that young Muslims are especially vulnerable these days is that they are the newest minority and Danish identity has not done much to embrace them, Scharf argues.

"Immigration is still something which is new to us," he says. "We have to understand that this is also about making sure that people who come from different cultures, people who come from other countries . . . should be able to identify themselves as Danish when they actually live here." Instead, the majority continues to do things, he insists, that send the message, "You might be born in Denmark, you might be raised and you've been educated, you've been working in Denmark, but you are still not really Danish."[30]

It's not a huge surprise, then, that a seven-year-old girl recently approached the Danish-Turkish MP Yildiz Akdogan on the street near her home in Copenhagen's Nørrebro neighborhood and asked, "So, are you a Muslim, too?"

Akdogan smiled at her and said, "I'm from Nørrebro, just like you."

And the girl insisted, "But you are a Muslim, right?"

It made Akdogan cringe.

"It's because everyone is asking her, 'Are you a Muslim?' or everyone is addressing her like that. She's not going to answer you if you ask her, 'Where do you come from?' She will not say, 'I am from Nørrebro. I'm a

Dane.' She will say, 'I'm a Muslim.'" This doesn't help create a sense of Danish pride among minorities. By focusing on identities that exclude people, she insists, "we are not contributing to the integration process."[31]

The latest iteration is a campaign in city councils to serve pork to children in kindergarten classes. The only reason to lobby for public pork provision, as Scharf puts it bluntly, is to tell people, "If you are Muslim, you are not really a Dane." Jews may feel offended or excluded, too, but, Scharf argues, they have a longer history of being a minority group and hence have more experience with such forms of subtle social exclusion. "I think Jews are much more used to the fact that they are confronted with these kinds of issues, and they have to work out their own solutions, they will have their own kindergartens, they will have their own schools."[32]

The sociologist Aydin Soei is skeptical about words themselves doing damage or leading to radicalization, but he has had his own experiences with being mistaken as a foreigner at home and as a native abroad. "It doesn't have to do with the tone itself, but it has to do with when people who have been born here or lived here their entire lives are talked about as if they were aliens in society, as if they are not Danish. So we have a problem with the narrative that you are only Danish if you are white," argues Soei. He was shocked, for instance, while living in New York, to be seen as white. "I lived in the Upper West Side and went for a walk in Harlem," he recalls. "The police stopped a black couple, and I just walked by. The black woman pointed at me and said, 'Why don't you stop that white guy over there?'" Soei, who has a distinctly Middle Eastern complexion and appearance, looked around, wondering where the white guy was, until he realized that she meant him. It was the first time in his life he'd been considered white.[33]

Another driving force behind the resentment of these angry young men is employment discrimination and lack of access to basic amenities of social life. Rather than submitting a CV with an address in one of Copenhagen's immigrant areas, many Muslim men fake it to give themselves a chance for an interview. Many of Copenhagen's nightclubs have quotas, according to bouncers, limiting the number of entries to twenty or so young men with immigrant backgrounds. Those who show up later in the evening get rejected. Soei has felt the sting himself.

Many of the young people from Nørrebro feel that their complaints disappear into a hole in the public debate and that they are not taken seriously in the same way that other citizens would be. They argue that the police have a monopoly on defining reality in media coverage of the riots. As several young men wrote in an op-ed after the riots, they just wanted to be treated like any other Danes by politicians and the media, rather than being sidelined or discriminated against "because of our names or skin color which still describe us as immigrants despite the fact that we were born here in this country."[34]

For Soei, the greatest paradox of the riots is that they are "likely to jeopardize the possibilities for young people to be perceived as citizens worthy of recognition in Danish society, while it is precisely this lack of recognition as morally accountable fellow citizens, that these youths so urgently seek."[35]

Espersen is dismissive of the complaints he hears from minorities and waves off claims of employment discrimination and other barriers. "There have been some young Muslims that have said to me, 'What about us? What can we do?' I say everything is open for you. If you think you live in a ghetto, move to Jutland, and you can have a house there. If you want to have an education, go and get one. What is all the complaining about?" he asks. "Denmark is one of the best societies in the world. Every option is open. You can go to university without paying. You get your books paid. You get a study loan. You get an allowance and everything. Everything is free. The world is yours."[36]

The French philosopher Pascal Bruckner generally agrees with the ideas of Espersen and others on the right when it comes to culture wars; he is best known for his scathing criticism of the left's apologetics for third-world dictators. To "excuse the atrocities of new nations by citing colonialism, imperialism, American influence, or whatever, is to start from an outrageous falsehood," he wrote. Rather than promoting justice, such apologists are helping newly independent nations "revert to forms of despotism that democratic tradition has already confronted and conquered," Bruckner argued in his incendiary book *Tears of the White Man*.[37]

But unlike Espersen, who is quick to dismiss all grievances, Bruckner is clear-eyed about the discrimination and anger among the children of immigrants today, something that most on the right dismiss as whining. Like Soei, Bruckner has seen firsthand the exclusion that was creating a counteridentity among the young French of the banlieues born to immigrant parents and not fully accepted as citizens. And like the angry young men in Denmark, he sees it happening in Paris.

"Born French, they now want to become French, but they feel themselves impeded by an invisible screen behind which they see their compatriots succeeding, working, and amusing themselves without inviting them to join the party. The color of their skin, and especially their social origin and their address constitute an insurmountable barrier," he wrote. For him, it was a negative form of integration. "France humiliated their parents and now ignores them, and their rage can also be interpreted as a cry of disappointed love, a way of saying: we're here, we exist."[38]

DESPITE THEIR RELATIVE SUCCESS IN EDUCATION AND WORK IN comparison with their brothers, Muslim women in Europe face their own dilemmas. Akdogan, the MP, recalls a recent talk she gave at a local school where many of the students were religious young Muslims. They asked Akdogan, in Danish, "What does it take for us to become Danes?" She looked at them quizzically and told them they already were and tried to convince them that their religious identity didn't define them. "All of them are born and raised in Denmark; they don't even speak their mother tongue," she told me, "and still, they don't see themselves as Danes."[39]

Messages that make minorities doubt their Danishness are frequent and sometimes come from top government officials, not just politically incorrect tabloids. In 2016, the prickly conservative former immigration minister Bertel Haarder asserted that Danishness means acceptance of gender equality, freedom of speech, hard work, and riding a bike, among other things, prompting a Danish-Iraqi writer who grew up in Syria to pen an op-ed letting him know that she had learned to ride her bike in Damascus, while a Danish-Pakistani reminded the minister that in addition to cycling to school every day for years in a working-class Copenhagen suburb, he had been raised by a hardworking mother.[40]

The story of Akdogan's own family, and how the broader society referred to them, is revealing. It is the story of how people went from being perceived as strangers to being regarded as a threat.

"In 1973, when my mother came to Denmark, she was a guest worker," the MP explains. The term recognized that she was actively participating in the society. Then in the 1980s, she became a foreign worker. "She had become a foreigner but she still was a worker" who was seen as contributing. Then, in the 1990s, she recalls, "there were these words like *Paki, Turkish,* or *black* . . . it was their national identity that was at the front." And finally, after 9/11, she became a Muslim. Age, gender, ethnicity, language, nothing else mattered. She was, Akdogan says, "reduced to one thing, and that was her religion."[41]

The fear of Islam that has gripped Denmark has also reshaped its political debate. During the 2015 election campaign, the so-called foreigner question took up over 40 percent of newspaper articles and TV coverage and set off a culture war over Danish identity that lasted long after the election. The shift in tone has had an impact. The Conservative Party's leader declared in the last campaign, "A Muslim culture from the Middle Ages will never become as valued here as the Danish culture that has grown from this old piece of earth," sounding more like a DPP candidate.[42] Anders Fogh Rasmussen, the former prime minister, once told a newspaper that it was the *kulturkamp,* not economic policy, that would be the determining factor in Danish politics of the future. He was right.

The dominant strain of politics these days emphasizes Danish culture and rejects anything foreign, especially if it's Islamic. It has even affected politicians who present themselves as libertarians. The widespread feeling is that Islam is "something that needs to be criticized, that needs to be seen as a threat," says Rasmus Brygger, who is twenty-seven and was until recently the youth leader of the Liberal Alliance, Denmark's most staunchly economically conservative party, before he had a falling out with the party over the immigration issue.

Brygger doesn't believe this new political climate is primarily the Danish People's Party's work, as others argue. "It's because of how the other parties reacted to the DPP," he insists. It is more a question of rhetoric than policies. "You see a lot of things being said, especially on social media but also by politicians today, that you would never have seen just five years ago and that would not even have been accepted if it came from the DPP," Brygger explains.

Despite his free-market libertarianism, Brygger is now seen as a leftist in the Danish media because of his views on immigration. This is a clear sign of how dramatically the political battle lines have shifted. Left and right used to be defined by economics in Denmark; now those boundaries are defined by immigration policy.

With the old predictable cleavages over welfare and taxes moving to the back burner, it is one's position on refugees and integration that now provides one's political identity. Politicians used to have real ideological positions, whether conservative or socialist, giving voters something to cling to when populist winds blew. But that era is over. It's dangerous, says Brygger, "because if you don't have an ideology and you don't have some kind of core principles, you can just go anywhere you'd like."[43]

The sudden obsession with Danish culture and identity is largely a reaction to the more visible presence of immigrants, many of whom are religious. In parts of rural Denmark, voters see it as a threat if they can't sell pork or publicly celebrate Christmas, says Brygger. "They see their culture under fire. So to them it's not a matter of economics."

But it's not necessarily those living side by side with new immigrants who are voting for the DPP. Brygger believes "if you have grown up with Mohammed as your neighbor, then you wouldn't have that kind of view." The kind of people who vote DPP, he says, tend to live in areas with very few Muslims. The electoral map confirms that the party has strong support in many lily-white parts of the country.

But as in Holland, in Denmark there is a powerful clash between what has become a staunchly secular society and a newly arrived population that is pious and practicing. "We are one of the most atheist countries in the world." It's rare to see Christians wearing crosses, so head scarves came as a shock.[44]

This is particular to countries like Denmark, Holland, and France, which pride themselves on a secular identity. Praying five times a day or eating halal meat is considered a sign of extremism by Danes who love their bacon and generally only go to church for weddings and funerals, if at all. As Brygger argues, no American Christian who prays regularly would ever be singled out in public debate as an extremist. In many parts of the United States, that is considered normal.

Arne Hardis, the conservative Danish journalist, believes that the extremely blunt public debate is a virtue. Talking about serving pork in public schools may make Americans laugh, he admits, "but it's about who should be tolerant of whom. There has to be an open discussion because it's an ideological fight," he insists.[45] But there is a difference between standing up for freedom of the press against Muslim imams making violent threats and needlessly provoking and marginalizing minority groups.

The problem is that what strikes Danes as a necessary frank discussion often sounds different to immigrants and their children. There are aspects of Danish culture that predate the arrival of nonwhite people and smack of a certain naivety and cluelessness about living in a diverse society. When I lived in Denmark as a teenager in the 1990s, it was normal to see chocolate-covered marshmallow desserts marketed as Negerboller (Negro Balls), and a popular video game at the time, the Mujaffa Game, featured a dark-skinned protagonist going through Copenhagen's streets stealing cars. What appears to some as fun and games is not always perceived the same way by those being mocked.

Media coverage of the immigration issue, like those antiquated traditions, reinforces the sense of nonwhite Danes as foreigners rather than fellow citizens. A study showed less than one percent of sources on Danish TV were of minority background. When they do pop up on TV, it's rarely to talk about taxes and health care.[46] They tend to appear only when the topic is integration or crime. Unlike in the UK, where BBC News is full of black and brown faces, that level of televised diversity seems nearly impossible in Denmark.

While Brygger agrees with conservatives about many of the problems surrounding immigration and integration, he sees a dangerous trend that many European intellectuals twice his age have failed to grasp: when a small Muslim minority is guilty of violence, which it is, "that can also legitimize solutions to that problem, which can hit all Muslims," he warns. In Denmark, the result has been that "we in our minds combine Muslims with radical Islam and terrorism, we combine immigrants with crime and rape," Brygger argues. "So you have this idea of a collective Muslim, and that's a very dangerous thing."[47]

5

Out of Sight, Out of Mind: Europe's Fantasy of Offshoring

THE DPP DOES NOT HAVE MUCH TO SAY WHEN IT COMES TO INTEGRATING the Danish-born children of immigrants and those who have lived in the country for many years. "They have no answer. They will say they have to act like a Dane, they have to be Christian, they have to go to church, they have to eat pork," says Thomas Gyldal Petersen, the mayor of Herlev, outside Copenhagen. As for those arriving now, he adds, "They have no answer, other than keep them out."[1]

Not talking about integration allows far-right politicians to sidestep serious social policy dilemmas. They want a simple and clear message, which essentially amounts to: refugees should just be sent home.

The DPP's deputy leader, Espersen, doesn't deny the charge that his party is trying to make Denmark look unappealing. He is very pleased about the negative ads Denmark printed in Middle Eastern newspapers. They helped, says Espersen. People understood that "the streets are not paved with gold here, and it's not paradise." He also has no qualms about sending a message that the party is not interested in integrating any more new arrivals, as many of the DPP's detractors charge. "Instead of what we've done in the past, automatically preparing themselves for staying, we should prepare them for going home," he insists. Espersen told me in April 2016 that the war in Syria would soon be over. "No war lasts forever, and of course there will be a time and then they must go back," he said. "The Palestinians, if they get their state, they must go back, too." He makes an exception only for those who are settled and have permanent residence and citizenship.[2]

He believes two years of provisional asylum would be fair. "Tell them from the beginning and let them know this is what it is. You have no future in Denmark." One of the party's key policy proposals is to offer asylum only on a temporary basis: "Take refugees, give them asylum but under the conditions that they go." It must be clear that "we don't want to integrate them. We give them asylum, we help them and everything, but the idea is that they should go back home; and maybe the education for the children here should be more English than Danish so that they can also use that when they get home."[3]

Those who do get sent home do not always get a chance to use their English skills.

For some asylum seekers, even if they are successfully integrated into Danish society, their place in it is not secure. Indeed, Denmark's get-tough policy has been deadly for some who lived in the country for years. Two Afghan brothers, Vahid and Abolfazl Vaziri, came to Denmark after fleeing Afghanistan with their family in 2006 when they were fourteen and seven. As members of the Shiite Hazara minority, they faced persecution in their home province. First, the brothers went to Iran, where their father disappeared; they eventually made their way to Europe and applied for asylum upon reaching Denmark. They were never approved. In June 2015, Danish police barged into their asylum center, forced them to pack, and took them to the airport. After several failed appeals, the brothers were cleared for deportation on the grounds that Afghanistan was now "safe" and that Vahid, then twenty-three, could serve as a guardian for Abolfazl, who was then sixteen. They were given approximately $3,500 in cash by Danish authorities and flown back to Kabul.[4]

Andreas Kamm, the head of the Danish Refugee Council—an organization devoted to helping refugees—is confident that Denmark's asylum appeals process is generally fair and reliable. "If you have a procedure, then you have to send the rejected people back," otherwise the system loses all credibility and effectiveness. Sixty percent of rejected asylum seekers do not go back—they stay illegally, he adds. But sometimes the system fails.[5]

In the case of the Vaziri brothers, they were robbed soon after arriving, and Abolfazl disappeared almost immediately after they returned to their home province of Wardak. Vahid searched for him in vain and eventually returned to Kabul to seek information from the authorities. Penniless, he slept under a bridge with heroin addicts. Two months later,

Vahid contacted his Danish lawyer to tell her that a group of Pashtuns had shown him his brother's body. He fled once again, following the same path he had as a child, heading for Europe through Iran.[6]

The case has been an embarrassment to Danish officials, but there has been no official apology nor any effort to locate Vahid and bring him back to safety in Denmark. Rather than make the country safer, this is the sort of case that can fuel a narrative of victimization among young Danish Muslims and recently arrived refugees.[7]

Khaterah Parwani, who came to Denmark as an Afghan refugee herself in the 1980s, knows this better than most. As a teenager, she was drawn to radical Islamist groups like Hizb-ut-Tahrir and was only pulled back by her parents. She now runs an organization seeking to deradicalize young Danish Muslims; it began with young women but quickly came to encompass young men who had joined radical groups and wanted a way out. She started working on hate crimes against young Muslims in 2013 after the founder of the DPP proclaimed that women choosing to wear a head scarf should take it off if they wanted to avoid becoming victims of street violence.[8] Parwani believes stories like that of the Afghan brothers will make the situation much worse. "Young Afghans used to blame the Taliban," she says. "Now they are blaming the West."[9]

THE DPP'S FOCUS ON TOUGHNESS DOESN'T NECESSARILY EXTEND TO sharing the burden with neighbors. When thousands of asylum seekers and migrants crossed through Denmark en route to Sweden in September 2015, Espersen was quite pleased that they moved on. "They didn't want to stay here. . . . They wanted to go to Sweden because they get 300 kroner more a month than we could provide," he argues, accusing them of welfare tourism. "We don't stop people that want to leave our country; we're not the DDR," he added, referring to the former East Germany. He believes that Eastern European countries are following a similar model— let people come because they're going to move on anyway. Poland is hostile to refugees, but it also knows that many will leave for Germany within a few weeks. But Espersen has bigger plans. He understands asylum seekers' desire to seek a better life but is adamant that Europe bears no responsibility for providing it.

The most elaborate of the DPP's policy proposals is to mimic Australia, with its offshore detention centers on remote islands like Nauru, an independent nation of ten thousand people that is one-third the size of Manhattan and located in the middle of the Pacific Ocean.

Espersen and his colleagues propose funding and staffing "Danish-driven refugee camps where they will be provided for, but the idea is that they should return."[10] And if they end up on Nauru or in Denmark's equivalent of it, even better. Then there is no question of integration at all. "We've actually called for an Australian model in Denmark," Espersen's baby-faced colleague Kenneth Kristensen Berth told me. "We would like to send people to other countries than Denmark to have their asylum complaint assessed." The goal is to outsource any processing of asylum complaints to other countries so there's no chance of refugees ever ending up in Denmark.

When I raise the issue of cost and the astronomical expenditures the Australian government has incurred by refusing to admit any asylum seekers, he seems unfazed. It would be cheap, he insists, "in comparison to what it'd have cost us to have all of those people come." Moreover, he argues, "you have to remember that this is also a deterrent," using the Australian government's favorite label. "Because if people know . . . we'll cross the Danish-German border, then we go from getting asylum in Germany to getting our case assessed in Tanzania, I wonder how many people would cross."[11]

ALTHOUGH IT RARELY MAKES THE NEWS, AUSTRALIA'S IMMIGRATION policy has become a beacon for Europe's new right. From France to Denmark, politicians point to the Australian model as the solution for Europe's refugee crisis, and they are not talking about the points system that Australia uses to determine the educational and skill levels of potential immigrants. The real attraction, especially since the massive refugee influx of 2015, is offshoring.

Spending taxpayer money to ensure that refugees never reach Australian shores has become a specialty in Canberra. Between 2013 and 2016, the government has spent approximately 9.6 billion Australian dollars (approximately $7.4 billion) to turn back boats, transport asylum seekers, and pay foreign governments and private security companies to detain them in foreign states, thus absolving themselves of legal and sovereign responsibility for the living conditions of the detainees and any obligation to grant them refugee status in Australia if their asylum claim is found to be genuine. The total cost is approximately 400,000 Australian dollars ($300,000) per detained asylum seeker.[12]

Rather than rescue people at sea, the Australian navy put intercepted asylum seekers into small orange lifeboat pods, sealed vessels that were then sent off to sea in the direction of Indonesia.[13] For those not turned back, the Pacific backwaters of Nauru and Manus Island were the only options, and the miserable conditions of confinement there were part and parcel of the deterrence policy.

For European politicians seeking to stop the flow of migrants and prevent their populations from even encountering suffering refugees fleeing Syria, lest they become sympathetic and welcoming, the Australian model of putting them out of sight and out of mind has undeniable appeal. It is a form of moral and judicial outsourcing.

In September 2015, after the body of three-year-old Alan Kurdi washed up on Turkish shores, Nigel Farage, leader of the UK Independence Party (UKIP), announced that "if the European Union had the right policy, people would know they would not be accepted by coming across the water, just as the Australians dealt with this problem, and that would stop the drownings from happening."[14] Douglas Carswell, UKIP's only member of parliament at the time, argued, "There are lessons to learn from Australia. It's come up with something that works."[15]

In October 2015, six weeks after being deposed as Australia's prime minister in a fit of intraparty backstabbing, Tony Abbott arrived in London to give the Thatcher Memorial Address at Guildhall. He praised the Iron Lady's resolve in the Falklands and offered paeans to Tory greatness before launching into a more self-referential discussion of Australia's immigration policy and how his government single-handedly put an end to the arrival of boat people.

He lectured the assembled Tories about the perils of loving one's neighbor as oneself, calling it a "wholesome instinct [that is] leading much of Europe into catastrophic error." Due to "misguided altruism," Europe was weakening itself, argued Abbott, and the only way to reverse the tide, he insisted, was studying and emulating Australia's policy. By Abbott's dubious account, no illegal arrivals had reached Australia in over a year and "the immigration detention centres have-all-but-closed; budget costs peaking at $4 billion a year have ended; and—best of all—there are no more deaths at sea." This, he claimed, was a truly compassionate policy.

Whether those turned away died in another country's waters or back in the countries they initially fled did not figure in his equation. By removing images of boats capsizing off Australia's shores from local television and ensuring that more migrants seeking asylum did not arrive in the country, his work was done. Nor was he bothered by the ongoing expenditure of billions of dollars for detaining asylum seekers offshore on Nauru and Manus Island and occasionally flying them thousands of miles at taxpayer expense for medical treatment in Australia.

The core of Abbott's argument was that "in Europe, as with Australia, people claiming asylum—invariably—have crossed not one border but many; and are no longer fleeing in fear but are contracting in hope with people smugglers. However desperate, almost by definition, they are economic migrants," he insisted.[16] By this tortuous logic, a Rohingya refugee who flees from Myanmar to Malaysia but is abused by police and arrested for trying to work—and cannot claim asylum because he is stateless and Malaysia isn't a party to the UN refugee convention—becomes an "economic migrant" simply by refusing to stop his journey. "Our moral obligation is to receive people fleeing for their lives. It's not to provide permanent residency to anyone and everyone who would rather live in a prosperous Western country," said Abbott.

The Australian model is not about efficient resettlement of refugees; it's about keeping them out. Abbott's policy prescription was simple: turn boats back, deny entry at borders, and build camps. Some force would be necessary and a lot of money, he admitted. Sounding a bit like the fictional French president in *Camp of the Saints*, he declared, "It will gnaw at our consciences—yet it is the only way to prevent a tide of humanity surging through Europe and quite possibly changing it forever." Abbott's real fear is the same as Raspail's—Western civilization being replaced. He even went so far as to criticize the EU and NATO naval presence between Greece and Turkey for being excessively compassionate toward refugees on capsized vessels. "As long as they're taking passengers aboard rather than turning boats around and sending them back, it's a facilitator rather than a deterrent."[17]

An anonymous Tory minister labeled the speech "fascistic."[18] Farage called Abbott "heroic."[19] Elsewhere in Europe, the right was watching closely.

UKIP AND THE DPP ARE NOT THE ONLY PARTIES ON THE EUROPEAN right looking Down Under for inspiration. Yohann Faviere, one of the Front National's local leaders in Calais, France, thinks it is the only viable model. "When they find a boat in the sea, they send the migrants back," he says admiringly of the Australians. He is bothered by the drownings but is adamant that Italy and Greece shouldn't be in the business of rescuing refugees. "The boats found in the Med need to be sent back to where they came from," he insists. [20]

Frits Bolkestein, the former leader of Holland's center-right VVD Party, who gave Geert Wilders his first political job, agrees that Australia is the answer to Europe's current problems. "The better we treat them, the more they come," he told me. "If you don't want them to come, you should not treat them all that well, which is what the Australians do." Bolkestein insists that Australian-style controls are the only solution as more and more of the world's poor, whether they are refugees or not, seek to move to Europe. "Look at the United Nations' statistics about African natality," he says. "It's most disturbing. Countries like Central African Republic, it's a failed state, and they go on producing children. Do we want them to come here? No, we don't, so what do we do? Australian solution."

When pressed on whether this would actually solve the problem of asylum seekers coming to Europe, he concedes that it wouldn't. "We are trained in the West to think that every problem has a solution," he tells me. "There's no solution to this, unless we adopt very nasty measures."[21] And nasty measures have become an Australian specialty.

The course of Australian immigration policy changed forever in August 2001. On August 26, a distress call went out from the KM *Palapa*, a vessel with over four hundred asylum seekers aboard sailing from Indonesia toward Australia's Christmas Island. Australian maritime authorities instructed any nearby vessels to attempt a rescue. The task fell to Captain Arne Rinnan at the helm of the MV *Tampa*, a Norwegian freighter that had just set sail from Perth heading for Singapore. Australian coast guard planes helped guide the *Tampa* to the site of the capsizing boat. Rinnan's crew hoisted over four hundred people onto its deck as the *Palapa* broke apart in heavy swells. It was then that the crisis began.

Maritime law requires a ship to take those rescued at sea to the closest suitable port, which was in Indonesia, twelve hours away. A group of asylum seekers refused to turn back to Indonesia and aggressively confronted the captain, asking him to take them to the closest harbor, which was Australia's Christmas Island—just six hours away. Several of those rescued were unconscious and sick with dysentery, and the ship, designed for cargo and a few dozen crew, only had sleeping quarters for fifty people. Rinnan agreed to head for Christmas Island, which was not equipped to dock a large freighter like the *Tampa*. On the evening of August 29, the *Tampa* declared a state of emergency aboard and approached Australian waters, despite lacking clearance. The government turned up the heat.

Although Australia had issued the initial call for rescue assistance, the conservative government led by Prime Minister John Howard had now changed its tune; that same evening, he introduced the Border Protection Bill of 2001 and threatened to prosecute Captain Rinnan for people smuggling if he entered Australian waters. Norway's government and the ship's owners warned Australia not to seize the *Tampa*, but when Rinnan eventually sailed toward Christmas Island, Australian troops forcibly boarded the freighter.[22]

Julian Burnside, one of the country's best-known lawyers, was called in to handle the case as the crisis deepened. Soon he was the senior counsel on the case, arguing, ironically, that naval officers had a legal obligation to detain the rescued migrants on Australian territory rather than hold them hostage aboard the *Tampa*.[23]

"The case that we ran started on a Friday night," he recounts. By the following Wednesday, the arguments were done and the judge went to prepare his ruling. It came down at 2:15 p.m. on September 11, 2001, Melbourne time—about eight hours before the first plane crashed into the World Trade Center in Manhattan—a federal court judge instructed the Howard government to bring the passengers to Australia, citing the judiciary's power "to protect people against detention without lawful authority."[24]

It was bad timing. Burnside lost on appeal a few days later. "All of a sudden, the discourse changed, and you didn't have terrorists anymore; you had Muslim terrorists, and you didn't have boat people anymore, you had Muslim boat people," he recalls.[25]

In late 2001, Prime Minister John Howard was in trouble politically. His response to the *Tampa* boosted him in the polls. Before the incident at sea, the nativist politician Pauline Hanson had posed a genuine challenge on the far right. Howard distanced himself enough to seem palatable to centrist voters but not so far that he would anger Hanson's followers. His own base, the so-called Howard battlers, were suburban working-class voters. Howard spoke to their fears, and when the aspirational white working-class bought into the anti-immigration message and when the strategy proved politically profitable, the party pursued it.[26]

What came to be known as the Pacific Solution was cobbled together during the legal proceedings. The intercepted asylum seekers were sent to Nauru aboard a troopship.[27] Burnside later discovered they were housed below deck next to the engine room. One of Howard's party colleagues, Jackie Kelly, reportedly ran up to the prime minister as he was on his way to address parliament. She was afraid voters were abandoning them for Hanson's One Nation Party. As legend has it, Howard waved his *Tampa* speech at her and said, "Don't worry, this will fix it."[28]

The numbers of boat people coming in 2001 were higher than in the 1970s and 1980s, when Vietnamese refugees had fled to Australia. Back then, the right, which had supported the American war effort, campaigned in favor of allowing South Vietnamese, and Prime Minister Malcolm Fraser remained committed to welcoming them.[29]

John Menadue, an octogenarian who has served at the highest levels of Australian government and business, points out that after 9/11, it was "much easier to appeal to an anti-Muslim sentiment than an anti-Vietnamese." The antimigrant backlash did not appear out of thin air, opportunistic though it was. Menadue has a longer political memory than most, and he remembers how Malcolm Fraser, Australia's conservative statesman in the 1970s and early 1980s, adopted a welcoming stance toward the Vietnamese that paved the way for their general acceptance. There was, however, "one politician at that stage who had reservations. That was John Howard," recalls Menadue. He spoke out against asylum seekers twenty years before he came to power, particularly in the mid-1980s.

Howard accused the asylum seekers of queue-jumping at every opportunity, framing them as cheats while "real" refugees languished in camps. In Australia, land of the "fair go," it was a powerful smear. By the late 1990s, Howard was going after the far-right supporters of Pauline Hanson's One Nation Party. Menadue gives him credit even if he sees the move as cynical and unnecessary. "In the end, he neutered that party by in effect adopting its policy, a very successful and skillful enterprise."[30]

The vocabulary of illegality that took hold in the wake of the *Tampa* crisis changed public attitudes. Even though there is nothing criminal about seeking asylum without a valid visa, many Australians now believe it is illegal. It's a twisting of basic definitions and legal concepts, but it has permeated everything. If all asylum seekers are illegal and hence criminals, then draconian policies are easier to justify. If it's a "war" against people smugglers, then military deployments are acceptable, and so is the rhetoric of national security threats, like the kind former immigration minister Scott Morrison repeatedly conjured with his talk of going to war on smugglers. The language is not an afterthought; it is part of the policy and serves as a justification for it.[31]

Within two days after 9/11, then defense minister Peter Reith linked asylum and terrorism by warning that boats could "be a pipeline for terrorists to come in and use your country as a staging post for terrorist activities." Never mind that the country's top intelligence official called the risk "extremely remote" and denied there was any evidence that terrorists were seeking to get to Australia by boat.[32]

As the scope of acceptable interpretations narrowed, civil servants started to mimic their superiors. A former labor minister, Chris Evans, noted that "public servants pick up the language of the politicians and they then start to demonstrate the attitudes that that language reflects."[33] It becomes self-fulfilling.

One of the public servants most responsible for shaping attitudes was Philip Ruddock, a short, gray-haired politician who represented Sydney's suburbs in parliament for over forty years and served as immigration minister under John Howard. Ruddock is proud of his role in transforming the national discussion about refugees. "I am probably more responsible for conditioning the Australian debate than any other public official," he told me. "We take the view that they should wait where they are first safe and wait a place in the queue."[34]

But not everyone can safely wait in refugee camps indefinitely.

Mohammad Baqiri fled the Urōzgān province of Afghanistan in the late 1990s as ethnic Hazaras came under attack from the Taliban. He was seven. Baqiri's older brother had left in 1999, and the family decided to follow. They lived illegally in Pakistan for two years, and then, after paying $16,000, he and a group of relatives traveled through Pakistan to Malaysia, then to Indonesia. It took a week for their boat to reach

Australian waters; during the journey, two women died, and a baby lost consciousness for six hours. Finally, they arrived in Australia—or thought they had.

As Baqiri recalls it, the navy circled their boat, telling them there was no way they would manage to enter Australia. A refugee on the boat who had previously been turned back lit a fire to force a rescue. After three hours of chaos, during which Baqiri's young nephew lost consciousness and several people jumped into the water, the navy rescued the passengers. They were taken to a detention center on Christmas Island. "The clothes that we were rescued in, that's what we had with us. For over a month, that's what we were wearing," he recalls. Then they were told that to have their claims processed, they would be taken to Nauru. "We had no idea where Nauru was."[35]

When the plane landed, Baqiri couldn't believe how small the island was. He remembers the mosquitoes the most—and seeing detainees suffering from malaria.[36] They were living in army tents. "There was no plumbing," he recalls. The passengers from the *Tampa* were there, too, he adds, and all of them were told they'd never get to Australia. Once on Nauru, he says, there was massive pressure to "stay here forever or go back to your country."

The list of abuses at Nauru is long and almost always contested by Australian officials. Health workers and inmates there have documented and reported dozens of cases of rape of female inmates, guards demanding sexual favors, denial of medical care, and countless incidents of self-harm, including inmates attempting to hang themselves and slit their wrists. One asylum seeker poured gasoline on himself and burned himself to death, and others have sewn their lips together in protest.[37] Baqiri was lucky. After spending three years as a child detainee on Nauru, during which time his brother joined a hunger strike and Baqiri watched him collapse three times and be carted to the hospital on a stretcher, in 2004, the family suddenly received news that their applications had been approved and they would be sent to Australia with temporary visas valid for three years.

When Australians talk about boat people, they do not usually imagine someone like Baqiri. He is young, hip, and dresses and speaks like most other men his age in Melbourne. But he has experienced a side of Australia that few natives or tourists ever see.

Things did not go well once the family arrived in Melbourne. Baqiri was bullied in school and had no friends. His older brother was working in the countryside two hours north of Melbourne, picking fruit. The family moved there, where there was work. Even Baqiri, just thirteen, would occasionally go into the fields. The local school was friendlier, and there were refugees from Iraq and other countries. He quickly became a star athlete, was chosen as a team captain in soccer, and won medals in track and field.

A decade later, in 2016, Baqiri was finishing up his undergraduate law degree and crisscrossing the country giving speeches. He is especially focused on talking to groups that have never encountered refugees, to union members, and to investors connected to companies that profit from detention facilities. At a shareholder meeting filled with investors in the company that manages part of the Nauru facility, there were discussions of how to increase profitability. "They were talking about numbers, about how much it's making. There were people like, 'What are you going to do to make it better so we can get more profit?'" Baqiri took the floor and told the audience and the media, "Look, I've been in that detention center. . . . Do you think it's ethically right to do this?" There was silence.[38]

RUDDOCK OVERSAW AUSTRALIA'S IMMIGRATION POLICY DURING THE years Baqiri was locked up on Nauru. He takes comfort in Australia's great diversity and top-four ranking worldwide in the number of foreign-born residents, along with Israel, Switzerland, and Luxembourg. "Initially, we didn't seek people with particular skills; we just wanted people who were like us,"[39] he told me, a vague reference to the notorious White Australia policy that explicitly barred Asian immigration and lasted until the 1960s.

Ruddock is quick to point out that it was his party, the right-leaning Liberals, who welcomed South Vietnamese refugees in the 1970s while the Labor Party opposed them. Back then, the most vicious antirefugee voices came from trade unions in Darwin. "They claimed that some of the boat arrivals were crime syndicate figures and brothel owners," recounts Klaus Neumann, a German historian who works at Deakin University in Melbourne.[40] Opponents tried to paint them as too wealthy to be genuine refugees because they arrived with all their earthly possessions, much like some Jewish Holocaust survivors who came in the 1940s or Syrians with nice smartphones today.

Ruddock likes to invoke the plight of the poor who wait in line in camps while wealthy asylum seekers pay smugglers, but it's not a meaningful distinction in international law; wealth is irrelevant in determining asylum eligibility.[41] One can be a wealthy Muslim landowner and yet be violently expelled by bigots who hate all Muslims. A rich woman who is raped by soldiers and chooses to pay a smuggler to escape her homeland has no less claim to asylum than a poor person waiting in a camp. Ruddock would never dare to question the legitimacy of refugee claims made by members of Berlin's Jewish aristocracy in the late 1930s, especially in his heavily Jewish constituency, but the logic behind denunciations of those who can afford to pay is the same.

As Madeline Gleeson of the University of New South Wales explains, Australian policy makers like Ruddock cleverly linked the two traditional sources of refugees in the public mind and "created the illusion of a queue" by setting those who are assigned for resettlement by the United Nations High Commissioner for Refugees (UNHCR) against those who flee on their own and make a claim upon arrival, in some sort of imaginary zero-sum equation. But in fact, Australia or any other country has no legal obligation to resettle a single UNHCR refugee. If they accept them, "it's goodwill," says Gleeson. "Asylum is something else."[42]

Ruddock remembers visiting refugee camps in Malaysia and Hong Kong as a young MP in the 1970s. "The first immigration of Vietnamese was extraordinarily well received, highly regarded. They worked hard. They were well educated. They were people who'd fought with the South Vietnamese."

It was in the 1980s that things changed, he says. Less-skilled Vietnamese with questionable refugee claims began to arrive. Unlike today's see-no-evil supporters of sending people home to danger, Ruddock had the honesty and curiosity back then to go investigate the situation on the ground. He went to Vietnam. "I wanted to satisfy myself that people being returned were going back in situations in which they were going to be safe," he tells me. Instead, he met a local Communist Party chief who told him about his children waiting to be resettled in the United States. That was the beginning of his skepticism. There was also the case of the Lebanese, whose admission Ruddock regards as a huge mistake. "We essentially got a very poorly educated, underskilled migration that came over five or six years . . . and has left us with a major and continuing problem," he argues. Finally, came the Chinese boat arrivals of the 1990s. Ruddock claims that today's detention regime initially arose out of law designed for handling stowaways.

The law was changed, he says, so that "if a person came into Australia without a valid entry permit, they would be detained until such time as they were either granted a visa or removed from Australia."[43] It passed with bipartisan support and became the basis of the mandatory detention regime that still exists today.[44]

Ruddock's innovation was to move it offshore, away from the view of journalists, citizens, and the review of Australian courts. According to the historian Klaus Neumann, Ruddock started in 1999 by making onshore camps "really inhospitable places," hoping to send the message to Afghans and Iraqis that it wasn't worth the trip. "That obviously didn't work," says Neumann, so Ruddock upped the ante with Manus Island and Nauru, broadcasting that "these are really hellholes, and you know, don't try to come here, because that's where you end up."[45]

When challenged about the ability of all the world's refugees to find their way safely to a UN-administered camp and patiently wait for re-settlement, Ruddock is defensive. "Your view is that those who've got no money and can't pay a smuggler and who have to wait in a refugee camp, even if their claims of persecution are far more heinous, should take second place to somebody who's got the money to pay," he asserts, assuming that no one seeking to pay a smuggler might face persecution or have a legitimate claim. "Look, we're not going to take every refugee in the world. There are sixty million now. We've got a population of twenty-two million; we're not taking sixty million. Okay?" he erupts.

I ask Ruddock what Australia owes asylum seekers with legitimate claims, if anything. Calming down, he argues, "They're entitled not to be returned to persecution, and as far as we're concerned, we're not prepared to have them here, and we have arranged that they can be elsewhere where they are safe." He is deeply suspicious of the many documented claims of abuse in the offshore detention centers. "If you've paid to come to Australia, your objective is to get to Australia, and you will say or do anything that will help pursue that objective in my view," he insists. "I don't necessarily accept at face value all the claims that are made. . . . I'm not convinced that the majority of it is true."[46]

There are many Australians who have similar doubts about Ruddock's commitment to the truth. Their skepticism stems from an infamous incident known as the Children Overboard affair.

In October 2001, just after the *Tampa* drama and one month before a national election, a boat under tow from the navy broke apart, and many asylum seekers were left flailing in the water. The government's leading officials, including Ruddock, went public with the story before verifying the details. They pushed a narrative of parents throwing children overboard to force a rescue; it fit the campaign theme of opportunistic and criminal asylum seekers nicely, even though the navy told government officials soon after the incident that no children had been thrown into the water.

Ruddock tells the story differently, though he does admit, in a roundabout way, that he misled the public. "There were people in the sea they believe jumped overboard in order to ensure that the vessel was taken . . . and it was reported to the naval headquarters in Darwin that there were children being held up and that they were being thrown into the water," Ruddock explains from his suburban Sydney office during the summer holidays. Those reports, he now concedes, "were inaccurate in that the children were not dropped into the water. Other people went into the water, presumably adults."[47]

But at the time, Ruddock acted on the initial, unverified information. "Bear in mind, we're in the middle of an election campaign. I was having a major press conference," he says in his defense. His aides received reports that children were being thrown overboard and briefed him. "I had to make a judgment," Ruddock tells me. "Do I say this is happening? Or do I sit on it?"

It was just over a month before the election, and Ruddock chose to go public. The prime minister then repeated the false reports, and the defense minister even released photos of children in lifejackets to bolster their claim. The event became a major trope in the heated campaign. After the election, there was an inquiry that determined what Ruddock and his colleagues had stated as fact was false.

I ask Ruddock whether he or Howard felt a need to retract. "Once you establish what the facts are, you accept the facts," he replies obliquely. When I ask whether it served a campaign purpose, he becomes defensive. "It wasn't contrived. It was an issue that arose in the campaign, which you had to manage," he insists. "I reported accurately what I was told."[48] If there is anyone to blame, he contends, it's the defense officials in the radio room when the reports came through, not the cabinet officials like him who repeated it to the world before verifying the details.

CHRIS KENNY, A COLUMNIST FOR RUPERT MURDOCH'S PAPER the *Australian,* is one of the only journalists to be granted a visa to visit Nauru—it costs $8,000, and there's no refund if the application is rejected. Kenny's exceptional success in getting a visa is something his critics chalk up to his right-wing politics. This outrages Kenny. Barring all journalists apart from the friendly ones like Kenny is an integral part of the government's policy, the *Guardian* reporter Ben Doherty argues. Even the foreign editor of Murdoch's *Australian* was scathing on this point: "The media has been consistently denied access to the refugee centres lest it actually report on the harrowing stories of these people and, by humanising them, generate some sympathy for them," he wrote.[49]

Kenny doesn't call it sympathy; for him, it's all lies. Like Ruddock, he believes that many of the doctors and NGO workers on Nauru have a political agenda and are fabricating stories of brutality, rape, and deprivation. "They just report what people tell them," he says of doctors and NGO workers. "There's a massive incentive for people to talk up hardship," he argues. "Are people being systematically abused and maltreated on Nauru? Obviously not."[50]

Those who criticize him are, he declares, "mealy-mouthed, tendentious, lying, left-liberal journalists trying to suggest that I tell lies." He challenges them to come up with "one fact I got wrong in the thousands of words I wrote." The problem with such a challenge, of course, is that his reporting can't be gauged against other journalists', because others haven't been permitted to visit.

When challenged on the moral fiber of their rousing humanitarian defense of the stop-the-boats policy, conservatives like Kenny refuse to consider that refugees might go and die elsewhere or be returned to persecution. To him, the central moral question is of secondary importance. "I see it as, like, a debating point," he tells me over coffee at a posh café in a Sydney suburb. "I mean, it's actually not what happens. If there are refugees in Indonesia, they're in camps; they work out what they're doing," he says, apparently unaware of the precarious existence of many refugees who live as illegal immigrants in a country that is not a party to the UN refugee convention. "If people are fearful for their lives in whatever country they've fled, they're not going to go back," he tells me breezily. "Most of them are not fearing for their lives; they're looking for a better future," says Kenny. "If you were turning back boats, and people were going back to be executed somewhere or to die in some other voyage, that would be a terrible thing. Who's come up with the example of that happening? It is just a hypothetical that hasn't occurred."[51]

According to Afghan refugee Mohammad Baqiri, who spent a bit more time on Nauru than Kenny, the camp authorities regularly tried to convince people to go back to Afghanistan and offered large compensation packages and promises of jobs. Many detainees accepted. "Out of those people, over twenty people have been killed by Taliban," says Baqiri. Such offers do not necessarily discourage future journeys, something that should give defenders of the policy pause. Among those who took the money, several of those who survived tried to come back to Australia twelve or thirteen years later, this time with their families.[52] Kenny had little to say when thousands of files from Nauru, detailing medical reports of injuries and abuse, were printed by the *Guardian* in mid-2016. Bizarrely, for someone who thinks abuse is vanishingly rare, he could only muster "nothing new" on Twitter.

Andrew Bolt, the best-known right-wing journalist in the country, is even more outspoken on refugee issues. Unlike Kenny, he does not try to put a socially respectable face on his harsh views. "I don't give a shit about international refugee conventions," he told me over coffee one morning. "People at the UN are determining what citizens of countries should decide. That's for us to decide."

Bolt is a great admirer of Jean Raspail and often sounds like the protagonist in *The Camp of the Saints*. "Immigration is increasingly colonization," he warns. The West today, he argues, has lost the "will to protect European civilization." Rather than defend the Western project, Bolt laments, "the West is wallowing in the sentimentality of wanting to seem good, not actually doing good," he told me. "Part is self-hatred. The left has got to bloody wake up."[53]

Australia's conservative journalists who defend the offshore detention policy rely heavily on the notion of queue-jumping. For every Syrian trying to make it by boat, Kenny argues, there are thousands waiting in

Jordanian refugee camps because they can't afford smugglers. If someone with money manages to come by boat, he argues, "they've jumped that queue." Kenny concedes that requesting asylum is not illegal, but he comes very close to equating the crime of the smugglers with the actions of asylum seekers themselves. "They're complicit in an illegal trade," he tells me.[54] Whatever horrors they're fleeing are secondary to the sin of paying a smuggler.

Refugees who have the money to pay smugglers are often more successful at reaching safety; it was true of many German Jews who fled in the 1930s. But the refugee convention does not discriminate based on one's income or mode of arrival. In the queue-jumping argument put forth by Ruddock and Kenny, a refugee who has been tortured or raped but happened to have the money to pay a smuggler has no legitimate claim in Australia, but the middle-class doctor who suffered no persecution and fled to the nearest camp when the bombs started falling is a viable candidate for asylum because he played by the rules.

Australia, for all the stereotypes of its laid-back surfer culture, is a society obsessed with rules and fairness, and the queue-jumping argument resonates perfectly with a population primed to think in terms of orderly regulations and where most people have never faced desperation, state-sponsored violence, or war crimes. By this logic, whether you have had your hand chopped off doesn't matter if you broke the "rules" to get to Australia.

Unlike Bolt, who is ideologically opposed to admitting foreigners, especially Muslims, Kenny, who once served as chief of staff to the foreign minister, seems more concerned about the optics and PR impact. He is adamant that they should be forced to stay in Nauru or go somewhere like Cambodia. "It's not a first-world welfare state like Australia; sure, we all understand that, but if your real problem is persecution and lack of freedom, you couldn't start a life in Cambodia?" he wonders. He even took his baby there on holiday, so it can't be all that bad, he insists.[55] So far, a grand total of seven asylum seekers have accepted resettlement there at a cost of two million Australian dollars ($1.5 million) and another fifty-five million ($40 million) in payments to Cambodia.[56]

Andrew Wilkie, an independent senator from Tasmania, regards offshoring as carefree spending on a policy with no direct economic benefits and one that keeps out needed workers in some industries and regions.

"We're a rich country; governments can afford to spend absurd amounts of money to pander to that xenophobia," he says. "Bizarrely, the feedback I get in my office from people in the community, it's not that tens of millions of dollars were wasted in Cambodia; it's whether or not an asylum seeker might be able to access welfare in Australia." Some of his constituents genuinely believe refugees are getting free cars and homes and call the office to complain.[57]

Kenny dismisses concerns about the huge expense. It would cost much more to host them in Australia, he insists, questionably.[58] "The offshore processing is the critical factor, because it denies the product—that is, getting into Australia—and access to not just our welfare but also our legal system," a clear statement that, in his view, there are certain rights refugees deserve to be deprived of.

Kenny does admit that not allowing those who have been admitted to work was a mistake. "If you go into regional Australia, places like vineyards and fruit orchards and whatever, growers have enormous trouble getting people to pick fruit," he says. But the issue is not economic, it is cultural. "I've spoken to the government, and they've thought all these things through," he confides. "They really want to make it clear that if you get on a boat, come across that water, you will not get to Australia."[59] The lesson was not lost on Denmark's government.

SØREN ESPERSEN OF THE DANISH PEOPLE'S PARTY HAS CLEARLY STUDIED Australia's Pacific Solution in detail, so I push him: Where would your Nauru be? "Morocco is a very good example of a country that would possibly do it for an amount of money," he claims. And Danish staff could run the camps. "We would do it ourselves. We would run the things ourselves and pay the Moroccan authority a fee. We would also make it possible for their local grocers or butchers to come and deliver goods."

I point out that it sounds quite different from Australia's notorious centers where hunger strikes, suicides, and attacks by hostile local islanders have become the norm. "That's not our style. We don't do it like that here," Espersen insists. "We would not treat refugees in that way. We would do it completely differently. There will be excellent service, I can assure you." In Denmark's offshore paradise, there would be education, too. Nobody will be "living in ratholes," he promises. "We've even got schemes here if somebody wants to go home. We help them with money, and these families, they can maybe come home with 10,000 pounds so that they can start a new life."[60]

The architect of the Australian model, Ruddock, doesn't think that European governments will be able to replicate it so easily unless the Syrian conflict is resolved. He also hints that a more humane approach might undermine the much-vaunted deterrent effect. "Our approach is not a menu; it's a recipe. It's not a matter in which you can pick and choose what you want to do. You've got to do it all. And that means the offshore processing, the return of boats, the mandatory detention, the temporary protection visas," he insists.[61] To him, it does not matter if people are bona fide refugees fleeing an ongoing war; they still don't deserve asylum in Australia.

Back in Copenhagen, Espersen openly questions many Syrian refugees' claims and whether they need asylum at all. "Why is it that they don't want to go home? That's a question you have to ask them. Why don't you want to go home to your country and help [with] rebuilding it?" as if there's an opportunity awaiting them tomorrow in the Aleppo construction trade.

Speaking in April 2016 before some of the harshest bombing of that city and Assad's second round of chemical attacks, he confidently asserted that with Russian aid "the war will stop. I believe in Syria it will stop before we know it." He also questioned the legitimacy of refugee claims, mentioning one family that was interviewed on television and asked why they waited so long. They replied that they had to sell their house first. "They come with wealth," Espersen insists.[62]

It is an assumption that Danish former refugees like Rabbi Melchior reject. People who own homes also need to flee bombardment, and they may need to sell their property to afford a perilous journey.[63]

Espersen imagines a world in which refugees are mostly fakes and face no danger, to the point that they will happily move home to the lands they fled and draw a Danish pension. An Australian-style solution to Europe's crisis is already taking shape in the form of deals with Turkey to send back migrants arriving in Greece, and a more aggressive form of offshoring, as Espersen advocates, could be on the horizon, especially if parties like his eventually gain enough power or influence.

The rapes, suicide attempts, beatings, and riots that have characterized Australia's experiment with offshore detention are not appealing to him; the economic and political logic is.

6

Terror and Backlash

JUST BEFORE 11:30 A.M. ON JANUARY 7, 2015, CHERIF AND SAID KOUACHI stormed into the Paris offices of *Charlie Hebdo*, a French satirical newspaper. They forced an employee at gunpoint to key in the security code, shot a maintenance worker, and sprayed the assembled editorial staff with Kalashnikov fire, calling out the editor Stéphane Charbonnier's name before shooting him and eleven others. The cartoonist Laurent Sourisseau, known as Riss, survived with a bullet wound to the shoulder.

The Kouachis gunned down a police officer on the sidewalk before fleeing the city. The brothers, who were born in France to Algerian immigrants and were orphaned at a young age after their mother's suicide, drove north as a nationwide search began. The manhunt continued for forty-eight hours as the killers hid in a forest, hijacked a series of cars, and eventually hunkered down in a warehouse near Charles de Gaulle Airport. On January 9, two runways were closed as police and soldiers descended on the suburban office park and placed it under siege, taking directions via text message from a warehouse employee hiding inside a cardboard box. At 5:00 p.m., after explosives were set off, the Kouachis emerged, guns blazing, and were shot by police just as their comrade-in-arms, Amedy Coulibaly, took hostages at a kosher supermarket in eastern Paris. He demanded that the Kouachis not be harmed and then killed four people before police raided the building and shot him.[1]

Two days later, several million marchers flooded the streets of Paris to denounce terrorism and defend free speech. The feel-good march, which featured an array of world leaders and France's entire political class with the conspicuous exception of Marine Le Pen, was billed as a defiant display of unity. Le Pen, who was excluded from the march by President

François Hollande—a politically motivated move that likely won her many new voters—held her own demonstration in the small southern town of Beaucaire, near Marseille. One thousand supporters turned out to hear her speak. "After tomorrow, the debate about what was done and what wasn't done must begin," she declared. "Have we put to work all the means at our disposal to fight the scourge of Islamist terrorism?"[2] A week later, she took to the pages of the *New York Times* to call for immigration restrictions, stripping jihadists of French citizenship, and reinstituting border checks.[3]

The wave of asylum seekers that streamed into Europe six months later was, for Le Pen, the greatest political gift imaginable.

IN THE MIDDLE OF THE AFTERNOON ON AUGUST 25, 2015, AS MOST OF Germany was enjoying the end of the summer holidays, a small government agency posted a message on Twitter that would shape the fate of hundreds of thousands of Syrians and many millions of Germans. "We are at present largely no longer enforcing Dublin procedures for Syrian citizens," read the seemingly unspectacular bureaucratic tweet, posted by the Federal Office for Migration and Refugees. But it meant something very different for the hundreds of thousands of refugees and migrants streaming through Turkey and seeking a way into Europe.[4]

A few days after the German announcement, a steady flow of Syrians, Afghans, Iraqis, and others began to arrive on the Greek island of Kos. As tanned Dutch tourists dodged refugee children wandering through the bike lanes, a middle-aged Syrian man showed me a screenshot of his itinerary on a tattered Samsung smartphone. A squiggly line snaked through a poorly drawn map of Greece, Macedonia, Serbia, and Hungary, with the prices of each point-to-point journey listed in dollars. The shortest and most treacherous, from Turkey to Kos, cost $1,500 (the hydrofoil fare for those blessed with visas and the right passports was $16). If they made it across alive, the weary refugees—many of them from Syria—would then trudge two miles past backpacker bars and package-deal hotels, passing occasional British revelers on the way home from a long night of drinking. They would arrive at the still-shuttered Kos police station before dawn. And then they'd wait.

It was there that I met Mohammed, a sixteen-year-old from the Syrian city of Latakia, who had made the journey from Turkey on a small dinghy with twenty-one others after the German announcement. He had been living in a tent on Kos's trash-strewn beach for a week. His companions, twenty-year-old Hatem and twenty-two-year-old Mahmoud, came from the Syrian cities of Deir ez-Zor and Hama, where some of the earliest protests against the Assad regime began in 2011. One bears a scar where he was shot through the knee. The other fled to Jordan, where he was beaten by police, before escaping to Turkey. Greek coast guard boats rescued their vessel halfway to Kos and brought them ashore.

The next day, the three men took an overnight ferry to Athens with hundreds of other Syrians. As word spread that Germany was opening its doors, odes to German chancellor Angela Merkel appeared on Facebook in Arabic, praising her as a "loving mother" and a lion.[5] By the end of the week, Mohammed had written to say that he'd reached the Austrian-German border. "I don't know anyone in Hamburg," he told me in a text message. But Germany had announced it would accept five hundred thousand refugees, so he crossed and took a train north.[6] Within days, the crowds stuck at Budapest's railway station began to do the same.

Germany's decision to welcome so many migrants is deeply rooted in its own past. What is today known as the Dublin Rule, requiring asylum seekers to request protection in the first EU country they enter, was originally a German idea. The German constitution was amended in 1993 to forbid asylum applications from anyone who had passed through a safe third country on their way from danger in their homeland to Germany. Since Germany was surrounded by safe states, theoretically it would be very difficult for a mass influx to occur; only arrivals by air would be eligible for asylum. "In the '90s, we had four hundred thousand asylum seekers, and this dropped until we had like thirty thousand," says Robin Alexander, a political reporter with the newspaper *Die Welt*. Many of the Balkan refugees eventually went home. "Wherever you go in the Balkans, people speak German today," he says.

And so the Dublin Rule was born. Nevertheless, "It always left a lot of German politicians with a bad conscience," says Alexander. It was a legal requirement that clashed with the spirit of much of the rest of the German constitution.

Contrary to popular belief, Merkel was not necessarily driven by compassion for refugees when she threw open the gates. At her core, says Alexander, who knows Merkel better than most journalists, she really

believes "that if Europe allows itself to be broken up into smaller entities," the European project could fall apart. And if the European Union
were under threat, how could it compete with China or stand up to Russia in Ukraine?[7]

Henryk Broder was having none of it. Broder, the son of two Holocaust survivors—his mother survived deportation to Auschwitz; his
father, Buchenwald—is one of Europe's most gifted polemicists. His
trenchant attacks on political correctness in the 1980s and 1990s skewered
Germans for their latent anti-Semitism and failure to reckon with their
crimes. In 1981, he wrote a scathing essay before emigrating to Israel for a
few years. "Auschwitz at your backs, but neither in your heads nor hearts,
today you can afford to debate about whether refugees fleeing Vietnam
are 'real' or simply 'economic refugees,'" he wrote caustically. "You count
the dollar notes and gold bars these people bring along—those fortunate
enough to survive their 'flight.' . . . These debates took place here once
before, when what was at stake was whether to let the wealthy Jews emi-
grate 'for a fee' or whether to kill them right off the bat."[8]

Back then, Broder went after his comfortable lefty intellectual friends
for being indifferent toward refugees and thinking they did not bear any
trace of their parents' Jew hatred. These days, he is less sympathetic to
those fleeing war. Broder now edits the right-wing website *Ach Gut!* (a
play on "Axis of Good") and has joined those denouncing the new refugees streaming into Germany. And because they are Muslims, he has few
qualms criticizing them. He told a Danish TV interviewer that Merkel
was "importing" millions of people who are "not used to democratic rules
of behavior." When challenged by the host about his own background, he
bristled. "The Polish Jews who came to Sweden and Denmark didn't take
with them their nasty habit of killing their daughters," nor did they try to
"impose their cultural habits" on their new societies, he argued. The rush
to welcome refugees, he insists, is because Germans didn't "use the chance
to go to a good shrink" and explore the residual burden from the Second
World War.[9]

For Broder, it's not about the numbers. It's the fact that "they concen-
trate in certain quarters" that become "no-go areas." He mentions Nørrebro in Copenhagen, which—like Kreuzberg in Berlin—is both an area
with lots of immigrants and the epicenter of bohemian hipsterism. Broder
insisted he's not a culture warrior. "I don't mind having a mosque in the

middle of Kurfürstendamm," he conceded, "provided that they don't store weapons in the basement."[10]

In Broder's telling, the German left has swung from being latent anti-Semites to blindly repentant do-gooders. But he insists Germany has no moral obligation whatsoever to take in refugees and is instead engaging in cultural imperialism by seeking to show the rest of Europe its moral superiority. Merkel's only obligation, he believes, is to her own citizens, and she never asked them.

Despite many Germans' enthusiastic welcoming of refugees in late 2015, all was not well in Germany. Large anti-Islam marches took place in major German cities, and hostels housing newly arrived refugees were attacked and burned. On October 17, a far-right activist stabbed the politician Henriette Reker in the neck while she was campaigning to become mayor of Cologne. She survived the attack and won the election by a wide margin. Merkel and other leading German officials condemned the attacker as a coward and lamented the radicalization of the refugee debate, but there is a growing section of the population that feels it is not being heard by political elites. Some of these angry citizens are turning to violence, and they are not necessarily unhinged madmen; in some cases, their stated motives are explicitly political and they are being egged on by far-right ideas. Ms. Reker served for years as the city of Cologne's director of refugee services and oversaw housing for asylum seekers. According to Der Spiegel, when the attacker was asked his motives, he told local police that "foreigners are taking our jobs" and warned that Sharia law was on its way to Germany.[11]

Three months later, Cologne was rocked by an even bigger scandal that seemed to confirm Broder's dark warning. On December 31, 2015, hundreds of women attending New Year's Eve celebrations were groped, attacked, and robbed. Several were raped. Most of the perpetrators were described as North African in appearance; some turned out to be asylum seekers. The press was slow to cover the story, and Mayor Reker and the police were criticized for not taking the investigation of allegations from over one thousand women seriously, fueling the already strong narrative that Merkel's policy had brought chaos to Germany. Riss, the Charlie Hebdo cartoonist who had survived the January attack, added fuel to the fire by depicting Alan Kurdi, the dead Syrian boy found on a Turkish beach, and suggesting, if he'd lived, he'd have grown up to be an ass-groper in Cologne.[12]

ANGELA MERKEL APPROACHES POLITICS WITH THE PATIENCE AND experimentation of the research scientist that she is (she has a PhD in quantum chemistry). As a former US ambassador to Germany noted, "If you cross her, you end up dead. . . . There's a whole list of alpha males who thought they would get her out of the way, and they're all now in other walks of life." That list includes her political mentor, the late Helmut Kohl, who tutored Merkel as she entered politics as a complete outsider, raised in Communist East Germany with no conception of how democratic political institutions worked. When Kohl became mired in scandal in 1999, Merkel had risen in the ranks to the position of party general secretary and she pounced, sending an op-ed to the conservative *Frankfurter Allgemeine Zeitung* calling for new, untainted leadership in the party. That was when most Germans first heard the name Angela Merkel.

The old Christian Democratic Union (CDU) establishment didn't know what hit them when Merkel came along.[13] As Merkel's biographer put it, "She's a learned democrat—not a born democrat." She couldn't comprehend why wealthy West German kids would have rebelled by joining the Baader-Meinhof Group; to her, they seemed like "spoiled children." But being from the East had its advantages. She was patient and disciplined, and she knew when to hold her tongue.[14]

Yet the refugee crisis and the attacks that followed it have presented her with a more explosive equation that is difficult to balance. When the backlash to Merkel's stance on refugees did arrive, it didn't come from the opposition or even other parties in her coalition; it came from within, from the head of the Christian Social Union (CSU), the CDU's counterpart in the state of Bavaria, the region where most of the refugees were arriving.

The CDU and CSU are known as *Schwesterpartei*—sister parties. When Horst Seehofer, the leader of the CSU, denounced Merkel's border policy, it seemed a grave threat to her authority. But the CSU does not exist as a party outside the state of Bavaria; Seehofer would never challenge Merkel on a national level, nor would he succeed if he tried. What was really driving him was political posturing to ensure that no challenge from the right threatened the CSU's majority hold on power in Bavaria, and that meant a hard-line stance from Seehofer to protect his right flank. His fear was that his voters might ultimately desert to the upstart far-right party, the Alternative für Deutschland, or AfD—an existential threat to the CSU.

Seehofer's fear has deep historical roots. The godfather of the CSU was Franz Josef Strauss, who famously declared that the party could never allow another conservative party in the democratic sphere to exist—that there could never be an opponent to its right. As the journalist Robin Alexander explains, the party's philosophy is "We do everything. We are left radical. We are right radical. We are liberals. We include everything. We speak for the worker. We speak for the boss. We speak for the town. Everything has to be inside our spectrum." It was dogma.[15] Even the liberals who didn't like it accepted it as their duty to allow space for a right-wing element within its big tent—with one exception.

There was one politician who challenged that dogma two decades ago: Peter Altmaier, the rotund, multilingual son of a coal miner, who is today regarded as the second-most powerful person in Berlin. An intellectually intimidating politician—he claims to have a library of six hundred books on Bismarck—he is now Merkel's chief of staff.[16] Back in the 1990s, Altmaier worried that the radical right, even if it was a fringe, would influence the party's agenda and endanger its role as a force of the center.[17] He is now a driving force in responding to the refugee crisis.

Until Seehofer publicly challenged Merkel's border policy, the two politicians offered two very distinct flavors of the same national party. Speaking with two faces was very effective at the polls.[18] Merkel is generally seen as quite liberal, and many Germans who wouldn't normally have voted for her but cannot opt for the CSU beyond Bavaria could tell themselves that she was part of the same party and vote CDU. Likewise, Bavarian voters who leaned left would refrain from supporting the Greens or Social Democrats in state elections because even though the local CSU might be adopting a hard line in the campaign, in parliament they'd align with Merkel, so everything would be fine. As a result, Merkel received the votes of those with much more conservative views, and Seehofer got the votes of reluctant liberals in local elections. The CDU-CSU alliance won nationally and in Bavaria; Seehofer kept control of his state, and Merkel stayed at the country's helm. It was a mutually beneficial pact.

Merkel's stance on the refugee crisis can be seen through the lens of Germany's postwar political thinking. There is an almost religious conviction that there cannot be another *Sonderweg*, or special path, for Germany. The most widely read history book among German politicians is

The Long Road West by Heinrich August Winkler. German history since the war has been largely focused on becoming part of the West. Merkel has insisted on a European solution and sees German generosity as a means to getting there, effectively giving other EU countries time to prepare for accepting refugees so they can be distributed across Europe.

But this clashes fundamentally with the allergy to a *Sonderweg,* argues Alexander. "This is very hard to swallow for older Germans because they learned to never do something alone."[19]

Merkel's border policy would have never been possible if she had been on her own politically. The Social Democrats, Merkel's biggest challengers in the September 2017 election, served in her cabinet; other key opponents were within her own party or coalition. Dissident CDU MPs won't attack their own party in advance of an election, and Seehofer's CSU is not a threat to her on a national level. And the Greens and many others on the left have staunchly backed her on the refugee question. But permanent support across the political spectrum is not guaranteed, especially when voters are shocked by violent events.

In 2016, a week before Christmas, Ariel Zurawski, the owner of a Polish trucking company, began to observe strange data signals from one of his eighteen-wheelers parked near Berlin. The engine was starting and stopping as if someone didn't know how to operate the ignition. The owner tried to call his cousin, the driver, who was scheduled to deliver a load of steel to a Berlin warehouse the next day. There was no reply.

Four hours later, the truck, emblazoned with Zurawski's name above the cab, plowed into a crowded Christmas market in the center of Berlin, killing twelve and injuring dozens more. Zurawski's cousin was found dead with a bullet to the head in the passenger seat. Frauke Petry, then the leader of the far-right AfD, immediately sought to capitalize on the carnage, calling the victims "Merkel's dead."[20]

ACROSS EUROPE, TERRORIST ATTACKS HAVE BEEN EXPLOITED BY THE FAR right as opportunities to stoke anti-Muslim sentiment; too often, journalists and intellectuals have played along. On March 22, 2016, terrorists detonated huge bombs at Brussels Airport and on the city's subways during rush hour, killing thirty-five people and injuring over three hundred. The *Charlie Hebdo* editorial published a week after the Brussels attacks was strikingly similar to the anti-Semitism peddled in the late nineteenth century during the Dreyfus Affair. These days, anti-Semitism isn't kosher, but there is no shame in targeting a new scapegoat.

The *Charlie Hebdo* editorial painted innocent Muslims as unwitting conspirators in a jihadist struggle to take over Europe, the tip of the Islamist iceberg. Its author was the cartoonist Riss who, six months earlier, had depicted a dead three-year-old refugee as a potential sex criminal.

He begins his article with the specter of Tariq Ramadan—a familiar villain—and his calls for a European form of Islam and for Western democracies to adapt and allow religion a place in public life. Ramadan would never shoot up a newspaper office or bomb an airport, Riss writes, others will do that instead of him. His task is to dissuade others from criticizing Islam through intellectual intimidation. He'll instill in young political science students, who one day will become elected officials or journalists, the fear of saying anything negative about Islam lest they be accused of Islamophobia. "That is Tariq Ramadan's role."[21]

Ramadan has been accused of fifth-column behavior before, most notably in Paul Berman's book-length takedown *The Flight of the Intellectuals*.[22] And it's true that some of his texts are at best apologies for, and at worse endorsements of, virulent anti-Semites and the Muslim Brotherhood's often reactionary ideology. But *Charlie Hebdo*'s big iceberg does not stop with Ramadan, whose intellectual track record is published for all to see. Riss targets the regular man and woman on the street, painting a picture of sleeper-cell fifth columnists on every corner, wherever one sees a veil or a beard.

Riss's next incognito jihadist is the pious woman on the street, brave and devoted to her family. She would never hide a bomb under her veil, but she makes us shut up and flee from debate, he argues. Her role, according to *Charlie Hebdo*, even if she doesn't realize she's playing one, is to silence criticism from those who feel uncomfortable seeing veiled or, worse yet, niqab-wearing women in the streets.

The next unwitting terrorist conspirator is the friendly neighborhood baker with a beard and a prayer mark on his forehead. He has replaced the old French baker, who retired. "He makes good croissants, is friendly and always has a smile for his customers. He's perfectly integrated into the neighborhood," Riss writes. His insidious sin is not offering ham sandwiches or bacon. And with that, the closet jihadist baker's role is fulfilled.

Now Riss moves to the morning of the Brussels attack. He writes of "a young criminal who has never opened a Koran in his life, knows nothing of the history of religions or colonialism." He calls a cab with two of his friends and heads for the airport with a bag packed with explosives. "They are not as learned as Tariq Ramadan, they don't pray as much as the baker, and they don't observe the precepts of Islam as well as the brave veiled mother," he writes.

It's here that Riss glides into the territory of the legendary nineteenth-century anti-Semite Édouard Drumont. Any Muslim, like the Jews in the anti-Semitic imagination of the Dreyfus Affair, becomes a threat to the nation. "At this precise moment, no one has done anything wrong," he intones ominously. But the terror that strikes when the bombs explode, shattering glass and leaving bodies strewn across the Brussels departure hall, "could not happen without the contribution of all of them . . . from the bakery that forbids you from eating what you like to the woman who forbids you from telling her that you'd prefer her without a veil," Riss concludes. "The path is drawn for all that will follow." For Riss, the terrorists' role is merely to "conclude what has already begun" and to tell us to "shut up forever, living or dead."[23]

One can muster genuine empathy for a man who lost most of his colleagues in a bloody attack just one year earlier, but his chilling conclusion has a great deal in common with the anti-Semitic tracts that paved the way for Vichy. Aside from the dubious logic of arguing that halal bakeries encourage terrorism, there is something much more sinister at work in Riss's editorial. In arguing that there is a direct line between the carnage in Brussels and the neighborhood baker who doesn't serve ham croissants, Riss is deploying protofascist rhetoric and actively insinuating that the most basic forms of religious observance pose a threat to society. It is scapegoating of the highest order.

Alain Finkielkraut, the well-known French philosopher, claims not to have seen the editorial, but he is familiar with the tip-of-the-iceberg theory and completely rejects the comparison to anti-Semitism. He argues that there is no resemblance between the two because the Jews scapegoated in the nineteenth century and during World War II were innocent; today's Muslims are blowing things up.

"There was no Jewish jihadism; it did not exist—that is, the Jews were seen as intruders, as a threat even though they were absolutely peaceful. . . . They had neither the intention to secede nor the intention to attack the citizens and institutions of the host country," he tells me. "On the contrary, they came to France with a feeling of gratitude and intense love. They came to France because it was the country precisely that had cleared Captain Dreyfus." And besides, he adds, Riss's editorial can't possibly be as dangerous as Drumont because "real racists do not read *Charlie Hebdo*."[24]

But Finkielkraut ignores the fact that the perceived Jewish threat and the actively fomented fear of it was a key component of the anti-Semitic imagination, and many were recruited to the cause by the framing of Jews as dangerous outsiders.

Like Finkielkraut, the Dutch Jewish academic Paul Scheffer doesn't see today's hatred and fear of Muslims as comparable to Nazi persecution of Jews in the 1940s. He regards the backlash against Muslims as occurring "in a context of violence" with no parallel in Jewish history. In other words, no Jews murdered well-known filmmakers, so hatred of them was indefensible. After Mohammed Bouyeri killed Theo Van Gogh, the argument goes, it's understandable. This ignores the fact that most people targeted and harmed by the current backlash are not guilty of any crime.[25]

Finkielkraut and Scheffer seem to forget the pretext for Kristallnacht—and that fears of radical Jewish communists and violent anti-British Zionists were once used as grounds for denying entry to Jewish refugees fleeing eastern Europe.[26] There is no reason that in the long run it couldn't happen in Europe again.

Instead of dismissing the analogy, we should learn from Europe's recent history—when the groundwork for mass murder was laid with talk of "them" and "us."[27] The fact that a small group of fanatical Muslims are engaged in violent terrorism does not mean that the entire group is guilty and deserves to be ostracized.[28]

Anti-Semitism remains a malignant force in France. But that form of racism has become unacceptable among major politicians and opinion leaders and has receded from the surface of political debate. Muslims have replaced the specter of the international Jew in mainstream discourse.

For the older generation of the French right, there was a direct line to Marshal Pétain and collaboration with the Nazis. Those old Vichyist Nazi sympathizers are dying off. Now it is the Muslim "who incarnates an international threat to France, who invades France, who threatens to take power in France," argues Daniel Lindenberg, a Jewish academic who specializes in the study of authoritarianism. The fear is that Muslims, like the Jews before them, will take power, that Sharia will be applied in Europe. In many ways, he argues, it is like anti-Semitism of the past. There are "the rich Muslims like Qatar's rulers, who replace the Rothschilds" as the wealthy usurping villains, he explains. "At the same time there are the very poor who are threatening because they come here with their large families" and threaten to outnumber and replace the native Christian inhabitants.[29]

What bothers Lindenberg the most is that there are now Jews who subscribe to this thinking and echo the views of the far right.[30] Éric Zemmour, an observant Algerian Jew who wrote the best-selling book *The French Suicide,* is the most visible, but Finkielkraut is the most influential.

Lindenberg knew Finkielkraut a bit in the 1980s and considered him "rather left-wing and anti-racist." Then, in 1989, the same year as the fatwa against Salman Rushdie, the debate over French Muslim girls wearing veils in school exploded. At that point, Finkielkraut started to become an intellectual of reference for the French right. It is a strange sight, Lindenberg admits, to see that "newspapers that are otherwise rather anti-Semitic are not anti-Semitic vis-à-vis Finkielkraut." The journal *Rivarol,* a wildly right-wing publication named after a French counterrevolutionary writer, still occasionally features baldly anti-Semitic material. However, says Lindenberg, "If there is an attack against Finkielkraut, there is always a reader who says, 'No, he is useful.'" For them, "the role of an intellectual like Finkielkraut is to give respectability to rather racist ideas."

The great irony is that the old identity at the core of this nostalgic vision is a conception of Frenchness that explicitly excluded Jews. "It is quite paradoxical because it uses against others the arguments of anti-Semitism," especially the idea of a foreign body that is unassimilable, says Lindenberg.[31]

The ambivalence toward Jews can be traced to two traditions on the French far right—that of Charles Maurras, a Catholic nationalist and monarchist whose counterrevolutionary ideas were in many ways protofascist; he called the collaborationist Vichy regime a "divine surprise."[32] For Maurras, the Jews were the antithesis of Frenchness par excellence and had to be excluded. Then there was Maurice Barrès, the right-wing novelist who wrote the novel *Les Déracinés* (The Uprooted) in 1897, lamenting rootless cosmopolitans and celebrating those grounded in the *terroir.* He was also a leading voice among the anti-Semitic propagandists during the Dreyfus Affair and spoke of his identity as rooted purely in his bloodline. "I defend my cemetery," he famously wrote, tracing a lineage back through blood and soil to generations past.

Yet as Finkielkraut himself acknowledges, the "immense pleasure" Barrès found in his heredity had a flip side during the Dreyfus Affair. "The other face of this pleasure was the physical and metaphysical disgust" that Captain Dreyfus inspired in him. Dreyfus was "very different from us, resistant to all the stimuli that our land, our ancestors, our flag and the word 'honor' stir in us." All throughout the Dreyfus Affair, Barrès remained obstinately attached to this view. As Finkielkraut wrote, "Dreyfus had betrayed because, a foreigner on the soil, he had treason in his blood. His crime was a product of his race. As a Jew, he is Judas, he conspired by his nature against the nation's identity."[33]

Barrès eventually accepted Jews as part of the spiritual family of France after seeing them die on the battlefields of World War I. But the seed was planted, and in certain quarters of the French right, these ideas never went away. Maurras never got over his fixation on the divide between the "real France" of authentic people rooted in the land and the "legal France" of paper citizens, an idea that is at the center of current debates about immigration, the books of bestselling writers, and the FN's campaign.[34] Maurras "is still alive, even among those who never read a line of him," insists Lindenberg.[35] And today, his ideas have found new form and a new scapegoat.

Still, Finkielkraut rejects any comparison between the hatred of Jews then and hostility toward Muslims today. The anti-Semites "were mistaken; they invented, it was a fantasy," he told me, dismissing the analogy. "But who can say that jihad is a fantasy? Who can say that Salafism is a fantasy?"[36] he asks. Lindenberg sees it as a dodge. It's intellectually lazy, he argues, to deny a similarity between the two eras even if today's Muslims aren't wearing yellow stars. The differences shouldn't prevent us from seeing that today they "occupy the unenviable position of scapegoats."[37]

As FRANCE OBSESSES OVER ISLAM, MARINE LE PEN IS APPEALING TO intellectuals of the left to join the so-called camp of patriots. She knows, Lindenberg writes, that there is total confusion and disarray among a group that was once "so sure of its identity."[38]

As Islam has taken center stage in political debates since 9/11, it has redrawn the ideological battle lines that once clearly separated Christian conservatives from secular liberals. Whereas Muslims were once whole-heartedly welcomed by the intellectual left in the name of solidarity with the third world, their cultural conservatism has now placed them closer, in terms of family values, to the positions of the old French right. But they haven't been warmly welcomed by those conservative Christians who see themselves as defenders of French identity. At the same time, the transformation in the eyes of French liberals of the poor oppressed immigrant into a Muslim making demands has "alienated the progressive left and made it possible to build a bridge" between the old left and those surrounding Marine Le Pen, argues the French expert on radical Isla-mism, Olivier Roy.[39]

Many on the old left are buying into the cultural argument of the new right because its leaders have shed the Catholic traditionalism and toxic anti-Semitism of the past and recast themselves as the defenders of French secular values. Lindenberg believes it's happening now because the same cultural anxieties animating the fears of ex-Communist workers in the industrial north are striking fear into the hearts of intellectuals in Saint-Germain-des-Prés.[40] Dozens of writers, even if they have no exper-tise in the field of religion, now pen books on Islam and talk about the Koran on TV; the most widely read is the pop philosopher Michel On-fray. "It's a bit like in the 1930s, there was . . . always the Jewish question," says Lindenberg.[41] Today, the Muslim question is everywhere. And when Islamists attack France or its neighbors, that question, and the blame that follows it, is thrust to the fore.

STÉPHANE CHARBONNIER WAS ONE OF THE TWELVE PEOPLE MURDERED at the offices of *Charlie Hebdo* on January 7, 2015. He was also one of France's best-known cartoonists. His book, *Open Letter*, was published posthumously. Charb, as he was known, presents a rousing defense of free speech and the right to insult any religion. He also rightly points out that *Charlie Hebdo* has a history of vicious mockery of Catholics and Jews; Muslims were hardly unique in that sense.

He insists that cartoonists were not mocking all Muslims when they drew a gun-toting jihadist, just as he was not mocking all Jews when he caricatured right-wing Israeli settlers. He is happy to equate "Jewish religious extremists who, for instance, stalk Palestinians in the West Bank by bulldozer and machine gun with jihadists who stalk infidels in Iraq or Syria." But Charb fundamentally rejects the concept of Islamophobia on the narrow grounds that it is fair to mock or fear a faith but that it is wrong to target the individuals who adhere to it, which would be simple racism. "The inventors of Islamophobia won't budge; they absolutely insist that Islamophobia be treated as anti-Muslim racism equivalent to anti-Semitism, which is anti-Jewish racism," he writes.[42]

This hairsplitting is a fair argument if Islamophobia is strictly defined as mockery of the institutional religion or fear of its most fanatical and violent believers. The problem is that most people engaging in Islamophobic behavior today do so out of fear and hatred of Muslims as individuals and as a group simply because of who they are, the God they worship, and what they wear.

The crux of his argument in the end is like Finkielkraut's—that hostility toward Islam today is different from hatred of Jews, and hence somehow more understandable and excusable, because Muslim extremists are killing lots of people. "Was there an international terrorist movement in 1931 that claimed to act on behalf of Orthodox Judaism? Were there Jewish jihadists threatening to establish the equivalent of Sharia law in Libya, Tunisia, Syria, and Iraq? Did Rabbi Bin Laden send a biplane crashing into the Empire State Building?" Charb fumed. "Jewish fundamentalism was not to 1931 what Muslim fundamentalism is to the twenty-first century."[43]

Given that Charb was murdered by Muslim extremists, his words carry added weight. Yet he did not foresee how the sort of violence that killed him might be harnessed politically to marginalize Muslims.

Hatred against a group can be mobilized when one of its members commits a violent crime. Whether the backlash should be characterized as simple racism or "Islamophobia" is a semantic debate that does not change the fact that collective blame is being ascribed—including by one of the murdered cartoonist's surviving colleagues—and where there is collective blame, collective punishment can soon follow.

Finkielkraut concedes that "at some point, there's a risk that the French will have had enough of Islam," because they already live to the rhythm of attacks and violence. Islam in its most violent form has become "a sort of permanent ambient noise, constantly being discussed in national politics." But for the moment, he believes, "French opinion is holding remarkably well. It is resisting the sirens of racism."[44]

The question is for how long, and whether figures like Finkielkraut will give an imprimatur of legitimacy to those who would rather join the sirens than resist them.

The conflation of individual Muslims and terrorist extremists is encouraged by people who claim they are attacking a religion but spend a great deal of time attacking its believers. It's a tactic that was used by those who deplored the influence of Jews in nineteenth-century France; anyone who dared to denounce anti-Semitism was accused of attacking freedom of expression.[45] Indeed, the title of the arch anti-Semite Drumont's magazine was *La Libre Parole* (Free Speech). These days, "very few of them express old-fashioned 'biological' racism," wrote Adam Shatz in the *London Review of Books*. "Instead, their 'cultural racism' portrays Muslims as an irremediable, jihadist fifth column."[46]

One of those who makes both arguments about Muslims today is the German central banker turned writer Thilo Sarrazin. His book *Germany Abolishes Itself* caused an uproar when it was released in 2010, not least because he was a member of the Social Democratic Party. Sarrazin, an economist by training, is more fixated on a Social Darwinist argument against immigration; he believes Turks are dumbing down Germany and endangering its competitive edge. But he also claims that Islamophobia can never be equated with anti-Semitism, because anti-Semitism was all invented and based on hysterical jealousies. Echoing Charb, he writes that discrimination against Muslims is acceptable because "terrorist attacks, honor killings, the furies of the Taliban . . . and the hangings of homosexuals are realities."[47]

But his analysis reveals a similarly static and racially driven view of Muslims. He blames Islam because Vietnamese immigrants have done better than Turks in Germany and ventures to argue the same is true in Britain because Indians tend to do better than Bangladeshis and Pakistanis. (He neglects to mention that British Indians also perform significantly better than white working-class British children, who are presumably not lagging behind due to genetic inferiority or their fanatical embrace of Islam.)[48] Sarrazin's dire warnings of cultural suicide sold 1.5 million copies. Even more people turned out in the aftermath of the *Charlie Hebdo* massacre to express solidarity with the victims.

Emmanuel Todd, a French sociologist, is convinced that there was something more sinister behind that great outpouring of patriotism. The fact that "millions of French people came out onto the streets to define, as a priority of their society, the right to pour scorn on the religion of the weak" reveals something deeper and more disturbing. "The focus on Islam actually reveals a pathological need among the middle and upper strata to hate something or someone," he writes in his book *Who Is Charlie?*[49] Nor is it driven by concern for Jews, who have been repeatedly targeted. Anti-Semitism is a very real problem plaguing France, but hardly any of those who so earnestly demonstrated after the *Charlie Hebdo* attacks raised their voices when Jews were murdered in Toulouse a few years earlier. French Islamophobia is a force that "casts Muslims out of the national community," and though a direct by-product of terrorism, it also, he argues, has the effect of provoking it.[50]

People like Finkielkraut and the famous feminist Élisabeth Badinter are part of this provocation. Badinter is known for likening veils in school to the Munich Agreement and boycotting labels that produce Islamic clothing. She sees attacks on Islam not as racist but as upholding secularism and women's rights. But as certain excessively clad visitors to French beaches would soon learn, this can lead to very concrete new forms of oppression by agents of the state.

Finkielkraut and former president Nicolas Sarkozy have gone so far as to protest the conversion of unused churches into mosques in a petition in the far-right magazine *Valeurs Actuelles*. The irony is jarring. Upholding secularism, apparently, now requires the restoration of churches. "It's no wonder," Shatz writes, "that, for many Muslims in France, including the silent majority who seldom if ever set foot in a mosque," *Charlie Hebdo*'s very large iceberg, was starting to sound like "a code word for keeping them in their place."[51]

7

Nostalgia, Fear, and the Front National's Resurrection

"IT WAS THE COLD THAT WOKE ME," WRITES MARINE LE PEN IN THE first line of her autobiography. It was 3:45 a.m. "It seemed like I'd just fallen asleep, when I awoke with a start, shocked by the cold and this strange silence. I was going to get up when I realized that my bed and my room were scattered with shards of glass."[1]

The twenty kilograms of dynamite that tore through the building shattered windows, collapsed steel columns, and catapulted the neighbors' baby—and the mattress that saved him—from the fifth floor into the foyer of the building. Marine and her older sisters were sent to neighbors across the street in their slippers and pajamas—"planted there in front of a cup of hot chocolate in the home of strangers. Completely lost."[2] She was eight years old.

November 2, 1976, changed the course of Marine Le Pen's life. It was that night that she was thrust into the reality of politics in the cruelest and most violent way possible. "I was 8 and learned brutally . . . that my father could die, that he risked dying and what's worse, that it was because people wanted to kill him," she writes. "I had gone to bed the night before like all other girls of that age. When I woke up I was no longer a little girl."[3]

The attack also planted the seeds of a deep resentment in her, one that persists to this day. "My father didn't receive the slightest sign of solidarity or compassion from the authorities. Not a sign or word from the head of state or members of government or the police chief. Nothing in the mail or even the shadow of a telegram," she recalls. "Only a young city councilor from the 15th arrondissement who came to the crime scene to meet the victims."[4]

The explosion that cut the building in two and left a gash sixty feet wide was one of the biggest attacks Paris had seen since World War II. "Even as a child, I could sense clearly that an assassination attempt against a politician—even one who wasn't yet well known—was a major event, yet the attempt against my father and his family would very quickly be filed away and passed over in silence."[5] Forty years later, she found herself running the party her father founded and leading in polls for the first round of France's presidential election.

The Front National's headquarters sit on a quiet street in the unassuming Paris suburb of Nanterre, near a car repair shop and a Portuguese restaurant, about six miles west of the apartment where Marine Le Pen was almost killed as a child.

Only when you approach the gray building with its mostly closed blue shutters do the armed guards come into view. In her modest second-floor office, surrounded by books and a cloud of vape smoke, Le Pen explains how she transformed a party known for calling the Holocaust a "detail of history" into a genuine contender for the presidency.

"Voluntarily or not, he gave ammunition to our adversaries," she says of her father's rhetoric. But she insists that she has now cleaned house. "I kicked out the people . . . who had stayed," she says, as a result of her father's complacency. "I fired them all from the FN . . . all those people who expressed an ideology or held views that I found unacceptable."[6]

When Marine Le Pen took the reins of the Front National in 2011, putting an end to the charges of anti-Semitism that had been leveled against the party for decades was at the center of her de-demonization campaign. In 2015, she went so far as to formally oust her father from the party and his role as honorary president.[7]

Le Pen is deeply resentful of past efforts to declare the FN beyond the pale. It is a visceral resentment, one that is rooted in her anger as an eight-year-old as she watched her childhood world shattered with scant sympathy from anyone around her. There are traces of that rage when she speaks about the *front républicain* and talk of a *cordon sanitaire* that have been mobilized in the past to sideline her party.

While she acknowledges the faults of her father's leadership and insists that she has purged all relics of that era, she believes her opponents are still tarring the party with the same brush and painting her as a clone of her father. "Today our adversaries no longer have that ammunition and they repeat on loop" slogans that no longer have any currency with French voters. "They've repeatedly used the arguments of racism, fascism, and xenophobia," she complains. But, Le Pen contends, "at a certain point, this argument loses its force . . . because voters see clearly that there's absolutely nothing in our platform that closely or even remotely resembles fascism or racism." She seems to sincerely hope that "if the person who embodies a certain politics changes, perhaps the vision that people have of the political movement, in fact, changes with it." In other words, that people will accept that she is not her father.

"They've tried everything against the FN—everything!" she exclaims, listing a litany of legal challenges and electoral reforms, "and nothing has worked." She remains extremely calm about it all, she says. "My goal is not to come to power by surprise," she told me one year before her election loss. "I would really like to be defeated based on what I stand for and not on the caricature that has been made of my platform."[8]

Julien Rochedy, a twenty-nine-year-old who was the head of the FN's youth wing from 2012 to 2014 and has since left the party due to clashes with Le Pen's top advisers, believes that the changes are real. Whereas the party leader once peppered his speeches with lines that made Jews' hair stand on end, today, if someone tells a racist joke within the party, "you will be attacked straight away," says Rochedy.

"There is such self-discipline these days. They are genuinely afraid of once again being labeled anti-Semitic or racist," he says.[9] But Le Pen's mission went beyond dissociating herself from her father's legacy; she wanted to clear the taint of homophobia, too. A survey showed that her share of the vote among married gay couples in the regional elections was over 32 percent, only slightly less than the number who voted for a left-wing party—up from just 19 percent in a similar poll from 2012.[10]

If there is a day when it became kosher for gays and Jews to vote FN, it was December 10, 2010. Le Pen was campaigning for the party leadership and declared in a speech to the party faithful, "I hear more and more firsthand accounts of how, in certain neighborhoods, it's not good to be a woman, or a homosexual, or a Jew—or even French or white."[11] It was not a dog whistle or a subtle reference; she was saying directly to gay voters:

I recognize that you're being victimized, and immigrants and Muslims are the cause of your pain. Or as Sébastien Chenu told *Le Monde,* "Who best protects the weakest? Marine Le Pen. A gay who is attacked for being gay is going to seek a strong law-and-order platform." Chenu, a cofounder of the gay rights organization GayLib, which was formally associated with Nicolas Sarkozy's party for a period and later split with the party when it refused to support gay marriage, is now a close associate of Le Pen's. In 2015, he was elected a regional councillor in the northern Pas-de-Calais region.[12]

There are others in the FN who cling to a more traditional Catholic conservative stance—namely, Le Pen's niece Marion Maréchal-Le Pen, the party's rising star. Marion Maréchal opposed the marriage-for-all movement. Chenu calls her position "an orthodoxy that is no longer in the majority."[13]

In 2013, when the country was riven by a debate over gay marriage, "the FN was split in two," recalls Rochedy.[14] The Catholic conservative camp was led by Marion Maréchal; the socially liberal camp was headed by Florian Philippot, who is gay and is now Marine's right-hand man. Marine stood above the fray, allowing her to dissociate herself from conservatives seen as homophobic. Even if her niece has taken a more traditionalist line on homosexuality, their divergent views have allowed the Le Pens to straddle the fence and project the FN as a big tent.[15]

As her inner circle has filled with more and more openly gay advisers, she has also made her pitch to Jewish voters more explicit. "For a lot of French Jews, the FN appears to be the only movement that can defend them from this new anti-Semitism nourished in the banlieues," Le Pen told me. "In a very natural way, they have turned toward the FN because the FN is capable, I think, of protecting them from that."[16]

By actively managing the party's image and courting Jews and gays, Le Pen is giving political expression to an idea that the philosopher Finkielkraut articulated more than a decade ago: that the left, not the right, poses the greatest threat to vulnerable minorities. He described the days leading up to the 2002 election as a mixture of euphoria and terror as anti–Le Pen protesters took to the streets en masse. "Unanimity reigned," he wrote in *Au nom de l'autre* (In the Name of the Other). The crowd's collective smile dripped with "moral superiority over the men of the past." Five days later, they succeeded, "as the ballot boxes brought down the

Beast . . . and the smile of protest became a smile of satisfaction." Although Finkielkraut voted against Le Pen, he did not, he writes, "join the party" and the masses reveling in the streets.[17]

It is a statement that evokes the final scenes of Albert Camus's classic *The Plague,* when the heroic Dr. Rieux, having banished the disease that nearly decimated his city, gazes out from his terrace listening to "the cries of joy rising from the town" but worries that the celebrations are premature because "he knew what those jubilant crowds did not know but could have learned from books: the plague bacillus never dies or disappears for good . . . and that perhaps the day would come when, for the bane and the enlightening of men, it would rouse up its rats again and send them forth to die in a happy city."[18]

Like a latter-day Dr. Rieux, Finkielkraut looked out at the rejoicing crowds dancing in the streets in May 2002 and worried that victory was never definitive and that the scourge might one day return to haunt France. But for Finkielkraut, the threat would not come from the Le Pen family; it would come from those celebrating the FN's defeat.

"Today it is the dancers who are making life difficult for the Jews," he wrote. "The future of hate is in their camp and not in the camp of those nostalgic for Vichy. In the camp of the smile, not of the grimace. Among the humane and not the barbaric. In the camp of the multicultural society and not that of the ethnic nation—in the camp of respect, not that of rejection."[19]

More than a decade later, sitting in his fifth-floor apartment, Finkielkraut remains adamant that the true danger facing France comes from the left. "Antiracism today frequently serves as a pretext for not seeing the true danger that threatens us," he told me in June 2016, on his sixty-seventh birthday. The French must, he insists, "avoid simplistic analogies with the 1930s. We must not mistake what era we live in. Europe doesn't only have demons; it also has enemies, and it needs to know how to fight those enemies."[20]

With so much in flux, longings for a bygone era have become an anchor, and peddling nostalgia is the centerpiece of many new right parties. In France, Marine Le Pen has promised a return to a time when the French had their own currency and monetary policy, when there were fewer mosques and less halal meat, when no one complained about nativity scenes in public buildings, and when French schools promoted a republican ethos of assimilation. Meanwhile, Finkielkraut unapologetically defends a nostalgic vision of France as the only thing that can save it. His 2013 book, *The Unhappy Identity,* depicted a France in crisis due to its unmooring from tradition. No one talks about belonging anymore, complained Finkielkraut.

In a January 2016 debate with the man who was then the presidential front-runner, Alain Juppé, Finkielkraut declared, "A growing number of French feel uncomfortable in their own country." He spoke of halal butchers and tea shops filled with only men, pleading that "the public good isn't in the clouds, it's made from tangible things—the French of Proust and Montaigne . . . the Jardin du Luxembourg and the cows of Normandy."[21]

At home on his couch, down the street from the Jardin du Luxembourg, he elaborates. "There's an anchoring in the French soil," he insists. "A people is built by its history. This heritage can be shared with newcomers but on the condition that there is a difference between he who is welcoming and he who is welcomed." And because the newcomers, in his view, are refusing to accept the culture of the receiving country, the place is fragmenting into parallel worlds. Finkielkraut talks about France reconquering its lost territories—meaning the suburbs surrounding Paris.[22] "Integrating people is not telling them, 'You are how you are and we are how we are.' . . . Integration means making them an integral part of our civilization." And if that doesn't happen, he warns darkly, "at best we'll have secession and at worst civil war." Increasing immigration today, he maintains, is nothing less than the "planned demise of Europe."[23]

Finkielkraut is no fan of the FN. Jean-Marie Le Pen has long traumatized the French Jews, because "he had anti-Semitism in his bones," he tells me. "His jokes, his slipups. Everyone knows them by heart. So it is difficult for the Jews to turn this page." Yet Finkielkraut believes the party has changed and argues that it "should be fought, but for what it is today and not what it was in the past, and not in the name of antifascism."[24] He also sounds startlingly like Marine Le Pen on issues ranging from the defense of secularism to denunciations of globalization.

Laïcité, FRANCE'S TERM FOR ITS PECULIAR BRAND OF STATE SECULARISM, was long a cause of the left. A 1905 law mandating the removal of institutional religious influence from the public sphere was a well-inten-tioned effort to render the state neutral in matters of faith and make all citizens equal before the law. In theory, it is a noble and democratic ideal. In recent years, however, the far right, once hostile to secularists out of attachment to the Catholic Church, has taken up the mantle of *laïcité* and claimed the cause as its own, transforming it into a weapon to be used against Muslims on matters ranging from Islamic dress to halal meat. "Everyone has the right to have a religion, the right to exercise it, but in the private sphere," Marine Le Pen argues. To her, the law is extremely clear, and it is Muslim immigrants who have eroded it. "Little by little, this secularism was nibbled away, precisely as a result of communitarian claims often emanating from fundamentalist Islamist associations."[25]

The author Jean Baubérot charges Le Pen with politicizing minor municipal clashes and turning them into national issues that helped fan the flames of Islamophobia and push voters toward the FN. The prob-lem today, he argues, is that the issue of secularism has been hijacked by the right as Le Pen "proclaimed herself the champion of *laïcité*." In-stead, a new ideology has supplanted the actual law of 1905 in public de-bate. Rather than keeping religious institutions—namely, the Catholic Church—out of public life, it has been used to target Muslims praying in the streets.[26]

During the same speech in which she presented the FN as the de-fender of gays and Jews, Le Pen spoke of 10 to 15 places where Muslims engaged in "an occupation" of French territory. When the editor of a conservative paper asked her if Muslims might be praying in the street because there isn't enough space in the mosques, she replied that they "would have to go pray at home"—a position that violates the 1905 law's provisions on free exercise of religion.[27] As the media frenzy ensued, Le Pen's 10 to 15 places ballooned in public debate to 185. "Marine Le Pen knows the art of playing billiards. She isn't just believed; she also suc-ceeds in creating beliefs that go far beyond what she has said," writes Baubérot. The word *laïcité* "comes easily to her mouth, but it is a falsified *laïcité*," he insists—a word that has been led astray with the explicit pur-pose of marginalizing one religion.[28]

The irony of the FN's defense of secularism as a principle is that Le Pen is an adamant defender of the purely Christian holiday calendar that celebrates countless obscure Catholic festivals but makes no mention of

Eid, Diwali, or Yom Kippur. And the odd nativity scene in a public building does not clash at all with her hallowed notion of secularism. When I
ask why, in a staunchly secular state, it's legal to display nativity scenes at
Christmastime in town halls and other public buildings, she scoffs.

To Le Pen, the Christmas decorations are "a symbol of culture. It
is our culture. It's traditional. It's not religious. When there is a nativity
scene in a town hall, people do not come to prostrate themselves in front
of it. We are a country of Christian roots, so we are a country of Christian
culture. Everything in our way of life comes from this," including calen-
dars featuring Pentecost and Ascension. She also claims that no one cared
until recently. "For a century, it was no problem for anyone. *Laïcité* was
not debated in France. It was practiced without anyone questioning it,"
she says, forgetting the Catholic Church's staunch opposition. She blames
political and religious groups resulting from increased immigration, who,
she claims, "have sought to impose their faith." *Laïcité,* to Le Pen, apparently does not mean the absence of religion in the public sphere; it means
promoting "our" religion and forcing others behind closed doors.

In her view, questioning nativity scenes is not a defense of secularism;
it's an attack on tradition. "Those who seek to have them removed," she
argues, "strike at the heart of the French, because it's part of their traditions."[29] This is an old and tenuous argument. Privileging Christianity,
even when it is cloaked in secular rhetoric, depends on legal acrobatics.[30]
To allow nuns to cover themselves while banning Muslim women's head
scarves is a fundamental violation of equality before the law. When a supposedly liberal state targets one religion's signs of observance and leaves
others alone, while observing one faith's holidays and ignoring those of
others, it is not neutral; it is effectively funding the arsenal of one faith in
order to defeat another.[31] Le Pen doesn't seem to mind.

Her view on halal and kosher meat is revealing; unlike nativity scenes,
they are not innocuous in her view, because they are not rooted in Christian culture and hence clash with her narrow and nativist brand of secularism. "People do what they want at home. No one has forbidden people
to eat halal and kosher. What we don't want is for everyone to eat halal,
because today 90 percent of slaughterhouses in Île-de-France [the region
surrounding Paris] are halal. People who eat meat slaughtered in Île-de-
France eat halal!"[32] To her, this is unacceptable. But pushing local schools
in FN-run cities to serve pork is absolutely fine—and a reestablishment of

French tradition.[33] Whether it's the imposition of meat or mores, Le Pen blames Islam. "In the twentieth century, there were two totalitarianisms, Nazism and communism. In the twenty-first century, there are two new ones: globalism and Islamism."[34]

Despite being Jewish, Finkielkraut's reaction is not so different. When I raise the issue of nativity scenes in public buildings, as clear a sign of a crumbling wall between church and state as I can imagine through American eyes, he is dismissive. Echoing Le Pen, he argues, "There will be nativity scenes in town halls because France is an old Catholic country," and anyway, he insists, they are completely innocuous. "Catholicism is part of the cultural heritage of France." In his eyes, it is not a state forcing religion down the throats of minority groups. "It is not at all the signal of a dominant religion that wants to impose its law."

Finkielkraut doesn't mind if France's brand of secularism is not seen as neutral by Muslim citizens. "Too bad," he exclaims, "maybe it's not neutral!" But that is the newcomers' problem, not France's, he insists. "The French no longer have the ambition to universalize their way of life," he says. That era is past. "They simply want this way of life to prevail within the borders of their own state."[35] But the country has a certain history, he maintains, and the burden is on the guest, not the host—or, as Finkielkraut likes to say, the welcomed and not the welcomer—to adjust. "The country in which they arrive did not begin with them. They come to a country which has its traditions, which has its customs. Secularism is part of these customs, as are the Christian festivals." He doesn't see this as a contradiction.

SECTION III

FROM TERRORISTS TO USURPERS

8

The Great Replacement

HARDLY ANYONE GETS OFF THE EUROSTAR IN CALAIS. ON A TRAIN WITH over seven hundred passengers, three or four disembark. The station, about five miles outside the city center, in the middle of green fields and highways leading to the Channel Tunnel, is surrounded by twelve-foot-high barbed wire fences for miles in either direction. A heavy iron gate is unlocked and quickly resecured each time a train arrives and departs. There are more police officers than passengers.

On the local platform, a short teenage boy is huddled in the semi-sheltered area. He asks me when the next train to Paris leaves. It's at 4:20 p.m., I tell him, more than an hour's wait. Farhad is barely five feet tall, fifteen, and from Afghanistan, and he has been waiting on the cold platform since 1:00. He's had enough of the Jungle, the colloquial name for the refugee camp on the outskirts of Calais, and is off to stay with an uncle in Nantes. He was one of the few who decided to leave and head south, rather than north, across the English Channel.

As you leave the station and drive through rolling fields and charming villages with stone houses, there are police stationed on every bridge crossing a highway or rail line, pacing back and forth in solitary boredom, anywhere that a migrant could potentially jump onto the road or the tracks. On rare sunny days, families with kids and young couples walk out onto the pier, watching the massive ferries shuttling hundreds of cars, trucks, and passengers back and forth to Dover across the English Channel. Near the entrance to the harbor, the ferries emerge slowly, putting their engines in reverse as they back away from the quay and turn eastward toward Dover.

It would not be difficult to jump in the water and swim thirty meters to the side of these lumbering vessels. The police, clearly, have thought of this, and a van of cops sits awkwardly at the edge of the pier among mothers buying their children ice cream and elderly couples strolling along the seafront.

The Calais Jungle, while it existed, was not a hospitable place for adults and less so for children. Built amid the dunes outside of Calais, the camp was a place of blowing sand and trash-strewn paths. There were makeshift shops built from plywood and garbage bags, selling fresh Afghan bread from windows as cars zoomed past on a highway overpass. When the traffic slowed, men would seek to jump onto trucks bound for Britain.

On a visit on a gray and blustery April afternoon in 2016, a group of eight-year-olds lead me deeper into the camp. When offered candy, they refuse and point to their decaying teeth. They don't want chocolate, they say; they want clothes. Near the highway on-ramp, where the children wait nervously for volunteers to unload a car filled with toys, a heavily armed French policeman takes a piss through a hole in the fence. The children are nervous and quickly grab a Spider-Man doll and a small remote-controlled car and run back to the camp. There are rumors that a Syrian child was raped by a local a few days before, and most parents wouldn't allow their kids to leave the camp.

For those who consented to having their handprints taken, there were over one hundred heated shipping containers in a secure part of the Jungle, each holding twelve men on six bunk beds, and there is a family section for women and children. Khan Ahmadzai, age nineteen, was one of those living in the heated containers. He hadn't heard from his parents in over a year and didn't know where they were, he told me. He left Afghanistan when the Taliban broke into his home and threatened to finish him off and kill his family if he refused to fight for them.

From Afghanistan, he fled to Iran and then Turkey. His journey to Europe took place in "a boat the size of a bed" with fourteen passengers. From Greece, he trekked to Bulgaria through the mountains and then Hungary and eventually Paris. Since arriving in Calais, he says he's tried many times to sneak onto trucks bound for Britain. "But the police catch you," he says. He decided to give up on England and moved into a shipping container with eleven other men, some of them strangers.[1]

In February 2016, French police bulldozed the southern half of the camp, leaving only two structures standing—the "school" and a make-shift church built by a group of Ethiopian refugees from plywood, plastic bags, and tarpaulins. At 3:00 p.m. every day, Khan comes to this school in the middle of a muddy field filled with blowing trash and the relics of the structures that once stood here—splintered wood and shredded tires. Those working there say the police knocked everything down but didn't touch the school because it was considered a safe zone. The teachers are a mixture of old women and dreadlocked hippies, most from the surrounding community. Khan comes for French lessons. He already speaks seven languages, he tells me, but finds French difficult and wants to learn. When I returned to Calais a month later, Khan was gone. Via WhatsApp, he told me he'd left the Jungle for resettlement in the southwestern town of Périgueux.

At dawn, a group of Afghan men begins to wait in line for showers, shooing away journalists pointing cameras at them. A line of over a hundred snakes down the road. Meanwhile, a group of East African men wash their feet at a tap along a small brick wall. Others fill five-gallon containers with water and haul it away in Carrefour shopping carts, wheeled miles from the closest supermarket.

Behind a row of bushes, eight Sudanese men huddle around a pit fire cooking a huge pot of lentils. Their encampment is on the edge of the demolished zone of the Jungle not far from Khan's school. But their most immediate neighbors are the last remaining inhabitants of the neighborhood before the Jungle arrived on the Rue de Gravelines: a cluster of run-down brick homes behind a giant gate. Building materials and old cars clutter the small parking lot on the other side of the fence. It's less than twenty meters away from their tents behind the trees. Larger homes sit behind dense foliage and larger fences with signs warning of dogs. "They don't like us," the Sudanese men tell me. "They look at us and shout at us." Down the road, café owners who complain of lost business are arming themselves.[2]

The restaurant Chez Abdallah occupies prime real estate in the Afghan section of the Jungle. It is also a warm respite from the biting wind and rain outside. Burlap sacks line the roof, and a few distressed Afghan and Persian rugs are scattered on the dirt floor littered with cigarettes, foil, and plastic cups. Thanks to a rattling generator, it also serves as the communal charging station.

When I visit the large wood-framed tent, a group of men huddle over cell phones as a teenager with wild hair dances to Arabic music while texting on his phone. Others sleep on hard wooden benches with their heads propped against blue tarpaulins. Many are Afghans, but the crowd is international; others are from Iraq and Kuwait. There are also a few Africans, including a refugee from Darfur who fled because, as he put it, "Omar Bashir will shoot you." He made his way from Sudan through Libya to Italy and eventually to France.

The men spend their days sleeping, smoking, and communicating with family via Facebook. Around 4:00 a.m., they would try to reach Britain. "We run very fast like Ronaldo and Messi," a twenty-three-year-old Afghan explains. If a truck is going slowly, one person will try to get on, but some are not so lucky and fall under the wheels. The day before, a man they knew had been found dead—run over on the highway.

Most of the men in the tent have family in the UK. The Afghan has a brother in Birmingham who has been there for two years and other relatives who arrived in 2001 and have since become citizens. For underage children, family reunions seem to work, he tells me, but at twenty-three, he doesn't have that option. His father owns a supermarket in Afghanistan, and his mother is a school principal, but he doesn't tell them where he is. "I don't talk too much about that," he says. "I don't want to make my mom nervous. She thinks I live in the city. If she knew I was living in Jungle, she would want me to come back. Jungle is for animals, not people."[3] As noon approaches, he occasionally gets up to serve customers bread or the spinach, pumpkin, and lentils simmering on burners above a discarded banner proclaiming "Kinder Treintje Te Huur"—a Dutch company advertising kiddie train rentals for birthday parties—that has somehow found its way here.

Amin Bagdouche, a doctor, is the head of Médecins du Monde in Calais. He is the child of an Algerian father and a gypsy mother and was born during the Algerian War. He treats refugees for everything from pneumonia to injuries sustained trying to jump on UK-bound trucks to lacerations from fistfights. "There are traumas that are linked to the physical violence between the refugees themselves," including sexual violence against both women and young men, he tells me.

He believes that the first dismantlement of part of the camp—and the final destruction—was purely the result of political pressure. The mayor of Calais, a member of the conservative Les Républicains party, feared the growing popularity of the FN. "It's purely electoral," he argues. And the northern corner of France is "a microclimate of what happens in Europe." It captures the full range of responses from the most violent to a warm embrace of refugees by locals like those teaching in Khan's school.

He likens the reaction to refugees to a spreading gangrene. Local politicians played with fire, he tells me, without ever thinking about what to do in the event of an explosion. In early 2016, right-wing groups from across France and Europe descended on Calais, trying to prevent NGO workers like Bagdouche from assisting the refugees. There was a clash with local police, and a decorated paratrooper and retired general named Christian Piquemal was arrested for participating in the march.[4] Members of the German anti-Islam group PEGIDA (Patriotic Europeans against the Islamization of the West) and their allies from elsewhere in Europe joined. Bagdouche believes it has become a real movement. "Now, there is information in the social networks that say that we must defend the French territory. They make calls, they target NGOs, they denounce, they put on their social networks the names of activists and volunteers," including people working for his organization. The clash has moved beyond the refugee issue, he says. "We have moved on to something that is on the order of real political conflict."

There was a camper van marked with the logo of his group, Médecins du Monde, sitting in a parking lot. It was set on fire at 8:00 one evening in Calais, he recounts matter-of-factly. Soon after, volunteers with the same logo on their car had their tires slashed. Bagdouche does not know who did it, but he points to a number of groups in the area that are agitating against refugees and NGOs, some more violent than others.[5]

I MEET THE LEADERS OF ONE SUCH GROUP, REPRENONS CALAIS (Retake Calais), in a public park across the street from the castle-like city hall. We sit on a bench near a fountain; some children play nearby, and a group of African migrants is visible at the far edge of the park.

The group's Facebook page features Guy Fawkes masks, blue-and-white Calais city flags, and photos from their recent demonstrations.

Samuel and Pascal are middle-aged men who lead the group's Internet community in their spare time. They have also produced videos for angry neighbors living adjacent to the Jungle.

It all started fifteen years ago, they tell me, but things got bad in 2013, when, by their count, the number of migrants shot up from five hundred to three thousand. They remember tents going up in the middle of a major boulevard. "People couldn't imagine that in Calais. Three years ago, there were fights between migrants in the middle of the city. The media minimized it or didn't even talk about it." They have no love for the city's center-right mayor, Natacha Bouchart. "Those who govern us are completely against us. It's bizarre because we're French, and they're against the French. The illegals, who aren't French, can do whatever they want." For them, even Marine Le Pen is too soft.

"Marine came here, walked twenty meters down the street" and not much more, Pascal recounts with a scoff. Only her niece Marion Maréchal represents their views, they tell me. "She has balls." But they have no desire to be part of any political party and take orders from superiors.

They talk approvingly of Donald Trump. He says the things that have to be said, declares Samuel. And while they worry about the mayor of London, Sadiq Khan, because he is Muslim, they are heartened by the fact that very few of the migrants in the Jungle actually want to stay in France. "It's thanks to us that they want to leave, because we're hostile. They know very well that the far right is growing here. They want to go to a country where they can live in peace. And now there's a Muslim mayor."

As for the refugees who choose to move elsewhere in France, like nineteen-year-old Khan, they have no patience. "They're sending them to all the little villages in France," says Samuel. After they start to open businesses and bring family members, "in two years the village will be dead."

"It's the great replacement," he insists, citing the title of a book by the anti-Islam author Renaud Camus that paints a dark picture of demographic conquest. "They want to replace us."[6]

Camus explains his theory in very simple terms: "You have a people and then, in an instant, in one generation, you have in its place one or several other peoples." He believes that a "great deculturation" inevitably follows and that it is the single most important thing to happen to France in centuries. He finds it scandalous that "a veiled woman speaking our language badly, completely ignorant of our culture" could go on TV and declare "to an indigenous Frenchman passionate for Roman churches, and the verbal and syntactic delicacies of Montaigne and Rousseau, for Burgundy wines, for Proust, and whose family has lived for generations in the same valley" that she, the veiled outsider, is "as French as you are." And for Camus, the most terrifying part is that "legally, if she has French nationality, she is completely correct."[7]

Camus thinks it is entirely appropriate to speak of conquest. In his view, what France and Europe have been doing for decades, through mass immigration, is allowing "counter-colonization or simply colonization" as Muslims seeking "mastery of the territory" flow into the country. There is also an anticapitalist element to his argument. Not only is the white Frenchman culturally threatened, he is also a "replaceable man, stripped of all national, ethnic or cultural specificity"—an exchangeable pawn.[8]

Camus's nostalgia is for an old France that he finds in the coastal provinces of the southwest, where there are apparently no housing projects plagued by unemployment and delinquency but only "old round fortified villages with narrow streets and houses clinging to each other."[9] It is this same nostalgic vision that inspires all of the new right's intellectual beacons, from the hard-edged white supremacists like Raspail, whose hero lives in a stone house in just such a coastal village, to the less aggressive purveyors of nostalgia like Finkielkraut, with his paeans to the cows of Normandy.

In Calais, the activists complain, nothing changes. "Everyone says one more year, and it gets worse. It takes a major event for the public to react," says Pascal as he tells the story of a ten-year-old girl who was kidnapped, raped, and killed by a Polish immigrant.

But the leaders of Retake Calais don't have much of a problem with Eastern Europeans. "We had Poles and Spanish and Italians. They totally integrated." By contrast, they point to the town of Roubaix, just outside Lille, which has a large Muslim population. "It's mind-blowing. Algerians, Tunisians, Moroccans, Turks. It's an African city in France. It's horrible. They don't come to integrate. They come for health care and a nice house."

For Samuel, the core issue is religion, even though he confides he's not observant himself. "I know an Algerian guy. He's as French as I am. He eats pork. He's not Muslim. He celebrates Christmas and Easter. He baptized his kids at the church." In fact, he adds, the Algerian guy hates Moroccans. "When he speaks, he's more racist than I am!" Samuel adds with a chuckle. But, he says, "a person like that is one in a thousand."

They also have no time for the local press, which published articles labeling their organization and similar ones like Calaisiens en Colère (Angry Calaisiens) xenophobic and fascist. "If defending one's country makes you a fascist, then I'm a fascist," Samuel declares.[10]

Dr. Bagdouche believes that a movement is beginning to coalesce. Groups like Retake Calais and Angry Calaisiens exist within this ecosystem. He respects the anger of neighbors suddenly surrounded by thousands of refugees. These are "people who are not millionaires. I can understand."

The problem, he contends, is that government decisions "have set up the perfect conditions for conflict" with little effort to defuse tensions. They allowed the camp to grow without trying to negotiate with the refugees or explaining the crisis to the local population. And there was little effort to build bridges. Essentially, they said, "Get along." He points to the FN's win with close to half the vote in the first round of the 2015 regional elections and with even better numbers in Calais. The situation, he says gravely, has become "ultrasensitive politically."

Bagdouche has been targeted before. His work has taken him to places like Afghanistan and Libya. He was not expecting to be harassed two hours from Paris. Abroad, he says, "we are targeted because we are French." In Calais, there is something different happening. It is one of the poorest regions in France, but that is hardly on the agenda. "We are not talking about the economic problems of this region at all." Bagdouche credits the FN with diverting attention or redirecting anger from the causes of economic problems to an easily identifiable scapegoat. "They won somewhere because they managed to move the cursor away from the problem, except that by moving it, they created a real political and global problem."

He views France's antipathy toward Arabs as rooted in the colonial past. "All that is Arab is a problem for the French," he contends. And this animosity has been easily mobilized into what he sees as a sort of "territorial vigilance" that attracts those in the police and military and others who are opposed to immigration.

The message is straight out of the great replacement, that "the barbarians must not occupy our country" or colonize France. It also resonates "somewhere beyond the law," he says, which encourages vigilante violence. There are alliances, he says. A retired general from the Foreign Legion who lives on the other side of France doesn't just show up at a protest in Calais "on a Sunday simply because he has nothing to do," says Bagdouche. He helped legitimize the movement, making other activists and protesters see themselves as soldiers with a role to play—part of the chain of command.

Bagdouche worries that the historical forces at work won't disappear or be stopped easily. "One does not prevent a historical movement like this one. We cannot prevent it." When Qaddafi was still in power in Libya, the country served as a barrier between Africa and Europe. That's no longer the case.

"I was in Libya, in Egypt. I know the mentality, the culture. There is no one who will stop the refugees," he says. And these days the people coming aren't Malians and Senegalese seeking a better life for the most part. It is people fleeing from decades of war. "They have decided to go to Europe, they will go there. They will not be afraid," he insists. "They simply do not want to stay in a country that is at war."

He finds the right's popular refrain that true patriots stay home to defend their country naive and childish. "Defend it against whom?" asks Bagdouche. Against Assad? Against the Russians? Against the Americans? Against ISIS? "This is not France against Germany. We're past that. . . . We're not on a Maginot line."[11]

TODAY, EUROPE'S MOST HEAVILY FORTIFIED BORDER IS JUST DOWN THE street. The Calais ferry terminal, the primary transit point for holidaying Brits taking their cars to the Continent, lies behind layers of tall steel fences and coiled barbed wire. It is only a fifteen-minute walk from the Jungle, and groups of migrants often pass by on the road leading to the departures area. There are few ways in; police patrol the entrances and exits, and even the departure ramp leading to the road for the few disembarking passengers who want to walk 1.5 miles into the center of town is enclosed in heavy mesh wire.

It's here that I meet Rudy Vercucque and Yohann Faviere, the local leaders of the Front National. Both men are anxious as they await a meeting with a visiting European Union official from Brussels. They insist on talking outside in front of the ferry terminal. Giant seagulls circle and squawk above.

More than anyone else, their ire is directed at the mayor of Calais, a member of Les Républicains. "She made the land for the camp available. It's she who has permitted this," Vercucque, a portly thirty-six-year-old, belts out angrily. And it was the former president Sarkozy, he reminds me, who negotiated the notorious Le Touquet accords, effectively moving the British border to where we are standing. "He has made Calais the cul-de-sac of immigration in France."

Faviere, bespectacled and bearded, is more soft-spoken. "I'm from here, and what we're doing today is trying to defend our city," he explains. He has few kind words for Sarkozy. "Sarkozy says he'll send the police, but you can't forget that it was he who eliminated thousands of police jobs in France. It's they who are responsible," he says, blaming the former president. "And to think that if they're reelected they'll change things, that's not possible."

After taking a call in the parking lot, Vercucque rejoins us on the rainy pavement outside the ferry terminal. "Today, you have weapons circulating in the Jungle, you have prostitution rings," he claims with alarm. "There's no tourism. Why? Because there have been riots in the center of town." As a result, the businesses of Calais are suffering. They pay their taxes," he assures me. "In the Jungle, the people don't pay taxes. Take a regular French guy who wants to make a bit of money for the end of the month. He opens a chip shop without declaring himself to the authorities—that would last two days. There it's been going on for months."

Revenues for businesses in central Calais are down 40 percent, including over the summer when tourism from the UK peaks.[12] The mayor, he asserts, "has no plan." The result is chaos, economic malaise, and a stagnating economy. "Find a doctor who wants to move to Calais. Find a surgeon who wants to move to Calais. If you bought your house for 250,000 euros, now with what's happened, you'll lose between 40,000 and 60,000! How are you going to sell?" he exclaims. "Can you imagine? You work your whole life, you pay off your house, and you lose money. It's not tolerable."

He mentions the case of Nadine Guerlach, who was threatened with expulsion from the house she'd lived in for decades, a rental from the city that directly borders the camp and who made a series of YouTube videos (with the aid of Samuel and Pascal from Retake Calais) lamenting the lost world of her youth when the Jungle was just a sandy expanse of dunes outside the city. She no longer leaves the house or does errands.

"You let a migrant come and move here totally illegally, and a Calaisienne who has paid her rent for thirty years, and now they want to kick her out because the house belongs to the municipality?" he asks, incredulous. "I don't think that's normal." He makes fun of the mayor's pleas for aid from the central government in Paris just before the last local election. "She's created a situation that she can't control anymore, and now she's playing victim because she can't accept the fact that it's her fault." Vercucque suspects that most of the migrants are not genuine refugees. He cites a census that showed 6,000 migrants and only 115 women and children among them. "If your country is at war or a boat is sinking, you send the women and children first," he tells me. "Are these really war refugees? I don't think so."

With all this anger directed at the current government, I ask if the FN's voter base is coming to them out of rage. The ever-diplomatic Faviere explains, "I don't think it's a vote of anger or a protest vote. I think today we really have people who adhere to our ideas . . . and that people really agree with us."

Vercucque puts it more bluntly. "We say out loud what people think deep down," he declares. "And now they're realizing that we're right."[13]

THIRTY MILES AWAY, IN THE SMALL TOWN OF GRANDE-SYNTHE ON THE outskirts of Dunkirk, a "second Calais" has sprouted, but under very different circumstances.

Grande-Synthe is a tiny, orderly town. It was built on the edges of Dunkirk to provide housing for the workers toiling in the nearby factories. It is much smaller than Calais, and everyone in the city hall seems to know one another. The town center is sleepy, with just a few shops, a brasserie, and a parking lot. The roundabouts are well manicured, and the streets' names tend toward the political, with some named after Socialist heroes like the slain Chilean president Salvador Allende. Grande-Synthe's residents have elected and reelected a Green Party mayor, Damien Carême, for the past sixteen years. It is also the first town in France to voluntarily build a refugee camp on its territory. "I told the government I would not accept deaths in my municipality," Carême tells me.

It is unusual for an area where the FN is gaining popularity. Carême proudly tells me that when Marine Le Pen was running in the 2015 regional elections, the FN only got 41 percent in his town, the lowest in the region—an area where Le Pen won a convincing 53 percent majority in the 2017 election.[14] Carême says there is no organized FN presence in the town and no committed activists for the party, although many have voted for it. He has still managed to win with comfortable margins for over a decade, winning an outright majority in the first round of the mayoral election with well over 50 percent of the vote.

Some of the town's politics can be explained by its history; Grande-Synthe was once an agricultural area. In the 1950s, it was a village, and residents used to walk across the fields to the seashore. Arcelor-Mittal, a steel giant, built a plant on the shore in 1963 with railroad tracks, new roads, and a huge dock for big ships transporting the steel. "It was a decision by the state to bring in factory workers," says Carême, including his father, who came from eastern France. "We came because there was work here," he recalls. Others came from Italy, Spain, and Portugal. Poles who had worked in mines in northern France came looking for work after the mines shut down. There were also workers from North Africa, recruited by French companies because they needed labor.

Grande-Synthe quickly transformed into a company town, and the population exploded, creating demand for more housing for all the new factory workers. In the span of less than twenty years, the town's population soared from 1,800 to more than 20,000.

The influx of refugees did not become grave until 2015. There were only thirty refugees in 2006, recalls Carême. "They stayed one night near the service stations and then jumped into trucks." As the numbers climbed, the municipality provided a heated tent and later multiple ones for men and women. Still the migrants tended to stay for forty-eight hours maximum. Their goal was always to reach England.

In the autumn of 2015, the numbers skyrocketed as more than a million Syrian refugees and other migrants made their way across Europe. The population of the camp went from 60 in July to 190 in August, then 550 in September. By October, there were 1,200 people, including many children. By the end of the year, there were 2,800 people living in increasingly unsanitary and overcrowded conditions. The bottleneck grew because the migrants all wanted to go to England, and border security, managed by the French police, was tight.

In August, Carême contacted the interior ministry, saying he wanted to take care of the people in his town. Initially, top officials in Paris were not enthusiastic and tried to dissuade him. They feared attracting more migrants and smuggling networks. "But I said I can't leave them in the conditions they're living in today. It's inhumane. I won't stand for it. There were three hundred children."

The growing camp, however, was on land that had been zoned for a new housing development. "I didn't know when it would stop. I needed to get the land back because I was planning to build housing on it," he adds, showing me satellite photos of the area. Moreover, local residents, their own immigrant heritage notwithstanding, were beginning to get irritated by the constant stream of volunteers from across Europe arriving with food, tents, and mattresses. "And the cops were there constantly. It was a huge mess. Residents were afraid that it would become like Calais," recalls Carême. "I told them I'd do something about it."[15]

In the summer of 2016, the new camp in Grande-Synthe sprawled between a freight rail line and a six-lane highway overpass on the outskirts of town. An old factory building loomed over the entrance; it was painted pale blue, and almost all the windows were broken.

When I visited, the camp was a collection of 367 small wooden structures scattered across a barren gravel expanse between the highway and the tracks. Each wooden shack was heated by a small gas stove. They were more durable than the plastic-and-cardboard homes forty miles away in the Calais Jungle but far from comfortable.

There weren't many people out, probably owing to Ramadan. Of the one thousand registered residents, I only encountered about twenty people, mostly young men in T-shirts and sweatpants walking to the bathrooms or the camp's phone charging station, where a few teenagers were playing foosball. Two young children rode dirt bikes up and down the gravel path. An elegant older man in a three-piece suit and Ray-Bans rushed from one shack to another, holding his veiled wife's hand.

According to the mayor's office, over 80 percent of the residents in June 2016 had come from Kurdish areas of Syria; prior to that, most were Iraqi Kurds. Graffiti advocating Kurdish independence adorned the walls of most of the shacks, and Kurdish flags were everywhere. The municipal government had posted red warning signs all over the camp with pictures of the highway, train tracks, and overhead power lines and the macabre message "Beware: Do Not Add to Recent Deaths," a reminder that most people do not intend to stay and their attempts to reach Britain generally involve crossing either the six-lane highway or the freight tracks.

Unlike Calais, where political opposition to refugees has been loud and occasionally violent, there was little reaction in Grande-Synthe. "My constituents have always been admirable on this issue," says Carême. There were no protests or petitions. He began writing monthly letters to constituents outlining his plans and the costs and reassuring them the original camp would be moved. "I told them there are new immigrants arriving here because there's war in their homelands and terrorism." Then he enlisted Doctors Without Borders to help advise on the relocation and design the new camp.

Carême believes that most politicians are driven to the right out of fear, telling themselves that support for the FN will increase if they don't act harshly. But that sort of electoral fear ends up entrenching far-right policies, whether or not the FN wins. Doing nothing amounts to "putting in place the policy of the Front National," Carême insists. "And for me, that's not how you fight them."

As for the right's claims that allowing migrants to stay encourages smuggling, he is dismissive. "Ten days ago, we arrested a major smuggler who'd come from Germany, so our fight against smuggling is working. We stopped twenty-two smuggling networks here. That hasn't happened in Calais, because we work with the police and the courts." Eventually, the national government came and paid for the day-to-day functioning of the camp. "They wrote a check. They saw that it worked. They announced that Paris is going to build one now like ours."

At the beginning, recalls Carême, "everyone said, 'He's crazy. He's going to have problems.'" The key, he is adamant, is keeping it within manageable proportions. "There were 2,800 refugees; I have a population of 22,000," an additional population of almost 15 percent to absorb and support in a small town. "It's a temporary solution. We responded to a need at a given moment," he says.

The closing down of Calais led to growth in Grande-Synthe. In April 2017, most of the camp was reduced to ashes after fires broke out, following fights between Kurds and Afghans, and most of its residents left for asylum-seeker centers across the country. Whether or not Carême rebuilds the camp, he's convinced that those who came to his town are only a first wave. "I think we're going to have climate refugees by the millions," the mayor adds, referring to those fleeing islands and low-lying coastal areas in countries like Bangladesh or drought in the Middle East. "We need to prepare for that."[16]

MAYORS LIKE CARÊME ARE MARINE LE PEN'S FAVORITE TARGETS. IN HER view, the last thing France needs to do is lay out a welcome mat. Le Pen blames the EU, more than any other institution, for encouraging and increasing immigration. "The European Union, through a whole series of structures, has been arguing for years that it would be necessary to welcome millions of immigrants to Europe because of the aging population in order to make the labor market more fluid," she tells me. "The reality is that Europe wants immigrants, and the people do not want them. That is the problem."

It's an argument that merges the FN's two greatest grievances—the threat from immigration to France's culture and economy and hostility toward the Brussels bureaucracy that is supposedly stealing France's sovereignty. The EU's objective "is to bring in lots of immigrants, not because of the aging population," she insists, "but to put pressure on wages, to push down salaries, because it believes that it will succeed there in gaining productivity in its global competition."[17]

It is yet another example of her co-opting the rhetoric of those who fancy themselves to be leftist and claiming it for herself. By framing the EU as capitalist villain, the FN becomes the defender of the little guy.

Once again, Le Pen's analysis sounds remarkably similar to that of Alain Finkielkraut. The philosopher also has harsh words for the global elites who jet between capitals without a second thought or from coast to coast in the United States, ignoring the so-called flyover states that voted disproportionately for Trump. "Our societies are now divided between the planetary and the sedentary, between the global and the local," between those who have the luxury of living without being grounded anywhere and the indigenous who have no choice.[18] For a Jewish philosopher who has written extensively on ethnic nationalism and anti-Semitism in French history, it sounds suspiciously like the vision of the nineteenth-century writer Maurice Barrès, who spoke of rootless cosmopolitans as a threat and idealized a French identity grounded in the cemetery with a direct bloodline from past to present.

"It's not necessarily the vision of Barrès," insists Finkielkraut, "but it's a completely natural view" because a people is a product of its history. And it is not just a difference in lifestyle and priorities; there is also an implicit value judgment and deep condescension at work, he believes. Those who are not rooted anywhere thanks to new technologies and "have the intoxicating feeling of forming a new global civil society despise the others. They despise the indigenous people. They treat them as stupid hicks and even bastards. The privileged today are not only better off economically, but in addition, they feel morally and politically superior."[19]

Le Pen's immigration policy is quite simple. She insists that France must reclaim its borders, and that means an end to the free movement of the Schengen era. "To reclaim the borders means being able to prevent people from entering the country when they are not invited, and I will send back to their country those who are illegally present on French territory," she declares. The massive refugee population that was until recently concentrated in Calais is the result of what she calls "a cul-de-sac problem. We do not have a border, and Great Britain has borders. Immigration is blocked in Calais. If we had our borders, by definition, we would push back the problem. But having borders is not enough. It's also necessary for France to create the conditions so that the country is not attractive to immigration."[20]

Le Pen's campaign manager, David Rachline, agrees. At twenty-nine, he is the youngest senator in France and one of just two FN members; he is also the mayor of the small Riviera town of Fréjus near Nice. In September 2016, Le Pen announced that he would run her presidential campaign.

Rachline, like his boss, enjoys a good argument. We sit outside the gilded and Versailles-like senate chamber on a sweltering June afternoon a few days after Brexit, which he describes as a "great joy."

The FN has many gripes with the European Union, but Rachline's is borders. The EU instructed its members "to remove our internal borders and replace them with external borders," he argues. "It will certainly not have escaped you that there are no borders at all, neither internal nor external." In Calais, there is the sea, which keeps many migrants away from the UK, but, he insists, "if there were no sea, the situation would be the same as in southern France," where, he says, "hundreds of thousands of immigrants pass through Italy and Ventimiglia," the town on France's border with Italy to the east of Nice. Europe, he claims, has become "a sieve, through which anyone who wants to enter can pass."

The day before we met, Rachline had accompanied Le Pen and a few other high-ranking party officials to meet then President Hollande and request a Brexit-style referendum in France. They knew the answer would be no; it was more for show. It would be too dangerous for Hollande to "let the people speak," he says, because they would reject his policies. "The European Union, as it exists, has strictly no legitimacy," Rachline maintains, because nonelected European commissioners make "rules that have not been validated by the French people." It is this, he argues, that "creates this rift between our elites and the people."[21]

In Le Pen's telling, immigration policy is not just about deterrence; it is about fairness. She argues, "Today in France, you are better taken care of for free when you're an illegal immigrant than when you're a working French citizen."[22] It may be an exaggeration—the refugees in Calais were often living in destitute conditions, although they did receive medical care at local hospitals—but it is an argument that clearly catches on with the sort of voters she is trying to attract.

Le Pen has no time for dual citizens and sees birthright citizenship as a threat to France. She doesn't use the term "anchor babies," but the idea is the same. Casting aside centuries of French tradition in the realm of nationality law, she insists that granting citizenship by birth is a disaster. "We must stop creating automatic French citizens," she argues, pointing out that the *Charlie Hebdo* killers were legally French.[23]

It is an argument with a long pedigree. It traces its roots to long before the time of Renaud Camus and his "great replacement." It started with Barrès. Before his vitriol was turned against Captain Dreyfus, Barrès was fuming about birthright citizenship just like Le Pen does today. He warned of new French citizens that wanted to impose their way of life. "They are in contradiction to our civilization," he wrote of the immigrants becoming French. "The triumph of their worldview will coincide with the real ruin of our fatherland. The name France may well survive; the special character of our country will be destroyed."[24]

The theme was picked up by Charles Maurras's followers in the 1920s. The industrialist François Coty, who owned the right-wing newspaper *Le*

Figaro, laid out the great replacement in more concrete terms in an editorial. The internationalists had decided, he wrote, "to replace the French race with another race." Having arranged for the destruction of the true French and the insertion of neo-French, these new citizens, with their French identity on paper, would become "naturalized enemies." For Coty, the most alarming problem was that these new citizens "could no longer be expelled; they are at home in our home; they have the same rights as us inside our own walls," he warned.[25]

Today's version of the argument is: if you don't behave appropriately, then you don't get a passport. "To give French nationality to someone without having taken the trouble to make sure that this person has the necessary morality to become a citizen and has the true wish to become one and to participate in the national destiny—it makes no sense!" Le Pen exclaims. And if it takes "a certain amount of time to see if the person has the right moral views," then the law should force people to wait until they are eighteen or twenty to apply. "So what" if they have to wait, she says. "I have friends who are French who went to live for fifteen years in Germany; they didn't become Germans. One can very well live as a foreigner in a foreign country." She mentions a study of French people who have lived in the United States for twenty years and want to become Americans. They "look at whether they have not stolen, raped someone, trafficked drugs—if they participate in the American way of life."[26]

What she doesn't mention is that a white French rapist or drug trafficker would not be subject to any extra moral scrutiny at age twenty according to her plan or risk losing his passport; only those with a drop of foreign blood need additional moral screening.

JULIEN AUBERT IS AN UP-AND-COMING MEMBER OF THE ASSEMBLÉE Nationale who represents a southern district near Avignon for the conservative Les Républicains party. He is on the rightmost edge of his party and is one of the people thinking about how to push back against Le Pen's narrative. At times his rhetoric sounds remarkably close to the FN's. In mid-2016, he wrote an article in *Valeurs Actuelles,* a conservative magazine that has embraced much of Le Pen's rhetoric, declaring that France was at war and would have to change its laws and priorities and renounce the comforts of peacetime. Like Le Pen, he denounced the political establishment for failing to call the enemy by its name. "Say it! Yes, Islamism has everything to do with Islam because all of our enemies identify with this religion," he wrote, calling for the bodies of dead Muslim terrorists to be incinerated—a deliberate violation of Islamic law's injunction against cremation.[27]

In June 2016, a few months before the primary that elevated François Fillon to the top of the Les Républicans ticket, he explained the party's strategy in countering Le Pen. "Absorb the centrists. Maybe recover the voters of the FN and therefore qualify automatically for the second round facing Le Pen," which he thought the party would win handily. When his party's nominee, François Fillon, became mired in scandal, this plan went out the window. Marine Le Pen beat Fillon by a margin of eleven percent in Aubert's district in the election's first round, and Emmanuel Macron won with 53 percent in the final round.

When it comes to winning back Le Pen voters, a lot of the people who devoted themselves to the subject are gone from politics, having lost elections. According to Aubert, his party is hamstrung by its broad tent approach. The FN has a unified and coherent message. Even where disagreements exist, they are generally smoothed over in the interest of party unity. "We do not necessarily agree on everything," he says, and more importantly, "we are accountable for the past. So rightly, people are telling us, 'You are the ones in charge.'" By contrast, he argues, the FN has the advantage of not being perceived as bearing any responsibility since it has never been in power. Not being seen as responsible for past failures means the party can get away with proposing policies that are completely impractical or financially unrealistic. "When you are in the FN, you can say anything," Aubert complains. "For us, nothing is forgiven."

For Aubert, the question of how to run against the FN hits close to home. In his region, the Vaucluse, the approach that brought Chirac to power so overwhelmingly in 2002 could backfire today. Le Pen's niece Marion Maréchal performed extremely well in regional elections there, Aubert notes. "You have 51 percent of people who vote Front National. It gets complicated. Do you establish a *cordon sanitaire* against half of the people?"[28]

In addition to courting Euroskeptic and anti-immigrant voters from the center and left, the other major shift in FN policy was to purge the party of its dinosaurs. The de-demonization efforts actually began long before Le Pen took over. It was after the crushing 2002 defeat that several party leaders became convinced that the image of an anti-Semitic and racist party needed to be purged if it was ever going to have a chance of electoral success.[29]

Le Pen's de-demonization campaign, culminating with the expulsion of her father, demonstrated a shrewd understanding of voters' "thin commitments" and the possibility of pulling some reluctant radicals over to her side by ditching the party's most damaging baggage.[30]

For all Le Pen's talk of courting Jews, she has not forgiven the community's leaders. One of the organizations she blames for treating the FN unfairly is the official organ of the French Jewish Community, known by its French initials, CRIF. "The CRIF is always trying to be on the winning side," she says mockingly. "It's socialist when it is the socialists in power; it's right wing when it's the right that's in power." And she believes they are stuck in a time warp. "To admit that for twenty years they had fought against the FN and while they were fighting against the FN, which represents no danger whatsoever to French Jews, they had not led any of the necessary fights against the fundamentalist Islamists is to admit that they have failed in their duty."[31] When Le Pen denied the French state's responsibility for the roundup of thirteen thousand Parisian Jews in 1942—by French police—and then appointed a man who had questioned whether the Nazis used poison gas to murder Jews to head her party during the final weeks of the election campaign, many French Jews found themselves reconsidering her claim that the FN no longer posed a threat to them.[32]

Whether or not Jews are flocking to her, she is confident that there is a "shy FN" syndrome. And like the shy Tories or shy Trump voters who didn't admit their voting preference to pollsters, she is adamant that a similar phenomenon exists in France. "You go down the street and you count. One, two, Front National. It's a fact." She is convinced that if people weren't afraid of being socially ostracized, they would admit their true preference. "I think there is still a form of intellectual terrorism in France that makes it impossible for you to say that you are FN. We whisper it to each other, we let each other know, but we do not dare say it, because if you do, public subsidies, relations with institutions, all of this is turned upside down."[33]

If such a hidden vote exists, it will spell trouble for the center right. If the 2017 election is any indication, Le Pen's 47 percent showing in Aubert's area in the final round suggests that she's right. Aubert has thought about this. The real question for him is whether the FN has simply become a normal right-wing party, in which case, he argues, "we must fight it as we would fight any party." But, he says, "if the National Front is a far-right party that uses a more smiling mask that allows it to attract voters, there is a danger."

He believes the party is riding the same wave Trump rode to victory in the United States. The driving force is the same: people who say, "We are declining, and we do not want to decline."[34]

9

Freedom of Religion—for Some

ON JULY 14, 2016, AS FRENCH FAMILIES AND TOURISTS STROLLED ALONG Nice's seafront promenade, a man of Tunisian background barreled around a corner in a large truck, running down everyone in his path and killing eighty-six people. Immediately, France, still reeling from the previous November's attacks in Paris, was thrown back into mourning. Less than two weeks later, two young men who had tried to join ISIS in Syria slit the throat of an octogenarian priest in his church near Rouen.

A month later, in mid-August, with most of France's population at the beach or near one, the mayor of Cannes declared that "burkinis"—a nebulous term for modest swimwear favored by many religious women who prefer not to bare themselves in bikinis or less—would be banned from the city's beaches.

Even France's ambassador to the United States, Gérard Araud, whose Twitter account often limits itself to disseminating images of works by famous French painters, joined the debate with a rousing feminist defense, declaring that "a burqa is not a neutral attire. It conveys a conception of the woman as a [sic] object of lust, a subject and not an agent of history."[1]

But for Araud and the staunch defenders of French laïcité, this was a clash of Huntingtonian proportions, and the battle to defend Western civilization necessarily required showing some skin. With the threat from Le Pen looming, the moderate right and even the socialists were keen to profit from the moment. After Le Pen declared that "the soul of France is in question here . . . France does not lock away a woman's body, hide half of its population," others raced to join the bandwagon to defend women's rights by insisting that they strip down to their swimsuits.[2] Former president Nicolas Sarkozy reacted by declaring "to wear a burkini is a political act, militant, a provocation."[3]

The argument that, at a time of heightened fear and sensitivity after the Nice attack, wearing "provocative" attire like the burkini could inflame public opinion and threaten public order is somewhat incoherent. It relies on the same dubious logic as those who argue that women should not dress in revealing clothing lest they provoke lustful men to rape. The actual problem in both cases is the harasser, not the woman or the garment; Islamophobic beachgoers, like aroused men, ought to be responsible for restraining themselves and not verbally or physically abusing a woman because of the clothes she does or does not wear.

The burkini bans led to discord at the highest levels of government with then education minister Najat Vallaud-Belkacem, herself a nonpracticing Muslim woman, calling the proliferation of burkini bans "unwelcome." Prime Minister Manuel Valls, concerned with appearing tough at a time when approval ratings for the Socialist Party were at all-time lows, insisted that the bans were necessary for public order. It was an easy way to win some points and look tough at a time when Le Pen was rising in the polls. "Women's rights imply the right for a woman to cover up," Rim-Sarah Alouane of the University of Toulouse told the Associated Press. "What is more French than sitting on a beach in the sand? We are telling Muslims that no matter what you do . . . we don't want you here." Remona Aly made the point more bluntly in the *Guardian*, arguing, "Politicians talk constantly about integration and inclusion, and then proceed to kick out to the fringes the very women they claim are oppressed and excluded from society."[4]

The harshest critics of hard-line French secularism tend to come from outside France. Ambassador Araud and others like him have hidden behind the intellectually lazy proposition that "a debate can't be understood from the outside."[5] While the French have little problem expressing shock at America's gun culture, the continued existence of the death penalty, and its lack of national health care, when it comes to France's civil religion, foreign criticism is off limits. Ironically, Araud followed his spirited defense of *laïcité* with a not-so-secular wish of "Happy Festival of the Assumption" to his thirty thousand followers.[6]

Context does matter, of course. And a society's legal traditions, history, and traumas are worth taking into account. But to argue that outsiders can't comprehend this debate and hiding behind context to defend a blatantly illiberal policy is tantamount to the American government choosing to defend the illegal removal of Arab and Middle Eastern passengers from planes by airline employees who had no grounds beyond the fears of fellow passengers who heard them speaking foreign languages or didn't like the way they looked.[7]

It is worth recalling that there were numerous violent attacks on Muslims and Sikhs (mistaken for Muslims) after 9/11, a moment when much of America, like France after the Nice attack, was understandably afraid of terrorist acts committed by men from the Middle East, but the highest officials of state did not attempt to excuse or condone those attacks.

Many French like to believe that a sprinkling of references to Catholic holidays and the odd nativity scene at Christmastime represent "French culture" and are therefore perfectly neutral and in no way infringe on the holy principles of state secularism. It is not seen the same way from the banlieues of Paris, where young women have been barred from wearing veils to their graduation ceremonies. In those forgotten corners of the republic, many young French citizens do not see themselves as fully French because they are not seen that way by the majority of the French.

FARHAD KHOSROKHAVAR, A SOCIOLOGIST AT THE PRESTIGIOUS ÉCOLE DES Hautes Études en Sciences Sociales and an expert on radicalization, has pointed to the gulf between *laïcité* in theory and its actual application that is angering and alienating many French citizens. This is due in part to the fact that France's conception of citizenship, "which strongly insists on adherence to a few exalted political values, has seriously eroded over time," he argues. While Germany opted for the more modest goal of lifting all boats through economic growth, France has remained, as Khosrokhavar puts it, "resolutely universalist and claims it still has both the desire and the power to enforce inclusion. Yet its assimilationist ambitions are increasingly at odds with everyday reality."[8]

There is an unrealized fantasy of absolute racial and religious equality, which is compounded by the fact that France forbids the collection of data disaggregated along those lines, meaning that there is no way to accurately measure whether the state is living up to its ideals or massively failing certain groups of citizens. It means that both successes and failures are invisible to policy makers, and those who are left behind in a society that hides behind the veneer of absolute equality between citizens are likely to become increasingly frustrated.[9]

This is especially the case in heavily minority communities where poverty is rampant and where young men who become radicalized tend to grow up. The pitfalls of harsh restrictions in the name of secularism are also dangerous on a strategic level if the state wants to reduce the appeal of Islamist recruiters. Implementing and encouraging the enforcement of laws like the head scarf ban and the current burkini row gives Islamists a ready-made pretext to accuse France of Islamophobia and lure angry young men into their orbit.

France has no doubt succeeded in integrating many North Africans and their children, but those left behind are far more bitter than in other countries. That is largely because the French model of integration is so rigid. Rather than fine every modestly clad Muslim at the beach, France needs to come to terms with the multicultural nation it has become and refrain from turning to the police to enforce secular morals.[10]

The political scientists and terrorism scholars Will McCants and Chris Meserole have attempted to quantify this argument by linking the number of foreign fighters in Syria from francophone countries to the radicalizing effect of strict *laïcité*.[11] Their methodology has come under attack, but the data is telling. France and Belgium have a hugely disproportionate number of citizens fighting for ISIS compared to other European countries on a per capita basis. The closest countries are Lebanon and Jordan, which are both direct neighbors to the Syrian conflict and have long histories of Islamist groups operating and recruiting.

According to the researchers, rigid state secularism like France's "helps jihadist recruiters who want to sign up Muslims who believe they don't belong." They point out that one of the primary goals of jihadist attacks is "to force western societies to over-react such that they start discriminating against their Muslim populations. In that sense, the ultimate goal of the violence is not so much to kill as it is to force the Muslims within those populations to make a black and white choice between identifying as Muslim and identifying as western," they explain. ISIS has a name for this strategy: eliminating the gray zone.

"When a state seeks to ban the niqab or hijab, *it forces that same choice*," they argue. While this may not be the proximate cause of radicalization for all French and Belgian jihadists, McCants and Meserole insist that there is a strong correlation, and their data backs this up. "For jihadist recruiters in the west," debates like the burkini spat "play right into their hands." Some French foreign fighters who have gone to Syria have cited the burqa ban as a catalyst for their radicalization. They regarded it as a law targeting only Muslims and it sent a message that Islam "was not welcome in France."[12]

There is no doubt that the news from the beaches of Cannes might have a similar effect on angry and alienated young men in some depressed corner of France, far from the rarefied diplomatic world that men like Ambassador Araud inhabit.

Critics will argue that this theory is yet another case of Western self-hatred, apologetics, and victim blaming, like Western leftists who reacted to 9/11 by focusing on the sins of US and European foreign policy rather than blaming the perpetrators of the attacks, or those who refuse to criticize totalitarian and fundamentalist governments on the grounds that Western standards do not apply in other cultures.[13] After all, it is France that has been attacked multiple times by Islamic extremists— why, they argue, should a proud secular democracy cave to the archaic demands and fundamentalist hypersensitivities of a group of people that refuses to live by the rules of a modern society?

But there is a crucial distinction between the justification put forward for the burkini ban—the state must protect women from being oppressed by a religious dress code—and the rousing defense of freedom of expression at the heart of Danish newspaper editor Flemming Rose's insistence on publishing and republishing the Mohammed cartoons.

When the French newspaper *Charlie Hebdo* decided to reprint those cartoons—an act that earned it the ire of Islamic extremists—the principle cited was freedom of expression and equal-opportunity lampooning of various religions. Many have argued that both *Jyllands-Posten* and *Charlie Hebdo* overstepped the bounds of decency and were needlessly provocative and offensive. That debate, like debates about permitting Holocaust denial and neo-Nazi marches through Jewish neighborhoods, is one worth having, but the bedrock principle that in a free society a citizen has the right to draw, say, and publish what she likes—short of incitement to murder—is an admirable one. Rose is correct that the right *not* to be offended should not exist in modern liberal democracies: it is a slippery slope as soon as speech (or beach attire) is banned in order to protect certain groups from potentially being insulted or provoked.

If Catholics or Jews or Muslims did not appreciate the offensive caricatures in *Charlie Hebdo*, they could choose not to buy the newspaper or organize a boycott. Those offended by the *Jyllands-Posten* cartoons had the choice not to read that paper and to purchase others. While upsetting, it did not fundamentally impact their freedom as citizens to move, dress, and assemble as they please. The burkini ban is different. For women who, for whatever reason, choose to cover up when they go to the sea, the immediate effect is the inability to visit a public space unless they remove certain items of clothing. They are effectively being banned from the local beach or forced to strip for police and wear attire deemed appropriate by the state. There is not another public beach they can visit.

Finkielkraut defended the bans on the grounds that "the burkini is a flag. . . . The women in burkinis only hide their bodies to better exhibit their submission and their separation. They offer to other beachgoers the doubly painful spectacle of servitude and rejection."[14] But there is a substantial difference between shrugging off the display of nativity scenes on Christmas, as he does, and instructing pious women to remove some of their clothes. It is the difference between looking the other way and active enforcement—in choosing when and how to police the boundaries of secularism and whom to punish for transgressing them.

When talking about secularism, Finkielkraut likes to say he's never asked for Yom Kippur to be a national holiday, and if he chose to fast, that was his personal business. Likewise, Christmas parties do not offend him. The difference, of course, is that no one forced Finkielkraut to refrain from fasting on Yom Kippur or to work on the Jewish Sabbath under threat of exclusion. Women who were asked to remove modest swimwear were either humiliated or excluded.

As one woman, Siam, complained after being forced by armed police to strip off her veil in Cannes "because people who have nothing to do with my religion kill, I no longer have the right to go to the beach! Because they carry out attacks, I'm deprived of my rights," the thirty-four-year-old woman told *Le Nouvel Observateur*. "Today we're banned from the beach. Tomorrow from the street?" she asked. "I'm disgusted that this can happen in France."

The incident was witnessed by a journalist and quickly gained national attention. She was fined eleven euros for not having "proper attire, respectful of good morals and secularism." The police did not intervene to stop a group of a dozen people shouting racist insults at her and her crying daughter, including "Go back to your country," and "France is a Catholic country."[15]

The insults were both upsetting and ironic given that Siam was, as she put it, "a bit française de souche"—a term used by nationalists and identitarians to denote deep French roots—having been born in France, as were her parents and grandparents. There is nowhere to go back to, as the racists on the beach demanded. In fact, she is more "de souche" than Finkielkraut, whose parents were Polish Jewish refugees, yet she was removed from a beach while he is hailed as a champion of French values.

Only by conflating true Frenchness with an explicitly Catholic or Judeo-Christian identity is it possible to exclude a third-generation French woman from the national community.

THE FAR RIGHT LIKES TO BLAME MUSLIM EUROPEANS FOR FAILING TO integrate, forming parallel societies, and rejecting their wonderfully generous new homelands. What they neglect to consider is that even second-generation Europeans, who in many cases were born in Europe and are citizens, are still not recognized as fully equal compatriots by society at large, dismissed as "French on paper" or not authentically Danish simply because of their skin color or name. And those who aren't citizens have it worse.

Unlike in the United States—aside from the white supremacist circles of Steve Bannon and Richard Spencer—in Europe, national identity is still largely perceived as being ethnically defined. A French citizen of Algerian heritage or a Dane with Moroccan parents will almost always be referred to, in casual conversation and in the press, as a Muslim or North African rather than by his citizenship. The populist right laments the failure of integration in these communities, and they are correct that there is a problem. But the lack of inclusion and recognition of fellow citizens in ways as basic as everyday language and newspaper references is also fueling radicalism and inhibiting the broadened notion of citizenship and national identity that critics of current policies tirelessly promote as a way to prevent extremism.

There are frequent public clashes that illustrate this problem. In early 2016, there was a debate about closing a mosque in the Danish city of Aarhus that was led by an extremist imam who was secretly recorded encouraging the stoning of adulterous women; he also reportedly encouraged radicalized young men to travel to Syria. "They are a kind of travel agency for Islamic State. Why should we accept it?" the Danish MP Naser Khader insists. It's no problem, he says, if a mainstream imam takes over this mosque. "The problem is not the house. It's what's in the house," he argues.[16]

The debate over closing the extremist mosque was in full swing during one of my visits to Denmark, and it focused on an obscure paragraph of the Danish constitution, which allows the government to disband groups instigating violence or seeking to use it to achieve their goals.[17] "Of course we have full religious freedom in the country. We stick to that," says the Danish People's Party's Søren Espersen. The DPP wants to use the constitutional provision to shut down the mosque. They also want to cut off all funding from abroad and from Danish local institutions. He complains that radical Muslim communities receive funding for everything from education to sports clubs.

The journalistic sting that sparked the controversy sent hidden cameras into the mosque, revealing things that rightly made most Danes shudder, including what sounded like encouragement of domestic violence. The imam was saying one thing in public and another in the mosque. Espersen was appalled. They were saying "if your wife does not want to go to bed with you, you can beat her up until she does and all these sort of horrendous things," and telling worshipers not to go to the police. He is convinced that "they have built up their own society with the Sharia law, and we cannot have that," Espersen insists. If groups preach violence and don't submit to the Danish constitution, "they must be shut down."[18]

Danish rabbi Bent Melchior is not convinced. "You fight it by getting the Muslim minorities into the mainstream of Danish life by giving them jobs, by educating them, and you'll find that, all right, the odd one person will fall out of this." He mentions Anders Behring Breivik massacring children in Norway, despite being a blond, blue-eyed Norwegian. "You have crazy people" everywhere, he argues, "but you don't solve the problem by closing down a mosque. It's ridiculous."[19] Even the police opposed shutting it down on the grounds that they knew where these people were and could easily place them under surveillance. Now, there was a risk that they'd go off the grid.[20]

Public debates like the one about shutting the mosque tend to fuel extremist sentiments, according to Jakob Scharf, the former Danish spy chief. Imams like the one filmed at Grimhøj Mosque "are not good for integration clearly," says Scharf, but, he adds, "it has absolutely nothing to do with terrorists, more radicalization, or extremism." Everything gets muddled in public debate, and while extremist imams might hamper integration, condone misogynistic behavior, and have a decidedly negative impact on their followers, they are not necessarily the catalysts for radicalization.

These days, argues Scharf, "the imams are not really relevant," because radicalization tends to happen outside through other actors, like recruiters, luring young men to Syria. Contrary to popular belief, "religion has very little to do with the terrorist issue." He describes the radicalization process in very different terms than most politicians. "People think this happens in mosques. That's not how radicalization takes place," he tells me. "It's also not top down. The individual is often looking for it" and seeks charismatic figures with strong views. These days, recruiting happens mostly online and through social networks.[21]

In Holland, like in Denmark, faith was not always front and center in politics. Those who were once defined by national origin overnight became labeled—and feared—because of their faith, even if they had never set foot in a mosque.

It was as if religious identity didn't matter, and then suddenly it did. This went for young Muslims as much as white Dutch people. No one was particularly interested in the fact that you were Muslim until the question of one's religion became politically loaded and required a response. Likewise, for angry young men feeling alienated, there wasn't much chance of becoming an extremist before everyone had Internet access at home and on their phones. Now it's not hard at all to find Salafi propaganda in dark corners of the Internet.

When the debate about integration did begin in earnest, its starting point was negative. "We were pushed to debate about it because of Theo van Gogh and Pim Fortuyn," says the Dutch politician Ahmed Marcouch. And when the Dutch talk about Islam, they talk about violence or oppression of women or the impossibility of reconciling it with democracy. Many Muslims hear nothing more and assume that society rejects them.

Marcouch, a former cop, was one of the first to talk about radicalization of young Dutch-born men. He was the chairman of a community organization in the neighborhood Van Gogh's killer came from. "There was no policy after the killing of Theo van Gogh; only the repression policy, but that's not enough." To prevent the next Mohammed Bouyeri, he is adamant, "we have to start in the education in the families." The schools and local institutions didn't want to take responsibility, he recalls, or they said they didn't have the right expertise.

Part of deradicalization, Marcouch insists, is presenting a different vision of Islam than what ISIS recruiters offer to young men. Instead of support from intellectuals and local government, he says the response is often something along the lines of "our tradition is different; we have separation of church and state." But just as abstinence education has proven to be a fairly useless tool in promoting safe sex among teenagers, pushing absolute secularism is not going to reduce the numbers of Dutch kids running off to Syria. The real problem, Marcouch argues, is that many Dutch people under the age of fifty have no idea how to talk about any religion, let alone Islam, because they have grown up in an aggressively and proudly secular society. The churches are empty in big Dutch cities, he points out, and the mosques are increasingly full.[22]

To make matters worse, the debate has largely taken place among secularist intellectuals, who are trying to explain and grapple with social phenomena that they don't understand. Holland has plenty of pundits eager to comment on immigration and integration, but few are steeped in the field that matters in a battle against extremist Islam. "The economists look for the economic roots of the problem, sociologists look for social causes, and the anthropologists try to explain jihadist culture, but none of them have any idea about theology," laments a government official who monitors domestic security threats. And that's what actually matters if you're trying to identify people who pose a genuine threat. Even those who study political radicalism tend to look at it through the paradigm of European history and the radical left. But looking at extremism through that lens won't help find the next jihadist terrorist. "It's easy to be a Marxist," quips the security official. "It's fucking hard to be a Salafi."[23]

A lot of key figures in Holland, Marcouch believes, have a traumatic relationship with religion. They want nothing to do with it. "Their mission is to make people separate from their religion." That won't work.

"We have to create conditions that make them feel secure," he says. And that means discussing how to make room for some form of Islam in modern society.

"It's very difficult to have nuance in this debate; it's either good or bad," he says. Dutch society's problem is its insistence on reducing people to a single identity and seeing those of Turkish or Moroccan origin only as Muslim rather than being Dutch, or a policeman, or an Amsterdammer, or a doctor. "People have lots of roots," Marcouch argues, likening young second-generation kids as trees blowing in the wind. When you start to make people choose, he says, "that makes people crazy."[24]

The narrowing of people's identities is dangerous, he argues. "You have a lot of these intellectuals and politicians that want us to have only one identity; to cut these roots. . . . When you do that with a tree, you know what happens; it becomes weak." A bit of wind, and it falls. And right now, he says, "the wind in the society is Wilders."[25]

By declaring immigration off limits for many years, elites in many countries let the issue fester. As the Dutch writer Paul Scheffer argues, ignoring the conflicts arising from large-scale change in working-class areas has made things worse. "For far too long, those who didn't live in the neighborhoods where migrants settled were the warmest advocates of the multicultural society while those who did live in them steadily moved out. Their opinions were ignored, or they were belittled for suddenly giving voice to their own latent xenophobia," he argues. Now they must pay attention. "The middle classes can no longer escape the changes migration brings—in part because they can no longer fail to notice migrants' children in the classroom."[26]

For Scheffer, the establishment's avoidance has been the key to Wilders's rise. Some of the current Dutch backlash against the establishment also has roots in the country's history when elite merchants known as *regenten* struggled against the masses who sided with the monarchy and the Calvinist Church. "The *regenten* were regarded as haughty, self-interested, and dangerously liberal," the historian Ian Buruma writes. They still are, and the word is still used to describe a certain type of Dutch politician or business leader not necessarily dripping with wealth or aristocratic like Eton-educated British elites. Instead they are men and women who give off an air of entitlement and ease with power, "ladies and gentlemen in sober suits who regarded it as their God-given duty to take care of the unfortunate, the sick, the asylum seekers from abroad."[27] And in a time when ideology no longer counts for much, these modern-day *regenten* have become easy targets, painted as out-of-touch elitists imposing their cosmopolitan pro-European vision on a less willing society.

Part of the reason is that there have been very real clashes of a sort that rarely happened before. "Old questions about the position of women have suddenly resurfaced and freedom of expression has become controversial," insists Scheffer, because migrants bring with them traditional beliefs that clash with a modern society. Hearing young Muslim women express fears about sexual purity strikes the carefree Dutch as an echo of a bygone era.[28]

"People have started to talk about blasphemy again, even apostasy," he laments. And like Pim Fortuyn told a journalist before his death, some battles should not have to be refought. "It may all seem familiar from recent history, but having to repeat the emancipation struggles of fifty years ago can hardly be described as progress," argues Scheffer.[29]

More jarring for many Dutch people are the pronouncements of certain extreme religious leaders. A Rotterdam imam shocked the country when he gave a sermon on homosexuality and declared "if this sickness spreads, everyone will be infected and that could lead to us dying out." It caused cognitive dissonance on the left, which was unaccustomed to conflicts between two minority groups; a member of one group the left saw as oppressed was now attacking another.[30]

In such an environment, it's also hard to be a practicing Muslim who supports gay rights. The stereotype that observant Muslims hate homosexuals is so entrenched on both sides that neither can believe evidence to the contrary. When Marcouch first joined in Amsterdam's legendary gay pride parade, which features floats on canal boats, he carried the Amsterdam city flag on the first boat, making him, as he puts it, the "first hetero-active Muslim" to participate. The gay community was worried about violence from extremists; conservative Muslims were baffled and angry. Both groups concluded, "Oh, maybe Marcouch is homosexual, too," he says with a laugh. Neither group could imagine a straight Muslim doing what he did.

It wasn't the only time Marcouch rankled Muslim radicals. His clash with a conservative cleric came into the national spotlight when he went

head-to-head with a radical imam on national TV in 2008.[31] The cleric
denounced him and wished death upon Ayaan Hirsi Ali. Marcouch told
him he was an irresponsible imam and that Islam is about love, not hate.
Conservative Muslims were angry at him for supposedly airing the community's dirty laundry in public.

For some Dutch viewers, it was the first awakening that the Moroccan community in their midst wasn't monolithic. The well-known investigative journalist Janny Groen from *De Volkskrant* told Marcouch that it
was the first time that some of her colleagues at the prestigious newspaper understood her in-depth articles about divisions among Dutch Muslims and how Salafi thinking had influenced Van Gogh's killer but was
rejected by most others.[32]

By 2017, the deradicalization program Marcouch started wasn't running anymore. "There's a lot of creating eyes and ears," he says. But "it's
not enough." Marcouch is observant but keeps to himself about it. Some
of his religious Muslim friends are afraid. They hear debates about banning halal meat or circumcision and worry, telling him, "They're trying to
take this from us. What's next?"

Marcouch gave a speech a few years ago in which he argued that
fighting radicalism went far beyond the pocketbook issues that politicians
talk about. "You can't emancipate or integrate only in a socioeconomic
way," he argues. The kids at risk were born in Holland. "They are infected
with ideas from outside. That means that the ideas from outside had more
power than the things that we teach them." For Marcouch, the reason
that jihadist ideas gain sway is because parents and schools have failed
to instill a strong alternative identity and non-extremist understanding
of Islam. If the message from ISIS is, "You are the one. You are the best.
You are the most important," and these young men have never heard that
from anyone before, it is enticing. Meanwhile, if the message in society at
large is, "Your religion is bad," then the choice is clear.[33]

His warning brings to mind a little-noticed article in *Le Monde* that
was published amid the mass mourning and obligatory moments of silence following the *Charlie Hebdo* massacre. Two reporters interviewed
teenagers at majority-Muslim schools in Paris's dreary southeastern suburb of Val-de-Marne. A seventeen-year-old girl told the paper, "I didn't
really want to do the moment of silence. I didn't think it was right to pay
homage to them because they insulted Islam and other religions too."

A fourteen-year-old boy was more direct: "I did it for those who were killed but not . . . for the guy who did the drawing. I have no pity for him. He has zero respect for us, for Muslims," he said. "But it wasn't worth killing 12 people. They could have just killed him," he added.[34]

Until young Muslims can feel an "inner safety" and a self-confidence that you can be Muslim and Dutch and accepted, Marcouch worries that the terrorism and radicalization problem will only get worse. There are now more than five hundred homegrown Dutch radicals; many have gone to Syria. "We've seen it. It's happened."[35]

THAT SAME REJECTION OF A SOCIETY THAT REJECTS THEM IS ALSO plaguing Denmark. It's primarily second-generation immigrants who are fighting in Syria, the former security chief Scharf points out. "These are individuals looking for an identity and community." They are not part of the first-generation community, and they are not accepted as Danish. It is a perfect recipe for anger and disillusionment. Some act it out on Danish streets; others go farther afield.[36]

It's a point that the Georgetown terrorism expert Daniel Byman has warned could plague Europe in the years to come. The problem is not that Syrian refugees will arrive in the West as radical extremists but that they could one day be radicalized if host societies fail to accept them. "If the refugees are treated as a short-term humanitarian problem rather than as a long-term integration challenge, then we are likely to see this problem worsen," Byman argues. "Despite their current gratitude for sanctuary in Europe, over time the refugees may be disenfranchised and become alienated."[37]

As was the case in the Orlando, Florida, attack on gay clubgoers, "the guy behind the terrorist attack in Copenhagen, he was not a very religious guy," Scharf points out. The same was true of the attackers in Paris and Brussels. Religion was used as an ex post facto rationalization, "a way of explaining . . . why terrorism is necessary."[38]

Rasmus Brygger, the Danish libertarian, makes a habit of engaging with groups he vehemently disagrees with. In that spirit, he has been attending meetings of the radical Islamist group Hizb-ut-Tahrir. He went to their open general assembly and found people complaining about hypocrisy regarding freedom of speech, arguing that "you would never find anyone talking about these rights for Danes, but Muslims don't have a right to be extremists."[39]

While freedom of speech in Denmark is formally equal, it is a source of frustration among young minorities. "It may well be that we legally have the same freedom of speech as everyone else, but what is it worth if we are seen as fundamentalists every time we say we've encountered racism,"[40] one young man complained. If it were only a matter of private gripes and wounded pride of teenagers, that would be one thing, but the argument of double standards is one that extremist groups are using as a recruiting tool.

After all, liberal democracies are meant to provide freedom of expression for those with illiberal ideas, so long as they do not incite violence.[41] During the Cold War, the West survived with Communist parties that received funding from Moscow. Likewise, today, people in open societies are free to call all soldiers murderers, denounce homosexuality as a sin, or advocate Sharia.[42] What's needed is more speech contradicting and discrediting those illiberal arguments. Instead, far-right parties have pushed for the banning of certain forms of offensive speech and the celebration of others. The cartoon controversy seemed to tell Islamists that "freedom of speech is very important to Danes, just not for Muslims," and the mosque closure debate, regardless of how vile the imam's words were, sent the message that absolute freedom of speech was not applicable to them. And so the Islamist recruiters told their audience that double standards are an example of why democracy has failed, a point they tried to hammer into potential new recruits.

Brygger also attended meetings of the Press Freedom Association, an anti-Islam group founded by one of the Mohammed cartoon artists that has united Marxists with hard-right Christian nationalists. A former Islamist and purported Danish spy, Morten Storm, came to address the group and advocated banning the Koran in a speech. That line, says Brygger, "got a lot of applause at the Press Freedom Association."[43]

For all their understandable anger toward Islamists, anti-immigrant groups across Europe are employing rhetoric and logic very similar to those used by the religious fundamentalists they so despise. What they present as a defense of liberal values is in fact an attack on those values.

Despite the populist right and religious Islamists seeing one another as sworn enemies, they actually share a worldview premised on the idea of an irreconcilable clash of civilizations. And when tensions explode, as they did during the mosque closure or the cartoon crisis, this logic is taken to an extreme. Offended Muslim clerics claim that they speak on behalf of all Muslims, and the Islamophobic right points to the angry crowds and says all Muslims are dangerous potential terrorists. The fact that many Muslims did not condone the violence or agree with the imams is lost. "The two sides feed off each other," argues the British writer Kenan Malik, "creating ever more exaggerated fears. . . . It helps create a siege mentality, stoking up anger and resentment, and making communities, both Muslim and non-Muslim . . . more open to extremism."[44]

Brygger's conversations at both ends of the political extremist spectrum led him to conclude that "they are definitely fueling each other—the extremist right and extremist Islam."[45]

JUST LIKE THE SELF-PROCLAIMED FREE-SPEECH ADVOCATES WHO PROUDLY advocate banning the Koran in Denmark, the debate over secularism in France has made for strange bedfellows and shifting alliances. As the French political scientist Olivier Roy argues, today's clashes over laïcité have blurred old battle lines and brought together those who were once viciously opposed. French secularists had always fought against the Catholic Church. These days, the enemy is Islam. It was, Roy writes, "as if the old structure of conflict were inherent to French identity and all that had changed was the religious actor."[46] And old leftists and Catholic conservatives are happy to join forces in the name of defending their narrow notion of secularism, even if it means trampling Muslims' freedom of religion along the way.

Today, those claiming to defend French secularism are more united by what they oppose—Muslims—than what they stand for. It is not just about any religion, Roy argues. "There is, in French laïcité, a specific fear of Islam" to the point that France seeks to "de-Islamize immigration or . . . reject immigration and the generations of French people descended from it in the name of a supposed incompatibility between Islam and Western values."[47]

This leads to bizarre self-justifications. Young women wearing veils are assumed to be forcibly manipulated—the veil being a symbol of servitude that a woman couldn't possibly choose to wear. According to this line of reasoning, the new defenders of secularism have no choice but to choose repression in order to liberate her.[48]

The greater tragedy of this form of state secularism that explicitly views Islam as its target and enemy is that it makes Islam an even more appealing identity for those seeking to rebel. When secularism becomes repressive, "we contribute both to putting religion at the center of the debate and presenting it as an alternative," Roy contends. It's no surprise, then, when Islam becomes the primary cultural marker among angry young men with immigrant roots.[49]

The Vatican didn't come around easily to accepting the French state's secularism after 1905, and when it did, it wasn't because of some religious epiphany; it was because the Vatican was forced to adapt itself to the inescapable fact that the French secular republic was there to stay. The path to a truce with fundamentalist Muslim believers is similar, Roy insists. Just as no one asks a Catholic cardinal "to declare that abortion is not a crime, but simply that he not incite fundamentalists to attack clinics that offer abortions." It is enough to demand adherence to the law.[50] Liberal societies all have members with certain illiberal beliefs or religious values that clash with those of the secular state. They do not need and cannot demand absolute conformity of belief among all citizens. If they did, they would cease to be liberal.[51] What they need is neutrality and equal protection under the law.

The burkini debate has exposed the fallacy of neutrality at the heart of the French model of *laïcité* as it is currently practiced. At the height of the scandal, Kenneth Roth, the global head of Human Rights Watch, published a photograph of a group of French nuns, covered head to toe, enjoying themselves at the beach without being told to leave or pay a fine. Similarly, no orthodox Jewish women, who generally cover themselves from shoulder to ankle and wear wigs to cover their hair, have been targeted by municipal laws banning their modest attire.

A supposedly neutral brand of secularism is being aggressively deployed against one group and celebrated by public officials who denounce religious women wearing modest swimwear in one breath and celebrate Catholic holidays in another. France's see-no-evil secularists often sound a bit like liberal Zionists in Israel, stubbornly beholden to an ideology that has an illustrious intellectual pedigree and sounds nice in theory but has become something altogether different in practice.

If the law is about defending secularism, then, like the school veil law, it must be enforced broadly and without preference or discrimination. Sikhs with turbans, Jews with kippahs, and Christians wearing large crucifixes were all, in theory, prohibited from doing so on school grounds. Whatever one thinks of that law and the fact that most of those disciplined under it were Muslim women, it was written in an eminently neutral way.

Indeed, if the burkini law were truly neutral and focused solely on preventing full coverage of the female body at the beach, then nuns and Orthodox Jews would be equally targeted for fines and removal, and any woman choosing to cover up—whether out of modesty, shyness, or a desire to avoid sunburn—would be suspect and a legitimate target for questioning. But despite the verbal acrobatics of certain intellectuals and public officials, the law always had a clear target.[52]

The more honest argument offered by proponents of the ban is their contention that the burkini is a garment that expresses affiliation with extremist groups. A ban on these grounds has little to do with defending secularism and more to do with preventing open display of terrorist sympathies. There is no proof that women wearing burkinis have such sympathies; on the contrary, most women arrested in France in connection with terrorist attacks all dressed casually in modern clothes. Moreover, if banning garments with certain extreme political messages were the true objective, then presumably France would also be banning T-shirts with ISIS logos or Osama bin Laden's face and the large market for neo-Nazi clothing and paraphernalia. There has been no ban of the sort.

In the end, it was the courts that saved the French government from itself. In response to an emergency application lodged by human rights groups against the southern towns that had banned burkinis, the Conseil d'État, the country's highest administrative court, declared on August 26, 2016: "The emotion and worry resulting from terrorist attacks and especially that committed in Nice on July 14 do not suffice to legally justify the prohibition contested here. . . . The disputed decree has thus infringed seriously and in a manifestly illegal manner upon the fundamental liberties—the freedom to come and go, freedom of conscience and personal freedom."[53]

Whereas other laws in Europe, like banning full-body burqas, had legitimate security rationales, this one did not. The hostility toward a single faith was blatant.[54] The problem with the Conseil d'État's ruling is that it set France's legal institutions at odds with an angry population that has become increasingly suspicious and even hateful toward Muslims. Surveys showed widespread popular support for the bans. As in Denmark, larger and larger numbers of French were calling for restrictions on

Muslims' religious freedoms and favoring openly discriminatory policies, a classic demand of majoritarian populists who proclaim themselves democrats but have no time for constitutions.

The dilemma, according to the Harvard political scientist Yascha Mounk, is that politicians in liberal democracies would either have to obey the will of an angry and increasingly illiberal electorate—which would inevitably lead to the violation of unpopular minorities' rights—or vest more power in unelected courts and bureaucracies that protect those rights. Either way, he argued, "liberal democracy is increasingly under siege" and likely to "decompose into its constitutive elements, facing us with a tragic choice between illiberal democracy (or democracy without rights) and undemocratic liberalism (or rights without democracy)."[55]

It is true that politicians will increasingly face such a choice, but in nations like France or Germany with strong legal traditions, independent courts, and deeply held reverence for core documents like the Declaration of the Rights of Man or the post–World War II German constitution, deferring to the courts—and the expert interpretation of the law—does not constitute a descent into undemocratic practices. It is an exemplary case of one democratic institution checking the power of another when the latter's decision-making risks being influenced by the fleeting political whims of the mob.

The French court's decision was not an exercise in undemocratic elitism; it was a show of resilience for France's long-standing democratic institutions and their ability to uphold French values that are far older and far more established than the passing wave of Islamophobia on the Côte d'Azur's beaches.

10

Barbarians at the Gates

As the refugee crisis spread across Europe in September 2015, Geert Wilders declared that the arrival of Syrian refugees in Europe constituted "an Islamic invasion" and warned of "masses of young men in their twenties with beards singing Allahu Akbar across Europe." He labeled their presence "an invasion that threatens our prosperity, our security, our culture and identity."[1] His stance had significant public support: 54 percent of Dutch voters did not want to accept more than the paltry quota of two thousand refugees per year even though the EU was calling on Holland to take nine thousand people.

At the grassroots level, citizens' groups formed to protest the resettlement of asylum seekers in their towns. In October 2015, Klaas Dijkhoff, the state secretary in charge of resettling refugees and asylum seekers, was attacked in the rural village of Oranje, a town with a permanent population of 150 people where the Dutch government had already placed over 700 asylum seekers.

Dijkhoff had come to deliver the news that even more asylum seekers would be housed in Oranje; in response, outraged villagers blocked the road leading to the vacant building where the government ordered the refugees to be housed, kicked Dijkhoff's car, and tore off its side mirrors.[2] Elsewhere, the violence was more threatening; in the town of Woerden, halfway between Amsterdam and Rotterdam, a group of twenty young men wearing ski masks stormed a local gym that was serving as temporary housing for Syrian and Eritrean refugees.[3] They threw fireworks, eggs, and smoke bombs into the center, known as an AZC (a Dutch acronym for asylum seeker center) housing 150 people, 50 of them children.

The police managed to arrest eleven people, and the government roundly condemned the attack, but the anger has not gone away.

According to Amanda Vermeulen, a former activist with a group called AZC-Alert in a rural area east of Amsterdam, "the major parties are on some sort of fantasy island. We have no voice." And as soon as anyone questions resettlement of refugees, she complains, "very fast you get a stamp on your head as racist." While she claimed the group was apolitical and focused on warning locals about plans for housing refugees in their midst, she acknowledged that some members support Wilders and that many more could soon join them because no one else in the government seems to listen.[4] Since that time, Vermeulen is no longer a spokesperson, and the group seems to have drifted more explicitly into the orbit of Wilders's PVV. Several AZC-Alert activists, judging from their Twitter profiles, double as local spokespeople for the party.[5]

Tanja Jadnanansing, a Labor MP who stepped down in late 2016, understands the anger. When one thousand asylum seekers show up in a village of a few hundred, "we should think more about where do we put them." But in cities like Amsterdam, there is not much of a problem, she claims. She describes a recent visit to Amsterdam Southeast, a diverse area where housing is cheaper and where many asylum seekers live after they arrive. Outside the office where they go to register, she ran into three Dutch locals having a beer. "The more, the merrier!" they told her. It was very different from what she heard in other parts of the country. Regular rank-and-file party members have come to debates at party meetings, and they tell MPs, "I understand that we have to let people in, but how about us?"[6]

That sentiment was on full display last spring in the provincial Dutch capital of Den Bosch, a pretty town in the country's south that is surrounded by a moat and endless green fields. The debate came to a head on April 18, 2016. A small group had descended on the provincial legislature to voice their opposition to refugee resettlement plans. Outside, the building was blockaded with almost as many police officers as protesters. Ten or twenty protesters gathered, clad in leather and black boots, and holding signs denouncing "multicultural terror." But the real action took place inside.

Members of AZC-Alert watched from the gallery in a blue-ceilinged chamber of the provincial legislature, a structure of modernist concrete festooned with paintings of seventeenth-century nobles. They applauded as the local PVV leader bombarded provincial representatives and the king's commissioner, an official charged with implementing the national government's policies, with questions about the construction of asylum-seeker housing. The tense session lasted for almost two hours before everyone gathered collegially for drinks overlooking the flying-saucer-like lobby.

The founder of AZC-Alert, Anita Hendriks, also works for the PVV's provincial delegation. She is a soft-spoken woman from the southern city of Eindhoven, who got angry when, as she puts it, the mayor "decided to start an AZC almost in my backyard—for seven hundred people." She complained but never got a meeting. Two weeks later, the asylum seekers were there.

"We're normal people with complaints," she said. "And we don't get heard." In her view, the government wants to show its power by deciding where to place people and "they neglect us." Her colleague, a man named Sander Booij, interjects with a quick feminist diatribe. "The people who do come think their culture is better. They think women are objects. We think women are equal to men." Holland is a Christian society, he insists, and they come from an Islamic one. Moreover, he argues, "there are seven safe nations between the Netherlands and Syria." As Hendriks tells me, the "real refugees don't come here. They stay in the camps."[7]

A few PVV officials on their way to the legislative chamber stop by our table to say hello to Hendriks. When I ask about their links, given her job as a secretary for the party, they explain that AZC-Alert is purely grassroots. But her colleague Booij, who once ran for local office on the PVV slate, admits, "The PVV is the only national party that shares our view."[8]

AZC-Alert spread largely on the Internet. "If there's a plan for an asylum center in a town, we try to contact locals in the town. We say, if you want, we can help you with the resistance against it," Sander explains. But they draw a line at more radical groups like the leather-clad, black-booted men outside the building. When I mention the German anti-Islam group PEGIDA, he explains, "We keep separate from them. . . . We think they're putting the resistance against asylum seekers in a bad light."[9]

Booij is intent on hammering home the message that "we're not fascists and we're not right-wing extremists. We're normal people with very big complaints about the refugee crisis, and we don't get heard." He comes from a small village with two thousand people. This plan, he says, could place centers with one hundred people in a town like his. "The provincial government is telling the little communities what to do," he complains. "They're saying to local governments, 'You're going to place these people, and if you don't do it, we'll do it for you.'" The government has simply decided, he says. "And the people didn't have anything to say about it."

He thinks that real war refugees need to be safe in their own regions, "if possible, in Turkey or Saudi Arabia." He is convinced that the real draw is Dutch benefits and generous immigration policies. "Our social welfare state is much better than surrounding countries'," he explains. And people are coming to the Netherlands, rather than Denmark or Germany, he believes, because Holland offers a shorter wait for family reunification.

Given that she works in the building, Hendriks is particularly upset at the lack of coordination. "They could ask me, 'Anita, how many people do you expect? What do you want to achieve?' No one asked me."[10] Hendriks feels that "democracy is under pressure now. We have to shut up." She gestures to the oversized bike-riding police force outside, mild by American standards. "You see here the crazy police force for a few people. They criminalize us." She compares it to a protest by environmentalists and angry farmers that she witnessed a few years ago. "They dumped pig shit outside the building," she says with a laugh. And nothing happened.

Apparently, public questions are quite common at most meetings of the provincial legislature, but tonight, it is strictly the elected officials who do the talking. Still, the PVV is taking Hendriks's concerns to the floor. Alexander van Hattem, the local party leader and also a PVV senator in the national government's upper house, lists the objections exhaustively, speaking for close to forty-five minutes in the chamber.

Arnoud Reijnen, the provincial government press spokesman, wears a suit and seems troubled that the one foreign journalist at the event has arrived in the company of the protesters. As he tells it, the Dutch agency COA, in charge of refugee resettlement and housing asylum seekers, was shrinking due to lack of demand. Then 2015 happened. The government needed to find short-term housing for people, and instead of letting them build camps like the Calais Jungle, the organization asked the various provinces and municipalities to provide emergency shelter for two to three years. It was a national government assignment. Municipal and provincial governments, along with COA, started researching where AZCs could be built. In some places, there were easy answers; one old military barracks, for instance, was used to house two thousand people.

Reijnen argues that there's actually a labor shortage that refugees could help fill. "If you're a plumber or carpenter, you have a job tomorrow," he says. Fleur, a middle-aged woman working for the cafeteria, is laying out coffee cups and comes to join us. She is Armenian and arrived in Holland as a refugee in 1971. She says among her neighbors and friends, "most of the people are worried; we don't have enough work for us."

Fleur views things differently because of her own history. "I think they can come—I was one of them." But she shares some of the complaints often heard from PVV voters. "I'm waiting for a house for six years now," she tells me. "I live with my mom now." Yet she sees new asylum seekers arriving and getting housing quickly.

Embarrassed by his employee's populist tirade, the press chief intervenes. "It's a problem. We had building of social housing until new cabinet came along."

Fleur continues, "When my dad came here, there was lots of work. Now our children go to school and they can't find a job." And much like Hendriks and the protesters, Fleur is also adamant that the refugees most in need aren't coming. "The people coming from there to Holland; they have money. The people who don't have money, they only go to Turkey. I know," she says with absolute confidence. "It's the reality." She says it was the same in the 1960s when the wealthiest Armenians left Turkey to come to Holland. "They had lots of money. . . . The people who don't, they're stuck in Turkey."

The reason that opposition to the AZCs ballooned so quickly is, according to Reijnen, "the coming of social media," which has allowed activists to mobilize crowds quickly—often far beyond their own hometowns. With popular anger increasing the PVV's popularity, he says, Wilders is able "to hold center and right-wing parties hostage."[11]

After the meeting, the man presiding over it seems mostly annoyed. The king's commissioner, Wim van de Donk, was asked to make sure that the province had enough space to host refugees, he explains. "This was not a political debate. The role that I play is debated in the national parliament. If they want to have a political debate, they have to do it at a national level. The policy was decided by the government, and they're in opposition." He scoffs at the complaints that the process is undemocratic. "I have an assignment from the national government. I'm a civil servant. I do not decide on the policy," he says, exasperated. The reason he was speeding up implementation was out of fear that another mass influx over the summer might hit Holland when it didn't have the capacity to take more people.

Van Hattem, the province's PVV leader, concedes that the provincial government doesn't have a formal role in making refugee policy, but he argues that the commissioner has overstepped his bounds by getting into matters of integration, social housing, and the local labor market. "That kind of policy belongs partly to local communities and the province." And if there is going to be a change in labor market policy, then, "as a democratic organ, we have to decide about the policy. But we've never had a discussion in the meeting hall about that."[12]

His PVV colleague Patricia van der Kammen, who served as a member of the European Parliament, is harsher. The government is telling citizens, "We are going to make a policy whether you like it or not." All they seem to care about, she says, is "how do we convince them that they want this?" She argues, like Wilders, that referenda are the solution to all these problems.[13] "The government has to listen to the citizens, and they don't. They don't look at what in opinion polls most Dutch people think about asylum seekers. They ignore it completely."

Asked if there could ever be too many referenda, she points to Switzerland. "Why not have twenty per year? On this, we think it's very wise for every local government to vote on this issue."

Van Hattem insists that the PVV is not trying to direct grassroots groups. "They tell us their worries. The initiative is on their side. We don't have relations to steer them," a dubious claim given that, at the event I attended, there appeared to be a near-total overlap between PVV supporters and the staff of the AZC-Alert leadership. Both are confident that the PVV will grow and that soon the larger parties will no longer be able to ignore them. "If the Dutch voters will make us big enough," he says hopefully, "they can't say anymore, 'We don't need you.' They'll have to work together with us."[14]

Although the party grew from fifteen seats to twenty in the March 2017 election, it did not meet expectations and was excluded from a right-leaning coalition government. Van Hattem did not get his wish this time, but the process that he, Wilders, and the angry citizens of AZC-Alert have set in motion is not going away.

It draws on reflexes and resentments that are deeply rooted in human behavior and are being activated by a perceived threat to the social order.

COUNTLESS ACTIVISTS, COLUMNISTS, AND POLITICIANS HAVE WEIGHED in on questions of integration and multiculturalism. What has been less examined but is of far greater consequence is how the encouragement of public displays of difference may impact voting behavior. The political psychologist Karen Stenner has argued convincingly that support for far-right parties is a direct result of members of the majority perceiving a threat to their culture, community, and way of life. Her work is a twenty-first-century revision of the famous F-scale designed by the Frankfurt School philosopher Theodor Adorno to measure fascist tendencies and other authoritarian personality traits, a study that has influenced much of modern social science since the 1950s.[15]

In her view, authoritarianism is not a consistent or ever-present personality trait; it is latent and activated by perceived threats to the comfort and familiarity of the status quo. As she argues, "Sometimes authoritarians behave like authoritarians but at other times [they] are indistinguishable from the pack."[16]

Rapid immigration and the arrival of significant numbers of people from distinctly different cultures—especially when those people bring different values and norms—is seen as a threat by certain people and activates their authoritarian predisposition and prompts them to resist.[17] Populist right-wing parties, whether intentionally or not, have masterfully exploited this reflex, painting themselves as the only ones who are listening to these voters' grievances and can preserve the stable order these voters cherish. The close ties between the AZC-Alert activists and the PVV in Holland are a case in point.

Stenner's research included the manipulation of subjects by using fabricated news stories designed to trigger their authoritarian reflex, a remarkably prescient research technique given the prevalence and influence of fake news stories in the 2016 election cycle. She found that "authoritarians will clamor for authoritative constraints on racial diversity, political dissent, and moral deviance under conditions of normative threat," by which she means clashing values and beliefs within a society and the perceived failures of its leaders.

On the other hand, they will not display these reactions when they feel reassured by unified public opinion and shared confidence in leaders.[18] The Swedish sociologist Jens Rydgren, writing on the rise of far-right parties in Scandinavia, came to a very similar conclusion. He found that "fragmentation of the culture" and "widespread political discontent and disenchantment" were predictors of voting for parties like Denmark's DPP.[19]

One of Stenner's more bizarre but telling findings is that authoritarians immediately abandoned hostility to immigrants and minorities when faced with an even more distant outside threat—in this case, the (fake) news of extraterrestrial sightings—which she regards as "a powerful demonstration of the potential for, and the potential benefits of, effectively altering the boundaries of 'us.'" Without actually harming any group regarded as outsiders, "the mere conjuring of *some* kind of greater difference," shifts authoritarian voters' reactions.[20]

Those with authoritarian reflexes are highly susceptible to political myth and will at a certain stage support an overthrow of the established order if led by a trusted leader promising renewal and salvation; traditional conservatives will not. If anything, they can be "liberal democracy's strongest bulwark against the dangers posed by intolerant social movements," protecting the status quo from demagogic promises of deliverance.[21] It is a fairly accurate description of Angela Merkel or Republican leaders and intellectuals from John McCain to Max Boot during the Trump campaign and early days of his administration.

Even so, the soil in 2017 is fertile for demagogues. "Unconstrained diversity," Stenner writes, "pushes those by nature least equipped to live comfortably in a liberal democracy *not* to the limits of their tolerance, but to their intolerant extremes."[22] To simply write these people off as racists is to miss the point and forsake any chance of winning the political battle with far-right parties.

Those who see themselves as globalists cheered when Merkel opened Germany's borders, but for the nationalists, like those protesting outside Dutch asylum centers, it was confirmation of their worst fears.[23] For Stenner's predisposed authoritarians, the uncontrolled arrival and government-decreed resettlement of large numbers of refugees was the ultimate threat to their perceived community.

It's absurd, the Dutch intellectual Paul Scheffer argues, to be a liberal country in a deeply illiberal neighborhood and simply open up the gates. "History has not ended," he says, referring to Francis Fukuyama's book *The End of History and the Last Man*. Europeans are surrounded by countries like Libya, Egypt, Syria, Turkey, and Ukraine. Policy makers need to move beyond crisis management and come up with a real vision.

The popular idea on the left that everyone should be able to move as they please is a rejection of the nation-state. The notion that citizens, whether long-standing or newly naturalized, should not enjoy any special rights over and above those enjoyed by noncitizens is exactly the sort of threat to the social order that triggers Stenner's latent authoritarians. If a passport means nothing and being born somewhere doesn't entitle you to any privileges in that place, it is the equivalent of charging a 100 percent inheritance tax on every family or a government spending as much on foreign medical aid as it does on health care for its own citizens, something that not even the radical left advocates.

Scheffer believes populism is "all about borders in the end. It's about protection, and if a state or a collection of states like the European Union doesn't offer protection, then you get withdrawal." He worries that others will fill the void. As President Trump signs executive orders to halt visas for visitors from several Muslim-majority nations, Scheffer's warning seems increasingly relevant. Politicians must "attempt to bring some order to it, because if migration is seen as a symbol of a world out of control, people will restore control," he warns. "And if it's not with liberal means, it will be with authoritarian means."[24]

As voters inclined toward authoritarian solutions perceive a threat to the nation and community they love, they react. Immigrants from Muslim countries have activated the backlash because they come not only with strange clothes and customs, but, like Orthodox Jews, they also make public requests for accommodations like single-sex transport, gender-segregated swimming pools, and special meals.[25] Whether or not these requests are reasonable, they are precisely the sort of threat to sameness that Stenner warns of. Once politicians exploit voters' fears, it can lead to "the kind of intolerance that seems to 'come out of nowhere,'" she writes. It is a reaction that produces "sudden changes in behavior that cannot be accounted for by slowly changing cultural traditions."[26]

In France, a country that stresses shared republican values, this dynamic has played out over the past few decades, and the fear of visible difference has had a clear electoral impact. Marine Le Pen has capitalized on it. A population trained to assume that everyone would assimilate quickly and easily saw that things were moving slowly in the realm of integration. Just as the FN was gaining strength, "a certain discourse on tolerance came clattering down from the elites towards the French lower classes" demanding that they respect the differences of immigrants, writes the sociologist Emmanuel Todd. "At the very same time as the lower classes were worried by the slowness of assimilation, their rulers were proclaiming that this assimilation was not necessary." As a result, they turned their resentment toward Arabs who were visibly different, while some immigrants turned their wrath toward the visible difference of orthodox Jews.[27]

In Todd's view, the new wave of Islamophobia and anti-Semitism has its roots in France's doctrinaire interpretation of republican egalitarianism, where sameness is sanctified even when real equality doesn't exist. Taking this logic to its extreme, he argues, if "human beings are the same everywhere, if the foreigners setting foot on our soil behave in ways that really are different, the reason is that they are not really human." The result of this "hysterical form of egalitarianism" is rejection of those who are perceived as not being similar although they should be.[28]

Stenner sees the excessive celebration of difference so popular among multiculturalists as preparing the ground for backlash because, she argues, it "generates the very conditions guaranteed to goad latent authoritarians to sudden and intense, perhaps violent, and almost certainly unexpected, expressions of intolerance."

It is a theory that has profound political implications. If politicians can celebrate the inclusion of immigrants as part of a shared national community—the sort of national unity often fostered by diverse national sports teams, for example—it could damage the populist right. If not, a backlash from Stenner's latent authoritarians is a real risk.[29] They are already mobilizing.

EDWIN WAGENVELD IS CONVINCED THAT EUROPE IS BEING TAKEN OVER by Muslims, and he intends to resist.

Although he has lived in Germany for many years, Wagenveld comes home to the Netherlands every so often to lead PEGIDA demonstrations in his homeland.

In April 2016, we met at a hotel on the outskirts of The Hague, known best as the favorite haunt of Hans Janmaat, one of Holland's pioneering anti-immigration figures. Wagenveld was planning a demonstration in the capital the following morning and was trying to minimize the chances of neo-Nazis showing up, whom he intended to tell they were not welcome, from the podium. Although Geert Wilders did once give a speech at a PEGIDA rally in Dresden, a fact Wagenveld is very proud of, he tries to steer clear of politics. Some on the far right have asked him to run for office, he tells me, but he's not interested. "I'm a protest movement; I'm not a party," he insists.[30]

Wagenveld spoke directly with Paul Belien, one of Wilders's speechwriters and spokesmen, to plan the Dresden rally and claims to have frequent contact with other PVV officials. He calls their ties "informal."[31] "I speak with a lot of people from the PVV. I speak with political people. I speak with voters." A few weeks before our meeting, he gave a speech at a protest in The Hague. "A few people from the PVV, political people, come to me, had heard my speech, and say, 'You are exactly saying what we are thinking,' and so I know," he tells me with pride.

He was hoping that there would be "maybe a little bit more working together," he says, but he sees PEGIDA as a street movement that has latitude politicians don't. "We can say a little bit more than the politicals say," he says with a smile. "On the street in Dresden, you have a lot of voice," more than in a parliament, he believes.

And the politicians know they need PEGIDA supporters to boost their numbers. He gives PEGIDA credit for changing the debate in Germany. "What we were saying on the podium in 2014 . . . now the politicians are saying the same. We say border closing, and now they did it. We say less refugees, and now they do it. I think we opened the discussion," insists Wagenveld. He wants to do the same in Holland.[32]

Wagenveld sees himself as unusually prescient. "What I am saying always is maybe my eyes are a little bit faster. I open them earlier than you," he tells politicians. He is originally from the pleasant university town of Utrecht, where Wilders also got his start as a city council member. Wagenveld depicts the city of canals and Roman-era cathedrals as a sort of apocalyptic Islamic wasteland. Twenty years ago, you never saw Muslims, he tells me. "Now, you go in the supermarket, people see the scarf."[33]

It is the specter of gradual colonization that great replacement theorist Renaud Camus writes about. And for Camus, PEGIDA is the hero of the moment. In his essay, "Pegida, Mon Amour," he praises the Islamophobic group as "a great hope rising in the East" and a "liberation front" that is fighting the "anti-colonialist struggle." For him, there is no hope

of living together in Europe when "there is a colonial conquest in progress, in which we are the colonized indigenous people" and the weapons
of sheer numbers and demographic substitution are used to subjugate the
natives.[34]

Wagenveld doesn't have much time for theory, but he resents the lack
of political action. "After Pim Fortuyn, they told us, 'We will change
something.' Nothing changed," he says. The lack of community reaction
after the Brussels attacks outraged Wagenveld. In the eyes of PEGIDA
sympathizers, whose worldview, like the *Charlie Hebdo* editorial after the
Brussels attack, paints all Muslims as part of the problem, it is evidence
that the whole community must be complicit.

When I ask about making halal meat available in schools, he is adamant that it must be forbidden. "We have to make it difficult for them to
live like a radical Islam." He is at least consistent in his application of pro-
hibitions, unlike some selective secularists in France. Asked whether his
preferred measures would apply to Jews, too, he is clear. "You can't make
a difference between Jewish, Christian, or Muslims. That's discrimination. When the scarf is forbidden, also the kippah is forbidden."[35]

As extreme as PEGIDA is in many people's eyes, its members can't
stand groups and individuals they regard as extremists. Wagenveld calls
people like Norwegian white supremacist and mass murderer Anders
Breivik "stupid idiots" who make it more difficult for activists like himself. He urges his followers to be peaceful and calm, and then people like
Breivik come along and ruin it. If a few members of neo-Nazi parties join
a PEGIDA march and play by his rules, that's fine, he tells me, but he
doesn't want anything to do with their leaders.

Wagenveld is dismissive of some of the other anti-immigrant groups
like AZC-Alert, though he generally agrees with them. "I only work
with people that are doing something in real life. Facebook is easy," he
says derisively.

As Wagenveld explains, he doesn't need the government or local authorities to tell him where asylum seekers are housed; he finds out himself. If he wants to organize a protest, he simply follows refugees home. "I
don't need an address where AZC is. I go to the marketplace, and I wait
until the first group is starting to walk. I walk behind them, and I find
where the AZC is."[36]

Wagenveld is an interesting and unusual spokesman for a vehemently anti-immigrant group. He himself is an immigrant—albeit a Dutch one in a country next door. On the issue of identity, his view is both rigid and revealing. When I ask if the situation would be better if young minorities were made to feel Dutch before Moroccan or Turkish, he replied, "Yeah, but you can only feel Dutch when you are Dutch," going on to explain his own time in Germany, where everyone sees him as a foreigner. "For more than twenty years already in Germany, I can't be German. I think I need a few things to get a 100 percent that identity. You have to be born here, or maybe come when you're two or three years old. . . . When you have a Moroccan culture, then I think it's not possible to say, 'I'm Dutch.'"

What Wagenveld seems to miss is that it's much easier for a white Dutchman to be accepted in Germany than for a nonwhite Moroccan to be accepted in Holland.

His family, he insists, is different. His kids speak German at home; when they drive over the border to Holland, they speak Dutch. When I ask if there's anything the state can do to integrate new immigrants more successfully, Wagenveld is blunt: "I think that time is over. There is no turnback point anymore."[37]

11

They're Stealing Our Jobs

IN EARLY 2016, AS WAGENVELD WAS ORGANIZING PEGIDA PROTESTS TO keep Muslims out of Holland, a group of freshly arrived refugees found themselves languishing in an AZC shelter, the kind of place on the edge of town that right-wing activists like to locate, protest, and occasionally burn down. The refugees were from Syria and Afghanistan and eager to start new lives. "They were doctors; they were dentists. Everything about them was academic," recalls Tanja Jadnanansing, then a Labor MP. "They were talking to me because they were asking me, 'What can we do? We get really tired of sitting in this shelter. We want to work.'"[1]

What was once a resentment of guest workers has now morphed into full-scale blame of refugees and foreigners stealing locals' jobs. In Holland, as in Denmark, this is causing tension on the left because of the risk it could pose to Dutch workers, especially if the refugees are paid a lower wage. They are generally not allowed to work for six months, and when they do, like a Syrian tailor and dentist profiled in the *New York Times*, they often do it for a significantly lower wage than their Dutch counterparts in the same professions.[2] While refugees may resent working for half the wage of natives, most of the skilled refugees Jadnanansing met "were just begging me, 'Let us work.'"

Both governments have made the same mistake when it comes to integrating refugees and immigrants; welfare states don't want people on the streets. Much like the Danish government's decision to park refugees and asylum seekers—some of them highly skilled—on welfare, the Dutch government has often opted to remedy the visible problem while leaving the invisible one to fester. "You don't want to have them as beggars in the stations. So you give them money, you give them an apartment, and you say, "Keep out of our lives," says Paul Schnabel, the former head of Holland's Institute for Social Research, which helps shape social policy.[3]

The risk today is new arrivals who are young and uneducated being left out of the job market or relegated to doing nothing. In contrast to the children of those who came in the 1970s, who are excelling in universities and public life, the latest wave is being left on the sidelines of the labor market, and it is a recipe for disaster. "If you want to have problems in society, you should have young male migrants who don't have work," Schnabel argues. They should be in school or in jobs. "If they are left to themselves, they become really a nuisance and even more dangerous than that."[4]

In both Holland and Denmark, the idea of paying lower entry-level wages to refugees who don't yet have language skills or local educational qualifications has been proposed as a possible solution, but both the left and the right have generally opposed it.

As more refugees entered Denmark in 2015, the issue of work became a dividing line in politics. The DPP and some unions railed about immigrants pushing Danes out of the workforce. A coalition of strange bedfellows has emerged from the right to the far left to support getting new arrivals into the workforce as soon as possible rather than putting them on welfare.

The risk of competition and conflict in the labor market has confused and divided the left, which likes to view itself both as supportive of needy refugees and as a defender of the working class. When refugees arrive in a new country, they tend to gravitate toward the capital and largest cities. In Copenhagen and its suburbs, there are fewer and fewer unskilled jobs available for Danes without an education or for foreigners who lack the language skills and qualifications to get skilled work. Much like parts of the Rust Belt in the United States, where manufacturing jobs have been replaced by a knowledge economy, the sort of stable blue-collar jobs that were once abundant have disappeared. "The old production facilities, they're gone. They're now in China or in Eastern Europe," says the mayor of Herlev, Thomas Gyldal Petersen. "Those companies, they're gone. What is left is jobs for highly educated people."

This economic backdrop has had an impact on the refugee debate, even at a time when some Danish companies wish they could find manual workers.[5] As far as Petersen sees it, there are two options: Pay refugees a low wage to clean floors and wash windows, and risk dragging the general wage level down, or, alternatively, invest in education to bring everyone up to a level where they can qualify for the new economy jobs that are available.

A new low-wage sector of the labor market could put pressure on workers on the lowest rungs. "We can't compete with China in producing cheap plastic stuff. . . . You can change the job market to match people's low skills, or you can change people's low skills to fit into the job market," says Petersen, like a true Social Democrat. "I have to choose the second one, because the first one is the way to making our society poor and weaker." Sweeping the floor for five dollars an hour is not a good life, he insists.[6]

For the DPP, it's quite simple: letting refugees in and letting them work "will toss out Danish persons who do not have skills from the Danish labor market," says the MP Kenneth Kristensen Berth. If the hordes descend on Denmark and there is no longer a strict minimum wage, he claims, then employers could pay workers five kroner (less than one dollar) per hour. The Liberal Alliance party has supported an entry wage, more out of hostility to the welfare state than out of empathy for refugees. "If nothing is done about the fact that people can just come to Denmark" and receive social benefits, Berth argues that will probably benefit the free-market right in the long term. Why would you be "willing to pay like 50–60 percent of your income in taxes if you are not absolutely convinced that this money goes to well-deserving people?"[7] he asks.

This is precisely the sort of outcome most feared by some welfare state scholars in the early 2000s; they worried that perceptions of undeserving welfare beneficiaries would sap support for generous welfare benefits and provide "openings for right-wing populist parties that combine anti-immigrant nativism with attacks on the welfare state."[8] But only half of that equation materialized.

That's because welfare cuts don't win elections in countries like Denmark—the staunchly free-market Liberal Alliance won just 7.5 percent of the vote in the 2015 election—and the welfare state is not in danger of disappearing. Indeed, the party that has benefited most from anti-immigration backlash is not trying to dismantle it; it wants to reinforce it. What has changed is that both the nanny state's boundaries and decisions about who deserves to be included among its members are being more closely monitored.

Berth's boss, Søren Espersen, is blunt on this point. All that the center right has left of its traditional policies "is lower taxation, which nobody listens to anymore," he scoffs. "They don't do that in Denmark. It's a discussion you don't have." The idea of a cradle-to-grave welfare state is still holy to most Danes, and American-style welfare cuts simply do not sell.[9] But welfare chauvinism does.

That may be one reason why the DPP's target has shifted. Social Democrats were once the biggest losers when it came to competing with the DPP. It is now the mainstream conservatives of the governing center-right Venstre Party who are at risk of having voters poached either because they are uncomfortable with gutting the welfare state or because they are staunch nationalists. "There's probably not that many left to gather from the Social Democrats," says Berth. "On the other hand, I think there's far more left in a party like Venstre."[10]

Espersen acknowledges that the DPP's support of the Venstre government makes for strange bedfellows. On economic policy, he admits, "we are miles away." The DPP is not a free-market party, but when it comes to immigration and EU skepticism, "this is what they come for," he says of the new voters. The DPP is even managing to draw voters from among Venstre's party officials, Espersen says smugly. He mentions a voter he approached during the last campaign, offering her a party leaflet. The woman declined, telling him she was on the board of the local branch of the Venstre Party. "Then just to be funny, I said, 'Well, you could vote for us anyway, couldn't you?'" recalls Espersen. She told him that she did. Later, he asked her what was going on. She explained she had friends in the party and didn't tell them who she actually voted for. "There were many of those types," Espersen says, echoing Marine Le Pen's conviction that there is a large silent vote fearful of ridicule or retaliation but steadfast in their support for the populist right.

"We don't want to change our welfare system," Espersen explains. The DPP wants to protect it for those who are deserving; and for him, that is native Danes and those with valid work permits. When it comes to the entry-level wage for refugees, "we are against that because it presses the wages down and also makes it impossible for Danish people that are citizens to get those lower-paying jobs. We have a minimum wage here of 180 kroner per hour [about $25]." The DPP line is very clear: state revenues should be spent on Danes, not on newcomers.

Espersen finds criticism from Americans particularly galling: "Sometimes when I am blamed by Americans about how horrible and rough we are, I just tell them, 'How many refugees did you take from Syria? Zero.' And those ones that come in illegally, they look after themselves. They can wash a car here and there. I don't think we need any advice, especially from the Americans." But if there's a lesson from Washington, he says, it's the model of low numbers and no safety net for immigrants.

"For me, it has never been about the money," Espersen says, mentioning that a drop in revenues from North Sea oil is straining infrastructure budgets for new train lines and other projects. "We can't do it anymore. We haven't got money now to subsidize this." And then the refugees come, and they "are entitled to a house and a flat and everything."[11]

A key to selling the DPP's argument is convincing voters that hardworking Danes are subsidizing the undeserving foreign poor rather than their down-at-heel countrymen who are deserving of solidarity. "If the idea spreads," says Berth, that taxpayers' money is going "to people who just don't want to work themselves or don't want to do anything for themselves, they just want to have money back, then, of course, people will not be willing to pay such a large amount of money in taxes."[12] What is left unsaid is that the DPP has been instrumental in spreading the impression that immigrants are leeches.

As Mayor Gyldal Petersen put it, the DPP has placed asylum seekers and everyone else in a catch-22. "Immigrants can't do right," he says. "When they're unemployed, they're a burden to society. When they're in a job, they just stole the job from a Dane."[13]

In a matter of two decades, the DPP has gone from being ostracized to being normalized. Espersen remembers the early days of the party, around 2000, when DPP officials were shouted down; it rarely happens anymore. Once upon a time, he needed protection. Now, says Espersen, "I can walk in peace now in the streets, and people will come over and say hi. There's never aggravation, not even from those circles that we are supposed to be in opposition to. I mean, the situation is very calm and very good, with the security getting less and less necessary."

The DPP now has 37 seats out of 179 in parliament; the prime minister's party has just 34 but governs with the support of the DPP and other right-wing parties. "What we have been saying and been warning about has now come true," Espersen argues, so of course "they will change their ideas about us."

When I first met Espersen in 2002, he was the spin doctor in chief for the DPP after its first big election victory, when the party gained 12 percent of the vote. Back then, his focus was on reducing immigration and getting out of the EU. These days, says Espersen, "these two items are the only things that are being discussed now, the only thing! And we've had that right from the beginning. So of course when other parties may start saying the same things, people will often go to the original and not the copy."

Espersen went into politics "to help save Denmark," he tells me. "I can see that's happening now." He marvels at how far his party has managed to shift the debate. "The Social Democrats now have moved such a distance that you cannot imagine it. It is absolutely incredible to hear what they are saying now and writing now" compared to ten to fifteen years ago. "That makes me very happy," says Espersen.[14]

In early 2016, the party leader, Mette Frederiksen, went to Stockholm to meet with fellow Scandinavian Social Democratic officials. There she gave a speech that rattled her Swedish and Norwegian colleagues. Frederiksen declared, "We social democrats must accept that there is a clash. . . . It is a very strong part of our identity that we help when people need help . . . but just as strong is our value that we must have a well-functioning welfare state." Frederiksen then dropped a bomb on the staid gathering of political allies. "My position is that a universally funded Scandinavian welfare state with free and equal access to healthcare, education and social subsidies is not compatible with an open immigration policy." From receiving lower wages to facing competition for housing and schools, "it's those who were already vulnerable who are being pressured." And without control over the numbers, the situation would only grow worse, she warned.[15]

Back in Herlev, Mayor Gyldal Petersen was looking sleep-deprived. The night before we met, there had been a shooting in the housing projects where he grew up—an extreme rarity in this small town of twenty-seven thousand. He doesn't believe that the Social Democrats have lost all appeal. On the contrary, he thinks they can expand their base and win some old voters back, but they have to speak openly; pointing to the shooting that shook his town the night before, he tells me, "You have to say it's a problem, and I want to do something about it."[16]

He is adamant, like the current party leader, Frederiksen, that a genuine commitment to social democratic values means ensuring social progress for everyone. While the left is very worried about mistreatment of asylum seekers, he fears that they have forgotten working-class Danes, making them low-hanging fruit for the DPP in much the same way that Donald Trump lured disgruntled blue-collar Democrats from the American Midwest across the aisle. "It is not social progress when people who moved into their apartments back in the '50s, in a good environment, good neighborhood, they had good relations to everybody. Forty years later, in the '90s, they are now retired, and they live in the same apartment; everyone around them are now immigrants speaking languages they don't understand."

Not everyone agrees with the direction the Social Democratic party has taken. Yildiz Akdogan, the Social Democratic MP who has tried to encourage young Muslim citizens to identify as Danes, was one of Denmark's first politicians from a minority background. Despite her trailblazer status, she didn't get much attention from the press when she first started out in politics, and certainly not from the women's magazines, because, as she puts it, "my story is not that interesting; I haven't been in a forced marriage, I haven't worn a head scarf, I haven't been in a radical group. My story is so normal that it's not a story."

She did once get an interview in a major newspaper as a new member of parliament, and it revealed a lot about how Danes view ethnic minorities, no matter how successful they are. Before the Danish political drama *Borgen* became an international TV sensation, there was another popular Danish television show called *Krøniken* that featured a character who represented the inner-city Copenhagen neighborhood Nørrebro in parliament. The fictional MP was also a Social Democrat. Akdogan called *Ekstra Bladet*, the country's largest tabloid, and told journalists she was the real-life version of the character in the show and happened to be a woman with a Turkish background. The paper seemed interested and arranged an interview.

The journalist's first question was, "So you are running for election—what does your father say to that?" She was furious. "I wanted to punch him," she recalls. "What kind of a stupid question is that? Do you ask the same question to my colleagues who are ethnic Danes?" The journalist insisted that her culture must present a challenge for a woman in politics. She told him her father didn't tell her what she should or shouldn't do. But it was clear to her that if you don't live up to the stereotype of being an oppressed Muslim woman in a head scarf with an overbearing father, then the media isn't interested.[17]

Akdogan believes the Social Democrats' biggest mistake was to move from ignoring the DPP to mimicking some of its policies. In the 2001 election, Prime Minister Poul Nyrup Rasmussen famously referred to the DPP's members as not being *stuerene,* a Danish word used to describe dogs who are not house-trained or, literally, clean enough to come into the living room.[18] By 2017, they had broken through the front door and moved into all its rooms. The Social Democrats, says Akdogan, ignored the DPP "for a long time, but then when we really took them seriously, we took them too seriously. . . . We should have also challenged their policies or their ideology, and we haven't really done that."[19]

AYDIN SOEI, THE SOCIOLOGIST WHO CAME UP WITH THE CONCEPT OF countercitizenship, is a leading advocate of letting refugees work, which angers many of his friends on the left who believe it will undercut wages for Danes. He is adamant that the state needs to "create another way of getting people into the labor market." He believes a lower minimum wage is necessary if uneducated people and foreigners who can't speak Danish well are ever going to find work.

"Denmark is a big welfare state. You get social welfare if you don't have a job. And a lot of refugees were just parked on social welfare instead of recognizing their education and their skills," says Soei. Even engineers have been put on welfare, he says, at a time when there is a projected shortage in the field. "If your motivation is to create a liberal society where the individual can create a good life for him- or herself, then you would have solved this problem years ago," he argues. Instead, the state has effectively provided newcomers with an allowance and keys to an apartment and ignored them, assuming that its work was done. The problem, says Soei, is that there is no political incentive to integrate asylum seekers into the job market. "It doesn't have consequences for the politicians . . . because they don't have the right to vote." Getting onto the first rung of the labor market ladder in Denmark is tough without

Danish fluency or local educational credentials. And arguing for a lower entry-level wage for refugees to allow them to work in unskilled jobs, as he has, is politically fraught, because Denmark's strong unions, not to mention the DPP, are opposed. Soei insists that the unions and the leftist parties are mired in an old way of thinking.[20]

Johanne Schmidt-Nielsen, the foulmouthed leader of the far-left Red-Green Alliance, doesn't buy the argument made by Soei. She is in favor of letting refugees work but not if it drags down wages for Danes. "If you go to some kind of company and you work there with a low salary, all your colleagues will say, 'Well, because of you, my Danish colleague got fired.'" That, she adds, is not good for integration.

Schmidt-Nielsen worries more about how public debate can influence young people who already feel angry and alienated. "Of course we have to talk about the problems. It's a big mistake not to talk about them, because then we can't change them." That said, some things are off limits. As she puts it, "Freedom of speech is not really the same as being a racist motherfucker." When politicians start competing to "be the biggest tough guy on immigrants," it can lead in dangerous directions.

Imagine, she says, being "a brown guy. I open the newspapers and all Muslims are terrorists, and I go into a shop, and the shop owner looks at me all the time because he thinks, 'Well, he's going to steal.' I try to get a job, and they say, 'Oh, your name is Mohamed.' . . . If all the time society tells you, 'Go away, you're not Danish,' at some point you say, 'Well, no, I'm not Danish. Fuck Denmark.' It's not an excuse for shooting people, but it's not difficult to understand."

She also claims that the right's rhetoric on traditionally left causes, like women's rights and gay rights, is purely opportunistic. "They don't give a fuck about women's liberation, because they don't do anything about the fact that there's 17 percent difference between what men and women in Denmark are paid!" she exclaims. And when it comes to gay rights, she points to the DPP's spokesperson on gay marriage, who responded to new laws by publicly asking, "What's going to be the next, that you can marry your dog?" Unlike Marine Le Pen's remodeled FN in France, some prominent members of the DPP remain mired in the old right's religious conservatism.

As much as Schmidt-Nielsen despises the DPP, she concedes that they have positioned themselves smartly on economic policy. "The DPP actually looks like a classic, social democratic party," she argues, except for the fact that they have supported the center-right Lars Løkke Rasmussen as the prime minister, despite his calls to cut welfare benefits. She thinks that the DPP's voters seem to have prioritized issues in a way that leads them to accept concessions on social benefits, because they care more about barring asylum seekers from the country.[21] Like the women and religious Christians who voted for Donald Trump because of his economic platform and pledges on Supreme Court nominations and despite his overt misogyny and philandering, some Danish voters on the right seem to care more about keeping refugees out than preserving their welfare benefits.

Given the left's stubborn resistance to low-wage jobs for refugees, Soei believes that seeking to change the left-wing parties' position is a lost cause at the moment. The focus, he argues, should be the unions, which he believes aren't being honest with the rank and file. The reason that the unions are opposed to the idea, argues Soei, is that they are worried about losing members. If they admitted to their members that refugees are doing work that Danes won't do and that Eastern Europeans, not refugees, are taking Danish jobs, then things would get better. "The political question is actually, do you want to be in solidarity with Eastern Europeans coming to Denmark to work here normally for a couple of years and go back, or do you want to be in solidarity with newly arrived citizens who are going to stay here?" says Soei.

The DPP simply wants these people to leave, so it has no interest in analyzing their skills or credentials. "They want people to move out," he says. "But if you look at the rest of the parties in Denmark, then it seems like a big mystery why we haven't done better." If the issue is framed as refugees taking jobs currently done by Eastern Europeans, then, he says, union members will accept it.[22]

Although they do not agree on much, Berth and Soei both believe Danes are effectively choosing to show solidarity with Eastern European temp workers rather than refugees who hope to remain in Denmark. "The fact that we have the chance for workers to move freely inside Europe has made it even more difficult to get refugees employed," explains Berth. An employer faced with the choice of hiring a Dane who wants a competitive salary, a refugee who speaks no Danish or English, and an Eastern European who speaks English and is willing to work for minimum wage or less is likely to choose the Eastern European.[23]

The DPP is also angry about Eastern European immigrants taking jobs, but one doesn't hear as much about Christian Poles as Muslim Danes on the radio or in parliament. The Danes call cheap EU labor "social dumping," with Eastern Europeans working for fifty to seventy kroner (seven to ten dollars) per hour with no safety regulations. Construction workers undercut by Polish builders might resent Poles more than Muslims; for them, social dumping is a major threat. Among the broader population, though, there is a different take. Many Danes see the Polish builders as a cheap and convenient way to get their home repairs done but are convinced that Muslim immigrants are criminals or terrorists.[24]

The DPP seems to have calculated that there are more votes to be won with the latter argument. Or, as the refugee law expert Thomas Gammeltoft-Hansen puts it more bluntly, "The best thing that could have happened for Jews or Poles is that Muslims came to the EU."[25]

THE DEBATE ABOUT IMMIGRATION AND WELFARE HASN'T BEEN WITHOUT its contradictions. The free-market right, when it lets principles take precedence over current political fads, favors free movement. Many on the left, as Soei's clashes with his leftist friends revealed, say they want to help refugees but balk at letting them work at lower wages out of fear that the welfare state will be undermined. Seeing the op-ed editor of Denmark's leading conservative paper argue for it didn't help sell it to the left.[26]

Nevertheless, Danish unions and employers have managed to hammer out a small-scale compromise with the government to experiment with an hourly "introduction wage" of as low as forty-nine kroner (seven dollars)—a sort of internship period—for refugees. It has been a very limited success. By October 2016, only thirteen eligible refugees had taken part in the program, and many traditionalists on the left remained worried that it would undercut wages for Danish workers.[27] But there are others on the left who insist that letting refugees work, especially skilled ones, rather than sitting around taking courses or receiving benefits, will not destroy the welfare state.

The same is true in Holland. The historian Leo Lucassen sees a great political irony in the strange bedfellows that have emerged. "You have this coalition of elite ultraliberal right-wing employers on the one hand and ultraleft people who think that we should have open borders," he says. He is skeptical of those who foresee an implosion of entitlements under the burden of new refugees simply because Holland has absorbed large numbers before without major economic consequences. In the 1990s, the welfare state didn't implode, and it isn't falling apart in Germany, which absorbed ethnic Germans from the Soviet Union and Balkan refugees in the 1990s and is now absorbing Syrians. Unless the numbers really sky-rocket, there won't be a collapse, insists Lucassen.

Nevertheless, the implosion argument is being used by Dutch free-market parties who have never had any great affinity for the welfare state and who now argue that immigrants "will wreck our society because they don't subscribe to Western liberal values."[28]

Danish free-market parties have shifted in the same way because they don't worry about alienating union voters the way the Social Democrats and DPP do. The free-market Liberal Alliance party used to campaign under the libertarian slogan, "Open borders, closed coffers"; anyone could come, but no one should automatically be entitled to welfare payments. These days, the party leader, Anders Samuelsen, says, "If you stay in Denmark, you have rights, and it's very lucrative. . . . Staying in Denmark with no social security, it would be a different situation."[29] While this position is distinct from the nativist defense of the welfare state offered by the DPP and is motivated by a desire to dismantle the welfare state rather than restrict who benefits from it, the impact on refugees is the same. It prompted former youth leader Rasmus Brygger to leave the party.

"I think a lot of people on the right wing like these ideas, but they don't like them in practice, because for them it means getting more Muslims here," Brygger explains. One of the most discussed issues in the Liberal Alliance, he says, was "Well, we can't open the borders until we have closed out the welfare state, and since that's not going to happen, we need to close the borders."[30]

During the 1990s, many Muslims refugees came to both Denmark and Holland from Bosnia, and they integrated quite well. The difference between the 1990s and today is that since 9/11, Muslims have become associated with terror. In the 1990s, there was grumbling, but people were complaining that the refugees cost money, not raising the specter of cultural conquest and calling for de-Islamization.

For Lucassen, work—or at least the chance to work—might actually be the solution. He believes that the labor market could solve many of the problems if only it were politically palatable to say so. Looking at the migration of Eastern Europeans coming to Holland and other wealthy EU members, "the labor market regulates these migrations quite well, and people contribute much more than they take out." He advocates expanding this system to the border regions of Europe, allowing anyone who passes a security check to come and seek work. Countries could even demand that they pay a deposit. The message would be "Good luck, but if you don't find a job, you're on your own," and they could only draw benefits after a certain amount of time, which would encourage regular work or going home.

With such a policy, getting to Europe would be safer and cheaper—the cost of a plane or ferry ticket. It would also put the smugglers out of business instantly. Of course, Lucassen admits, "it's possible that a billion refugees or asylum seekers will be on our doorsteps as of tomorrow; then you have a problem, because there are limits," but the right's argument that the EU has reached this saturation point is, he says, "bullshit."

The labor market approach could eventually work, he believes, just not in this political climate. Like Australia, with its untilled fields and offshore detention centers, Holland is too "locked in this populist anti-Muslim nativist kind of atmosphere to really think clearly."[31]

12

The Rise of White Identity Politics

THIERRY BAUDET IS THE SLICK-HAIRED SOPHIST BEHIND THE DUTCH new right. He runs a think tank called Forum for Democracy, which has now transformed into a political party. His group helped support the successful April 2016 referendum against an EU association agreement with Ukraine, earning his party the label "pro-Russian" in some circles.[1] He has referred to Bashar al-Assad as the only solution in Syria. "Once the neoconservative folly in Syria is over and we just restore Assad to power, and things will go quiet, which is what we should do," he argues. As for the refugees, "they can go back," he says breezily.[2] His website features photos of him lying atop pianos, he boasts of his time studying with the conservative philosopher Roger Scruton at Oxford, and he has been named the most important public intellectual in the Netherlands—by himself, but apparently no one else.[3]

Baudet is dismissive of politicians. "They are incredibly stupid people. . . . They are essentially brain-dead," he told me in April 2016. "I think their lives are incredibly trivial and their brains show incredibly little activity."[4] In late September, Baudet declared his intention to become one. And in March 2017, he and a colleague from his new party won two seats in the country's 150-member parliament.

His work often reads like a repackaging of foreign ideas for the Dutch market.[5] Baudet wrote a book called *Oikophobia* (Greek for "fear of one's own home"), a treatise on self-hatred expressing ideas very similar to his professor Scruton's own essay on the subject.[6] He also once studied under

Paul Scheffer before tacking sharply to the right, and some of his writing on the importance of borders has strong echoes of his onetime mentor's work.[7]

Baudet relishes attacking the left for abandoning its own ideals. "It's so obvious that the Muslim immigrants bring with them a whole set of pre-modern values . . . , which are at odds and in conflict with so many things that the left has been fighting for," he argues. But rather than merely de-nounce the left's well-known hypocrisies on issues from the Rushdie affair to the Khmer Rouge, he goes further. Baudet believes the left never even cared for ideals like women's rights. "They were tools to destroy something. They were actually not in favor of feminism; they were just against the patriarchal society," Baudet argues.[8] He goes on to cite the heavily foot-noted but academically tenuous work of the PVV's second-in-command and the brain behind Wilders, Martin Bosma, who wrote a book in 2015 denouncing the Dutch left's support for the anti-apartheid movement on the grounds that the movement's objective "was to destroy the stronghold of the West" in South Africa, as Baudet puts it. Bosma's book argues that South Africa's white Afrikaners—who ruled over a disenfranchised black majority for almost fifty years—have in the democratic era been reduced, as the books title states, to "a minority in their own land" and that the native Dutch will face a similar fate as a Muslim great replacement usurps Holland.[9] Baudet believes the current silence toward the excesses of fun-damentalist Islam is "maybe because the left is not really interested in jus-tice and human rights and all those things, but actually they are interested in destroying the West. That's their real agenda."

Baudet sees the future of Europe taking one of four paths: the Israel scenario (terrorism, military in the streets, low-intensity violence); the South Africa scenario (what he believes to be a mass exodus of whites); a utopian Canada scenario (successful multiculturalism); or what he calls the "reverse Algeria option," an academic way of describing a forced pop-ulation transfer. As he puts it, "The Algerian option, where four million French people that have been living there for two generations were just pulled out, thrown out of the country. And that's also an option, that there will be such a big conflict that Europeans will, like they did in 1492, reconquer their lands," or, in other words, to follow his analogy, expel the Muslim "settlers" from Europe.

Baudet claims he longs for a rosy Canadian scenario. "I really hope for the Canadian model; I think every sensible person hopes for it, but

I think the Israeli model is more likely," he says. And to avoid that, he believes the first sensible step is "to stop immigration from Muslim countries and to try whatever we can to have a program of national integration and everything," but he doesn't have much faith it will succeed. He brings up Scotland and Catalonia—odd examples for an ardent proponent of reclaiming a strong national identity. "Spain failed with Catalonia, the English failed with Scotland," and treading on even thinner ice, he adds, "the Germans tried to integrate the Jews for a thousand years."

Quickly backtracking from an argument that might call into question his vehemently pro-Israel public persona, he says, "I don't think Judaism as a religion has many rules that are opposed to a liberal society, which I think is the case with Islam." (Evidently, he has never seen an ambulance pelted with stones for the sin of driving through an Orthodox Jerusalem neighborhood on Yom Kippur.) His disturbing reference to the ostensibly poorly integrated German Jews who were murdered by Nazis, he assures me, was just to point out that "there are not many examples of successful integration of different ethnic, cultural, religious groups into societies."[10]

Like Wilders, Baudet is full of praise for Israel and the Jews.[11] But unlike the ethnic nativism of the stage-managed party leader who wears his Islamophobia on his sleeve, Baudet's lurks just beneath the surface. As in France, there is a fantasy on the Dutch right of purging society of unwanted "colonizers"—by which they mean Muslim immigrants—who, they insist, must leave or be expelled.

When it comes to the contemporary Dutch debate over refugees, Baudet is uninterested in discussing strains on the national budget. "I don't think the problem is essentially about money. . . . I think it really is about the very legitimate concern that these people might not be here to join our way of life." He worries about a violent breakdown of society, and although he believes that his ideas and the right-wing politicians espousing them will win in the end, he concedes gloomily, "there is a very probable scenario that we will just lose. . . . It's very possible that in fifty years Europe will not exist anymore."[12]

Or more precisely, Europe will not exist "as a predominantly white-skinned, Christian or post-Christian, Roman-law-based kind of society that we know it as today. It might be some kind of Middle East, Arabian kind of world."

Cultural and demographic anxiety about dwindling native populations and rapidly increasing immigrant ones—especially Muslims—lies at the heart of all nativist parties' platforms and the theories that underpin those political programs. Many of them can be traced to the apocalyptic visions of Enoch Powell and Jean Raspail, the two men whom Renaud Camus, the man responsible for popularizing France's great replacement theory, cites in an epigraph to his book.

Even Christopher Caldwell, the most thoughtful and measured of the right-wing commentators on Islam and immigration, opens his book with a reference to Powell, pointing out that the author of the notorious "rivers of blood" speech was mathematically correct even if he was considered morally beyond the pale. In other words, he accurately predicted the number of nonwhite Britons who would be living in the UK in the early twenty-first century. For that demographic projection, Powell deserves some credit—less so for the paranoid vision of the Tiber, or the Thames, foaming with blood.

Caldwell adopts the same vocabulary as Baudet when talking about immigrants as colonizers. "If one abandons the idea that Western Europeans are rapacious and exploitative by nature, and that Africans, Asians, and other would-be immigrants are inevitably their victims," he writes, "then the fundamental difference between colonization and labor migration ceases to be obvious."[13] This leaves out the small matter that European colonialism was enforced at the barrel of a gun by settlers with political and economic control, whereas Muslim guest workers had to receive permission and visas before coming to do menial jobs in Europe.

Caldwell makes a legitimate argument when he asserts that large numbers of religious Muslims could change Europe's culture in significant ways; he is on far less solid ground when likening the arrival of impoverished factory workers to the brutal Belgian conquest of Congo, slipping from reasoned argument into the nativist paranoia of Renaud Camus and Jean Raspail.

Caldwell also falls into the trap of assuming some sort of Islamic exceptionalism in the realm of reproduction. Muslims, he warns, "might not go through the same demographic transition that their hosts did. Muslim culture is unusually full of messages laying out the practical advantages of procreation," as if Catholicism and Orthodox Judaism do not similarly encourage believers to have large families.[14] Indeed, it's the same sort of argument one heard about Catholics in nineteenth-century America or that is common today among secular Israelis resentful of their ultrareligious compatriots who often have a dozen children and receive state benefits.

More importantly, it is an argument that ignores the data on demographic convergence between immigrants and natives after one or two generations, often due to the cost of living. Furthermore, there is no evidence in Europe that religiosity of any sort increases birth rates. In Europe, the countries with higher church attendance (Poland and Portugal, for example) have the lowest fertility rates. It is staunchly secular countries like Iceland and Denmark and Sweden that have the highest birth rates per woman.[15]

As with the Republican congressman Steve King, who praises Geert Wilders and worries about the impossibility of restoring "our civilization with somebody else's babies," the fear on the European right is about *who* is having the new German or Danish babies and the fact that it is not white Germans or Danes.[16] This is best captured by Thilo Sarrazin's borderline eugenicist rant against immigrant reproduction in his book *Germany Abolishes Itself.* Sarrazin's two greatest fears are a declining white population and the number of kids being born to less-educated parents, who, in his view, are always immigrants. He cites Darwin in arguing that acquisition of intelligence is hereditary and warns that if the low-educated population grows faster than the highly educated (because immigrant women, whom he believes are intellectually inferior, are at the moment having more babies than whites), then Germany will disappear.[17]

Sarrazin is terrified that the Muslims are going to replace the Germans and that the great—and supposedly more intelligent—German race will vanish. He accuses the Germans of being "too lazy and indolent" to keep up their fertility rate to compete with the demographic conquerors, alarmingly pointing out that a third of children born in Paris and half in London are nonwhite.[18] It is a vision of multiracial hell straight out of the pages of Raspail.

Bent Melchior, the Danish refugee-turned-rabbi, isn't convinced by Caldwell and Sarrazin's apocalyptic predictions. He believes that the European way of life will rub off and that people will eventually integrate even if they hold on to some of their religious traditions and language. There's an old expression in Danish about "the villa, the Volvo, and the dog. Little by little, the Muslims see that this is a pleasant way of living."[19] Gradually, he says, they will have two or three kids rather than eight.

His theory is supported by evidence from neighboring Germany, where the birth rate in the 1970s was 4.4 for Turkish immigrant women and had by 2010 fallen to 2.2, almost exactly in line with the population at large. In France, the situation is similar. Whether it is due to adapting to the cost of living or cultural norms, the numbers are converging.[20] It is something he has seen close up in the Jewish community, he says. "In the long run, the majority conquers."[21]

The most interesting part of Sarrazin's book features an extended conversation with the mayor of Neukölln, a largely Arab and Turkish area of Berlin, where dependency on social welfare is a real problem. The mayor, who clearly knows a great deal more about the challenges of integration policy than Sarrazin, tells the author that the women "who wear the veil most rigorously are often the ones who master the German language best"[22] and come from cultivated families. "Orthodoxy, culture and the veil can go together perfectly well."

Ignoring his well-informed source, Sarrazin proceeds to conclude that further immigration will lead to a dumber Germany where churches will turn into mosques and schools will no longer teach German—a future in which "the country of my grandchildren and great-grandchildren will be in large part Muslim; where we speak mostly Turkish and Arabic, where the women wear veils and the daily rhythms are marked by the calls of muezzins." In Sarrazin's Eurabian dystopia, "Germany will not die all at once, it will disappear quietly along with the Germans and their intellectual potential, eaten away by demographic developments."[23] It, too, has an echo of Raspail. "We're going to die slowly, eaten away from the inside by millions of microbes injected into our body. Little by little. Easily, quietly. No pain, no blood," he wrote in *The Camp of the Saints*.[24]

Like Sarrazin and Raspail, Holland's newest right-wing actor on the parliamentary stage, Thierry Baudet, is terrified of a great replacement—the disappearance or "dilution" of what he considers a superior white civilization. To him, it is an existential question. "If I go to a museum, and I look at these portraits, they are essentially people like me that I can see. In fifty years it won't be," he says wistfully. "People will walk in the Rijksmuseum or the Louvre, and they'll look at these faces and say, 'Yeah, those were the people that once were.' Rather like we look at Roman emperors."[25]

PEOPLE LIKE BAUDET WOULD HAVE NEVER FOUND THEIR WAY INTO parliament without an assist from the new right's media arm. Just as the FN has become a huge presence on social media in France, the right is in the midst of conquering Dutch media. *Geenstijl*, a popular Breitbart-style news and video site in Holland whose name means "no style," deploys an army of snide commenters across mainstream sites. It began as an irreverent blog and drifted more explicitly to the right, becoming a home for those who felt politically homeless after Pim Fortuyn's murder. It has now become ubiquitous, and its commenters are a formidable presence on Dutch Twitter. The site draws on the Dutch penchant for irony and pushing the limits of acceptability. Some politicians confess that the first thing they do when they arrive at their offices in The Hague is look at *Geenstijl*.[26]

It has also helped shape what the journalist Kustaw Bessems sees as a new form of political correctness. In the old days, he says, there were taboos enforced by the left: badmouth immigrants and "you were immediately called a racist and extreme right and basically pressured to shut up. Now, it's the other way around," Bessems argues. As in Denmark, where the Muslim question has taken over public debate, in today's Holland, "as soon as you say anything else than 'immigration is a problem' or 'Islam is the cause of terrorism' . . . the thought police immediately jump on your neck to correct you."[27]

In addition to hijacking the concept of free speech and redefining it as the right to insult Islam, the new right's greatest success has been to reframe the debate in stark cultural terms to the point that ideological cleavages over economic policy, foreign policy, and other issues that were long the bread and butter of political debate have almost disappeared from the discussion. Geert Wilders is a prime example.

Early in his career, he was advised by a rising intellectual star of the Dutch right: Bart Jan Spruyt, a neoconservative in the American tradition, who wanted to roll back the cultural revolutions of the 1960s and 1970s and saw in Wilders an opportunity to establish a conservative movement in that mold. By 2006, the two had fallen out and parted ways.[28] The cultural shift was far too entrenched. And to Wilders's credit, he was smart enough to realize that the old right's moralism was not a winning position in modern Dutch society, especially after Fortuyn. He grasped that Holland's unique political and cultural preferences meant that there was no space for that sort of conservatism; being both socioeconomically right wing and culturally right wing was a nonstarter.[29]

Fortuyn laid the groundwork for right-wing populism in the Netherlands; but it wouldn't have succeeded if others hadn't followed his lead. Dutch elites tend to adapt; the massive changes in the 1960s and 1970s would never have happened if not for the political elites standing aside, seeing which way the wind was blowing, and accommodating that change.[30] The only convincing explanation for the durability of Fortuyn's ideas is that he succeeded in introducing a new form of cultural opposition, and the other parties have for the past fifteen years played along.[31]

That cultural opposition cannot be ignored. Fortuyn and Van Gogh both embodied a peculiar but essential national trait—a very Dutch pride in causing offense. What Van Gogh seemed to miss was that, to some, his words actually mattered. He sounded the alarm about extremism before most, but, as the historian Ian Buruma writes, he never expected the outside world to "intrude on his Amsterdam scene, with its private ironies, its personal feuds, and its brutal mockery that was never intended to draw more than imaginary blood." Such rhetoric works well among friends or in small countries. "Its destructive power can be cushioned in a narrow society where everyone knows the rules of the game. When it is exposed to outsiders with a less playful view of words the effects can be devastating."[32]

Websites like *Geenstijl* are particularly effective at enforcing the new politically correct orthodoxy when these cultural flashpoints emerge. There has been a debate in Holland in recent years over the holiday Sinterklaas, a peculiarly Dutch pre-Christmas ritual that features a character known as Zwarte Piet, or Black Pete, who, like Santa's little helper, brings gifts to children. The character is a cultural icon as deeply entrenched in popular culture as the Tooth Fairy. People often dress up in blackface to play Zwarte Piet.

For decades, there was no discussion about it; in the past few years, it has become a national debate as black Dutch citizens of Surinamese origin and other activists have called for an end to the tradition. Everyone from radio hosts to the prime minister has weighed in. White Dutch people never faced questions about their traditions and still tend to react by arguing they're innocuous. The reaction from many of them has been outrage at the left's political correctness and a demand that when it comes to this holiday tradition, which appears to most foreigners as crude and racist, you can't take it from us.

The fact that Holland has a beloved blackface tradition in 2017 says something about its ability as a society to handle diversity.[33] The whole Black Pete debate is really about whether a minority group has a right to criticize Dutch national traditions. The Irish became white Americans, as did the Jews, but the shrill debate over Black Pete suggests that despite the Surinamese speaking Dutch as a mother tongue, a lot of people have never accepted them as Dutch.

The same is true when it comes to celebrations of diversity. Debates about public observance of non-Christian religious holidays such as Diwali for Hindus, Eid for Muslims, or Yom Kippur for Jews usually boil down to: we have just Christian holidays, and that's it.[34] It is the mark of a country that has yet to grapple with even the most superficial and innocuous embraces of diversity.[35]

The debate can be traced to Holland's amnesia about its colonial past. There is a widely held view that because Holland was not a great power like some of its neighbors, it is superior by virtue of not having a violent nationalist tradition.[36] Such a self-perception also drives the debate about apologies and accommodation of minorities. If we haven't been as oppressive or brutal a colonial power as our Belgian or German neighbors in terms of body counts—a dubious honor—then the conclusion is we don't need to redeem ourselves. Memories of the Dutch army's brutal campaigns in Indonesia are conveniently forgotten. And it is not just white Dutch people who have no sense of the country's dark history.

As Bessems, the *Volkskrant* journalist, points out, many among the younger generation are not learning about any of the country's darker chapters. And in lower-level schools (Holland is notorious for its tracking of students into vocational, higher, and academic tiers), there is not much emphasis on history. As in France, there are Dutch children of Muslim background who are exposed to Holocaust denialism or attracted to it out of hostility to Israel.

It is all the more troubling because Holland has never fully confronted its not-so-distant historical demons. It is a country that, unlike Denmark, did very little to save its Jewish population. In fact, the Dutch were among the most zealous in rounding up and exterminating what was once a large and prosperous community. Only Poland was more murderous. The outside world is familiar with the story of Anne Frank. Less known is the fact that over 70 percent of Dutch Jews were sent to Nazi concentration camps.[37]

Paul Scheffer is adamant that everyone in the country should learn that history, and he finds it offensive and condescending when some commentators argue that schools shouldn't bother Turkish children with the bloody history of World War II in Holland on the grounds that it's not *their* history. To Scheffer, this is just another version of the abdication that he claims leads some extreme cultural relativists to say it's fine for Muslim men to beat their wives because it's "their culture."[38]

By the same token, he believes that a young Algerian in France has every right to ask why he isn't taught about French-led massacres in the 1960s or that a Dutch-Surinamese student should be able to ask her teachers about colonialism. The presence of minorities "forces you to rethink institutions like education and the welfare state," argues Scheffer. It also means asking, "What is the history you're teaching? If we talk about history and we think it is important to know where you come from, then we have to talk also about how vulnerable we have been as an open society to these forms of barbarism."

He mocks right-wingers who deride Muslim intolerance and forget their own history. Wilders's supporters like to talk about how Holland has had religious freedom since the seventeenth century. "Well, why did Catholics have to hide, and why was it forbidden by law for Jews to marry Christians?" Scheffer asks. Those who defend equal treatment for gays, he adds, "should remember that fifty years ago, this was absolutely not accepted in the Netherlands either. It's a very recent discovery." By all means defend it, Scheffer argues, "but then understand how vulnerable it has been."[39]

Some of these dilemmas arise because the modern left doesn't know what to say when minority groups say or do offensive or illegal things, be it an imam denouncing gays, the Cologne attacks, or Holocaust denialism. "People find it hard to say, 'No, you're wrong.' . . . It's ludicrous and it's vicious and it's very damaging for a society to deny a genocide," Bessems argues. Confronting the Christian establishment was one thing; it's quite another when the clash is with a less powerful group. "Left wing, liberal, and progressive people have found it hard to make the same points against Muslims, because they felt they were stepping on the minority."

Nevertheless, he insists, "if you believe that values are universal, if you believe in personal freedoms, if you believe in equality despite gender or sexuality or race or whatever, then you will."[40]

Bessems spent four years working in The Hague. "I was really astounded by how little of the outside reality actually penetrates into this bubble. . . . The only thing they are worried about is the image they project," he says of the country's political class. "Events are not real events anymore. They are factors in this image management." The result is that Dutch politicians can be inaccessible to the point of absurdity. Leaders rarely talk to media unless it is perceived as helpful to their immediate political interests. Even low-ranking party members across the spectrum tend to behave as if they are celebrities and eschew the press—or demand the review of quotations before publication.[41]

Parliament has become a sort of theater, detached from society. For voters, this leads to more disillusionment with the establishment. "There's no sense among voters that there is a connection between their vote and what happens," argues Bessems. "A lot of very important issues have been transferred, of course, to the European level in a very dishonest way." Of course, politicians might say, you voted for us and the decisions are politically legitimate, because it was elected parties that transferred authority to Brussels. But voters don't buy it, and it helps Wilders win the votes of the frustrated, and others, fearful of losing more voters to him, start to parrot his policies.

Bessems recalls visiting officials in The Hague at the height of this mimicking trend. "When I talked to politicians, I used to say that sometimes I wish you would just close your eyes for ten minutes and pretend that Wilders doesn't exist." He would ask them what they really believed and their considered positions on actual issues. There were few answers. "I think they've become totally reactive. They're reactive to Wilders, they're reactive to media, they're reactive to public outcries, they're reactive to opinion polls."

Bessems blames the growing number of PR consultants in politics, who regularly outnumber journalists. "They have whole armies of spokespeople in between when a politician is on the record." In this stage-managed political landscape, the ghost of Pim Fortuyn looms large. He was "someone who was prepared to think out loud, who enjoyed confrontations with his critics," says Bessems, by no means a fan of the late populist leader.

Fortuyn's style now seems a thing of the past. "He was not a classic populist in the sense that he was always trying to please his electorate," recalls Bessems. "He would say things that his own electorate would probably not like," and then explain himself, something almost unimaginable in today's political environment. Bessems wonders how Fortuyn would have fared in this era of gotcha journalism. "We as media have . . . a very big and damning influence," he admits. Political reporting is not generally focused on substance. "Basically, you ask a politician something and you hope it's either not in line with their party or not in line with the coalition partner or not in line with something they said three years ago," says Bessems.[42]

Fortuyn was transformative because he went beyond what politicians generally attempt. Whereas many politicians merely mirror what the masses think, Fortuyn tried to sculpt them, seducing them into sharing his views.[43] The results are plain to see. Fifteen years after his death, people are saying things that politicians got prosecuted for in the 1980s.

DUTCH POLITICS TODAY IS ALMOST ENTIRELY DEVOID OF SUBSTANCE, and moral commitments are frowned upon. It has descended into a sort of popularity contest where the most theatrical get the most attention.[44] Wilders, of course, with his dyed-blond streak of hair, is the most colorful and plainspoken politician. While he is no Pim Fortuyn, he attracts attention in the theater that parliament has become.

He can also say things that others cannot. Wilders has perfected a populist rhetoric that blames foreigners for all that ails the Dutch working class at a moment when they feel they no longer have any control over their neighborhoods or society. What Wilders has done, Bessems argues, is to tell these frustrated voters, "I can give you that control."[45]

He appeals to these sorts of voters because he breaks a taboo in Dutch politics—he is perfectly comfortable being blunt and with issuing moralistic messages. Other politicians "talk in a very abstract way," says the former Labor MP Ahmed Marcouch. "The people don't understand." Wilders by contrast "is very clear," speaking directly in blunt sound bites like "De-Islamize Now" and "No More Islam."[46] It's no wonder that in January 2017, Dutch prime minister Mark Rutte fired an opening shot in the campaign for the March 15 election, which he won, by telling immigrants and their children who don't like the Netherlands that they should "act normal" or, if they don't like it, leave.[47]

For Wilders, unlike the prime minister, follow-through is not so much of an issue. "I think it's a complete utopia that he tries to sketch for his voters, and I think he can never deliver what he is promising," argues Bessems. He doesn't have to.[48] Wilders is not in the cabinet and not directly accountable to any specific constituency or for any ministerial portfolio. The lack of responsibility for actual policymaking allows a lot of freedom. Wilders and PVV politicians can say almost anything without consequences, and it might even attract more voters to their side. By leaving major economic crises festering and unresolved, they also ensure an ongoing receptive audience for their message, so long as they are never blamed for the problem.

WHILE HE WAS STILL ALIVE, PIM FORTUYN WAS MORE VOCAL THAN MOST about feeling threatened by young immigrant men, but he was not the only one. Among Jews and gays, there is a palpable fear of being targeted. And, as in France, it has made right-wing parties seem a palatable option for these groups in a way that was never possible before.

Bram, a pseudonym for a prominent supporter of Geert Wilders's PVV party in Holland who wishes to remain anonymous, recently told me, "It's an outdated reflex for Jews to always say the problem is the extreme right. We have new enemies, and we need new ideas." It's an echo of what the French philosopher Alain Finkielkraut wrote in 2003: "If we want to face reality we must saw through the bars of our retrospective prison." Both insist that seeing today's anti-Semitism as a reincarnation of Europe's past is misguided.[49]

The threat, Bram is adamant, is not Wilders or Le Pen or the AfD in Germany. It's the left and Islam.

"We shouldn't discriminate between the socialist anti-Semites and the right-wing anti-Semites. Jews are always fucked in Europe. We should go for the short term. . . . It's a historic anomaly that we're not in danger. We should be active and vote for parties that are good for us *now*." And right now, Islam is the biggest enemy, he says emphatically. And in his view, Geert Wilders is the only politician standing up to it.

As far as Bram is concerned, "we're at war with Islam," which means the Dutch government should be cutting off satellite TV, WhatsApp, and trade with and travel to certain countries. "If Iran can do it, we can," he insists. Bram would also remove the idea of equality of religions in the constitution, effectively demoting Islam. He would ban all mosques for a period; he would forbid or penalize conversion to Islam. He even believes that internment camps might become necessary, although they "could be reduced to targeted administrative detention," he allows. "Chamberlain was a much more pleasant man than Churchill, I'm sure," he says. "But we're at war, and we need war leaders."[50]

Bram ended up in PVV circles because his interests were security, the EU, immigration, and, as he puts it, "they liked the fact that I was Jewish." Geert Wilders is famous for arguing that Holland must be de-Islamized and calling for "no more Islam." Bram is not short of ideas about how to accomplish this. His policy vision is blunt and punitive when it comes to immigrants. No more Muslim schools. No more extremist mosques. Stop exporting Dutch welfare payments—a reference to immigrants who allegedly send remittances to their families drawn from state subsidies. Much more stringent punishments for crime—a "three strikes and you're out of the country" program. "You can incentivize people to leave," he insists. That said, he adds, "I don't think there will be a kickout program. It's not in the DNA of Geert Wilders to go against the rule of law."

When pushed on the question of education, he argues that "you can't close Muslim schools, but you can cut public funds to them." He admits that there would then be calls to withdraw public funds from Jewish and Catholic schools, too, but he views these religions as fundamentally different and deserving of recognition in a way that Islam is not. That's because, as Wilders is fond of saying, "Islam isn't a religion, it's an ideology."

"The Islam we currently see is not part of our culture," Bram argues. "Currently it is so against what we find pleasant here" that abandoning a few core liberal democratic values is acceptable in his view. "It's wrong to put equality of laws first," insists Bram. "The protection of Islam should be excluded from the constitution."[51]

Wilders didn't do as well as expected in the March 2017 election, but he may win without ever coming to power. "You can have a lot of influence in politics by steering the debate. . . . The PVV has shifted the whole political discussion to the right," Bram says. He is convinced that the battle has already been won on some level, regardless of the election outcome. Pointing to France's 2016 burkini debate, he says approvingly, "Sarkozy is saying, 'Let's change the constitution,'" and a socialist government contemplated closing mosques. So even if Le Pen loses, he told me six months before her defeat, "they're making elites move to the right," and that is precisely what is happening in Holland. "The Labor Party is saying exactly the same thing Geert Wilders said five years ago," he tells me with evident satisfaction.[52]

The Labor Party's policy shifts on immigration have had political consequences. In late 2014, two Dutch-Turkish lawmakers, Tunahan Kuzu and Selçuk Öztürk, broke away from Labor and formed their own party, Denk (Think). Kuzu, the leader of the new party, told the press that all the traditional parties had moved too far to the right on integration and asylum. Painting himself as the anti-Wilders, he argued that he had no choice but to leave Labor.

Ahmed Marcouch is not so charitable toward those who left his party to form Denk. He argues that his erstwhile colleagues Kuzu and Öztürk split off because they were opposed to the Labor Party's stance on recognizing Turkey's massacre of Armenians as genocide (Holland is home to a significant Armenian diaspora) as well as their disagreements over integration policy.

They also saw an opportunity. The Dutch Labor Party is hemorrhaging votes; it has gone from being the country's largest party to winning only 9 seats (out of 150) in the March 2017 election, a staggering loss of more than three-fourths of its seats, including Marcouch's own. "They are infected with the success of populism," Marcouch told me before the election with evident disdain for his former colleagues. "They want to be the Wilders of minorities."[53]

Kuzu made headlines in September 2016 during Israeli prime minister Benjamin Netanyahu's state visit to Holland; in a receiving line, Kuzu refused to shake Netanyahu's hand, outraging the Israelis and many Dutch politicians.[54] Bram, who is a huge Netanyahu supporter, was not at the event but claims he "would have liked to punch Kuzu in the face" had he been there. Nevertheless, he concedes the cold shoulder was a political masterstroke and predicted it would win Kuzu's party a couple of seats by galvanizing the anti-Israel vote among Dutch Muslims.[55] He was right; Denk exceeded all expectations and won three seats in the new parliament.

But for Marcouch, Denk is playing a dangerous game. The party risks taking Holland back to the 1950s, when pillarization separated communities, schools, and resources along religious lines, allowing Catholics and Protestants to live almost entirely separate lives. What the new Denk party is doing, he insists, is similar, and Holland cannot go back to that model. They institutionalize discrimination by creating a party based on ethnicity, he argues, and when ethnicity is so central, then voters' views are very simple.[56]

For Dutch Turks, there is a strong counterpull on their identity by leaders like Turkish president Recep Tayyip Erdoğan, who broadcasts a strong Turkish nationalist message to the diaspora in Europe. And Denk is vehemently pro-Erdoğan. This came into full view just days before the March 2017 Dutch election when Turkey sought to send its foreign minister to Rotterdam to campaign for a referendum that Erdoğan eventually won, giving him almost unlimited executive powers. Wilders denounced the Turks; Erdoğan called the Dutch "Nazi remnants." As the journalist Bas Heijne remarked, "Geert Wilders has his mirror image in Erdoğan."[57] Both are peddling nationalist identity politics. In the end, the Dutch government refused landing rights to the foreign minister's plane and expelled another Turkish official. Rotterdam's Moroccan-born Muslim mayor replied to the Turkish Nazi talk by asking publicly, "Do they not know I am the mayor of a city bombed by the Nazis?"[58]

It may have been enough to shore up the centrist prime minister's shaky support just days before the election. Rutte won convincingly, Marcouch lost his seat, and Baudet is now in parliament.

Unlike some of the nationalist supporters of the PVV, Bram is not motivated by unquestioning love of country. He has a fraught relationship with Dutch culture and does not see Holland as an inherently friendly and innocuous country. Bram's great-grandfather obtained exit permits for his five daughters to leave Germany in 1937 but ripped up the tickets, assuming that Jews would be safe. Only two of the daughters survived.

"He did not worry enough," says Bram. And on the other side of his family, in Holland, "it wasn't the Germans who pulled my grandparents from their home," he tells me. "It was the Dutch." The municipal government gave the occupiers a detailed map showing where all the Jews were living, and local police and collaborators made the roundups and deportations possible.

Given that history, Bram's default assumption is that the capacity for murderous violence is always lurking beneath the surface of society. "Anne Frank was not betrayed by the Germans," he reminds me. "But by

Dutch. Regular Dutch. Neighbors." The fact is that Jews might need to find new allies in a new war, he argues, because they will never be safe.

"The trains for the Jews will always come," he declares ominously. "I'd rather be wrong than be too calm." Bram is convinced that until the West wins its war against Islam, Jews will be in danger. "I'm not under any illusion," he tells me, that being a prominent PVV supporter "will buy me a ticket off the trains. It might delay it."[59]

When we discuss the details of our respective family histories—many of his relatives were killed by the Nazis in the years after my own family fled Berlin for South Africa—he stands by his position on welcoming refugees to Holland today. "South Africa shouldn't have taken your relatives," he tells me. That would be akin to Holland and Germany accepting Syrians today. Many are genuine refugees, like the German Jews of the 1930s, he concedes, "but they should have been taken by neighboring countries," he contends, rather than going somewhere thousands of miles away.

For Holland to take German Jewish refugees during World War II was appropriate by this logic. Today, he argues, "Saudi Arabia should be taking them all." That neighboring countries should absorb refugees is an argument that makes sense on the surface but overlooks the fate of those German Jews who were denied entry when they sought refuge far away and were then resettled in countries near Germany, most famously the passengers aboard the MS *St. Louis*. The ship, carrying 937 passengers, was turned away by Cuba amid large anti-Jewish demonstrations by the Cuban right in 1939. It then sailed north, and the Jewish passengers sought refuge in the United States. The passengers were rejected; at the time, they sailed so close to Florida's shore that they could see Miami. They cabled President Roosevelt, asking for asylum; he never replied. The ship turned back to Europe on June 6, 1939, and the passengers were mostly resettled in European countries deemed safe at the time—primarily Belgium, Holland, France, and Britain. All in Britain survived, except one killed in an air raid. Some of those resettled in continental Europe were relocated a second time after their safe havens were occupied by the Nazis; those in countries bordering Germany were not so lucky. In the end, more than 250 of those sent to Belgium, France, and Holland were killed in the Holocaust.[60]

Even today, "Europe is not so civilized," Bram maintains. "There's a thin line between the guys who danced after Srebrenica" and everyone else—a reference to the members of the Dutch peacekeeping force during the Bosnian war who withdrew from Srebrenica, clearing the way for the mass killing of Muslim citizens, and later celebrated the end of their mission with drinking and music on their way home to Holland. It's an odd reference for someone who blames Muslims for most of Europe's current problems, but Bram is not entirely unsympathetic to the plight of European Muslims. He even sees parallels to the persecution his family faced. But he does not believe it is Jews' role to defend the new victims.

"At this time in history, Jews can't be heroes. . . . I don't think in politics Jews have the luxury of choosing their allies." And he can't stand it when left-wing Jews stand up for Muslims. "When a rock is thrown at a Jewish synagogue or home, there is no public condemnation. When a little Molotov cocktail is thrown at a mosque in the middle of the night, we are the first to weep."[61]

Though they occupy opposite ends of the political spectrum, the Green Party's Zihni Özdil and Bram agree on one thing: there is a deep and potentially violent strain of racism lurking beneath the surface in Dutch society. "After Poland, the Netherlands is the country where the Holocaust was the most successful," Özdil reminds me. The local police went "Jew-hunting . . . they were so eager. Not SS officers, not Germans—Dutch police officers!" he exclaims.[62] Like Bram, he has no illusions; he is holding on to his second, Turkish, passport.

"If I were a Muslim in Europe at this moment, I'd be very uneasy," Bram admits. "If Europeans regain their manhood, it could be bad. It's the history of Europe to treat foreigners terribly. We Jews know that." And for that reason, he argues that "every Muslim should be happy Geert Wilders exists." If he didn't and "if someone else channeled these hateful feelings, it would be much worse," Bram says menacingly. "Wilders is civil. He is a democrat. He is not the new Hitler."[63]

THE NEW NORMAL

13

When the Right Turns Left— and the Left's Voters Go Right

IN THE POSTINDUSTRIAL FRENCH TOWN OF HAYANGE, THE MAYOR IS A thirty-eight-year-old gay vegetarian who used to be a left-wing activist with a group called Workers Struggle. Things have changed. Now the young mayor, Fabien Engelmann, fears the great replacement and sees halal meat as a harbinger of Islamization. Despite his own diet, Engelmann sees the absence of pork as truly worrying—"a conquest of France through its dishes." On September 30, 2016, he moved to evict the well-known charity association Secours Populaire from its local office, accusing it of being pro-migrant and in league with his old Communist Party comrades.[1]

According to Andrew Hussey, a British-born academic teaching in Paris, you can't understand the rise of the FN without looking at the demise of the French Communist Party, which was the continent's largest on this side of the Iron Curtain. As the party collapsed, its members and adherents were left rudderless. "Where do the people who were Communists go?" asks Hussey. The Socialist Party technocrats who graduated from the prestigious École nationale d'administration, "are so disconnected from ordinary people" that, even if their roots are in Marxist politics, old leftist voters shun them.[2] Distrustful of the establishment and searching for a state that protects them, many have turned to the FN.

Whether or not there is an ethnic (or culinary) great replacement happening in France, it is unquestionably happening in politics. In France's postindustrial north and east, uneducated working-class people, whom the left once saw as its base, now vote for Le Pen.[3] Whereas once the FN relied on the south, with its religious Catholics and many *pieds-noirs*, or settlers, who fled Algeria during the early 1960s, it now has an additional base. And unlike in the United States, where a new coalition of enfranchised immigrants, progressive millennials, and professional college-educated whites was almost enough to offset the Democratic party's losses in the Midwest, there hasn't been a similar phenomenon in France's economically ailing regions. In Britain, UKIP's former leader, Paul Nuttall, has for years focused the party's electoral strategy on winning votes in old Labor strongholds—but in France, where Marine Le Pen won over 50 percent across large swaths of the northeast, the Socialist Party's loss of the working-class heartlands is nearly complete.[4]

"I think you've got a big political question here about who looks after you; this is a very communist way of thinking. It's a paternalist way of thinking," argues Hussey. In his view, there are two large sections of French society that feel excluded: the white working class and Muslims. Because the left no longer speaks to these groups, they find new homes with Le Pen or extremists. "Nobody believes that the left is going to help them," Hussey argued. "The left is disconnected in Paris. . . . They don't live in the banlieues."[5]

With Marine Le Pen having discarded the image of fascists and skinheads, ex-leftists are now at the center of the FN's modernization campaign. After the economically conservative François Fillon's ill-fated victory in the 2016 Les Républicains primary, Le Pen tacked to the left. She clearly believed that there were more votes to be won from the old left than from Catholic conservatives.[6] Although Le Pen prefers to avoid the phrase "welfare state" ("That's a socialist concept," she insists), she has appealed directly to this yearning for a large, nurturing state that fights for the little guy and not the rich. "I defend fraternity—the idea that a developed country should be able to provide the poorest with the minimum needed to live with dignity as a human being. The French state no longer does that," she told me. "We're in a world today in which you either defend the interests of the people or the interests of the banks." And she has seen results. She pointed to the 2015 local elections in the northern Pas-de-Calais region. "It was socialist-communist for eighty years," she says. "I won 45 percent."[7] She took over 52 percent there in 2017.

In much the same way that Donald Trump swept the American Rust Belt states with high union and ex-union membership that have historically voted Democratic, she is appealing to traditionally left voters who resent the capitalist class but no longer see Socialists as representing their class interests. As Democrats in the United States and Socialists in Europe have joined the Davos class while paying lip service to the working class, the workers are looking elsewhere. The divide today, Le Pen argues, is no longer a left-versus-right ideological split. "The real rift," she maintains, "is between those who think the nation is the only structure capable of assuring their security and prosperity and defending their identity and those who have a postnational vision—who consider the nation-state an outdated concept, who want to get rid of borders and sovereignty."

For all these reasons, Le Pen had hoped to run against a socialist or a leftist candidate rather than someone on the right. This surprised some of her supporters, but her strategic logic was sound. "There is a porousness to the right-wing electorate that is important, and because the right-wing electorate is, I believe, freer than the left-wing electorate. It responds less to instructions, it does not obey orders, whereas voters on the left tend to obey orders more," she told me a year before the 2017 election.[8]

In a race against Fillon, had his campaign not foundered on corruption allegations, she would have been competing for center-right voters who tend to see their interests represented by the moderate right's candidate; she would have faced the same challenge as her father—the specter of a united front against the FN that would rally Socialists and Greens to the moderate right's candidate, as was the case when Chirac trounced the elder Le Pen in 2002. On the other hand, if she ever has the chance to face a Socialist candidate, especially an unpopular technocrat like François Hollande, Le Pen told me she believes she would get plenty of working-class votes and could lure a substantial share of the moderate right to her side because they would not obey instructions to defeat the FN and would be unlikely to rally behind a leftist. She didn't have a chance to test her theory, because Emmanuel Macron was no Hollande and managed to draw voters from both the center left and center right while the far left sat out the final round in large numbers. He beat Le Pen 66–34 percent, but Le Pen's prediction may have turned out to be more accurate had she faced a weaker and more explicitly Socialist candidate.

Her campaign manager, David Rachline, blames the left for its own losses. "It wasn't us who changed our position. We have always fought for the identity and sovereignty of our nation and against globalization!" he exclaims. "It's the left that has betrayed the working class. The

Communist Party, who, rather than defend French workers, have spent their lives defending foreign workers, immigrant workers." Where have their voters gone? he asks snidely. The Communist Party used to have five to six million voters. They now vote FN, he argues, "because we cannot at the same time defend French workers and be for globalization. One cannot at the same time defend French workers and support free competition. It's not possible," he insists. "What did those people do when they were in charge or when they supported the socialist governments? They produced all these treaties, they produced the European Union. Immigration, it was them; free-market Europe, it was them; redundant workers, it was them. So the French clearly saw who had betrayed the workers."

Rachline has his own history of ties to unsavory characters, whom he now disavows completely. As a teenage activist, he flirted with the ideas of Alain Soral, an openly anti-Semitic writer and political partner of the comedian Dieudonné, who is notorious for promoting anti-Semitic ideas among France's youth, especially in the impoverished banlieues. As a successful black man speaking truth to the establishment, he has become popular. Dieudonné is all business these days. He sells mugs and T-shirts. Soral, in addition to his anti-Semitic online videos, sells wine and survivalist kits online.[9] He even stages events for survivalists in the forest. But they are not purely a joke. According to Soral himself, their electoral list was financed by Iranians.[10] They received only 1–2 percent of the vote in metropolitan Paris, but in certain banlieues—in what is usually the electoral desert of the housing projects—they got many more votes. There, their anti-Jewish conspiracy theories found a sizable audience.

When I mention Soral, Rachline bristles and insists they have parted ways. "He has nothing to do with the Front National, that man." He admits that at the time, Soral had criticisms of Israeli foreign policy and an economic analysis that was "interesting," but as soon as he went beyond that, he had nothing to do with the FN. When he was in the party, leafleting and singing karaoke alongside Marine Le Pen,[11] Soral never strayed into anti-Semitism, insists Rachline. "We would have immediately distanced ourselves from him."[12]

For his part, Rachline, who has Jewish roots himself, dismisses any charges of residual racism or anti-Semitism stemming from his youthful indiscretions when he was a teenage FN party activist.[13] Like Le Pen, he touts the party as a defender of minorities. "It's done. . . . We showed that this was not true. And we demonstrate daily that on the contrary, we will be shields for these people—for French Jews, for French homosexuals," he promises. "Today these people know full well that they have nothing to fear from us, and even better, I think they know that we are the only ones to truly defend them," he adds.

Rachline believes that demonizing and sidelining the FN was the only way that the establishment remained in place for so long. "It was their only chance to try to discredit us." He is adamant that these days the FN would turn no one away.

Noncitizens are a different story. "We should expel all those who are not allowed to be here," he insists. "Delinquent offenders will be expelled, long-term unemployed foreigners will be expelled, and obviously, those who are clandestine, those who have no residence permit." I ask him, if the FN's dream of an EU collapse occurs, would the Poles and Hungarians be kicked out, too? He claims that they are rarely recidivist offenders and seldom long-term unemployed. But, he adds, "any additional immigration will be banned."

Rachline doesn't think the economic impact would be so bad. "We have the same rate of trade flows with Germany as one hundred years ago. So the European Union did nothing." On the contrary, he argues, "it destroyed three hundred thousand jobs in France."

I mention that sometimes the FN's tirades against free-market capitalism start to sound a lot like the far left. Rachline doesn't like the comparison. He admits that their analysis sometimes approaches that of the radical left or Greens but, he insists, the way politicians do, "the reality is that our proposals are diametrically opposed to theirs."[14]

His boss is less defensive. Her refusal to use the term "welfare state" aside, Le Pen does not seem embarrassed to sound like the old left. France's major parties and Macron's new one are all the same to her. "They all defend the interests of the great financial powers, the big multinationals, the banks," she tells me. "We defend the interests of the people."

She blames the EU for turning France into a rudderless, impotent country. "We no longer have territorial sovereignty, we no longer have economic sovereignty, we no longer have banking sovereignty, we no longer have monetary sovereignty. We cannot pursue an economic policy in a country if we do not have those choices." Running France, she says, is "like trying to drive a car that has no steering wheel, no gearbox, and no accelerator pedal." She affirms her commitment to a market economy, lest she be confused with the socialists she detests. But as with her endorsement of "fraternity" and a state that lets people live with dignity rather than using the term "welfare state," she argues that France must "admit that we are in a reconstruction economy. Our situation is as if we're emerging from a war." The state "must reinstate regulation and reestablish rules in the economy."[15]

Marine Le Pen's populism borrows more from the left than the right. "Even if she dresses it up with extreme right-wing semantics, it is the people against the elites. The little guy against the bosses," says Julien Aubert, the MP for Les Républicains from the southern region of Vaucluse, near Avignon.[16]

The FN's rising fortunes are partly a result of its shift from a purely nativist stance to a broader political platform, even before Marine took the reins. The elder Le Pen shifted to an antiglobalization and anti-EU position, adopting some rhetoric familiar to the French left. This new formulation, combined with a robust defense of the welfare state, had the power to draw in new constituencies.[17] If there is an ideological comparison to Le Pen's current program, it is Peronism in Argentina, Aubert maintains. "She has tried to combine the legacy of her far-right father with a left-wing program."[18]

Indeed, Le Pen is no fan of the financial industry; the book *Banksters* has a prominent place on the shelf behind her desk, and her critique of economic policy is perfectly calibrated to appeal to both young antiestablishment radicals and old leftists who resent fat cats at the commanding heights of the economy. She insists that socialists have forsaken whatever claim they may have had to representing the interests of workers. Sounding more like Bernie Sanders than Donald Trump, she argues, "The financialization of the economy has done us great harm; we want economic patriotism, we want an industrial policy that defends the strategic interests of France."[19]

Le Pen did not win this time, but if voters conclude that she or a future far-right leader has genuinely shed the FN's racist baggage and the centrist parties fail to address the grievances of Le Pen's angry supporters, then Aubert believes, in 2022, "there will be nothing left to oppose the National Front."[20]

IN DENMARK, THE DANISH PEOPLE'S PARTY HAS, LIKE MARINE LE PEN, tacked sharply to the left on social policy, starting to sound like trade unionists in their calls for a bigger public sector and more welfare.[21] As the unions and the Social Democrats have drifted apart, the DPP has exploited the rift. Historically, there was just one working-class party in Denmark. Now there are two.

The great unanswered question of Danish politics is whether the DPP will one day realign with the center left. The party has always been an awkward match with the welfare-cutting, free-market right, an alliance premised on a common understanding about immigration. Now that the Social Democrats have moved so far to the right on immigration issues, they appear, on paper, to make much more sense as allies, given their broad agreement on social policy issues and the preservation of the welfare state.

There is even a chance that, as their platforms drift closer on immigration, the DPP and Social Democrats could one day form a coalition. Apart from the symbolism and dramatic break from tradition, it's a coalition that would make more sense ideologically than the current arrangement. It is a "realistic scenario," says Johanne Schmidt-Nielsen, the far-left leader. "Luckily, they don't have enough." But the two parties together would not be far off. At a time when the distinctions between left and right on economic policy have been largely eroded, a party's policy on "immigration and refugees becomes the difference that makes the difference," she argues.[22]

The DPP's deputy leader, Søren Espersen, concedes that the Social Democrats are a better match for the DPP on economic issues. The question is whether they would ever accept the DPP in a coalition. "We have here a very good relationship on the personal side," he says. The DPP leader Kristian Thulesen Dahl and Mette Frederiksen, the Social Democratic leader, easily "could sit down and have a cup of tea."

After the last election, when coalition negotiations began, Prime Minister Lars Løkke Rasmussen reportedly wanted the DPP in the government. "I am not joking; we could practically have chosen any ministerial post that we wanted except the prime minister. But it was to be on his terms, and we didn't want that," Espersen explains.[23]

By staying outside a formal coalition, the DPP doesn't have to take responsibility for the government's unpopular policies. It enjoys the best of both worlds: the government needs it more than it needs them. It can influence popular policies and take credit for them while standing clear and washing its hands of others that might alienate its voters.

In the eyes of Mayor Thomas Gyldal Petersen, the DPP has engaged in a masterful circular form of politics that ensures the party's self-preservation by keeping voters' key grievances unresolved. It is similar to what Geert Wilders's PVV has done in Holland—a sort of political arbitrage.

"What the DPP does, besides saying that the immigrants are a problem, they support a right-wing government" that has in the past and is currently making it more difficult to invest in the social policies at the heart of the Danish welfare model. "They are cutting down on the education system, they are cutting down on the municipalities' budgets, they are cutting down every tool that we use to make social progress and integration work," argues Petersen.

The result is the indefinite extension of the social problems driving voters into the DPP's ranks, which means their pitch to voters continues to resonate. "They do two things: they talk about a problem, make it high politics, and on the other hand, they make it more and more difficult to solve the problem," argues the mayor. "That's smart, because that makes this problem eternal" and gives the DPP's voters an eternal reason to support them.[24]

Espersen is confident that at some point in the near future, Denmark's peculiar system of forming governments—illustrated for the outside world in the hit TV show *Borgen,* which features a smaller party's leader ascending to the premiership when others fail to form a government—will land his party in power.

After an election, the party leader chosen by the largest number of other parties goes to meet the queen and has the first shot at forming a government; it does not have to be the party with the most votes and often is not. It is a negative formula. "You don't have to have the majority for you. What it requires is you mustn't have a majority against you," Espersen explains. He is confident that if it gets to a third or fourth round, the DPP could form a government, especially if it becomes the largest party. And then support from the Social Democrats might materialize, or at least an absence of opposition.[25]

If the DPP and Social Democrats were to realign and govern together as a sort of left-nationalist bloc, it would be a watershed in Danish politics. It would require 90 out of 179 seats. Current polls put the two parties just short of that, and few Social Democrats will publicly discuss the possibility of such a coalition for fear of alienating supporters already upset at their rightward shift. The DPP is happy to entertain the possibility. "That would be an interesting situation," the MP Kenneth Kristensen Berth says. "It's not party policy that we can only cooperate with a Venstre government. We can also cooperate with the Social Democrats."[26]

The far right's courting of former left-wingers isn't limited to Scandinavia and postindustrial France. The populist right in Britain is now openly courting disgruntled working-class voters who for years watched the Labour Party transform into a staunchly urban middle-class party less interested in the views of the working poor, who are these days often dismissed by leftists as uncultured relatives too embarrassing to invite to dinner.[27]

TWELVE YEARS BEFORE BRITAIN'S 2016 REFERENDUM ON EU MEMBERSHIP, a writer named Michael Collins warned of a protest vote coming from "working-class whites in poor areas who believe they have been neglected and ghettoized." He lashed out at "the pundits who dismiss these concerns as part of populism's manifesto." He lamented the way that middle-class progressives, who had once fought in the name of the working class, now derided them as chavs—a term comparable to the American epithet "white trash"—who "loved Gucci; loathed the Euro" and were "racist, xenophobic, thick, illiterate, parochial" types who "survived on the distant memory of winning one world cup and two world wars and were still tuning in to the ailing soap that is the House of Windsor." Collins's rage at this caricature prompted him to write a book about his working-class childhood in South London that has the tone of an elegy. "All they represent and hold dear was reportedly redundant in modern, multicultural Britain. It was dead."[28]

Reviews of the book seemed to confirm his thesis—class prejudice among media elites was rampant—whether the reviewers were black or white. Roy Kerridge mocked the book in the conservative magazine the *Spectator.* The black broadcaster Mike Phillips, writing in the *Guardian,* accused Collins's social history of his family and neighborhood of stoking up "a self-pitying and half-hidden resentment," while comparing it to Enoch Powell's rhetoric and arguing that the book "appeals to the most destructive form of nostalgia." Only the *Telegraph* was vaguely positive, offering some faint praise for the book: "To the extent that it forces us to confront our 'acceptable' prejudices, it is most welcome."[29]

Collins isn't the only writer to point out that class hatred plagued the left and right. The *Guardian* columnist Owen Jones devoted a book, *Chavs*, to the phenomenon. It has become an "integral, respectable part of modern British culture," he wrote, to openly express contempt for the white working class on the grounds that "they were themselves a bunch of racist bigots."[30] Jones, a fixture on the far left, was equally scathing toward lefty journalists who felt no qualms bashing lower-class whites as chavs.

"It would be nice to dismiss chav-hate as a fringe psychosis confined to ranting right-wing columnists," he wrote, but it had also become a "liberal bigotry" allowing people who fancy themselves as progressives to "accept that massive discrimination against ethnic minority groups explains issues like unemployment and poverty and even violence," while refusing to "believe white working-class people have such excuses." He pointed to minorities slamming working-class whites by claiming "we seize opportunities these slobs don't want."[31]

He blamed the myopia of liberal multiculturalism and a fixation on racism that "understood inequality purely through the prism of race." The effect has been to turn the white working-class into another minority group, encouraging them "to develop similar notions of ethnic pride, and to build an identity based on race so as to gain acceptance in multicultural society." And this new racial group didn't have a place in the new multicultural order.[32] It was only a matter of time before some enterprising politician sought to create one. As Labour support in working-class areas faded, the British National Party (BNP) emerged and presented itself as the white workingman's alternative.

Mark Simpson, a writer better known for coining the term "metrosexual," was fed up with Collins's poor reception. When Collins was accused of being "an intellectual outrider for the BNP" on the radio, he fumed that "all those do-gooding right-on middle-class types were the real recruiting sergeants for the BNP." In precisely the way that Karen Stenner described latent authoritarians being provoked into intolerance, he argued in one of the few positive reviews that "by telling the white working class that anyone or anything that acknowledged they even existed was 'racist' they immunized them to the charge of 'racism' and pushed them into the hands of a straightforwardly racist party."[33] The BNP has now faded from the scene, but its emergence as an electoral force between 2000 and 2010 was a sign of things to come.

Daniel Trilling, who wrote the definitive book on the BNP's rise, noted how the East London area of Barking "in a short space of time changed from a settled, mainly white community to an ethnic mix that began to resemble the rest of London." The local Labour Party MP saw the writing on the wall in the late 1990s, warning that ignoring working-class voters to appeal to Middle England would provoke a backlash.[34] Tony Blair's New Labour Party wasn't focused on helping the working class; if anything, they encouraged escaping it.[35]

Between 2002 and 2010, the BNP posted impressive scores in local elections, winning thirty-three local council seats across the country in 2006 with an average of 19 percent of the vote. UKIP, a "BNP in blazers," as some called it, started to steal its thunder after 2010, and by the time of the Brexit referendum in 2016, had all but eclipsed them.[36]

The rest of Britain, and perhaps some of the reviewers who panned Collins's prophetic book, seemed to finally notice in the early hours of the morning on June 24, 2016.

Brexit should have been the left's wildest dream—a genuine mass working-class revolt against Westminster elites, except the revolt was directed at an idea that the new left held dear. The problem was that the revolutionary class of Marxist dreams had parted from the vanguard. "In an almost comical reflection of the sacred lefty belief that any worthwhile political movement will necessarily be built around the workers," the writer John Harris observed, "the foundation of the Brexit coalition is what used to be called the proletariat, . . . even if some of their loudest complaints are triggering no end of anxiety among bien-pensant types, and causing Labour a great deal of apprehension."[37]

Amid all the shock and disbelief at the *Guardian,* Harris explained the outcome to a readership that had almost unanimously voted to remain. He described visits to rural Lincolnshire where UKIP leader Nigel Farage "could pitch up and do back-to-back public meetings to rapturous crowds." People were angry about lack of housing, a lousy labor market, and sanctimonious pitches from politicians at election time—pitches that amounted, in Harris's view, to the "suggestion that the only thing Westminster can offer working-class people is a specious chance of not being working class anymore." A poor woman on the fringes of Manchester put it succinctly. "If you've got money, you vote in. . . . If you haven't got money, you vote out."[38]

UKIP was started as a party with a singular focus on leaving the EU. Yet in an era of populist backlash, it has "almost by accident, stumbled across this potent new social division and given it a voice." Nigel Farage, the party's long-serving leader, vowed that one day UKIP would have more ex-Labour supporters than Tories, and its post-Brexit leader, Paul Nuttall, made courting the old left his explicit strategy.[39]

The media elite, much like those who panned Collins's book, had missed this entirely. They were so busy denouncing UKIP and the right as reactionaries that they missed the political lesson: it was their former base that had fueled UKIP's rise and helped the leave vote win. The same was true of left-wing parties and media organizations across Europe. By denouncing their own former voters for holding certain unsavory views rather than engaging and seeking to understand their fears, they lost the political battle. "The alienation of the people charged with documenting the national mood from the people who actually define it is one of the ruptures that has led to this moment. . . . The press and television are the focus of as much resentment as politics," wrote Harris in the pages of a paper that was as guilty as any.[40]

Harris couldn't believe Labour MPs' shock; "How did they not know?" he marveled. Well-paid media and finance professionals in London were immune from competition from Polish plumbers, but in Sunderland and Essex, that wasn't the case. There was no doubt a heavy dose of outright xenophobia and bigotry behind the vote, as the heinous attacks on Poles and other immigrants in the weeks after Brexit proved, but there was also a rational economic protest. Even if the referendum was more about giving the political establishment a black eye, the numbers should have been a warning. During the 1990s and just after 2000, about 60,000 migrants came to Britain from Europe each year. Between 2004 and 2012, it was 170,000 per year. By 2011, there were 654,000 Poles living in the UK.[41]

There was also an element of the old and angry outvoting the young and optimistic—and taking a momentous decision that would shape a world many of them would not live to see. Youth resentment peaked the week after the vote, and, for Harris, their complaint echoed Orwell's description of Britain as "a family in which the young are generally thwarted and most of the power is in the hands of irresponsible uncles and bedridden aunts." But the fact is there were many such forgotten distant relatives hiding in the countryside.[42]

It was those who left for the suburbs of Essex and Kent who helped Brexit win, the last group "that the chattering classes are happy to hear mocked and attacked." They now live in "those suburbs where the fluttered folk of the white flight settled," amid bungalows with "half-finished walls and slabs of stacked paving, awaiting the DIY mood of the next Bank Holiday." Even among the young who can't remember where their families came from, nostalgia reigns. Collins finds young men "searching for an identity or clinging to a past they never knew," who speak with an exaggerated cockney. These are people who fear the crime of the city might reach their suburbs. They don't want asylum seekers, and they are united in "a desire to protect themselves from further disruption."[43]

As Harris argued the week before the referendum was held, "for millions of people, the word 'immigration' is reducible to yet another seismic change no one thought to ask them about, or even explain." Like the Dutch and Danish voters who flocked to the far-right, there was a sense that massive change was under way without any sort of consultation.

Both Collins's book and Harris's *Guardian* articles had accurately foreseen the result. Much like the American punditocracy living inside its Washington, DC, beltway bubble that dismissed Trump's chances of winning the primaries, most of the British media elite (apart from Brexit cheerleaders at the *Telegraph*) were not looking far beyond the M25. Those who had been watching carefully from beyond the capitals were well aware that both Brexit and a Trump nomination were likely.

One exception among London journalists was David Goodhart, writing in the *Financial Times,* who saw the referendum as "an early-21st-century 'peasants' revolt'"[44] of those left behind. It was also a clash between the millennial identity of achievers and those clinging to a more nostalgic identity, like Collins's old mates from Southwark who felt they had been written out of history, people who still live a few miles from where they were born, for whom identity is more tribal and geographic.

Resentment of new arrivals and the perception that they must compete with outsiders for their paltry share of diminishing benefits was making working-class Brits angry. And the strategy that propelled the welfare nationalists of Denmark and France, calling for more social benefits—but for us, not them—has become a rallying cry far beyond Europe.

14

Xenophobia Beyond
Black and White

MARY LOUW ISN'T YOUR TYPICAL XENOPHOBE. SHE VOLUNTEERS AT A
school in a poor neighborhood where the children are varying shades of
brown; she's openly lesbian, was once a member of the Young Communist League, and quotes liberally from Marxist-Leninist doctrine. She
doesn't hate Muslims, and she isn't white; she isn't even European.

Xenophobia is not just a matter of wealthy white Europeans slamming their doors in the face of poor brown Muslims fleeing war and
tyranny; it is a universal phenomenon that can arise anywhere where
economic angst, frustrated expectations, and the need for a convenient
scapegoat converge. And in South Africa, a young constitutional democracy modeled on the liberal laws of Canada and Germany, the situation
has become acute. South Africa's pattern of resentful native-born citizens
mobilizing against fellow Africans from neighboring countries is almost
identical to what is happening in Europe, but it tends to go unnoticed in
the international press because it is far away—and both the victims and
the perpetrators are black.

The grievances of South African blacks angry about immigration
today are remarkably similar to those among working-class Europeans.
Poor London East Enders after World War II voiced the same discontent. As the British writer David Goodhart recounts, "No sooner had
the working class there come into its inheritance after the sacrifice of the
war years than it was snatched away by the arrival of people who had had
little to do with that story." After years of being kept below stairs and
laying down their lives for Queen and country, there was a sense that the

downtrodden working class had finally been accepted as full members of society and were owed a debt. To them, the arrival of immigrants—and the competition they brought to the lower end of the labor market—amounted to the state taking back the gift it had granted.[1]

For South Africa's majority, finally granted freedom after decades of oppression, the influx of better-educated foreigners was a similar shock. The native-born had an understandable sense of entitlement to redress from the state after forty-six years of apartheid rule and many more of colonialism before. For newly arrived skilled immigrants from countries like the Democratic Republic of the Congo and Somalia, there was no such expectation, and they were willing to work or sell goods for far less than native South Africans would. Like the East Enders of the 1950s, black South Africans—at last recognized as full citizens of their own country—felt that their hard-fought inheritance was being snatched away.

After the democratic transition in 1994, "I was one of the people who was very much optimistic about the change in the country," Louw recalls. It was a moment of hope, "knowing that apartheid will come to an end. We will be free as black people," she tells me, perched on a plastic chair in an elementary school parking lot as trains rattle past a nearby station and the smell of grilled meat wafts from the platform. Two decades later, she is outraged by the foreigners in her midst, and she blames South Africa's most revered icon, Nelson Mandela, for opening the doors.

Today, Louw's priority is kicking foreigners out of her neighborhood. She blames them for all of inner-city Johannesburg's crime. "They are everywhere," complains Louw. She claims they steal cell phones and citizens' identity cards. "There is no proper control over them, and that leads to the anger. . . . We feel they should rather leave," she tells me. "We are slaves of this democracy, not recipients," she wrote in a recent message to a WhatsApp group of similarly minded friends.[2] South African citizens are "sweating day and night for the future of our own children, yet the foreign rapists of our freedom and economy seems to be the only beneficiaries," she thundered.

Louw comes from a political family. When she was in high school, she started a student league of the South African Communist Party, "trying to educate and teach my fellow students about Marxist and Leninist theory. Just in-depth knowledge on Karl Marx and Che Guevara," she tells me matter-of-factly.[3]

These days, she remains active in local politics. She lives in Hillbrow, once a student neighborhood and now known mostly for its soaring crime rate. She is active in the grassroots leadership of the Communist Party. The frustrations of South Africans like Louw who expected great things only to find themselves politically free but economically trapped are widespread. Politicians made promises of homes and jobs that went unfulfilled; instead, they found themselves living surrounded by foreigners from elsewhere in Africa.

South Africa tends to remain off the radar when it comes to debates about refugees and immigration. It shouldn't be.

For the past decade, it has had one of the highest rates of asylum applicants in the world. Migration is not a new phenomenon in South Africa; it has been a cornerstone of the economy for over a century. During the apartheid era, migration was widespread, but it was strictly regulated and used as a means of bringing cheap labor to the gold, diamond, and platinum mines. Thousands of workers from neighboring countries came south to toil underground.

Since the end of apartheid in 1994, the Rainbow Nation has become a destination for refugees fleeing wars across the continent or seeking a better life. With genocide in Rwanda, war in the Democratic Republic of the Congo, and the deterioration of neighboring Zimbabwe, South Africa received a flood of refugees and migrants from across the continent. As was the case in Britain when EU freedom of movement went into effect, the country received far more people than it expected. Many of them are better educated than South Africans and quickly find jobs as teachers, waiters, and engineers. Car guards, who hustle for loose change in exchange for keeping an eye on parked cars, often hold advanced degrees from universities in war-torn nations like Congo or Somalia.

In 1996, South Africa produced a startlingly liberal constitution that entitled foreigners and their children to almost all the same rights enjoyed by citizens, apart from voting and running for political office. But there was a countervailing force in immigration policy. In the immediate aftermath of the 1994 transition to democracy, Nelson Mandela appointed his rival Mangosuthu Buthelezi as the head of the Home Affairs department.[4]

In 1999, Buthelezi called on "good patriots" to report illegal immigrants to the authorities and argued publicly that the much-touted post-apartheid reconstruction and development plan would be a failure if scarce resources had to be shared with foreigners.[5] It was a sign of things to come.

South Africa was a beacon for both refugees and economic migrants across the continent due to its comparatively healthy economy and new-found stability, but the new immigration policy didn't provide economic migrants with a legal route to work. As a result, "lesser-skilled economic migrants turned to the asylum system alongside genuine asylum seekers, capitalizing on the minimal barriers to entry and the work entitlement granted to asylum applicants while their claims are being processed." The surge in applications overwhelmed the bureaucracy and had the perverse effect of denying the claims of genuine refugees, who were classified as economic migrants by officials struggling to disqualify people as fast as they could.[6]

South Africa is unique among African countries in that it doesn't require refugees to live in camps; it allows them to move into communities, work, and send their children to school. Setting up the processing of claims is expensive but far cheaper than building camps and providing for their residents. Like European governments in the early days of guest workers, South Africa never anticipated the challenges of integrating large numbers of foreigners who would be living and working alongside locals.[7]

Then the numbers began to balloon. While the government's data is often incomplete, it is clear that between 2006 and 2011, South Africa received more asylum applications than almost any country in the world. In 2008, there were more than 200,000 requests, and in 2009, it peaked at over 340,000 filed claims.[8] By 2015, South Africa was second only to Germany—after the massive influx of Syrians—in the number of unresolved claims.[9]

Part of the reason was the implosion of neighboring Zimbabwe. After years of mismanagement and cronyism under president-for-life Robert Mugabe, the economy had by 2006 spiraled into hyperinflation and the finance ministry was racing to add zeros to the banknotes. As Mugabe's government began to crack down harder on the political opposition, inflation exceeded 6,000 percent annually. The denominations ascended to the absurd—bills worth $100 trillion were printed—before citizens reverted to using US dollars and South African rands.[10] Several million Zimbabweans fled south to their wealthier neighbor. The strain on South Africa was palpable.

IN THE 2009 OSCAR-NOMINATED SCI-FI FILM *District 9*, LOCAL RESIDENTS go to war against giant armored alien prawns who descend upon South Africa's cities. American audiences ate up the human-versus-alien violence and the high-tech weaponry on display. Some reviewers looking for a political message saw the heavily armed police vehicles fighting the aliens as an allegory for apartheid. It wasn't; it was quite literal.

The scenes at the beginning of the film featuring poor local residents who advocate killing "them," burning their businesses, and kicking them out were based on actual footage from the year before in which real people rather than actors were talking about the immigrants in their communities—not extraterrestrial crustaceans.

The film came out one year after mobs of South Africans went on the rampage, torching shops owned by immigrants, burning one man alive. Sixty people were killed, one hundred thousand were displaced, and thirty thousand homes were destroyed.[11] The violence did not let up; in 2010, a string of murders of Somali and Ethiopian shopkeepers—often preceded by threatening letters—forced many to close down or leave town. In Khayelitsha, the sprawling shantytown outside of Cape Town, twenty-two Somalis were murdered in just three months. In 2013, a Mozambican taxi driver died after being tied and dragged behind a police van. And in Port Elizabeth, cell phone footage emerged of a twenty-five-year-old Somali being stoned to death while trying to protect the goods in his looted shop. That year, the Somali Community Board estimated that one thousand of their countrymen had been murdered in South Africa since 2004.[12]

The award-winning South African writer Jonny Steinberg devoted an entire book to the life story of a Somali refugee, Asad Abdullahi, who had fled war in Mogadishu as a child and made his way on a treacherous journey through the Horn of Africa to Kenya and, eventually, after thirteen years on the move, to Cape Town. After nine years in South Africa and the killing of several of his friends and family members, he found himself applying for asylum again—in the United States—on the grounds that South Africa was too dangerous.[13] The story is all too common, but most are not as lucky as Abdullahi; they are not able to flee to safety a second time.

In April 2015, the South African government launched Operation Fiela (meaning "to sweep clean") with the ostensible goal of reducing crime.[14] In practice, it turned into a crackdown on immigrants, leading to mass arrests, detention camps, and deportations. The government boasted that nearly four thousand foreign nationals were arrested in May and sent to the Lindela Repatriation Centre, an immigration prison outside Johannesburg. Human rights lawyers denounced the roundup as "a show of institutional xenophobia."[15]

As much as government officials have sought to deny the existence of widespread xenophobia or dismiss it as the unfortunate work of criminals, surveys of the South African population show deep-rooted suspicion and dislike of foreigners even though the sort of terror-related fears that stoke hostility to foreigners in Europe and the US are completely absent in South Africa. Both crime and persistent poverty are huge problems, but they do not explain some brow-raising statistics: two-thirds of the population believe that refugees don't deserve police or legal protection, over half of South Africans surveyed want to deport all migrants not contributing to the economy, and one in four would prefer to expel all foreigners. When asked to explain the causes of the pogroms that raged across the country in May 2008, more than 60 percent of respondents blamed migrants for taking jobs from South Africans or causing crime. More than half either supported the violence against foreigners or were indifferent.[16]

Baron Mukeba, a Congolese man with the build of a fullback, was left for dead in early 2015 when he was attacked with an ax to the head near the mining town of Rustenberg, two hours north of Johannesburg. "They can attack you easily," he says with a shrug. "The things that happen at night . . . it's the law of the jungle," Mukeba told me, speaking French over a drink in a small Ethiopian-run bar near his home in Johannesburg.

It took him fifteen days to recover, and his attackers were never caught. "The police didn't even try. They don't give a damn. They didn't even do an investigation. . . . There wasn't even a trial," he recalls. After being released from the hospital, he fled. Faced with this kind of terror, immigrants have turned inward for security. The Johannesburg neighborhood of Yeoville, perched on a hill overlooking the city, used to be almost exclusively Jewish. These days, it is full of Congolese and Ethiopian restaurants—a safe zone. South African taxi drivers and xenophobic gangs are afraid to go there, something that makes local residents happy. "It's not easy to come here and attack a foreigner. It has become a stronghold," Mukeba tells me.

The sort of impunity Mukeba describes is rampant. Mukeba's friend Prince Abenge Médard, a fiery speaker who works with the Congolese opposition in exile and various immigrant groups in Johannesburg, says that francophone immigrants have it worse than others. "They are hostile to all the foreigners," he says of South Africans, but "francophones are worse because they are really foreign. . . . To have a linguistic connection is already something. From the start, we are foreign."

He is convinced that xenophobia has been deeply inculcated into most South Africans and is being directed from above. He doesn't hesitate to make analogies to Europe, but he insists that there is one crucial difference. "In Europe, it's from the bottom up," Médard argues. "The leaders feel the pressure of the people against foreigners, and they're reacting to it. Here, it's top down." He blames the ruling party—or segments within it—for spearheading violence or condoning it. Only after the dust settles do they hypocritically speak out, like arsonists masquerading as firemen. "They organize marches after having killed 350 people," he scoffs.[17]

Marc Gbaffou, the head of the African Diaspora Forum, an immigrant lobby group headquartered in the stronghold of Yeoville, also claims that the green light for anti-immigrant violence comes from above. "Many close to the pinnacle of power have expressed openly xenophobic views," he points out. President Jacob Zuma's son declared publicly that foreigners are a ticking time bomb and could take over the country.[18] "When you tell someone who is not educated that, they take it seriously," Médard argues. "People need to be conscious that we are in a hostile country."[19]

Immigrants in South Africa, and especially shopkeepers, have come to be known as walking ATMs. It is not because they are particularly rich but because South African laws make it difficult for immigrants to legally acquire weapons and for those without a longtime fixed address to obtain a bank account. As a result, they are known to often carry large amounts of cash and to lack the ability to defend themselves.[20]

For many of the diaspora forum's members, the South African reality they experienced upon arrival was very different from the rosy image they had of "the most open and welcoming country on the African continent." Soon after moving there, Gbaffou laments, "people start losing the image of South Africa that we all believe in."[21]

DESPITE MARY LOUW'S UPBRINGING IN COMMUNIST PARTY CIRCLES, foreigners were never part of the democratic South Africa she dreamed of. As we sit in the school parking lot, she vents. Louw complains that she routinely sees foreigners waiting in line at the social security office for food grants, foster care, or child support. "They benefit more," she says. The government must "recognize us before they even think of recognizing foreigners."

In late 2016, Louw started a lobbying group, organized on WhatsApp, called "Proudly SA Citizens." The message espoused by its members is not subtle, and the accompanying texts leave little to be imagined. The chats feature calls to evict foreign families from their homes alongside emojis, including a running black man, Nigerian and Zimbabwean flags, knives, guns, and swords.[22]

Louw believes that all violence in inner-city Johannesburg is the fault of immigrants, and she insists that locals are the only victims, even if crime statistics show that plenty of robberies and murders are committed by South African citizens.[23]

But as in many European countries where immigrants have come to be seen as competitors, the real lightning rod is jobs. The anger of poor South Africans is not directed at Japanese or Italian businessmen; it is fellow black Africans competing for the same jobs who are the targets of their xenophobic rage. Louw lost her job as a third-grade teacher, as she tells it, because Zimbabwean colleagues lied to her boss and alleged that she'd corporally punished a student—an offense in South African schools. She was unemployed when we met and had trouble returning my calls until a friend offered her a five-rand (thirty-five-cent) top-up for her cell phone. "If you go to many South Africans who are presently unemployed, they all sing the same song. 'I lost my job. A Zimbabwean lied about me to my boss,' or 'A Mozambican lied about me to my boss, and I ended up losing my job.'" These foreigners are also "criminals," Louw insists. "They are pushing us out of jobs."[24]

For a country that prides itself on having the world's most liberal constitution—guaranteeing housing, health care, and education—the spectacle of angry locals attacking foreigners and burning down immigrant-owned shops does not look good. But political leaders, sensing that defending the rights of foreigners won't win them any votes, have largely remained silent.

AS IN EUROPE AND THE UNITED STATES, NOSTALGIA IS A CENTERPIECE of anti-immigration rhetoric in poor South African communities. "It's always an image of how things were. How things used to be. How things could be," says Ingrid Palmary, a professor at the University of the Witwatersrand in Johannesburg. What is different and deeply ironic is that some of it is yearning for a time during the apartheid era.[25] She interviewed members of the Greater Gauteng Business Forum, a grandly titled group that brought together angry locals who wanted to push foreigners out of Johannesburg's townships.[26]

Their complaints echo Louw's grievances, coated with the language of reconciliation that pervades South African politics. "We had to battle for so many years against apartheid. . . . Now we are in the process of rebuilding the country to trust each other, to get to know each other, get to tolerate each other, to live with each other . . . to heal, and without any disturbance from them," said one member.

The business forum went to great lengths to push "them" out. Threatening letters were sent to foreign-owned shops but always with a quasi-legalistic tone.[27] There was no shame in the threat; those who wrote listed their names and phone numbers. Looters often made a point of getting their faces on TV when camera crews came. The business forum unapologetically recounted how they would raid immigrant-owned shops to carry out searches for weapons with no sense that vigilantism was illegal.

Ultimately, they were demanding rights for themselves that they believe foreigners should not be entitled to. "South Africa has got freedom, that freedom is not yours, it is a South African freedom," another member of the forum told Palmary.[28]

Just like Europe's purveyors of white identity politics, who warn of Muslim usurpers, many black South Africans regard foreigners from elsewhere in Africa as new colonizers, the vanguard of a great replacement that prevents South Africans from enjoying the fruits of their hard-won liberty.

The South African government was initially shocked by the various pogroms. Worried that it might be accused of failing to fulfill its international human rights obligations, officials soon settled on crime as a convenient explanation. If the violence was simply the work of common criminals, there were no fundamental societal ills to address. This approach has deep roots. During the post-apartheid Truth and Reconciliation Commission, the key factor determining whether someone could request amnesty was if his violence had been politically motivated violence or simply a "crime." It was a moral line in the sand.[29]

Many murderers walked free after confessing apartheid-era transgressions and requesting amnesty; those who were deemed common criminals without a political motive ended up in prison. In leaders' responses—and dismissals—of xenophobic pogroms today, there is an echo of this moral distinction. In 2010, the minister of police called attacks on foreigners "just crime." Five years later, President Zuma insisted that most South Africans weren't xenophobes and the violence was driven by "criminal elements."[30] The implication was that crime is an unfortunate nuisance but ultimately something that can simply be written off.

Denial is rampant, even among people who see themselves as progressives and liberals. At a conference in late 2015 that assembled various left-leaning NGOs and academics devoted to helping immigrants, a trade union leader took the floor and gave a rousing speech about how black South Africans couldn't possibly be blamed for hateful violence, because they had always lived happily alongside Mozambican neighbors. Prince Abenge Médard, the Congolese activist, was sitting at the table next to him. Infuriated, he rose to show the union leader pictures of the dead and mutilated bodies of slain immigrants on his cell phone.

For black South Africans who have joined the middle classes, the places where these clashes are occurring—on the edges of townships and in shantytowns—are far away from the world they now inhabit. Like the well-meaning European progressives who never lived in immigrant neighborhoods and were blissfully unaware that rapid immigration sometimes leads to resentment and violence, many South Africans who have moved up the economic ladder refuse to believe that there is a problem.

In much the same way that the European right complains about political correctness and the erosion of free speech, Louw believes the South African constitution is too liberal when it comes to foreigners and is not living up to its promise to its own citizens. Louw, like the Dutch AZC-Alert activists protesting asylum seeker housing in their neighborhoods, insists that her speech is being silenced. "We have a democracy and . . . we have all this beautiful rosy constitution that says you have the right to freedom of expression and freedom of speech and freedom of association."

But, she is adamant, "we are deprived of that. If you don't want to associate with foreign nationals, you are being labeled as xenophobic."[31] She also rejects the idea of hate crimes legislation, which would undoubtedly criminalize some of her own statements.

Legal scholars across the world point to the South African constitution as a model document. On the streets of Johannesburg, and at the grassroots level of the ruling party, there is a very different view. "As rosy as it might look in theory," Louw told me, "in practice, it's not working for us."[32] It's a remarkably similar refrain to Samuel and Pascal, the French activists opposing refugees in Calais, who complained of foreigners being treated better than native French.[33]

Louw sees absolutely no problem with Germans and other Europeans wanting to send Syrian refugees home and insists that the same must happen in South Africa, echoing the refrain of the European right, which routinely portrays young male refugees as cowards and deserters for failing to stay behind and fight against Assad, Hezbollah, the Russians, and ISIS. "Why go and seek refuge in another country?" Louw asks. A true fighter, she insists, "it's one who lays down his life, her life for their people, right in the midst of where those things are happening." If gays were under attack in South Africa, Louw says, she would stay and fight rather than become a refugee. "I feel I have to fight for my fellow homosexual people; I will never run to another country."

For many observers with a knowledge of South African history, the violence against immigrants from African nations is all the more alarming because many of the victims come from neighboring countries like Zimbabwe and Mozambique that sheltered South Africa's liberation movement leaders during their decades in exile. Louw has no time for this argument. She says she owes no debt to the nations that sheltered exiled leaders. Her own brother was killed by the notorious apartheid-era police. "There are South Africans who fought with stones. . . . If my family died here and they refused to go into exile, why should I owe my loyalty to the central African countries? Mandela and his family owes it . . . but not my family. They fought against the same system, but they did it right here at home."[34]

Louw is preparing for a new battle, and she is not ashamed to advocate forced removal. "Presently, the government is refusing to listen to us," she says. "The only way for the government to listen, it's through violence."

A group of schoolchildren stroll past on their way to the train station, and two men living in wooden huts emerge from the small structures with laundry hanging in the windows as ash blows from a barbecue on the nearby platform. Children duck the fence and return to school with Styrofoam containers filled with grilled meat. A two-wheel trailer inscribed with the words *Thuleni Burial Society* lies in a corner under shade, next to an empty parking spot.

"This is what we are going to do," Louw tells me. She will apply for a protest permit and make sure her group is accompanied by police. "Wherever you are going to target those people, it mustn't be regarded as an unlawful picket or an unlawful march," she explains methodically.

"I believe we should actually drive them out. It's the only way," she tells me calmly. "When I say drive them out, we should actually use force. Not force in terms of burning their shops but telling them we are kindly asking them to leave." That polite request, she explains, should be backed by the threat of violence. Louw has no qualms brandishing weapons outside of immigrants' homes until they leave the country if that's what it takes.[35]

I ask if that could lead to injuries or deaths. "I think it's worth the risk. How else are we going to do it?" she deadpans. So what if people die? I ask. "It shouldn't be the price to pay, but maybe it's the only way that it will shake the government," she tells me. Sounding every bit the populist, she tells me they need to "come down and listen to the people."

Even when Louw acknowledges that plenty of foreigners work hard and don't commit crimes, she still demands their expulsion. In her view, the innocent are "silent criminals," because they will have children who might commit crimes one day or take South African citizens' jobs. "They are even more dangerous than the one who openly shows he's a criminal," she tells me.[36]

Five thousand miles from France, and without a hint of hatred toward Muslims, Louw's logic echoes the European backlash after the Brussels bombings of March 2016 and the frightening vision of *Charlie Hebdo*'s very large iceberg, where even the innocent are guilty when any one of their kind commits an offense.

South Africa is far from Europe and the Middle East, and fear of Islam is not the animating force behind the populist backlash there, but the pattern of resentful native-born citizens mobilizing against foreigners and politicians responding to their rage is very similar to what is happening in Europe. South Africa's experience should serve as a warning that the virus of xenophobic violence lurks beneath the surface in all liberal democracies. Jealousy, resentment of competition, and a refusal to share the fruits of a liberal state with outsiders is a scourge that can emerge in any society, even when religious difference or fear of terrorism are not the catalysts.

There has not yet been an explicit politically endorsed backlash against immigrants in South Africa. For all the violence at the local level, no national political party has openly campaigned on a platform of kicking foreigners out.[37] But as the ruling ANC loses ground to the opposition parties, or as others see that the issue is a sure way to win votes, a movement like France's FN or Denmark's DPP could one day emerge.

If other parties in South Africa start blaming the ruling ANC for failing to curb illegal immigration or failing to tackle unemployment, the ruling party could crack down on foreigners to regain lost power.[38] The process may have already begun.

In December 2016, Johannesburg's mayor, Herman Mashaba, from the opposition Democratic Alliance, declared that all illegal immigrants should leave the city. "I want them to understand that they are criminals," Mashaba announced a few months after ousting the ANC from city hall. "They are holding our country to ransom and I am going to be the last South African to allow it." He promised to contact foreign embassies to give notice that their citizens were in South Africa illegally.[39]

Louw was thrilled, despite being a staunch ANC supporter. Seeing police arrest dozens of foreigners made her "fall in love with this city Johannesburg," she wrote giddily to the anti-immigrant WhatsApp group. "Herman Mashaba has won my hearts admiration by refusing to baby sit these alliens [sic]. He has proven . . . that he is committed to drive them out of this city," she gushed. "Finally someone commits to do something instead of labeling us as xenophobic. I salute the mayor's initiative."[40]

Foreigners in Louw's view do not deserve the rights enshrined in the constitution, such as the freedom of expression she holds so dear herself. In another message to the group, she alerted her friends that immigrants were protesting at the mayor's office and urged all members to "put an end to their madness, . . . otherwise these people will take over our country by force." She went on to call for sit-ins at asylum reception centers and even temporary tent cities built to shelter immigrants already driven from their homes. Like the PEGIDA and AZC-Alert protesters in Holland, their goal is to find foreigners and intimidate them.

When politicians in Africa's richest country condone anti-immigrant violence or use xenophobic rhetoric toward refugees from poorer nations, it does not receive the same scrutiny as the pronouncements of neo-Nazis and Islamophobes in Europe. Seen through a Eurocentric lens, where xenophobes must be white and the oppressed immigrants dark-skinned, it doesn't compute. But the problem, and the threat to the country's liberal constitutional order, is just as grave.

A savvy political organizer, Louw drew a lesson for her beloved ANC from Mayor Mashaba's surprise move. "If we fail to deliver, those who previously had confidence in us will seek assistance from the opposition parties and we cannot blame them," she wrote. "If we continue to babysit and nurse foreigners in our midst, on the basis that they kept our leaders in exile, someone else will deliver with deportation that will win the admiration of many SA citizens. . . . Someone will take over parliament as a brand new party to run the country come 2019."[41]

Mary Louw is not a minister or a mayor, and her outraged missives and political commentary are read by just a handful of other angry inner-city residents at the lower rungs of the ANC's party structure, but her xenophobic views are not unique; they are widely shared. And if one day, the party follows her advice, her fantasy of expelling all foreigners could come true.

15

Willkommenskultur vs. Guantánamo

SOUTH AFRICAN XENOPHOBES ENTERTAIN THE FANTASY OF SENDING ALL foreigners back to where they came from. Australia is unique among modern Western democracies in having actually tried to do this—if not sending them home to danger, then morally and legally outsourcing responsibility to remote Pacific islands.

It represents the opposite of the policy adopted by German chancellor Angela Merkel at the height of the 2015 refugee crisis: a clash of visions and values between the Refugee Convention and Guantánamo Bay—on one side a foundational text of the postwar international order and on the other the post-9/11 fantasy of creating extralegal spaces, where people deemed undesirable can be detained indefinitely beyond the reach of the law and in some cases sent back to war-torn homelands despite ongoing threats to their lives.[1]

Over 51,000 asylum seekers arrived in Australia by sea between 2009 and 2013, the equivalent of over 750,000 arriving in a country the size of the United States. It was a time of media frenzy and a "boiling point" within the immigration department.[2] Bringing back control of the border was the political mantra of the day.

In 2011, Australia's Labor government struck a deal with Malaysia. Under the proposed agreement, Australia would send eight hundred asylum seekers who had arrived by boat to Malaysia in exchange for four thousand people already certified as refugees by the Malaysian government.[3] Human rights lawyers successfully challenged the government on the grounds that Malaysia wasn't a party to the 1951 Refugee Convention and couldn't guarantee legal protection. Their victory buried the deal, pulled the rug from under the Labor Party as elections approached, and arguably paved the way for something much worse.

Despite his left-leaning tendencies, the Australian éminence grise John Menadue believes it was a mistake to kill the Malaysia deal. "My good friends in the NGO movement torpedoed it," he says politely. "They wanted a three-course meal when only one course was available."[4]

The Labor Party tried to get tough just before the 2013 election by foreclosing any possibility of boat people ever reaching Australia.[5] The party was hamstrung. They were being squeezed like European Social Democrats by a shrinking working-class base that abandoned them for the far right, and the cosmopolitan urban left was starting to leave them for the Green Party. Labor was hemorrhaging in both directions.

Kevin Rudd, the Labor prime minister, responded with a policy of talking tough but humanely. He wanted to do both. The stated target of the policy was now people smugglers. "It was a subtle but actually very important shift," says Waleed Aly, Australia's young television superstar, beloved by millennials on the left and detested by many on the right. "It meant that harsh asylum-seeker policy suddenly became recast as compassionate."[6] The right quickly seized upon this politically popular argument.

Self-styled compassionate conservatives began to cast the smugglers as villains and the asylum seekers as pawns who needed to be saved. They were conflating two separate problems, as Aly pointed out. "Is it the nature of the journey that concerns us, or the fact that the boats often arrive on our territory?" he asked. "One approach is about protecting the rights and well-being of asylum seekers; the other is about protecting ourselves."

Today's right in Australia has reached "a point where debate proceeds on the basis, real or feigned, of compassionate concern for the fate of asylum seekers. It seems the boat people must be stopped not for our sake, but for their own," Aly wrote.[7] And that meant recasting draconian policy as benevolent. The shifting humanitarian argument was best captured in a political cartoon. The old version read "Fuck off, we're full." Now it was edited to read "Fuck off, we are very worried about you drowning."[8]

Two Syrians, Ahmed and Marwan, had the great misfortune of arriving in Australian waters in the middle of that policy upheaval, on a cursed winter day in late 2013. Ahmed, now in his forties, is a university-educated accountant who worked in Syria before escalating violence forced him to flee. He fled the country for Australia, where he has relatives who are citizens, planning to send for his wife and children later. He and his fellow detainee, Marwan, both claimed they were inspired by Australia's criticisms of the Syrian government for violating human rights.

While they were at sea on a small boat from Indonesia to Christmas Island, Australia's government changed the rules. Henceforth, all "illegal maritime arrivals," a euphemism for anyone arriving by boat without a visa, would be barred from ever being resettled on Australian territory.

Some asylum seekers on the boat they traveled on have received temporary visas, permitting them to remain in Australia. Ahmed and Marwan were not so lucky. Instead, the two were sent to Manus Island, a remote part of Papua New Guinea, under the new law. "I don't know the news because I am in the ocean," Marwan recounts in broken English. By the time their boat reached Australian waters, the new law was in effect and their fate was sealed. At the time we met, Ahmed's family remained in an ISIS-controlled part of Syria, and his daughters had been in hiding for more than a year for fear of being raped by ISIS soldiers.[9]

The new policy was a shock even to those on the right. Not even they had proposed so draconian a measure, but once the bridge was crossed, it was something they were happy to leave in place. It is a policy that has stranded men like Ahmed and Marwan in detention and laid the groundwork for years of harsh policy because once in power the right had no incentive to roll it back.

After people are sent away, Australia conveniently wipes its hands and claims that because no one is shooting or torturing them, it has committed no sin. But the safety of refugees is not in fact a foregone conclusion.

The local islanders were not uniformly thrilled about the arrival of the asylum seekers. In February 2014, Reza Barati, a twenty-three-year-old Iranian detainee, was killed during a riot when asylum seekers tried to escape from the detention center on Manus Island and local residents and police stormed the facility. Recalling the cases of Somali refugees who fled war only to be assaulted and killed once in South Africa, many lawyers believe it's valid to argue that Australia has violated the Refugee Convention if locals pose a new threat to the refugees sent to Manus Island or Nauru, the other Pacific island Australia uses for offshore detention.[10]

Melissa Parke, a human rights lawyer and ex-politician, contends the new policy was premised on a bogus argument. "If you really cared about saving lives, you'd care about what happened to people whose boats were turned back. Do they drown?"[11] The assertion that the refugee problem has been resolved when boats stop coming is as misleading as a hospital turning away every ambulance and then claiming that no one in town is sick or injured.[12]

Australia's entire stop-the-boats debate boils down to an argument about utilitarianism. The TV host Aly offers an example that tests the moral and economic commitment of the faux humanitarians. He asks seriously, if they care so deeply and would spend whatever money it takes to save lives at sea, then why not charter a cruise ship and assess asylum claims on arrival? No one would opt for the rickety boats of the smugglers. "We become the people smugglers; all lives are saved," he says. It is also cheaper.

To prove the point, he and a friend calculated how many asylum seekers could fit on a luxury liner and booked every cabin at the full commercial rate per passenger. "We had enough money left over to have a budget every week for a concert on board from the Rolling Stones, Coldplay, Radiohead. And then we still couldn't spend all the money that we're currently spending," he says with a laugh.

The real question, then, is whether the policy's goal is actually to save lives or simply to stop refugees from sharing the wealth of Australia's welfare state. For Aly, it's about keeping foreigners out and preserving generous benefits for "us." And when that's the case, he argues, economics doesn't matter.[13]

FOR ALL THE TALK ABOUT THE RULE OF LAW, AUSTRALIA IS PUSHING THE boundaries of what one expects from a liberal democratic nation. In 2015, it enacted laws threatening whistle-blowers with prosecution if they went to the press rather than voice their complaints internally through the immigration minister, including in cases of child sexual abuse in detention centers.[14]

It is not the only questionable legislation. Gillian Triggs, the president of Australia's human rights commission, is one of the right's favorite punching bags and the person in charge of ensuring that international human rights treaties are not violated.[15] The fact that United Nations agreements aren't enshrined in domestic legislation makes her work difficult. Australia was a prime mover in negotiating and signing almost all the UN's original human rights treaties, but today's leaders, fearing being held accountable, have deliberately avoided codifying them in local law so they are immune from charges of violating international legal norms. In 2015, the government passed legislation striking references to the Refugee Convention from domestic legislation.[16]

Then, when legal challenges forced parliament to admit that no existing law permitted the state to fund or facilitate the detention of people not accused of a crime, Australian lawmakers found a solution: they simply passed legislation and applied it retrospectively, an increasingly common practice when the government finds its policies running into legal hurdles. The most Kafkaesque result of the Australian government's penchant for passing retrospective laws is that babies born to detained mothers inherit the status of their parents—an illegal maritime arrival. "Our law says they arrived on a boat even if they were born in a Melbourne hospital and never set foot on a boat," explains the human rights lawyer Daniel Webb, an intense man who wears dark-rimmed glasses and speaks in full paragraphs. "It would be laughable if it didn't trigger such serious consequences," he adds. The immediate result of the law was that Australian-born babies risked being subject to mandatory detention and removal to remote Pacific islands like Nauru or Papua New Guinea.[17]

It was lawmaking based on the political whims of the moment with no regard for enduring principles or values. "I think that we have become inured to it," says David Manne, another human rights lawyer who has sued the government over offshore detention. "It's become normalized. The nation hasn't flinched." To Manne, Australia is on a slippery slope when groups who are marginalized and in need of protection have come to be seen as a threat. "People, including children, babies, can be politically expendable. . . . The real threat is to the life of our nation under the rule of law," he warns.

As we sit in a trendy restaurant in an area packed with students, hipsters, and yuppies, Manne muses, "If you asked most people here to lock up children indefinitely, I think they would be outraged about the idea," but few know that it's happening so close to home, he adds. "It's actually only eighteen kilometers up the road that it's going on."[18]

THE VILLAWOOD DETENTION CENTER ON THE WESTERN OUTSKIRTS OF Sydney is a far cry from the mosquito-infested detention camps of Nauru in the South Pacific. The center is modern and colorful. Apart from the heavy security presence, x-ray machines, and heavy iron doors, the public areas resemble those you'd find in an elementary school or children's hospital. Visitors bring food and drinks and sit on brightly colored faux leather benches alongside the detainees; the bathrooms are shared by everyone. But among these men (and a few women), there are several who have come from a much darker place, often for just a few weeks of medical treatment before being sent back offshore.

Down the street are several small brick houses. This is where families in detention live. An Iraqi family was relocated here after spending several years on Nauru. About two years ago, their teenage son started having psychological problems—"fighting with himself," as his parents put it. He was put on various medications and became jittery and began fighting with security guards, who slapped him and detained him in the local jail, sometimes for a few hours and another time for a whole day.

To avoid being accused of detaining people illegally, Australia's government suddenly declared in 2015 that no one was being detained in Nauru because the camp was "open" and asylum seekers technically had the right to leave. "At first, a lot of people were afraid to leave the camp," says the father, because of the native Nauruans. "They're all big. . . . They look at you walking in the street." For the final two months in Nauru, with the right to move freely, the father worked for a wage of $2.50 per hour (a fraction of Australia's minimum wage) doing carpentry for the Nauruans for twelve to thirteen hours per day. "The Nauruan people have good hearts," says the father, but alcoholism is rampant. "They drink a whole carton of beer per day, and then they fight. They come bang on your door in the middle of the night, and in the morning, they're your best friend."[19]

A Rohingya man in detention at Villawood who wishes to remain anonymous told me he fled Myanmar's Rakhine State in 2007, going first to Thailand, then Malaysia. He tried to work there, but police arrested illegal employees and demanded bribes from them—mostly money but sometimes their shoes. He would have stayed in Malaysia, he says, if he had been able to work without the threat of arrest hanging over his head. "I had to come here," he says. But when he arrived in Australia by way of Christmas Island, he was immediately flown to Nauru. He still has no right to work there, and the Nauruan police, he claims, constantly ask him for bribes.

In his view, Myanmar's much-celebrated move toward democracy has meant nothing for people like him. When asked about Daw Aung San Suu Kyi's emergence as a leader, he is dismissive. "It's all bullshit. . . . People are still being killed. If anyone tries to leave the village, you get shot." He was in Villawood for medical treatment, and the Australian immigration authorities planned to send him back to Nauru. He's even asked to be returned to Myanmar, a solution that Australia usually encourages. "I've been asking them for two years to go back," he insists, "but they said, 'No, it's too dangerous. You have no papers and are stateless.'" Rohingyas like the man in Villawood have been stranded on a small island they had never heard of and never sought to reach. "I have no alternative country," he says, "not Australia, not Myanmar, only Nauru."[20]

For refugees of other nationalities, even when they are fleeing ongoing wars, the Australian government has no qualms sending them back into danger. It is framed as voluntary but in fact is far from it. "We are returning refugees to refugee-producing countries," argues the human rights lawyer Webb. Australia is essentially telling legitimate asylum seekers to pick their poison—human rights violations at home or on Nauru and Manus Island—while immigration officials engage in an Orwellian twisting of definitions. "The more you understand about the conditions in which we are keeping people," he says, "the more you understand that it is not a voluntary choice."[21] When circumstances in detention become so terrible that detainees begin to think they have no choice but to go back, Webb insists, "it's like standing on the edge of a cliff and holding a gun to someone's head and saying, 'Jump, or I'll shoot you.' And then when they jump, saying, 'Well, I'm not responsible for your death because you chose to jump.'"[22] The metaphor may sound violent, but he is adamant that the government is "deliberately forcing people to choose between two deeply harmful and dangerous scenarios."

Rahul, a Sri Lankan asylum seeker who eventually made it to Australia, was detained in Nauru for over three years and dealt with this conundrum daily.[23] He was told it might take five to six years to process his case. It was an effort, he says, to convince people to go home voluntarily with the United Nations' International Organization for Migration

(IOM). Money was offered on the condition that they leave before their refugee applications had been processed. If they were rejected, the offer of money was off the table. According to Mark Isaacs, a young Australian who worked for the Salvation Army in the Nauru camp, the Australian government was "attempting to create an environment in Australian-approved centers that was worse than the oppression the men had suffered in their home countries, and then used IOM to offer them 'voluntary' repatriation."[24]

For his part, Philip Ruddock, the architect of offshoring, is proud of the fact that once refugees are sent off to the Pacific, there is generally no access to Australia's considerably more advanced legal system. He is satisfied that the Australian government no longer has any responsibility or jurisdiction over them. "We've satisfied ourselves that if a person is a refugee, they will not be returned to persecution," he says, and if they are intercepted by the Royal Australian Navy and sent to a third country, Australia has no further obligation to process them.[25] "If the situation changes back home, and it's safe for them to return, you can return them," he adds. The risk, human rights lawyers are quick to point out, is *refoulement,* the legal term for forcing an asylum seeker back into danger, which is prohibited by the Refugee Convention.

Ruddock is a savvy lawyer, and he knows how to find ways around international legal concepts. "The obligation is non-refoulement," he argues. "It is not an obligation to give people permanent residency . . . and it doesn't mean you have to give your family and all your offspring an entitlement to come," hence his idea of temporary protection, which was initially dismissed as draconian but then wholeheartedly embraced when it proved politically useful. As Ruddock puts it bluntly, "Because you can't refoule them, then don't give them anything more than you have to." But he is not particularly concerned about verifying the safety of the situation they're returning to. "There's no obligation to verify," he tells me. "We can't send our officials in to see whether or not you're abusing your nationals," he says.[26] In other words, someone could be sent back to a place that isn't safe at all.[27]

Ahmed and marwan, the syrian refugees who were adrift at sea when Australia changed its laws, were also at Villawood in early 2016, after having been transferred for medical reasons. Their problems started in March 2014, when another riot swept through the detention camp on Manus Island where Reza Barati was killed and private security personnel put it down; several asylum seekers were beaten by the guards. Ahmed was assaulted by a guard and later had a heart attack. He was flown to Brisbane, more than 1,500 miles away, at taxpayer expense, for treatment. He was placed on suicide watch after threatening to kill himself if returned to detention. Nevertheless, he was flown back in April, and he soon had another heart attack and was diagnosed with PTSD.[28] Once again, Ahmed was flown to Australia because facilities in Papua New Guinea were deemed inadequate. The various doctors treating him noted acute anxiety about being deported to Syria or returned to the scene of the riot; they recommended releasing him into the care of his relatives living in Australia, who had offered to financially support him. Instead, he was kept in detention.

Considering his circumstances, Ahmed is a relatively jovial man. He eagerly tells his story as he chain-smokes. "Manus was like a hell," he says. "I was starving there. I saw death there. We were attacked by the locals. They said, 'You should go back to your country.'" The first time we met in January 2016, he was worried that his eldest son would be conscripted into the Syrian army. The next time we spoke, he told me his son had reached Slovenia and was trying to get to Germany.[29]

Marwan looks far less well. He is thin (he lost over thirty pounds during his six-month hunger strike), nervous, and easily distracted. His eyes dart around, and his legs occasionally shake. He is visibly worried when talking about his wife and son still in Syria. His niece and nephew in the house next door were killed when a bomb fell on it. He told doctors that soon after arriving on Manus Island, there was a riot "with dogs tearing people and people being shot at and people being killed . . . , which was like what I experienced in Syria." He told the doctors, "I swear on God I will kill myself" if ever returned to Manus. He tells a similar story in person, sitting in a covered outdoor visitors' area within the Villawood detention center as a torrential thunderstorm sweeps through Sydney.

"There was no humanity," says Marwan. "I was there when the Iranian died," he adds, referring to Barati. He is furious at Australia at this point. "Give me one month to go to any embassy," he says, exasperated. "Let me have a chance!" he exclaims. "If we do something wrong, put me in the jail. . . . You have the choice to refuse me, but you don't have the choice to put me in PNG third world. I ran away from war!"[30]

Ahmed and Marwan's fears are well founded. In late 2015, there were eighteen Syrians in detention in Australian or offshore centers. The nineteenth Syrian, a man they both know, was sent home and offers a cautionary tale. The Australian TV journalist Ginny Stein tracked down the man who, in despair over his indefinite detention and encouraged by immigration authorities, signed papers permitting him to be voluntarily repatriated. Declassified government e-mail records show that the IOM, which usually assists with such repatriations, refused to get involved. The IOM bluntly told the Australian government that it does not take people back to Syria because it refuses to "return individuals to situations of vulnerability."[31] As the Syrian's case proved, Australia has no qualms doing so.

The Australian government gave him just over $2,300 before he left.[32] The man's intention was to escape in transit and fly to Turkey, where he could seek safety in a refugee camp, but he couldn't escape immigration officials in Qatar when changing planes. He was singled out as soon as he arrived in Damascus with a wad of foreign currency and was accused of financing the Syrian revolution. Then, he claims, he was tortured for twenty days before being released. Soon after his return home, he was injured by shrapnel from an artillery shell that landed four meters away; it killed his father. Still, he told the journalist Stein, "I am free."[33]

WHEN LEADERS TRY TO DO THE OPPOSITE OF WHAT AUSTRALIA HAS done for the past fifteen years, as Angela Merkel has attempted in Germany, there is a political price to pay.

Merkel was the exception in 2015 in a world overcome by fear and reaction; her vision was the opposite of Australia's effort to exert total control over its borders, even when it required callous indifference to the plight of refugees and a willingness to treat them terribly to deter others from coming. She rejected the Australian model that so many on the European far right dream of replicating, but she may have overreached in her leniency and compassion. There were dissenters in Merkel's party who warned that there would be political consequences for her border policy; no one quite imagined how dramatic they might be.

On September 4, 2016, almost a year to the day after she opened the country's borders, Angela Merkel's CDU was defeated by the upstart far-right party, AfD, in the small northeastern state of Mecklenburg-Vorpommern. The new party took 21 percent of the vote. It was the latest in a string of setbacks that began in March, when the AfD had strong showings in two other states. But Mecklenburg was different; it is Merkel's home turf. She grew up in the East German town of Templin, just north of Berlin, and watched the wall go up as a seven-year-old. Two weeks after losing her home state, a similar battering occurred in Berlin's municipal election, where the CDU suffered its worst-ever result, taking under 18 percent of the vote while the AfD came in third with almost 15 percent.

Finally, Merkel accepted some direct responsibility, telling the press, "If I could, I would turn back time by many, many years to better prepare myself and the whole German government for the situation that reached us unprepared in late summer 2015." She maintained that her policy had been "absolutely right," but admitted that it had "led to a time when we did not have enough control over the situation."[34]

It was not Merkel's only political headache; two months later, she was humiliated at the CDU party congress by a junior colleague almost half her age. Jens Spahn, the deputy finance minister and a rising star in Merkel's CDU, stood just a few feet away from the chancellor when he took the microphone to weigh in on the internal party debate about whether Germany should ban dual citizenship, a law that Merkel had reversed in recent years in a deal with the Social Democratic Party (SPD), allowing foreigners—mostly Turks—to keep their foreign passports and become naturalized Germans. Taking the floor after Merkel's interior minister and the party's general secretary had spoken in favor of her plan, Spahn declared, "Of course you have to make compromises in a governing coalition, but we're at a party convention." As the *Spiegel* reporters in the room wrote, "The applause was so loud that it was immediately clear that he would emerge victorious."[35] Spahn had accomplished a rare feat: he'd stood up to Merkel and won.

When the refugees started to arrive en masse, it was a moral question for many people. But for Spahn, it was a political one, especially for his own party. "We have lost the trust of too many people," Spahn told me when we met in the cafeteria of the Bundestag on a sweltering July day.

For him, the refugee policy was decided on the fly. "Would we have been able to withstand this in a public debate?" he asks. "Can we survive it?" But there was not a public debate, and he and other CDU members who dissented within the party ranks lost the internal one.[36]

Suddenly, the influx of one million people was a fait accompli. Spahn worries that the CDU, once the party of law and order, is losing the trust of voters on the issues that have always been its bread and butter. People no longer feel safe on trains and public transit, he says, a sentiment that only worsened last summer after a spate of attacks throughout southern Germany and in the wake of the Berlin Christmas market horror that struck just ten days after he confronted Merkel at the party congress.

Spahn says he is fighting back against a party he believes has been "too accommodating of a liberal elite that has become convinced of its own moral superiority." He is concerned that his party could start hemorrhaging voters to the AfD the way that other centrist parties in Europe have—from British Labour to Denmark's Social Democrats—and refuses to allow them to "co-opt issues like family or the fear of Islamism." Nor does he think it helps to "immediately cry 'racism' when somebody voices anxiety that immigration is eroding the homeland."[37]

Spahn has another trait that differentiates him from most members of the conservative CDU—he's gay. Spahn famously came out in a speech to the assembled conservative party representatives by telling them he never wanted to be the victim of an attack while walking down the street with his boyfriend. Some of the more traditional conservatives still don't quite know how to speak about his sexuality, resorting to odd formulations about his "family situation" or calling him "a pleasant homosexual."[38]

Spahn didn't realize at the time that his sexual orientation might also prove politically useful. He speaks of his move from rural Germany near the Dutch border to the middle of Berlin as a "liberating experience" and seems to realize that being gay gives him flexibility that other politicians don't have. He calls it "leg room." The sentence "not every culture is an enrichment," for example, doesn't grate in the same way it might coming from an old, straight conservative.[39]

Spahn is fully aware that the refugee influx and the emergence of the AfD has made some strange bedfellows. "The most funny thing about it," he told me, "is that now the conservatives in my own party start to defend women's and gay rights." Spahn admits that "it's ironic, yes." But, he continues, "if you have repeated it publicly often enough, you start to believe it."[40]

In much the same way that the late Pim Fortuyn's homosexuality was instrumentalized to help redefine what it meant to be right wing in Holland, Spahn's rise within the CDU may be doing the same for Germany's conservative establishment—and is perhaps helping to shut the AfD out of that ideological space despite their selection of Alice Weidel, a thirty-eight-year-old lesbian, as one of their top candidates.[41]

Spahn was not the only dissenter in the CDU ranks. "I was actually skeptical from the very first day," insists Philipp Lengsfeld, a young bespectacled member of parliament who represents the CDU in Berlin Mitte, the heart of the capital and a district that straddles the old wall between East and West. "Parts of society were on the verge of hysteria. . . . It sent the wrong signals to the wrong people," he told me in July 2016, two months before the election debacle in Berlin.

He doesn't blame Merkel alone. "It was the whole society," he says. "It was the media, church, all sorts of NGOs, activists, and so forth. Everybody was like, 'Welcome! We have to save the world.'" There is something very German about this impulse, according to Lengsfeld. "Either we want to conquer the world, or we want to save the world; it's always a little over the edge," he adds.[42] It is also a particularly West German sensibility that lingers more than twenty-five years after unification. For Lengsfeld, who grew up in East Germany, this savior complex is foreign. His personal history is deeply bound up with East Germany's. Both his grandfather and stepfather were Stasi officers, the latter spying on his mother, Vera, a well-known human rights campaigner in East Germany throughout the 1980s, when Philipp was growing up.[43]

As the refugee crisis grew more acute in September 2015, with the corpses of refugees found in a truck outside Vienna and the body of Alan Kurdi washed up on a Turkish beach, there was pressure to act. The message from Germany's opinion leaders was "we are so strong, we are so good, we are an example to the world. This is all West German thinking. It has nothing to do with the reality of the eastern states," Lengsfeld insists. People in the east weren't feeling "we are so wealthy, we need to share. . . . This is all luxury thinking of the West, of the liberal people from the West who never even saw that there is an East Germany. Who always lived in virtual Europe," he argues.

This West German thinking, he insists, explains why so many more voters in what was once East Germany are abandoning the CDU and other mainstream parties to vote for the populist AfD. As a German foreign ministry official puts it less generously, "People complain about the harsh anti-refugee backlash in Hungary and Poland. We have our own central Europe within Germany."[44]

Lengsfeld isn't hostile to refugees, but he is convinced that many who crossed the border last September were not fleeing persecution. Young men were, as he put it, "sitting in Casablanca watching the news and said, 'Wow, *Willkommenskultur* in Germany, that's the place to go.'" For some, it wasn't about fleeing; it was about a better life. And by declaring the German borders open, the government effectively gave an incentive to people in the Balkans and North Africa to try their luck, he contends. "This was all mixed together; everyone was called 'refugee' regardless of origin, background, hopes, expectations."

As the CDU debated its policy, a minority challenged the chancellor's position. "It doesn't make sense at all," Lengsfeld recalls thinking. "What is the plan? Are we inviting the world? Are we getting millions of migrants . . . in an uncontrolled, unchanneled manner? That was no plan. The counterargument was we cannot change it, this is like a natural catastrophe," he recalls, visibly frustrated. "The majority of the party was on our side," he adds. But Merkel made a decision and the party followed her, he says, "because we are loyal. We are conservative. We follow our leaders."[45]

The business community went along with the policy, too, Lengsfeld believes, because "they were desperate for arguments," but there were no good ones. It was "lies, all lies." The idea that the German workforce was aging and needed a fresh infusion of labor was a popular theme in the media in late 2015, but it was a fantasy, he insists. They were hoping to train new workers, but it was a stretch. "You don't solve that by uncontrolled asylum migration," Lengsfeld argues. "How can you expect that people from a totally different culture, who don't speak a word of German, who are not able to read and write, to go and to solve our high-tech job issue? It's crazy!"[46]

Spahn agrees. There were many people in government and corporate circles who thought an infusion of young people would be good for the labor market. To him, it was all "wishful thinking." All these people under twenty-five might have looked appealing to a country with one of the oldest workforces in the world, but they all still needed language skills and training. "To make it a real demographic relief," Spahn maintains "we need two-year-olds to come, not twenty-year-olds."

In the United States, there's hardly any social safety net, so people who arrive, whether legally or illegally, immediately seek work. By contrast, in Germany, "you can survive for ten years without ever having to work," Spahn argues. But for him, the question is not about whether the economy profits from the influx. Spahn is certain it won't in the near term. "To make it an economic plus, at least half of them must add more to our economy and our GDP than the average German."

The best thing Germany can do now, he says, is try to integrate as many people as possible so the financial burden is low. In the 1990s, when hundreds of thousands of refugees from the former Yugoslavia came, unemployment was high so there wasn't a question of letting people work. Now there is a need, but the skills don't match apart from a few engineers and doctors among the refugees, says Spahn. "The very best case is if this is, in ten or twenty years' time, an economic plus."[47]

Aydan Özoğuz has a rosier view, as one would expect from the German government's commissioner for immigration, refugees, and integration. She is a member of the Social Democratic Party but serves in Merkel's coalition government. She has been at the center of the government's policy response and its shifts as the open-door policy has become less popular, including the negotiation of Merkel's controversial deal with Turkey, the country her parents came from.

Although Özoğuz was born in Hamburg in 1967 and grew up in Germany, she did not acquire German citizenship until 1989, a function of Germany's then extremely strict jus sanguinis citizenship laws that for decades granted nationality only to those with German blood. She is not the only famous person in her family. Her cousins are the leaders of the Istanbul-based punk bank Athena, and her two brothers run a notoriously pro-Hezbollah and pro-Iranian website that has been under surveillance by the German intelligence agencies for years; she has publicly dissociated herself from her brothers' work and political views.[48]

Despite all the criticism of Merkel's policy, Özoğuz insists, "I think we did quite well. They were knocking on our doors. The alternative would have been to tell them to just go away." Germany didn't have the luxury of ignoring them. "We have a humanitarian policy; we have to live this."

And she doesn't see refugees as the greatest threat to Germany's social fabric. She believes that the emergence of far-right populist parties could pose a much greater risk to the fabric of society than the refugees. "I think it's quite dangerous" when a party publicly suggests that all Muslims might be a threat as the AfD has done. "On social networks, they say every Muslim is kind of an extremist." In much the same way as the *Charlie Hebdo* editorial implied that a bakery selling only halal croissants and a veiled woman walking down the street were somehow part of the problem, this leads to a sense that perfectly peaceful Muslim citizens are some sort of fifth column. "It is alarming," says Özoğuz. "I am a Muslim, I was born in Hamburg, I grew up in this country—am I a part of this country or not?"

She admits that the refugee crisis is straining the fabric of the European Union, but she remains optimistic. Where she does agree with Lengsfeld and Spahn is that the refugee issue should be strictly humanitarian and not be touted as some sort of economic panacea or subjected to cost-benefit analysis. "We shouldn't look with this eye of economic interest," even if, she adds, helping them may also help the economy one day.[49]

Integration is a less fraught topic in Germany than in Holland or France. While France and others remain fixated on the nineteenth-century German concept of a *kulturnation*, Germany has largely moved on. Given its history, nationalist nostalgia simply doesn't sell in the same way.

Many German Turks still do not have citizenship, but Germany's immigrants and their families are not as socially marginalized and geographically isolated as many minority communities in France or Holland. Kreuzberg, the heart of Turkish Berlin, also happens to be the epicenter of hipster Berlin and the neighborhood of choice for many young people visiting or living in the city.

German politicians who opposed Merkel's policies in 2015, like Lengsfeld and Spahn, are fully aware that many of those who came are there to stay and that integration will be a major issue in the years to come. Unlike Le Pen and many on the French right, they do not insist on absolute and immediate assimilation. The key, for them, is numbers and focusing on truly humanitarian cases rather than anyone arriving seeking a better life.

"They are in the country now. We have to deal with it," Spahn says frustratedly. Many are low skilled and will need a lot of training. Integrating asylum seekers through the labor market will, he thinks, take far longer than most people think. Lengsfeld insists that Germany needs to talk about quotas to limit the number of asylum seekers coming into the country and ensure that they are not economic migrants. "The Germans are not used to this type of differentiation; that maybe has something to do with the past," he adds, pausing, because "we also selected in Auschwitz." But that historical discomfort must not be allowed to drive current policy, because selective immigration policy can't in any way be equated with the murderous Nazi regime. And being strict is essential, he maintains, because not everyone is a true war refugee.

The far-right politicians refusing to take any Muslims are, in his view, just as misguided as the leftists who insisted that everyone crossing the border was by definition a refugee. That said, it is harder to integrate people with doctrinaire religious views. "If you don't accept a female teacher, female managers, female policemen, if you don't accept that your daughters and wives are working in and interacting with the community, you have an issue," he argues. Unlike some politicians further to his right, he notes that the Muslim community is not monolithic, and fundamentalists are a problem for moderate Muslims, too. "Do you think that a young Turkish-origin woman in Germany is happy," he asks, "if some Afghan village people are coming with their medieval view on life and trying to implement this in modern Germany?"[50]

For Spahn and Lengsfeld, spending money on integration is not even in question. The alternative is doing nothing and then waiting to see what happens. That, they maintain, will be much more expensive in the long run if integration fails. "We are a democracy. We have the rule of law. We have procedures for everything," says Spahn. "So you just can't say, 'Go.'"[51]

But by 2016, increasing numbers of voters were arguing just that.

GERMANY'S POPULIST BACKLASH CAME MUCH LATER THAN MOST. GIVEN its history, the country has long shunned anything resembling the far right. Looking back fondly to the first half of the twentieth century is simply off limits. Until 2006, when Germany hosted the World Cup, it was unusual to even see the national flag flown at sporting events. Many Germans thought that they, unlike other European nations, were immune to the far right. For decades, conservatives had tried in vain to start a moderate right-wing party. The only thing that existed to the right of the CDU was the neo-Nazi National Democratic Party (NPD). Some smaller new parties had made it into local parliaments only to collapse and disappear. Then came the AfD.

Much as the French establishment has for decades tried to place the Front National behind a *cordon sanitaire*, Germany has long sought to sideline the far right. But according to *Die Welt*'s Robin Alexander, attempting to cordon off the AfD doesn't work and won't dent their popularity. "They even tried to stop the TV stations inviting AfD politicians to discussions," he recalls. "That old strategy of keeping them outside collapsed."[52] The party is here to stay.

The impulse to marginalize a growing force on the far right is understandable in Germany, but it could be driving even more people into the arms of the AfD. They were called "aggressive mob people," Lengsfeld says, referring to supporters of PEGIDA. "I think this is dangerous." There has been a change in what Germans fear, and this, he argues, leads to dismissive political responses. Germans are accustomed to the standard bogeymen of the left. "I'm more used to all this left-wing fear about nuclear energy, climate change, and all the rest of it. Now we also have right-wing fear, Islamophobia, and so forth," he explains. If voters say they are afraid of Islam, politicians can't just tell them that discussion is off limits. "That makes no sense," says Lengsfeld. "We need to approach this openly, but fairly."[53]

Shutting down discussion or pretending that there is no problem either drives the opposition underground or, as the CDU and others on the right have learned the hard way, into the arms of new political parties seeking to profit from the growing anger of certain voters.

Christian Schmidt was part of the AfD before anyone had heard of it. He helped set up the party when it was an anti-EU movement and nothing more. Frauke Petry, the leader at the helm for the party's major victories in 2016, wasn't yet involved. The key players were Bernd Lucke, an economics professor, the disgruntled CDU politician Alexander Gauland, and Konrad Adam, a conservative journalist. As Schmidt explains, "At this point, immigration was not an issue at all."[54]

The party was pro-sovereignty and focused on law and order. It argued that Germany shouldn't be providing social security for the rest of Europe by bailing out countries like Greece. The message resonated at a time when the Greek crisis was very much in the headlines. The AfD took a little under 5 percent of the vote in the 2013 elections, just shy of the threshold needed to enter parliament, but they won seven seats in the EU parliament in 2014. The press labeled them as being to the right of the CDU, a characterization that suited them just fine. It was the first time in thirty years that a new party had done so well in Germany.

But no sooner had the AfD won its first victories than it began to change. All the voters for the failed right-wing parties of years past—and some who supported even more extreme movements—"were still around," says Schmidt. "Those who didn't make it in other parties saw it as another chance . . . and they used our structure of the AfD to hijack it from within."

All of a sudden, "more lunatics and weirdos and people with strange ideas and conspiracy theorists joined our ranks," he tells me. One of them was Björn Höcke, the AfD leader in the eastern state of Thuringia, who has called the Berlin Holocaust Memorial a "monument of shame." "When I hear Höcke," Schmidt says, "I think it's 1937 again. Like Goebbels in the Reichstag."[55]

At the same time, as Schmidt puts it delicately, "more reasonable people started to leave the party." He estimates that about six thousand members who shared his views left and about ten thousand with more extreme views, especially on immigration, joined the AfD. "People joined who were no longer tolerable. I left mentally in mid-2014," says Schmidt wistfully. "I physically left at the end of 2014."[56]

Robin Alexander sums up the AfD's early program as "Let it be 1985 again," but they were also tapping into something deeper. "I think more Germans had right-wing views than dared to express them . . . because the right-wing parties were always super horrible, and you have to be an absolute asshole to vote for the NPD," says Alexander. But if you felt uncomfortable, now you had an address to turn to. "Bernd Lucke wasn't a Nazi. He was a conservative professor. He was okay. He was not saying, 'Invade Poland.'" But then once you had this respectable new force, argues Alexander, "all the right-wingers, all the madmen, they filled their ranks."[57]

Frauke Petry emerged as a key figure in 2015 and was, as Schmidt recalls, more moderate at the beginning. But she quickly saw her chance and "like a chameleon" adopted a strident anti-immigration position. Others also reinforced the right flank of the party, and in a showdown in mid-2015, before the refugee crisis arrived on Germany's borders, they defeated Lucke 62 percent to 38 percent at a party congress. The founder of the party was forced to leave.[58]

The AfD has performed the best in the east. Schmidt believes that the party has special appeal in places like Dresden, where many people feel they have been on the losing end of Germany's boom. "People who were party officials in East Germany are sitting at home twiddling their thumbs. They're easy prey," says Schmidt. Also, Dresden is famous for being cut off from all Western media during the Cold War, since TV and radio signals didn't reach the city. It became known as the "valley of the ignorant," which was one explanation for its staunch support for the DDR—the old East Germany—until the fall of the Berlin Wall. The city that was once the epicenter of true believers in the DDR is now the home of PEGIDA. It's the states with the fewest refugees where the fear is greatest, says Schmidt. "Because you don't know anybody, you're more fearful," he argues.

Schmidt himself is no cheerleader for Merkel's refugee policy. Like Spahn and Lengsfeld, he mocks the "national euphoria of the business community," which subsided quickly, and he worries about Germans being crowded out of affordable housing or having their wages undercut by new arrivals. Still, he thinks the AfD is selling a false bill of goods. "It's like Trump—build a wall. It's simplistic." They have called for closing mosques and using live ammunition at the border if masses of people try to cross again. "They know very well that they'll never get it, but it's popular to say so," he argues. "And by that, you fuel hatred toward foreigners."[59]

As Schmidt and others from the party's early days jumped ship, Alexander Gauland stayed on board as the party swung right; he became its deputy leader—and one of its top two candidates in the 2017 election. The AfD's rise "started with the opening of the border by Angela Merkel, and the total uncontrolled influx of totally different people who didn't belong to the European culture, who didn't belong to the Christian faith," says Gauland, a bald seventy-six-year-old who peppers his answers with an encyclopedic knowledge of postwar German politics and occasional references to Bismarck.

He was a loyal member of the CDU for forty years. Merkel, he says angrily, has moved the party steadily toward the center, to the point that "the party has no longer a conservative wing, it has no real liberal wing, it has nothing." The final straw for Gauland was the government's 2010 decision "to rescue Greece, and to keep the euro, whatever it costs." He left the party after the first Greek bailout agreement and began to form the AfD with Schmidt, Lucke, and others.

By September 2015, many voters seemed to be following him, and they were fleeing parties across the political spectrum. "They are coming from CDU, from the Left Party, from former nonvoters. A lot of protest voters, and we have a lot of voters from the Social Democratic Party," he says, clearly satisfied that some on the left who share the Islamophobic Social Democrat Thilo Sarrazin's views are now voting for the AfD. "It's all around."[60]

As Gauland tells it, they are people who feel that the CDU's move to the center has left them without a voice in parliament. As the *Willkommenskultur* of late 2015 reached its pinnacle, there was, he says, a large group of people who wanted nothing to do with it. "We took up the refugee crisis . . . because all other parties said refugees welcome, and let's say half of the German people said, 'No, we don't welcome refugees.'"

Some of them joined PEGIDA marches; others kept their views to themselves or around the dinner table—people who no longer feel anyone in parliament speaks for them, because, according to Gauland, "all parties have the same policy." With the only genuine opposition to Merkel's policy coming from within her own party and from the CSU in Bavaria, there wasn't a genuine public debate. "That's the real problem of German democracy. There is no real opposition," he complains. "The left and the Greens have the same idea about securing Europe with much German money and a refugees-welcome policy."[61]

Gauland is adamant that Germany isn't learning the lessons of the 1970s. He argues that the country "wanted a workforce, and suddenly we had a new society." Now there is a massive new influx at a time when the country still hasn't solved the problems of the last wave, he says, "and now you bring in a lot of new immigrants. Often these are young Muslim men, and it is very difficult to integrate them in society." He is dismissive of the economic arguments made in favor of welcoming refugees. If there is a labor shortage, he says, why not find native Germans who speak the language to fill the jobs?

Gauland makes it clear that he believes Germany is not destined to become a melting pot like America, and he hasn't been shy about expressing his antiquated and politically incorrect views. He famously declared in an interview that most Germans wouldn't want to live next door to Jérôme Boateng, a half-Ghanaian soccer player who is a star of the beloved German national team. The next day, lawmakers from other parties showed up in the chamber wearing Boateng jerseys.[62]

"The United States, Australia, Canada, and New Zealand, they are immigration societies. Germany is not an immigration society," declares Gauland. "We have immigration, but the majority of the German people is not interested in this immigration. They get used to it, yes, but they would prefer otherwise if they could choose." He also insists that Muslims pose a unique challenge compared to other immigrants, a problem he attributes to Islam never having undergone a reformation as Christianity did. "It is only the Muslims that can't separate the state and the religion, or they don't do it." He concedes that Christianity once had the same problem but credits Martin Luther with solving it.

As for becoming the face of the far right, a concept that evokes greater fears in Germany than elsewhere, Gauland is adamant that his party hasn't been infiltrated by neo-Nazis and skinheads. He stresses that the AfD is "not the parliamentary arm of PEGIDA," although he does acknowledge that "a lot of people who march with PEGIDA in Dresden are people who could be members, or friends, or voters of the AfD."[63]

What is clear is that no matter how well the AfD performs in the 2017 election—with the traditionalist Gauland and the lesbian Weidel as the joint leaders of the party's list—it will not seek to govern in a coalition. Maybe in ten or twenty years, the AfD could join a coalition, but doing so now, Gauland explains, "would be disastrous, because the people would call it treason." He points to the record of small parties in West Germany who joined coalitions. "All these parties have been destroyed by the CDU. They have been sucked up . . . , forgotten." For a small party, it's far better to remain in opposition, he insists.

As in Denmark and Holland, winning power is not necessarily the prime objective. The far right doesn't want to take the reins of government, lest it be blamed for failure. Shouting from the sidelines without taking political responsibility is a far less risky proposition.

The immediate goal is to influence and drive debate. Gauland clearly derives great satisfaction from the way that his party has changed the national discourse about refugees. He proudly cites a Green Party mayor in the town of Tübingen who broke with party orthodoxy and called for tougher border security. "It has totally changed; the discussion has totally changed. This is what we have done."[64]

16

Camp of the Saints at the White House

IN THE HEART OF BUCOLIC LANGUEDOC WINE COUNTRY IN SOUTHWEST France, the Front National has a sympathizer in city hall. Mayor Robert Ménard is an eager rabble-rouser. From his perch at the Béziers town hall festooned with tricolors, he holds forth on the failures of the French left and explains why he went from being a Trotskyist radical to the country's best-known right-wing mayor.

Ménard was supported by the FN in his race for mayor and claims that he agrees with Marine Le Pen on "80 percent" of the issues, but he has several major policy differences and insists that she won't ever win unless she changes.

Chief among his grievances is the FN's obsessive hatred of the EU that Le Pen and her campaign manager, David Rachline, constantly harp on. He describes her stated desire to leave the euro as a "colossal error." "Leaving the euro would weaken France," he told me in June 2016, a year before Le Pen's defeat.[1]

He thinks the strong state she dreams of resurrecting, or reinforcing, is a chimera. "I don't think for a moment that her economic policies can be implemented . . . [b]ecause it's a statist program. . . . The French only want one thing—to be left alone," says the ex-Trotskyist.

Ménard used to be seen as a leftist. Now he is calling for immigration to be halted and was filmed kicking Syrian refugee families out of public housing in Béziers. What changed? According to Ménard, his ideas ran up against reality. "You say, 'Long Live Integration,' and then you go into a school . . . and you see it just doesn't work."

Ménard tells the story of visiting a local school in a tough neighborhood where he once lived. He went to eight classrooms and, much to his chagrin, on only one occasion did the teacher ask the kids to stand. Ménard was incensed by the lack of respect. "How do you educate kids when the mayor of the city, who is an adult, enters the classroom? . . . You say, 'The mayor is coming, stand up, stop talking, and listen,'" he fumes. "Either you give up and say, 'That's how it is.' And the entire left is giving up and saying, 'That's how it is.' Or you say, 'Maybe things have to change.' And so I changed," he tells me.

"How are you going to integrate kids when instead of teaching them and their parents French in after-school hours or outside class we are teaching them Arabic or Turkish?" he asks, dismayed. "You won't integrate in a school in Béziers when two-thirds of the kids are Muslims. You won't integrate anyone, because you integrate when people are a minority, not when they're two-thirds of the class."

Sounding very much like Le Pen, he argues that to integrate the people who are already in France, you have to stop letting new people in. "You have to stop family reunifications. You have to stop birthright citizenship, and you have to get rid of the social advantages that attract economic migrants to France," he argues.

The other issue hampering integration, he says, is that France has lost its pride in itself. Ménard likes to quip that France celebrates its defeat at Waterloo and not its victory at the Battle of Austerlitz. "That lacks all common sense!" he exclaims. France, he maintains, is consumed by self-doubt. If the country "can't seduce its own population, how is it going to appeal to a number of people who are French on paper and not in their hearts?"[2]

His latest gambit has been to rename a street commemorating the accord that officially ended the war in Algeria. He has rechristened it to honor Hélie de Saint Marc, a World War II hero who later joined the rebel generals who defied de Gaulle and attempted a coup in 1961 to prevent Algerian independence. Ménard regards the Évian Accords that ended the Algerian war as a "capitulation" and those who tried to preserve French Algeria as heroes.

Ménard comes from a family of *pieds-noirs*, or French settlers, in Algeria who were forced to relocate in 1962, part of an exodus of seven hundred thousand. Béziers is home to many of them, and they are a reliable source of votes for him and for the FN. These days, the debate over identity is most heated in this region, where many *pieds-noirs*, like Ménard's family, arrived after fleeing Algeria. The Algerian war and decolonization is an open wound in southern France in much the same way that slavery still haunts the American South.

The wound has certainly not healed for Ménard. "In the official history of France, we present March 19, 1962, as the cease-fire because Charles de Gaulle signed the Évian Accords," he tells me. "There were more victims among the French of Algeria and the harkis after the cease-fire than before," he adds, referring to the massacres of Algerians who fought with France, but neglecting to mention the many Algerians and French soldiers who were murdered by diehard French colonialists after the cease-fire.[3] It's "historical revisionism to try to make people believe it was a cease-fire," he contends. "We all know it's a lie." Although there has been an outcry about the decision to rename the street, Ménard brushes it off. "No one's removed the plaque. It's still there."[4]

Ménard sees no contradiction between his current stance and his prior work as an advocate for press freedom. In fact, he began to change as a journalist, becoming outraged by corruption in Africa and Western aid to governments he believed were corrupt. "In France, when you lead an organization defending human rights, it's assumed that you're on the left because it's only the left, sir, that defends human rights," he says sarcastically, "it's only the left that's for equality, it's only the left that takes care of the poor."[5]

Pascal Bruckner is another Frenchman of the 1968 generation who has followed a similar political trajectory, but he is more clear-eyed in his appraisal of France's woes. Like Ménard and Finkielkraut, he is unsparing in his attacks on the left's blindness to certain problems and many leftists' hypocritical embrace of third-world villains. Yet he is not at all nostalgic for some imagined past idyll, as they are.

"Identity is not a cage but a point of departure that allows us to add onto the past, to turn it in a different direction," Bruckner writes. "A people, unless it buries itself in its own mausoleum, has to be able to break with its customs, trample on them in order to recharge its batteries."[6] France has not been honest about its own dark chapters. Rather than celebrate them, as Ménard does, Bruckner wants the filth out in the open. France "has long lived under a system of deferred truth, struggling to unveil the secrets that have been fermenting like a puddle of pus for years," from the delayed reckoning with the crimes of Vichy to the Algerian war. "It took almost sixty years for France to pay lip service to the Setif massacre in Algeria on May 8, 1945," he notes.[7] Bruckner doesn't want to dwell on the past and ruminate on the nation's sins, but he is honest enough to acknowledge them and to see a nation's strength in its ability to face the past squarely, as Germany has done, rather than sweep it under the rug.

Ménard prefers his nostalgia served raw. His latest crusade is to place a moratorium on the opening of kebab shops in Béziers. He caused an uproar when he declared war on the town's many Turkish-run restaurants, which on a Monday at 10:00 p.m. are among the only places open in the town center. "There are twenty to twenty-five. That's enough," says Ménard. "I'm for culinary diversity; the problem in Béziers is the diversity is in the other direction," he rages, like the vegetarian mayor of Hayange, who fears creeping Islamization of the national palate. "For me, the problem is defending the restaurants in the center of town that are not halal."[8]

In May 2016, Ménard organized a conference for the French right in Béziers, seeking to unify the FN supporters with disparate other groups—those backing Sarkozy, the so-called Identitaires movement, which opposes immigration and Islamization and argues, as Barrès does, that the French are rooted in their cemeteries and soil. Renaud Camus, the author of *Le grand remplacement* (The Great Replacement), was on hand to sign books, and Marion Maréchal-Le Pen, Marine's niece, represented the FN but ended up walking out halfway through the proceedings due to attacks on the party by other participants.

One of those in attendance was Julien Rochedy, the young conservative who served as the FN youth wing's leader from 2012 to 2014 before falling out with some members of Le Pen's inner circle. Rochedy went to the Béziers conference hoping the right could unify; he came away disappointed. He is still a committed conservative, yet he was convinced a year before the election that the FN would not get much more than 35 percent of the national vote in 2017 because of its backward-looking rhetoric. He was right. According to Rochedy, "They just want to go back thirty years." Their platform, he maintains, "doesn't at all take into account the world as it is and what France has become; it's a purely nostalgic discourse."

Rochedy has seen the FN from the inside, and he believes that they face a real challenge in reconciling a nostalgic vision with practical policies. "There is a difficulty for these parties, and for the FN in particular, to see things as they are," and try to respond—"not with answers that come from the '60s and the time of General de Gaulle" but with policies that address the challenges France faces today. He is aware that appeals to make France great again will win some votes, much as Trump touched nostalgic nerves with his slogan and his pledges to bring back jobs that moved abroad decades ago. "Unfortunately, today, European populist parties are winning with impressive margins because they draw on this nostalgia." It exists, Rochedy concedes, "but it won't win because nostalgia never wins." It might win with "those who have lost everything, who are really truly angry. So that's twenty to thirty percent of the population, but it can't go beyond that."[9]

He argues that the politics of nostalgia have a clear appeal, but not necessarily for the sort of voters one might expect. France is different from both Britain and the United States because of a generational divide that keeps older voters, even those angry about immigration, from voting for Le Pen. The reason, he insists, has less to do with ideology and more with caution and conservatism in the most literal sense.

Whereas young British voters overwhelmingly voted to remain in the EU and the elderly voted to leave, in France, opinion about the EU tends to run in the opposite direction. That's because appeals to nostalgia work better with the young, who dream of an era they never witnessed, than with the old, who lived through the good and the bad of an era Le Pen promises to restore. "Marine Le Pen can't win [among the elderly] because those people are afraid of leaving the euro," Rochedy told me in 2016. "They are afraid of huge changes. . . . She is scaring all the old people."

There is also a deeper cultural reflex. "The French are Vichyists," he insists, and not in the sense of racism and anti-Semitism. "Since World War I, the French have accepted foreign domination," he explains. "What matters, what they want, is jobs, security, and all that." But anyone seeking to run a campaign on the idea of France reclaiming its independence, as Le Pen has, is not likely to attract older voters. "It no longer speaks to them," says Rochedy, "There's a Vichyist mentality in the sense that as long as I'm living well, I don't mind if someone else is ruling me." As a result, the elderly vote for the parties that want to remain in Europe and the euro. Meanwhile, more and more of the young vote for the FN.

Rochedy was convinced then that if Marine Le Pen would just stop talking about leaving the euro and the EU, she would rise to 40 percent in the polls. Instead, she stood by her staunch Euroskepticism until the final days of the campaign. The results confirmed his analysis. Those in their sixties and seventies voted overwhelmingly—over 70 percent—for Macron.

As much as Rochedy is sympathetic to some of the broader goals of the FN and their views on immigration, he is a pragmatist, arguing that "these parties are living on the moon." As he sees it, "the far right in France lives off two fantasies," either what they call re-immigration, the idea that tomorrow they could "expel fifteen million people, which has never happened in history, or the total assimilation of fifteen million people, which also has never been seen in history." As an opposition party, the FN can say whatever it likes, but if it ever wins power, it will have to return to earth. "I understand what they want, and it's legitimate, I think, but it has absolutely no chance of succeeding," he adds.

When talking to FN leaders, including Le Pen, the idea of assimilation, rather than integration, is a favorite talking point, but Rochedy thinks it is just as misguided and impractical as their attempt to rewind history. "The FN wants to act as if the immigrants, the people who have entered France, never came. Their platform is to say, 'We'll assimilate them, all of them, whatever their origin, whatever their religion, and make them into perfect Frenchmen.'" It won't work. Their policy sells well with many voters, "except that ignores the fact that more than ten million people have entered France over the past thirty years. I believe that we will have to accept these communities, we will have to accept the communal fragmentation of France—a vision more in line with the American model."

That model is poorly understood in France, "but it is the only possible one," he argues. "We cannot make fifteen million people into native French. . . . It won't work anymore. Believing that is a failure to look at the world as it is. All they are doing is pleading to return to the way things were thirty years ago, but that serves no purpose at all, because it is impossible."[10]

As the 2017 election approached, France's nostalgist in chief, or at least its best-selling one, was Éric Zemmour. Having sold half a million copies of *The French Suicide,* Zemmour is the most widely read of the new French reactionaries. The ideology of the moment is nativist nostalgia, and Zemmour, despite or perhaps because his roots are in Algeria, channels it perfectly. The Jewish writer happily quotes a legendary anti-Semite, noting that "Maurras once exalted the 40 kings who made France; henceforth we will have to count the 40 years that unmade France."[11] He even had the chutzpah to defend the collaborationist Vichy regime in front of a synagogue audience, arguing that Jews had too much power in the French economy of the 1940s and that the Vichy regime's anti-Semitic decrees were merely discriminatory but not exterminationist.[12] Zemmour seems to believe that the sort of anti-Semitism that stops short of the gas chambers is acceptable.[13]

His five-hundred-page tome doesn't seek to connect the disparate dates marking France's slow progression to the grave. Zemmour is concerned primarily with providing a list of enemies and their crimes.[14] His pantheon of traitors includes feminists, Eurocrats, and lefty intellectuals. He denounces the *sans-papiers,* or undocumented immigrants, who were a favorite cause of the French left as a new "ideal Jew" and the return of a "Christ-like figure, a poor persecuted foreigner" who had come to save a sinful and corrupt France.[15]

But his most frequent target is Muslims. He doesn't attempt to hide his hatred for them or his hopelessness that their situation can be remedied. Like the Danish People's Party and Marine Le Pen, he has little time for integration—it's a lost cause. This extends to the national soccer team, often celebrated for its multihued representation of modern France. In Zemmour's telling, Les Bleus are a cesspool of barely literate converts who eat halal meals—an incarnation of the new white proletariat that will emerge from "reverse integration" if those of solid French stock are left to remain in the festering banlieues in the era of the great replacement.[16]

Zemmour's account of France's self-immolation apportions its blame equitably across the political spectrum. "The right betrays France in the name of globalization; the left betrays France in the name of the Republic. The right has abandoned the state in the name of liberalism; the left has abandoned the nation in the name of universalism," he writes. Most egregious, in his view, "The left has betrayed the people in the name of minorities."[17] And for a Maurras admirer like Zemmour, minorities are just paper citizens who do not belong to the "real France." They are not part of "the people."

Zemmour, the observant Jew with a soft spot for Vichy, laments the fact that "political elites have forbidden Europe to refer to 'its Christian roots,'" calling it a "premeditated suicide that brings back the storms that we fended off in the past," transforming France into a pathetic purgatory stuck between "tourist attractions and Islamic fortresses, between Disneyland and Kosovo." For him, as for Finkielkraut, the ideology of antiracism is the real threat.[18] Along with globalization and multiculturalism, it will be to the twenty-first century what totalitarianism was to the twentieth—"a messianic progressivism" that will eventually have the effect of replacing war between nations with wars within them.[19]

Rochedy rejects the best-selling nostalgia of people like Zemmour, but he is equally harsh toward the left and those who denounce any form of restriction on immigration. That path will lead to disaster, he believes. "What's amusing for us is that left-wing journalists, American Democrats, liberals who have a kind heart, those who want to open Europe up—by preventing a halt in immigration, they will lead France and other European countries to civil war." He is convinced that the road to hell is paved with good intentions and that failing to reduce immigration as much as possible while obliging politicians to accept legal immigration will lead France "straight for a catastrophe, and that's when there will be racism, hatred, and violence," the sort of dystopia Stenner imagines when the latent authoritarian reflex is fully provoked.

Rochedy is not sure anything can be done at this point to prevent conflict; some of it, he believes, is inevitable. Looking at tensions between young immigrants or their kids and native French in certain poor areas, he says, "I think it's too late. For my generation or the next, it's going to be horrible."

Whereas secularism was once a neutral glue that held the country together, it no longer serves that purpose. "It worked because it was French patriotism. French identity is no longer religion, it is no longer Catholicism; it is the republic, the homeland," he says, somewhat nostalgically for a twenty-nine-year-old. But state secularism has become a wedge issue rather than a unifier, a rallying cry for the FN on everything from butchers to burkinis. He argues that immigrants were once attracted to that strong sense of identity. "They wanted to become like that and part of that. . . . That's why France was able to assimilate a lot of immigrants," says Rochedy. "Now, there's nothing left. It's an open space."[20] And many voices have flocked to that void, including some who are far to the right of Marine Le Pen and some who are simply angry citizens like the neighbors of the Jungle in Calais. Others join the Identitaires movement, which glorifies a Frenchness rooted in white blood and a specific soil. Still others gravitate to right-wing websites like Francaisdesouche.com, a Breitbart for the ethnic French that hides nothing in its name.

Jean raspail does not like receiving visitors. He is furious that another journalist shared his unlisted phone number, but when I show up at his apartment in Paris's seventeenth arrondissement, he is eager to talk about his forty-four-year-old novel that everyone from Marine Le Pen to Donald Trump's adviser Stephen Bannon is fond of citing. "It's not a migration," Bannon said in a January 2016 Breitbart interview about refugees in Europe. "It's really an invasion. I call it the Camp of the Saints."[21] Bannon's obsession with the novel prompted a flurry of belated reviews in early 2017 by Anglophone critics discovering Raspail for the first time.

Published in 1973, just five years after the heyday of French student radicalism, *The Camps of the Saints* was roundly panned by the French intelligentsia, and Raspail was denounced as a reactionary neocolonialist. Now he feels vindicated.

Raspail's tone was scornful in the 1970s; he is even more bitter now, at ninety-two. Frail but sharp, Raspail declares, "The political situation in France is chaos. It is heartbreaking, it is sad, all these people are puppets." He never belonged to a political party and does not see a way out. "It bothers me because I am French, and I find that my country has become completely pathetic."[22]

Raspail is an old friend of Jean-Marie Le Pen and tells me that he has known Marine "very well since she was two years old." But he isn't a fan of where the FN is going. It was never a party of power, and it shouldn't be, in his view. "It was a party that had its usefulness," he argues. "It was a party that pissed off others, . . . raised important issues, and put on a good show."

Raspail believes the FN was always more effective at shaking things up and bringing new ideas into the political debate. "That's why people vote for them," he adds. Their strength is in the field of ideas. But now, he laments, "they want power, they want to have a lot of MPs," to gain real weight in the National Assembly. That, in his view, was their mistake.

Whatever the party's electoral fate in the coming years, Raspail paints a dire scenario for France. "There are peoples who have disappeared without massacre, . . . they have been absorbed ethnically, intellectually, legally. They entered into another civilization and they disappeared." And Europe is next. "We will become a minority, we white Europeans," he assures me.[23]

Raspail does not like mixing; much of his writing focuses on disappearing tribes and languages. "We are a country, a civilization, a language, a way of life. . . . That is what made the country. If we blend it with something that does not correspond at all to what we are, it won't work and we'll be lost." He says the same is true of Germans or the English, and it won't mean the apocalypse, but the essence of what he considers Frenchness will disappear. Here, Raspail sounds a lot like Renaud Camus in *Le grand remplacement*, or Barrès with his hallowed cemetery. "France will continue to function very well. It is a beautiful country, there are resources, . . . the railroads will work," he imagines. "But it will not be the same people at all. It has nothing to do with me, so I do not want it. I was born in a civilization that is mine, surrounded by people who will be my compatriots. That is my reason for living!" he exclaims. "I do not want to share it with people who may not all be ill intentioned but who will inevitably come to muddle and blur all of this."

He posits a theorem about assimilation: "Any minority that refuses to adapt is lost. Second, any minority that adapts is lost. There is no solution." He believes France is moving in the direction of adapting to Islam. He raves about Michel Houellebecq's novel *Submission*, which chronicles an Islamist takeover of France beginning with a moderate, well-meaning Muslim candidate to whom the left rallies to keep the FN from power. "Houellebecq picks up where *The Camp of the Saints* left off. . . . I had foreseen a lot of things, and he, he finally understood that the great danger is not the invasion like in *The Camp of the Saints*, although that is what we are now witnessing. Instead, we will be damned by our own weakness, by our cowardice." The French, he argues, sounding a lot like the woman he has known so well since she was two, are being asked to adapt to Islam and "a generalist global consensus . . . , which is as dangerous to me as Islam."[24]

Four decades after he wrote it, Raspail's book is mostly denounced for its overt racism or lauded as prophetic by right-wing anti-immigration activists. But what is most striking about the novel is the way it captured the tone and content of both sides of a fictional debate that has today become all too real. Raspail's chief villains are the liberal editors and radio hosts who lay out the welcome mat for the refugees. "When the heart gives way, it's a Turkish bazaar," he wrote disdainfully. The radio shows led by liberal hosts "paid for the inserts in those catalogues called newspapers, whose editors, decked out in suede, and barbecue-fed, with their Riviera tans, cried out for human liberation through an end to profits, preached rejection of money, that enslaver and corrupter of souls, called for doing away with all social constraints and for abject equality," he wrote. "It hit the spot. It sold. Whereas nothing else did." He imagined priests "frantically scribbling with an eye toward the following Sunday" as ready-made sermons came across the airwaves.[25]

Today, Raspail sees the European dilemma in the same way his protagonists did then. His heroic right-wing newspaper editor, Machefer, tries to raise his own militia, telling readers, "Unless the government orders the army to take all possible steps to prevent this landing, it's the duty of every citizen with any feeling for his culture, his race, his religion and traditions, not to think twice, but to take up arms himself."[26]

One of the book's heroes is the captain of a Greek ship who rams flailing refugees in the water. Other heroes include a not-so-fictional South African leader who threatens to fire on refugees without a second thought, a policy that Raspail's protagonists advocate in France as the fleet approaches. A naval captain advises the French president, "We have to make a choice. Either we open our doors to these people and take them in. Or we torpedo every one of their boats, at night, when it's too dark to see their faces as we kill them."[27]

The novel's climactic scene occurs when the French president is giving a radio address and falters just as he is about to give orders to fire on the refugees coming onto French shores. In his speech to the nation on the eve of the refugee fleet's arrival, the president declares, "Today it's the poor who are on the attack, with their ultimate weapon. . . . I have, therefore, ordered the army to open fire, if need be, to prevent the refugees from effecting a landing." But then he hesitates, backing off his orders and "asking every soldier and officer, every member of our police—asking them from the depths of my conscience and my soul—to weigh this monstrous mission for themselves, and to feel free either to accept or reject it."[28]

I mention that Frauke Petry, the leader of Germany's AfD, called for using live ammunition if Germany's borders were overrun by refugees. In the novel, Raspail's character backtracks at the last moment, but for the author, the question of whether to fire or not to fire is the essence of the book and forty years later captures the dilemma Europe faces.

"I don't concern myself with their motives," Raspail says of the refugees and migrants arriving in Europe today. "They are poor, they are on the run, there are women and children. They are millions. If they enter, there will be millions more that will arrive after them. What do we do? Do we pull the trigger?" he asks. The answer for the book's fictional president is no, but it's clear Raspail sees his character as spineless. "We are encumbered throughout Europe, by the ex-Christian phenomena of compassion," he says. "Compassion is fabulous, . . . but it is obvious that without the use of force, we will never stop the invasion."

"We do not send them home, we help bring them in," he says. This, he maintains, is due to misguided impulses rooted in "two thousand years of Christian charity." In Raspail's view, that charity was "for the neighbor, for the people nearby. . . . Christian charity did not say to love the totality of the world," he tells me. Raspail, a Catholic, is even willing to criticize the pope. "He does not know what Europe is. He is not a European. It does not interest him much," he laments. Whereas Pope John Paul II talked about nations and borders, Pope Francis is "willing to get along with the Muslims," he complains. Indeed, his only sign of mercy is for fellow Christians. Should France open its arms to Christians from Syria? I ask. "We have to welcome them," he says bluntly.[29]

MANY CRITICS HAVE ACCUSED RASPAIL OF BEING A WHITE SUPREMACIST. Although his heroes in the book are mostly white and Christian, there is one assimilated Hindu who joins them in their last stand against the "invaders." When the refugee boats arrive, only a small band of patriots holds out, including the murderous Greek captain, the editor Machefer, and the Indian man. They gather with the old professor in his stone house to keep a tally of the body count as they shoot down the "invaders." Being white, Raspail likes to say, "is a state of mind."[30]

In person, his views closely resemble those of his characters. For Raspail, so many years after he wrote *The Camp of the Saints,* it is still about religion and whiteness. Poles once came to France en masse, he recalls. "All the mines in the north were populated by Poles. But perfect gentlemen, . . . they are Christians, they are European, and they are white. A Western civilization, then, it goes very well," he says approvingly. Raspail begins to get angry when I ask him what he would do now.

"I am not the president of the republic," he snaps. But eventually, he responds, "My answer is this: we are fucked."[31]

Raspail sees a movement taking shape today, much like the small band of men who face down the refugees in his novel. "We're fed up; we've seen enough. . . . In Marseilles, there are more Muslims than Christians now. They say, 'It's all right, they're French, they're going to vote.'" He rejects this. "No, there is going to be a resistance movement, and it has begun. . . . There are alliances that are being built unconsciously. Catholic movements, identity movements," Raspail tells me.

As Amin Bagdouche, the doctor who treats migrants in the Calais Jungle, sensed after seeing his tires slashed and his van set on fire, the conflict has moved beyond the refugee issue. Something is brewing, a movement that attracts both ex-generals and hooligans, that posts the names and addresses of people to target on social media, and that has an appeal that exists "somewhere beyond the law."[32]

The two men—a white nationalist celebrated by the anti-immigrant right, and the half-Algerian doctor who became a humanitarian activist—could not be more different, but their dark vision is strikingly similar.

"If the situation becomes the one I predict—catastrophic—there will certainly be resistance that is both tough and armed. . . . People will want to liberate their city," the man who four decades ago foresaw a mass influx of refugees in Europe assures me.

"There is something that will explode, I cannot tell you what, I cannot tell you if I wish for it, I don't know," says Raspail. "But something will explode."[33]

Epilogue

In our modern age, nationalism is not resurgent; it never died.

—ISAIAH BERLIN

ON THE MORNING OF NOVEMBER 9, 2016, I FOUND MYSELF GIVING A TALK to a hundred people, some angry and some on the verge of tears, at the Open Society Foundations in New York.[1] It was meant to be a small lunchtime seminar on the European far right. Given Donald Trump's shock victory less than twelve hours earlier, it quickly became a discussion of "How could this happen here?"

The crowd was international and diverse. A woman with a German accent stood up and asked whether the proper way to respond to Trump was to resist, to recognize his voters' pain but reject their misguided politics, or accommodate them. I told her that none of these solutions would help reverse populists' advances in the United States or anywhere else they have gained influence and power.

Seeking to eradicate xenophobic sentiments, as many anti-Trump and anti–Le Pen activists seem to believe they can, is misguided. They forget that tens of thousands of midwestern voters who supported Obama in 2012 voted for Trump in 2016.[2] The Michigan Democratic congresswoman Debbie Dingell predicted it might happen in her state. She was dismissed as crazy. "At Rotary clubs, local chambers of commerce, union halls and mosques, I noted that we could see a Trump presidency," she wrote in the *Washington Post* two days after the 2016 election.[3] Even after Bernie Sanders upset Hillary Clinton in the Michigan primary, Democrats continued to ignore the state until literally the last minute.[4]

I'd felt the same fear as Dingell as I drove along a highway lined with Trump-Pence signs on the way to Detroit's airport the day before the election, listening to radio reports that Obama had just flown in for a pro-Clinton rally—this in a state where Obama had decisively defeated Mitt Romney, the son of Michigan's former governor, by a ten-point margin.

"I knew the Downrivers would support Trump both in the Republican primary and in the general," wrote Dingell, referring to the blue-collar postindustrial sprawl to the south of Detroit that was once dominated by union households and staunch Democrats. "I witness the emotions and passions of their residents every day, and I believe they are what elected Trump president."[5]

The distance from the northern tip of France, where Marine Le Pen took 57 percent of the vote, to the southeastern corner of Michigan, where Trump won 58 percent, is not so great, and the grievances of voters in both places are strikingly similar.[6] They resent factories that close down and send jobs abroad, they fear both Islam and the growing number of immigrants they see in their towns (or hear about on TV), and they bristle at the triumphalism of the globalist class that appears to be succeeding while they fall further behind.

At the end of my talk, a man who worked in the IT department stood up to make a comment; he was the last person to raise his hand, and many in the audience had already left. He explained that he came from the border of Ohio and Pennsylvania, and most of his family members had voted for Trump, and not because they were racists or hated Muslims. Many of those who remained in the room looked genuinely shocked. They couldn't imagine that anyone would vote for Trump for any other reason.

Since November 8, 2016, there has been a lot of blame among Democrats and a healthy dose of self-flagellation, too. Some blame Clinton's Wall Street ties; others find fault in the modern Democratic Party's obsession with identity politics. But the assumption that Americans have to throw gays and blacks under the bus in order to appeal to working-class whites is false. Building an electoral coalition is not a zero-sum game, and a party can have both objectives. There are real tensions, however, between the identity-politics model of progressivism and the old-fashioned leftist politics of class, and they need to be reckoned with.

Too many people of my generation have barely any memory of a left focused on the economic interests of the working class; to them, progressive politics is mostly associated with identity-based movements from transgender rights to Black Lives Matter, and those supporting a candidate like Trump are too often seen as incorrigible racists rather than alienated ex-Democrats. As the British writer Nick Cohen observed, "When the liberals despise the working class the opportunities for back-lash politics are boundless."[7]

The irony is that nativist politicians like Trump or Holland's Geert Wilders are not particularly concerned with bread-and-butter issues, and their economic policies aren't terribly helpful to workers and the poor. But because there is often no class-based counterargument coming from the left, it is easy for right-wing populists to seize that political terrain; it is an open space.

Trump's popularity among working-class whites shows that rheto-ric and cultural appeals matter more than details in an environment where there is no clear policy debate. Once the old battle lines disap-pear, realignment becomes very easy. The challenge for today's left is to acknowledge these voters' fears and offer policies that help address their grievances without making the sort of moral concessions that lead toward reactionary illiberal policies.

MANY HAVE COMPARED THE RISE OF DONALD TRUMP IN THE UNITED States to the ascendance of populist parties in Europe. During the cam-paign, grassroots right-wing activists from Calais to The Hague expressed admiration for Trump and praised him as a reflection of their own ideals. Wilders even attended the Republican convention in Cleveland, where he headlined an LGB-Trump event along with Pamela Geller and Milo Yiannopoulos—speaking in front of a wall featuring photos of bare-chested men, Make America Great Again hats, and a "Don't Tread on Me" flag.

Wilders tried to take a page from the Trump campaign by becom-ing a social media sensation, but in the end, he lost the election. While Trump's Twitter feed no doubt fueled his popularity in certain quarters, Wilders failed to learn a second lesson from his American idol. Trump campaigned tirelessly across the country, often holding three or more mass rallies per day. Wilders barely left his office, hoping to win an elec-tion simply by regurgitating his familiar anti-Islam slogans on Twitter.

Trump has been extremely successful at mobilizing a segment of the American population and earning their enthusiastic support, but his followers represent a declining demographic, which bodes ill for the long-term success of his brand of white identity politics. As Robert P. Jones wrote a few months before Trump's victory, during the Obama years, white Christian America became a minority for the first time in US history, falling from 54 percent of the population in 2008 to 45 percent in 2015. "The passing of a coherent cultural world—where working class jobs made ends meet and white conservative Christian values held sway—has produced this powerful politics of white Christian resentment," he wrote.[8] Trump voters felt it viscerally.

Fear of decline and of small numbers can be a powerful political force, especially when a group accustomed to being on top sees its power wane while an opportunistic leader fuels the fears and resentments of its members.[9] A few months before Trump's victory, Jones wrote in the *Atlantic*, "It is the disappearance of white Christian America that is driving their strong, sometimes apocalyptic reactions."[10] It would be naive to ignore them, because many members of this group are perfectly capable of fighting a rearguard battle to preserve their dominance.

It is an argument at the core of J. D. Vance's devastating memoir, *Hillbilly Elegy*. Vance grew up in Appalachia and the Rust Belt, in desperate places where heroin addiction is widespread and a majority struggle to make ends meet against a backdrop of shuttered factories and desolate downtowns.[11]

Trump has filled a void precisely because, as Vance argued in an interview, "the two political parties have offered essentially nothing to these people for a few decades. From the Left, they get some smug condescension, an exasperation that the white working class votes against their economic interests because of social issues. . . . From the Right, they've gotten the basic Republican policy platform of tax cuts, free trade, deregulation, and paeans to the noble businessman and economic growth," a tone-deaf approach, Vance insists, when the local small business owner has just fired your brother. Suddenly, Trump comes along, a guy who relishes attacking elites and openly criticizes companies that outsource jobs. His campaign was music to their ears.[12]

Just as white Christian America was fading into minority status—the sort of power transition that leads to war between nations, according to certain international relations theorists—Obama was elected.[13] A well-dressed, well-educated black president who was a good father and whose wife told Middle America to stop feeding their kids junk added to this sense of smallness and being eclipsed.[14]

Studies after the 2016 election showed that it was not just economic resentment but cultural anxiety—a fear that an America these voters knew and had once dominated was disappearing—that drove the election results. Trump's numbers among white working-class voters with such anxieties were staggering; after he skillfully stoked their rage, 80 percent of those who felt things had changed so much that they felt like strangers in their own country supported Trump in 2016.[15]

The New York and Washington echo chambers that elites and intellectuals from both parties inhabit are very different from the world these voters live in. In their world, there is little trust in the press, and there's no check on the Internet conspiracy theories that have come to rule the digital world.[16] Today's meritocracy, by contrast, has become a circle of winners that listens only to itself. When those outside this winner's circle "come to view all formal authority as fraudulent, good governance becomes impossible," writes the MSNBC journalist Chris Hayes, setting off "a vicious cycle of official misconduct and low expectations."[17]

Only by listening to and understanding marginalized voters' rage can activists and mainstream politicians hope to win them back. The left so far has failed to make them a better offer, and belittling them doesn't help.[18] Considering that a large number of Trump voters in Michigan and Wisconsin voted for Obama at least once if not twice, getting them to return to the fold matters.

The alternative is far worse; denouncing and disparaging these voters can, eventually, lead to a desire for authoritarian solutions, especially when major media institutions are distrusted by large sections of the population. "If the experts as a whole are discredited," Hayes wrote in 2012, "we are faced with an inexhaustible supply of quackery."[19]

Those lines perfectly anticipated the Trump campaign of 2016 and the culture of distrust that made it possible. Trump hired Steve Bannon, the head of the rabble-rousing right-wing site Breitbart News and a great admirer of Jean Raspail, to run his campaign after the revelations about his Putin-coddling campaign manager, Paul Manafort, became too much of a liability. A purveyor of fringe quackery had reached the inner circle of a major party's presidential campaign and then secured a key role in the White House.

ON THE MORNING OF APRIL 23, 2017, AS THE POLLS OPENED IN THE ninth arrondissement of Paris, an old man with a cane positioned himself in front of a bright yellow mailbox and began to scrape. After a few minutes, he sauntered away toward the markets of the rue des Martyrs, leaving a torn and scratched relic of the modified hammer-and-sickle logo of the hard-left candidate Jean-Luc Mélenchon's party, France Insoumise (Rebellious or, literally, Unsubmissive France).

The old man, no fan of Mélenchon's anticapitalist, anti-NATO, pro-Russian rhetoric, had reason to worry. In neighborhoods like this, the epicenter of Paris hipsterdom, Mélenchon polled well. Everyone from student protesters to academics and the well-to-do scions of one of the city's wealthiest families told me they were voting for the ex-communist firebrand. His soaring oratory and rage at the system captivated the left and almost propelled him into the second round; he finished with almost 20 percent of the vote, just 2 percent less than Le Pen.

After the results came in, Mélenchon was the only defeated candidate who did not call upon his followers to back the centrist candidate Emmanuel Macron against Le Pen in the second round. He instead consulted 250,000 of them online and found that two-thirds refused to support Macron. In the days leading up to round two, there was panic on the left.[20] Even the former Communist Party organ *L'Humanité* printed op-eds calling on readers who had voted for Mélenchon to grudgingly back Macron.[21] According to postelection polls, only half of Mélenchon's voters did so; many simply stayed home, contributing to the highest abstention rate in decades (25 percent) and the largest number of blank or spoiled ballots (over four million, or 12 percent of all votes) ever recorded.[22]

Le Pen and Mélenchon together drew nearly 50 percent of the youth vote in the first round, splitting the 18–34 age bracket evenly. Unlike in Britain's Brexit referendum, the young did not support the status quo; they voted for extremists who want to leave the EU.[23]

Those who believe millennials are immune to authoritarian ideas are mistaken. Using data from the World Values Survey, the political scientists Roberto Foa and Yascha Mounk have painted a worrying picture. As the French election demonstrated, belief in core tenets of liberal democracy is in decline, especially among those born after 1980. Their findings challenge the idea that after achieving a certain level of prosperity and political liberty, countries that have become democratic do not turn back.[24]

In America, 72 percent of respondents born before World War II deemed it absolutely essential to live in a democracy; only 30 percent of millennials agreed. The figures were similar in Holland. The number of Americans favoring a strong leader unrestrained by elections or parliaments has increased from 24 to 32 percent since 1995. More alarmingly, the number of Americans who believe that military rule would be good or very good has risen from 6 to 17 percent over the same period. The young and wealthy were most hostile to democratic norms, with fully 35 percent of young people with a high income regarding army rule as a good thing.[25] Mainstream political science, confident in decades of received wisdom about democratic "consolidation" and stability, was ignoring a disturbing shift in public opinion.[26]

There could come a day when, even in wealthy Western nations, liberal democracy ceases to be the only game in town. And when that day comes, those who once embraced democracy could begin to entertain other options. Even Ronald Inglehart, the celebrated eighty-three-year-old political scientist who developed his theory of democratic consolidation more than four decades ago, has conceded that falling incomes, rising inequality, and the abject dysfunction of many governments—especially America's—have led to declining support for democracy. If such trends continue, he wrote in response to Foa and Mounk, "then the long-run outlook for democracy is indeed bleak."[27]

Part of voters' disillusionment stems from the political establishment's failure to confront very real tensions and failures of integration, either sweeping them under the rug by pretending violent extremism and attacks on free speech were not problems or implementing policies that failed. These legitimate debates have been eclipsed by an obsessive focus on Muslims after 9/11 that paints them as somehow different from earlier immigrant groups, members of a uniquely violent and unassimilable religion. This image has played a crucial supporting role in legitimizing the rhetoric of anti-immigration parties and opened the door for a web-savvy army of right-wing propagandists who put forth arguments that are both offensive and easily digestible.

Christopher Caldwell's provocative 2009 book, *Reflections on the Revolution in Europe,* stood out from the chorus of shrill and alarmist writers who warned that mass migration posed a fundamental threat to European culture and stability.[28] His was a serious and carefully argued book.

The central question he posed was, "Can Europe be the same with different people in it?" He held that the erosion of old Christian values and a strong sense of national pride in much of Western Europe weakened the cultural identity of countries to the point that they were no match for the all-encompassing identity offered by Islam.[29]

But Caldwell failed to pose a crucial and closely related question: Can Europe be the same if it abandons its core political values? What he and others contending that Muslim immigrants threaten the West's cultural fabric have neglected to ask is whether the threat to liberal democracy could originate from within, rather than from outside.

What if genuine refugees are sent home to face persecution and death? What will happen to the social fabric of democratic countries if foreigners are treated as second-class citizens and denied the same rights as the native-born? And what if, in reaction to the challenges of mass migration, liberal democracies abandon their constitutional principles and adopt exclusionary policies that erode their long-standing commitment to human rights?

Writers like Caldwell don't seem to have considered that European nations' harsh reactions to outsiders could reduce them to democracies on paper but not in practice or that their leaders, facing extreme electoral pressure from angry citizens and right-wing parties, might sabotage their own painstakingly crafted democratic institutions.

Caldwell's declaration that there is no political force in secularized Europe capable of matching the all-consuming identity offered by Islam seemed prescient when it was published, but it was premature.

As the events of the past two years have proved, there is in fact a powerful countervailing form of extremism that is alive and well in Europe: white nationalism. It was not strong enough to put Marine Le Pen in power, but it did garner over one-third of valid votes cast in France's presidential runoff. It is a competing ideology that is in many ways a mirror image of radical Islamism. Both share a nostalgic obsession with a purist form of identity: on the one side, a medieval Islamic State; on the other, a pure white nation unpolluted by immigrant blood. Both extremist visions feed off one another, and they have the power to tear Europe apart.

The nagging question today is which Europe will ultimately win. In the wake of Emmanuel Macron's impressive victory in the French election, it is tempting to think that the plague of populist nationalism has been banished. But that would be naive.

WITHIN MINUTES OF MACRON'S VICTORY ON MAY 7, 2017, THE triumphalism began across the world. MACRON DEFEATS RADICALISM, proclaimed Spain's *El País*. FRANCE STEMS TIDE OF POPULIST REVOLUTION, Britain's *Independent* cheered. WHITE NATIONALISM GETS THUMPED, declared David Leonhardt in the *New York Times* the next morning.

The euphoria that greeted Macron's victory is understandable but dangerous. Marine Le Pen's FN won over 10.5 million votes, double the number her father received in 2002. She ran a serious and competent campaign, unlike other far-right figures. As with Holland, where Geert Wilders's weaker-than-expected showing in the March 2017 election was interpreted as a signal that populism's march had been halted, there is no cause for celebration.

Wilders performed poorly because the few times he did campaign, he was surrounded by a phalanx of armed guards in small villages filled with supporters. Le Pen, by contrast, stumped all across the country and braved crowds throwing eggs at her in staunchly anti-FN Brittany. She even tried to upstage Macron in his hometown, Amiens, where he waded into a hostile crowd of striking Whirlpool workers and, rather than pandering, told them he wouldn't make any "airy promises" to avert the closure of their factory.[30] When Le Pen heard he was going to visit, she descended on the site with her entourage first, seeking to bolster her credentials with workers whom she knew would not be receptive to Macron's free-market message. It was a bold move akin to Trump's visit to an Indiana air conditioner factory a few weeks after the election, where he sought to show that he was already saving American jobs.

Even in Paris, where Marine Le Pen's posters were routinely defaced with the word "SATAN," there was no unanimity about how to fight her. Unlike in 2002, the *front républicain* that had battered Le Pen the elder did not materialize this time. Macron's victory, with 66 percent of the vote, was a convincing one, but it was nowhere near Jacques Chirac's 82 percent score—a testament to what Marine Le Pen has achieved. She has almost doubled her father's share of the vote, having drawn in supporters from both the far left and center right.[31]

After the FN's loss, Le Pen gave a concession speech that sounded more like a campaign rally for the upcoming legislative elections. Marion Maréchal, Marine Le Pen's niece, the more likable and telegenic face of the party, openly entertained the idea of overhauling the party on national TV and perhaps further rebranding it to create a broader conservative movement. A few days later, Marion Maréchal announced she was leaving politics; few doubt she will be gone long.[32] If the FN finally abandons its name and the baggage that comes with it, younger leaders may be able to de-demonize the party in a way that Marine Le Pen could not.

Too many people on the European left scoff at nationalism, mistaking their own distaste for evidence that the phenomenon no longer exists or is somehow illegitimate. If 2016 and 2017 have proven anything, it is that this sort of visceral nationalism, or loyalty to one's in-group, still exists. It can be manipulated in ways that lead to chauvinistic violence, or it can manifest itself in innocuous displays of national pride, like waving the team's flag at the World Cup. But it is not going away.

Pretending nationalism is passé may be popular among globe-trotting university students and tech entrepreneurs but is not a political proposition likely to win national elections. As the Israeli academic Azar Gat argues, "Ethnic and national affinities have deep roots in the human psyche and have been among the most powerful forces in human history." It is not merely a phase or some sort of "atavistic relic in a liberal, cosmopolitan, and universalist age."[33]

That humans need to belong to a group as much as they need food is an idea that goes back centuries.[34] As the philosopher Isaiah Berlin once argued, nationalism is a "pathological form of self-protective resistance" in the face of patronizing or condescending outsiders—"the inflamed desire of the insufficiently regarded to count for something."[35] Berlin wrote those words in 1972, but they could equally be applied to anti-EU Brexit voters and Le Pen's supporters today.

Those who dismiss this sort of national sentiment as backward and immature do so at their own peril. People across the world, even the jet-setting members of the transnational elite, occasionally feel pangs of nostalgia for home cooking or a welcome ease when speaking their native tongue. This is not an irrational feeling; it is simply a fact of life. The problem for many on the globalist left is that they falsely believed it could be purged.

As Berlin argued more than forty years ago, "There really are sincere and genuine liberals who . . . sometimes discount the very existence of certain facts" that might impede their goals. As if he were talking about the Brussels bureaucrats or self-assured American Democrats of 2016, he warned that some see the "existence of nations, of national feelings, as obstacles and nuisances, . . . something which ought to be cleared away for the purposes of creating one great united human race."[36]

What these globalists miss is that not everyone has the luxury of leaving. A well-educated multilingual Londoner with friends and family abroad could easily find work in Brussels or Frankfurt; for her, the EU represents great opportunity. For the resident of a small rural town, with no education beyond high school and no foreign language skills, the EU is a threat, especially when he is forced to compete with Poles and Romanians for construction jobs. Those who don't have the education and skills to travel abroad often resent those who do. To compensate, they identify strongly with the place they come from and support politicians who promise to protect them from both genuine and imaginary threats. They do not have the luxury of voting with their feet, but their protest is felt at the polls.[37]

PAUL SCHEFFER, THE MAN WHO STARTED THE DUTCH INTEGRATION debate in earnest, says he entered the political trenches when he found himself asking, "Why is my tolerance falling apart?"

Scheffer warned in March 2016 that it was a mistake to dismiss Donald Trump or to argue that he was fundamentally different from European populists or less likely to win. He also pointed to the supporters who don't fit easy stereotypes—pro-Trump Latinos, Surinamese Hindus who voted for Pim Fortuyn, or Dutch Moroccans who say Wilders is right, even if they won't support him.

Holland, like many EU countries, has entered a postideological age where the cleavages that used to define parties and politics no longer exist. Years of coalition governments spanning the center left and center right emptied Dutch debate of genuine ideological clashes. This postideological moment is precisely what has made the ground fertile for populists and confused everyone else.

The assumption that ignoring populist politicians or even declaring them beyond the pale will make them go away has been repeatedly proven false. The Dutch center-left party, D66, won almost as many seats as Wilders in the March 2017 election, largely by taking him on fearlessly. "If you don't stand up and point out where he's wrong, that the issues are real and their solutions are fake," insists Sjoerd Sjoerdsma, the party's immigration spokesman, then the debate will continue to move further to the right and politicians like Wilders will win the battle of ideas, even when they do not win power at the polls.

The populists can't simply be ignored. With or without actual control of the government, they have proved they can exert influence and shape debates without ever wielding formal power. Those who oppose populism need first to understand it. To dismiss the populist impulse as something completely alien is to miss the point and to preemptively lose the political debate.

"When people talk about populism, it starts with the presumption this is irrational," says Scheffer. The starting point instead needs to be "there is fear on all sides and that there is irrationality on all sides," he insists. "And then we start arguing."[38]

Accepting that these views exist is not a moral concession; it is political realism. Recognizing that strong nationalist sentiments are not going away does not mean giving in to the policy preferences of the populist right; it means taking them seriously, engaging with their ideas, and defeating those ideas by proving they are unrealistic and will not help people. To ignore and marginalize nationalists by denouncing them as retrograde fascists while advocating completely unfettered immigration policies that add to their sense of cultural anxiety simply makes things worse: it provokes those predisposed to authoritarianism to support strong nationalistic leaders.[39]

Those arguing for wide-open borders tend to be extremely self-righteous, casting their position as morally unassailable. They are not only making a political mistake likely to cost their side elections; they are also exhibiting a lack of foresight. Many of the arguments for free movement and generous refugee and skilled immigrant quotas are morally appealing, but one cannot honestly argue for complete openness without acknowledging that it could result in huge demographic shifts in Europe, America, and poor nations if there is catastrophic climate change in crowded countries. A purely free market of movement could in a few generations cause Greece to become majority Egyptian, mineral-rich African nations like Zambia to become majority Chinese, and poor ones like Mali or Sierra Leone to lose their entire populations to wealthy countries like France and the United Kingdom—economies that are not at the moment prepared to absorb and integrate huge numbers of newcomers in an effective and sustainable way.[40]

TODAY'S FAR RIGHT LEADERS ARE DANGEROUS NOT BECAUSE THEY ARE fascists in the Hitlerian sense but because angry voters, under the right conditions of cultural and economic anxiety, will latch on to their ideas and follow them, falling victim to new political mythologies without any resistance.[41] That can eventually take a country in a dangerous direction.

The first step in any coherent political project to counter right-wing populists is to reject the fear that fuels their popularity and resist the temptation to adopt their policies. Very few leaders have done this. In Holland and Denmark, the center right and the Social Democratic left have largely caved and adopted certain planks from the populists' platform. The left has lost much of its old base by appearing to care only about free trade, technological progress, and limitless diversity. This scares many people who used to vote for the Democratic Party, British Labour, or European Social Democrats.

It is possible for the left to "feel their pain," without adopting a Trumpian or Le Pen–style agenda. It is not so difficult to tell voters that their resentment of companies that have sent jobs abroad is legitimate or that they are entitled to be uncomfortable about a large influx of immigrants in their hometowns. Whatever one thinks of Bernie Sanders's policies, his campaign managed to attract millions of working-class voters almost entirely based on economic appeals while denouncing Trump's nativism and Islamophobia. Others can do it, too.

In Europe, there are only two leaders who have unequivocally rejected the nativist vision of the far right. Angela Merkel has remained steadfast in her openness to refugees while admitting she has made some policy mistakes. And Emmanuel Macron, France's new president, has forthrightly refused to take the bait, telling Marine Le Pen to her face during the vicious final presidential debate on May 3, "Who plays upon people's fears? It's you, the high priestess of fear is sitting in front of me." He doubled down on this argument in his May 7 victory speech, insisting to the crowds at the Louvre, "we will not succumb to fear, . . . to division."[42]

This is easy to say after winning an election; it will be harder if there is another attack. Macron's challenge will be to stand by his lofty rhetoric when there are bodies in the streets and crowds are baying for blood. Some of Le Pen's views on terror and immigration have become commonplace even among those who voted against her; the knee-jerk reaction after attacks in most European countries is to tighten immigration controls, but as Macron told her during the debate, closing borders doesn't stop terrorism, especially in a country like France, where most of the attacks have been perpetrated by French or EU citizens.

Terrorist attacks have in most cases not been connected to the recent wave of refugees, but the two have been conflated in the public's mind because Le Pen and those afraid of losing votes to her have deliberately linked the two. The overwhelming majority of French Muslims are just as afraid of terrorism as the FN's voters; they have been its victims twice over, killed in many of the attacks and collectively punished in their wake by a society that blames all Muslims for the crimes of a few.[43]

If Macron can continue to divorce counterterrorism policy from the immigration debate and prove that liberal democracies can be tough on terror without calling for Trump-style travel bans or punitive laws that target Muslims and no one else, it will be a huge achievement, demonstrating that France can fight Islamist terrorism mercilessly without declaring war on Muslims and eroding the rights of the country's largest minority.

IF TERRORISTS ONCE AGAIN MANAGE TO STRIKE AMERICA, PRESIDENT Trump will likely seek emergency powers just like British and French leaders have in the past—but with far more dire consequences. It is one thing for leaders committed to democratic norms to seek temporary powers to fight terrorism; it is quite another to grant such powers to a nativist authoritarian who regularly flouts those norms by denouncing judges, targeting Muslims for differential treatment, and firing independent officials for disloyalty.

Security crackdowns and states of emergency after shocking acts of violence are designed to show strength at moments of vulnerability, but ultimately, they can target not just terrorists but other groups as well. As the British law lord Leonard Hoffman wrote in a 2004 decision condemning indefinite detention of foreign terrorism suspects, "Terrorist violence, serious as it is, does not threaten our institutions of government or our existence as a civil community." He added, "The real threat to the life of the nation, in the sense of a people living in accordance with its traditional laws and political values, comes not from terrorism but from laws such as these. That is the true measure of what terrorism may achieve."[44]

The immediate reaction to the Manchester terrorist attack on May 22, 2017, seemed to confirm those fears. Within hours of a suicide bombing that killed twenty-two people at a concert, Katie Hopkins of the *Daily Mail* declared on Twitter, "We need a final solution," proving that even members of the media elite are not above raising the specter of ethnic cleansing in the heat of the moment. She quickly deleted the overt Nazi reference and apologized, only to declare two weeks later that "our process for dealing with terror cannot be words or vigils. It must be internment and deportation. And we keep deporting until our house is in order."[45]

Liberal democracies are better equipped than authoritarian states to grapple with the inevitable conflicts that arise in diverse societies, including the threat of terrorist violence. But they also contain the seeds of their own destruction: if they fail to deal with these challenges and allow xenophobic populists to hijack the public debate, then the votes of frustrated and disaffected citizens will increasingly go to the anti-immigrant right, societies will become less open, nativist parties will grow more powerful, and racist rhetoric that promotes a narrow and exclusionary sense of national identity will be legitimized.

The mainstreaming of xenophobic views and policies could eventually undermine the liberal democratic model of government in countries that we today regard as progressive and tolerant. The result would be a watered-down form of democracy that deprives immigrants and ethnic and religious minorities of basic rights. And at worst, it would mean a resurgence of the ugliest nationalist ideologies that marred the history of the twentieth century.

Acknowledgments

THE TRAVEL AND RESEARCH FOR THIS PROJECT WOULD NOT HAVE BEEN possible without the generous support of the Open Society Foundations. The Open Society Fellowship allowed me to devote an entire year to researching this book and to visit the eight countries covered in it, as well as a few others, for reporting. Thanks especially to Bipasha Ray, Steve Hubbell, Lenny Benardo, Zach Seltzer, and Milap Patel in New York; Sipho Malunga and Fatima Hassan in South Africa; and Jordi Vaquer and his colleagues in the Barcelona office.

This book was written under many roofs and occasionally outdoors in the middle of nowhere, when I needed to be far away from people and farther from a reliable internet connection. Thanks to William, Michael, and the zebras at Fonteinskloof; to Hilka and Linden in Noordhoek; and to Mario and family at Pera di Basso.

I am grateful to everyone who hosted me over the past two years. Thanks to my mother, Val Polakow, and stepfather, Simon Baseley, for housing and feeding me during two stints of fourteen-hour-per-day writing sprees in Ann Arbor and for taking pity on me and giving me a nice new monitor after seeing me try to write a book on a little laptop; to my father, Len Suransky, for providing me with an air mattress, wheels, and a printer while in South Africa; to my stepmother, Carolina, and my sisters, Sarafina and Sonya, for putting me up on many visits to Holland and giving me occasional advice on the intricacies of Dutch politics; and to my brother, Shael, and sister-in-law, Cynthia (and most recently my niece, Selah), for welcoming me on many whirlwind visits to New York.

Thanks to Eubie and Nduduzo in Johannesburg; Louise, Hans, and Jasmine in Amsterdam; Sune, Lindsay, Sofia, and Viggo in Copenhagen; my uncle David in St. Ives; Anna Rubbo and Diana Hosking in Sydney;

Benjamin and Evelyn Choi in Hong Kong; Sepideh Farkhondeh, Thomas Williams, and Valentine Faure in Paris—and especially to Marlow Cora Williams, the most astute analyst of French politics under the age of five, for temporarily moving out to allow a *remplaçant* with a strange accent to colonize her bedroom.

A book like this is never possible without the many connectors who lead journalists to their sources by sharing e-mails, phone numbers, and addresses. There is a long list of people who do not appear in the text or endnotes but without whom I would never have managed to find those I've quoted. I am indebted to Søren and Kresten Schultz Jørgensen, Sijbolt Noorda, Saïd Mahrane, Zoé Reyners, Clélie Mathias, Olivier Guez, Sascha Lehnartz, Thomas Bagger, Don Markwell, Mran-Maree Laing, Monique Corah, Anthony Bubalo, Katie Engelhart, Abdelkader Benali, Chantal Suissa-Runne, Haroon Sheikh, Sisonke Msimang, Jennifer van den Bussche, Atossa Abrahamian, Thomas Bøje, Tarek Omar, Arnon Grunberg, Jacques Faisant, and others whom I've probably forgotten to include. I am especially grateful to the more than one hundred people who agreed to be interviewed for this book, especially those who were happy to talk despite our political disagreements.

Thank you to Isabelle Daumont for her excellent transcriptions of several French interviews and to Vinti Vaid and colleagues at Indian Scribes for their transcriptions of many others. Thanks also to Erwan and Guillaume at the Jungle in Calais for letting me in and showing me around and to the Tällberg Foundation for inviting me to Lesbos to see the refugee crisis up close in Greece.

I am grateful to Reihan Salam, Daniel Levy, Stéphanie Giry, Dimi Reider, Dan Smokler, Sameen Gauhar, and Adam Kuruvilla Lelyveld for their friendship and advice; to Benjamin Moser, Thijs Kleinpaste, and Felix Marquardt for connecting me with sources and offering detailed editorial suggestions; to Sune Haugbølle and Eusebius McKaiser for being both generous hosts and scrupulous editors; to Elaine Pearson, Timothy Snyder, James Angelos, Ben Doherty, David Caron, Maureen Eger, and Rasmus Brygger for reading portions of the manuscript and offering valuable comments; and to Sewell Chan, Trish Hall, Clay Risen, Aaron Retica, Rebecca Appel, Louise Loftus, Ceylan Yeginsu, Steve Erlanger, Alison Smale, and all my former *New York Times* colleagues for their advice and support along the way.

Meline Toumani and Seth Anziska deserve credit for introducing me to Scrivener and telling me (correctly) that forty-dollar software could change my life as a writer. Dan Kurtz-Phelan assured me at a low point in the editing process that cutting thirty thousand words from a manuscript is really not so much. Ivan O'Mahoney told me about an Australian reality TV show with a title too good to forget. And Jonathan Shainin and David Wolf at the *Guardian* pushed me to write an early overview of this book as a "Long Read" and helped shepherd me through their merciless but ultimately rewarding editing process. I owe all of them.

I'm also indebted to my friends Josh Yaffa, Noy Thrupkaew, Bill Wheeler, Andrew Woods, and Shahin Vallée, who offered comments when this was just a grant application and a half-formed idea. Tom Mayer, Basharat Peer, and Sonia Faleiro gave advice on early versions of the proposal and, more importantly, introduced me to the Wylie Agency. Tracy Bohan, Kristina Moore, and Andrew Wylie believed in this project from an early stage when some others were hesitant to take it on, and they have been there for me every step of the way. Their unwavering commitment to big ideas and serious nonfiction is refreshing.

I am grateful to my editor, Alessandra Bastagli, for her advice on restructuring the book and for her patience through numerous drafts that were invariably submitted late. Thanks also to Michael Dwyer and Jon de Peyer at Hurst in London for their early enthusiasm for the book and for helping bring out the UK edition; to Stephanie Summerhays for getting the book through the production process; to Sara and Chris Ensey for carefully copyediting it; and to Josie Urwin, Lindsay Fradkoff, and Alison Alexanian for making sure that people see and read it.

Stuart Reid's keen editorial eye (and scalpel) was crucial; without his expert help, this book would not have been finished anywhere close to its deadline or prescribed length.

And finally, thank you to Jen Choi for putting up with my constant travel (and joining me for some of it)—and for her love, support, and understanding ever since that morning in February 2015 when I woke up before dawn, announced I would quit my job, and started frantically typing the proposal for this book.

Notes

Introduction: The Threat Within

1. Angelique Chrisafis, "'It Looked like a Battlefield': The Full Story of What Happened in the Bataclan," *Guardian,* November 20, 2015, https://www.theguardian.com/world/2015/nov/20/bataclan-witnesses-recount-horror-paris-attacks.

2. Michel Houellebecq, *Submission* (New York: Picador, 2016).

3. Alain Finkielkraut, *L'identité malheureuse* (Paris: Gallimard, 2015).

4. Éric Zemmour, *Le suicide français: Ces quarante années qui ont défait la France* (Paris: Hachette, 2014).

5. Finkielkraut's parents were Polish immigrants. Zemmour's parents came from Algeria and, as such, were not technically immigrants. They held French nationality at the time they left Algeria for mainland France because Algeria, at that time, was still a French colony and regarded as France.

6. My citations are drawn from the French translation of the book. Thilo Sarrazin, *L'Allemagne disparait: Quand un pays se laisse mourir,* trans. Jean-Baptiste Offenburg (Paris: Editions du Toucan, 2013).

7. Bat Ye'or, *Eurabia: The Euro-Arab Axis* (Madison, NJ: Fairleigh Dickinson, 2005). Bat Ye'or is a pseudonym for Gisèle Littman, an Egyptian-born Jewish writer.

8. Doug Saunders, *The Myth of the Muslim Tide: Do Immigrants Threaten the West?* (New York: Vintage Books, 2012), 15–18.

9. Ibid., 14.

10. Bruce Bawer, *The New Quislings: How the International Left Used the Oslo Massacre to Silence Debate About Islam* (New York: Broadside, 2012), e-book.

11. Jean Raspail, *The Camp of the Saints,* trans. Norman R. Shapiro (Petoskey, MI: Social Contract Press, 2015), 260.

12. Marine Le Pen's Twitter feed, posted September 1, 2015, https://twitter.com/mlp_officiel/status/638959623215706112.

13. Raspail, *The Camp of the Saints,* 53.

14. Ibid., 67–69. When his beloved refugees land, France is thrown into chaos, his wife is raped, and he is shot.

15. Ibid., 4.

16. Ibid., 164–165.

17. The French legislature debated a similar law and voted it down, though Marine Le Pen vowed to pass it if she became president.

18. Timothy Snyder, "Donald Trump Acts Like He Wants Regime Change— in the United States," *Guardian*, February 6, 2017, https://www.theguardian.com /commentisfree/2017/feb/06/trump-authoritarianism-judiciary-regime-change.

19. These minorities could be electoral minorities or ethnic ones.

20. Cas Mudde, "The Populist Radical Right: A Pathological Normalcy," *West European Politics* 33, no. 6 (November 2010): 1167–1186.

21. Opposition to decisions made by the European Union is far more defensible given that those institutions are more recent and less democratically accountable to citizens of member countries.

22. There are of course many examples of Jewish violence. Violent attacks by the Irgun and Lehi terrorist groups targeted British officials and property before Israel's independence in 1948 and were used as an excuse in the late 1940s for barring European Jewish refugees from entering Britain, Australia, and Commonwealth countries.

23. Jonathan Kirsch, *The Short, Strange Life of Herschel Grynszpan: A Boy Avenger, a Nazi Diplomat, and a Murder in Paris* (New York: Liveright, 2013), Kindle edition, 42.

24. Timothy Snyder, "'In the Cage, Trying to Get Out,'" *New York Review of Books*, October 24, 2013, http://www.nybooks.com/articles/2013/10/24/herschel-grynszpan-cage -trying-get-out/. This was especially true for the many Jews who were residents but not citizens due to Germany's granting of citizenship by blood descent, not one's place of birth.

25. Kirsch, *The Short, Strange Life of Herschel Grynszpan*, 82–83.

26. Ibid., 92–94, 104–106.

27. Ibid., 108–109.

28. Ron Roizen, "Herschel Grynszpan: The Fate of a Forgotten Assassin," *Holocaust and Genocide Studies* 1, no. 2 (1986): 217–228.

29. Kirsch, *The Short, Strange Life of Herschel Grynszpan*, 112–113, 124.

30. Ibid., 119–121.

31. Ibid., 121–123.

32. Roizen, "Herschel Grynszpan: The Fate of a Forgotten Assassin"; Kirsch, *The Short, Strange Life of Herschel Grynszpan*, 121–123.

33. Kirsch, *The Short, Strange Life of Herschel Grynszpan*, 124.

34. Roizen, "Herschel Grynszpan: The Fate of a Forgotten Assassin."

35. Kirsch, *The Short, Strange Life of Herschel Grynszpan*, 121–125.

36. Roizen, "Herschel Grynszpan: The Fate of a Forgotten Assassin."

37. Ernst Cassirer, *The Myth of the State* (New Haven, CT: Yale University Press, 2009), 293.

38. Peter E. Gordon, *Continental Divide: Heidegger, Cassirer, Davos* (Cambridge: Harvard University Press, 2012), 23. See also Peter E. Gordon, "German Idealism and German Liberalism in the 1920s: Remarks on Ernst Cassirer and the Historicity of Interpretation," in *The Weimar Moment: Liberalism, Political Theology, and Law*, eds. Leonard V. Kaplan and Rudy Koshar (Lanham, MD: Lexington Books, 2012), 338.

39. Gordon, "German Idealism and German Liberalism in the 1920s," 341.

40. Cassirer, *The Myth of the State*, 278.

41. Ibid., 280.

42. Ibid., 296–297.

43. Ibid., 280–282.

44. Ibid., 295–296.

45. Azar Gat, "The Return of Authoritarian Great Powers," *Foreign Affairs,* July 1, 2007, https://www.foreignaffairs.com/articles/china/2007-07-01/return-authoritarian -great-powers. Far-right parties in Europe and the Trump campaign in the US also enjoyed the enthusiastic support of Vladimir Putin's Russia.

46. Fareed Zakaria, "The Rise of Illiberal Democracy," *Foreign Affairs,* November 1, 1997, https://www.foreignaffairs.com/articles/1997-11-01/rise-illiberal-democracy.

47. Fareed Zakaria, *The Future of Freedom: Illiberal Democracy at Home and Abroad,* revised ed. (New York: W. W. Norton, 2007), 115–116.

48. Ibid., 26, 250.

49. Ibid., 101–102.

50. Zakaria, *The Future of Freedom,* 162, 181, and 254. Writing in 2003, Zakaria eerily predicted the rise of Donald Trump. "America is increasingly embracing a simple-minded populism that values popularity and openness as the key measures of legitimacy," he wrote. "As the political party declines further, being rich and/or famous will become the routine path to high elected office." Zakaria was not alone in worrying about the rise of demagogues in democratic countries. Michael Signer, a political theorist who is now the mayor of Charlottesville, Virginia, wrote a book focused on popular leaders who come to power through democratic means and use that power to subvert democracy—demagogues. As democracy expands, Signer wrote, "it increases the potential for its own destruction." He set out four criteria that define the demagogue: a leader who presents himself as a common man, depends on charisma and a deep emotional connection with the people, exploits his own popularity to satisfy his political ambitions and, finally and most crucially, having achieved power, openly challenges or breaks accepted norms and laws in order to implement his goals. Writing in 2009, Signer saw the United States as a model of democratic resiliency—a place that has at times flirted with demagoguery, for example, in the era of Andrew Jackson and Huey Long, without ever succumbing. In late 2015, over a year before Trump's inauguration and his attacks on federal judges over his immigration order, he changed his tune about America. "Just as an autoimmune disease attacks the body through its own defenses, demagogues are a disorder native to democracy itself," Signer wrote in the *Washington Post.* "We'd be wise to accurately diagnose it now." Michael Signer, "Donald Trump Wasn't a Textbook Demagogue. Until Now," *Washington Post,* December 2, 2015, https://www.washingtonpost.com/posteverything/wp/2015/12/02/donald-trump-wasnt -a-textbook-demagogue-until-now/?utm_term=.468b89285b31.

51. Barry James, "French Leader Takes 82% of Vote in Showdown with Extreme Right: Chirac Routs Le Pen in Runoff," *New York Times,* May 6, 2002, http://www .nytimes.com/2002/05/06/news/french-leader-takes-82-of-vote-in-showdown-with -extreme-right-chirac.html.

52. Cas Mudde, "The Intolerance of the Tolerant," *OpenDemocracy,* October 21, 2010, http://www.opendemocracy.net/cas-mudde/intolerance-of-tolerant; Elizabeth Kolbert, "Beyond Tolerance," *New Yorker,* September 9, 2002, http://www.newyorker.com /magazine/2002/09/09/beyond-tolerance.

Chapter 1: The Guests Who Overstayed

1. Paul Scheffer, *Immigrant Nations* (Cambridge, UK: Polity Press, 2011), 131.

2. Ian Buruma, *Murder in Amsterdam: The Death of Theo van Gogh and the Limits of Tolerance* (London: Atlantic Books, 2006), 13.

3. Christopher Caldwell, *Reflections on the Revolution in Europe: Immigration, Islam and the West* (London: Penguin, 2010), 35.

4. This changed in the 1990s and with the new citizenship law of 2000.

5. Christian Joppke, *Citizenship and Immigration* (Cambridge, UK: Polity, 2011), 26–27.

6. Ibid., 36.

7. Rogers Brubaker, *Citizenship and Nationhood in France and Germany* (Cambridge, MA: Harvard University Press, 1996), 22–23.

8. David Goodhart, *The British Dream: Successes and Failures of Post-War Immigration*, (London: Atlantic Books, 2014), 118–121.

9. Patrick Weil and Nicolas Truong, *Le sens de la République* (Paris: Grasset, 2015), 37.

10. For a longer analysis of how the Gulf States treat guest workers and barter citizenship, see Atossa Araxia Abrahamian, *The Cosmopolites: The Coming of the Global Citizen* (New York: Columbia Global Reports, 2015).

11. Buruma, *Murder in Amsterdam*, 21.

12. Caldwell, *Reflections on the Revolution in Europe*, 46.

13. Pascal Bruckner, *The Tyranny of Guilt: An Essay on Western Masochism*, trans. Steven Rendall (Princeton, NJ: Princeton University Press, 2012), 2.

14. Ibid., 34–36.

15. Doug Saunders, *The Myth of the Muslim Tide: Do Immigrants Threaten the West?* (New York: Vintage Books, 2012), 128–129.

16. Ibid., 121: "They warned that the strict and unchangeable sexual inequality of Catholic doctrine imprisoned women, and that Catholic immigration set back the cause of female equality," writes Saunders.

17. William H. Pryor Jr., "Moral Duty and the Rule of Law," *Harvard Journal of Law & Public Policy* 31 (2008): 153; Brian Kelly, "Victim of the Klan: Father James Edwin Coyle, Alabama," *Catholicism.org*, February 23, 2009, http://catholicism.org/victim-of -the-klan-father-james-edwin-coyle-alabama.html.

18. Radley Balko, "The United States Also Denied Refuge to Jews Fleeing Hitler, Fearing They Might Be Nazis," *Washington Post*, January 25, 2017; Dara Lind, "How America's Rejection of Jews Fleeing Nazi Germany Haunts Our Refugee Policy Today," *Vox*, January 27, 2017, https://www.vox.com/policy-and-politics/2017/1/27/14412082 /refugees-history-holocaust; "Voyage of the St. Louis," United States Holocaust Memorial Museum, accessed March 27, 2017, https://www.ushmm.org/wlc/en/article.php ?ModuleId=10005267.

19. Paul Blanshard, *American Freedom and Catholic Power* (Westport, CT: Greenwood Press, 1984).

20. Saunders, *The Myth of the Muslim Tide*, 116.

21. Ibid., 119.

22. Caldwell, *Reflections on the Revolution in Europe*, 205–206. For all his grave warnings about the Islamic menace, Caldwell acknowledges this history and the political backlash it produced. He points to the 1850s in Boston as the moment when the city's WASP establishment began to feel uncomfortable. As the Irish Catholics began to have children and shape the culture and rhythms of the city, "the natives began to voice intolerant opinions, to mutter openly about the newcomers' higher birthrates, to form radical and secret political parties, and to take active steps to exclude the Irish from their

institutions." It was the beginning of the Know Nothing Party in American politics. Caldwell likens that period to the current one in Europe, especially as immigrants and their children who have become citizens start to exert their power at the ballot box. What he does not acknowledge is that Boston turned out reasonably well and was not culturally decimated. His real fear, much like that of the suffragists of the early twentieth century, is that the political demands made by a religious minority will irrevocably transform society for the worse. "The question for the future is not whether the Muslim vote will shift the electoral balance on today's contentious issues," writes Caldwell, "but whether it will change the issues themselves, reopening aspects of European society that are today considered settled."

23. Han Entzinger in *Multiculturalism and the Welfare State: Recognition and Redistribution in Contemporary Democracies*, eds. Keith Banting and Will Kymlicka (Oxford: Oxford University Press, 2006), 193–199.

24. Catherine Fieschi et al., *Recapturing the Reluctant Radical* (London: Counterpoint, 2012).

25. Kenan Malik, *Multiculturalism and Its Discontents: Rethinking Diversity After 9/11* (London: Seagull Books, 2013), 47.

26. Kenan Malik, *From Fatwa to Jihad* (London: Atlantic Books, 2009), 20–21.

27. Ibid., 21, 94–95.

28. Paul Berman, *The Flight of the Intellectuals* (New York: Melville House, 2011), 171–176.

29. Gilles Kepel, *Les banlieues de l'islam: naissance d'une religion en France* (Paris: Points, 2015), 154–156.

30. Jean-Yves Camus and Nicolas Lebourg, *Les droites extrêmes en Europe* (Paris: Seuil, 2015),144–145, 177.

31. Ahmed Marcouch, interview by author, The Hague, September 14, 2016.

32. Ibid.

33. Ibid.

34. Ibid.

35. "Enoch Powell's 'Rivers of Blood' Speech," *Telegraph,* November 6, 2007, http://www.telegraph.co.uk/comment/3643823/Enoch-Powells-Rivers-of-Blood-speech.html.

36. Michael Collins, *The Likes of Us: A Biography of the White Working Class* (London: Granta Books, 2004), 182–186.

37. Ibid., 188–189.

38. Ibid., 207.

Chapter 2: When Integration Fails

1. Ayaan Hirsi Ali, *Nomad: A Personal Journey Through the Clash of Civilizations* (London: Simon & Schuster UK, 2011), 171–175.

2. The headline in Dutch suggests drama but the connotation is tragedy or disaster.

3. This party is known as the Partij voor de Arbeid, or PvdA ("party of the workers") in Holland—I will refer to it as the Labor Party. At this point, Hirsi Ali herself was working for the party's think tank on integration issues before taking a turn to the right a year later and running as a candidate for PvdA's center-right rival, the VVD.

4. Paul Scheffer, "Het Multiculturele Drama," *NRC Handelsblad,* January 29, 2000.

5. Ibid.

6. Scheffer, *Immigrant Nations,* (Cambridge, UK: Polity Press, 2011), 39–40 and 82.

7. Ahmed Marcouch, interview by author, The Hague, September 14, 2016.

8. Ian Buruma, *Murder in Amsterdam: The Death of Theo van Gogh and the Limits of Tolerance*, (London: Atlantic Books, 2006), 53.

9. Frits Bolkestein, interview by author, Amsterdam, July 4, 2016.

10. Merijn Oudenampsen, interview by author, Amsterdam, April 20, 2016.

11. Buruma, *Murder in Amsterdam*, 56–57.

12. Andrew Osborn, "'I Shot Fortuyn for Dutch Muslims,' Says Accused," *Guardian*, March 27, 2003, https://www.theguardian.com/world/2003/mar/28/thefarright.politics.

13. Frits Bolkestein, interview by author, Amsterdam, July 4, 2016.

14. Ibid. All quotes in the preceding paragraphs are also drawn from this interview.

15. Buruma, *Murder in Amsterdam*, 29–31.

16. Frits Bolkestein, interview by author, Amsterdam, July 4, 2016.

17. Buruma, *Murder in Amsterdam*, 64.

18. Ibid., 31.

19. Ibid., 1–3.

20. The original Dutch letter can be found at http://www.volkskrant.nl/binnenland /-open-brief-aan-hirshi-ali~a706350/. The English version is available at http://www .militantislammonitor.org/article/id/312

21. Ibid.

22. Ayaan Hirsi Ali, *Infidel* (New York: Free Press, 2007), 322.

23. Buruma, *Murder in Amsterdam*, 11.

24. Ibid., 15; "When smugness is challenged, panic sets in," he writes.

25. Bas Heijne, interview by author, Paris, March 15, 2016.

26. Ahmed Marcouch, interview by author, The Hague, September 14, 2016.

27. Buruma, *Murder in Amsterdam*, 48.

28. Han Entzinger in *Multiculturalism and the Welfare State: Recognition and Redistribution in Contemporary Democracies*, eds. Keith Banting and Will Kymlicka (Oxford: Oxford University Press, 2006), 187 and 196.

29. Paul Scheffer, interview by author, Amsterdam, March 24, 2016.

30. Leo Lucassen, interview by author, Amsterdam, April 22, 2016.

31. Willem Schinkel, interview by author, Rotterdam, April 18, 2016.

32. Ibid.

33. Ibid.

34. Christian Joppke, *Citizenship and Immigration* (Cambridge, UK: Polity, 2011), 140.

35. Willem Schinkel, interview by author, Rotterdam, April 18, 2016.

36. It is the opposite of *autochtoon*, which means "indigenous."

37. Zihni Özdil, interview by author, Amsterdam, March 22, 2016.

38. Paul Schnabel, interview by author, Amsterdam, April 21, 2016.

39. Zihni Özdil, interview by author, Amsterdam, March 22, 2016.

40. Zihni Özdil, *Nederland, mit vaderland* (Amsterdam: De Bezige Bij, 2016).

41. Ibid., 48.

42. Rinus Penninx, interview by author, Gouda, March 21, 2016.

43. Ibid. All quotes from Penninx in the preceding paragraphs are drawn from this interview.

44. Paul Scheffer, interview by author, Amsterdam, March 24, 2016.

45. Zihni Özdil, interview by author, Amsterdam, March 22, 2016.

46. Ibid.

47. Bas Heijne, interview by author, Paris, March 15, 2016.

48. Rinus Penninx, interview by author, Gouda, March 21, 2016.

49. Zihni Özdil, interview by author, Amsterdam, March 22, 2016.

Chapter 3: The Nativist Nanny State

1. Bent Melchior, interview by author, Copenhagen, March 7, 2016. The preceding paragraphs draw on the same interview.

2. Sasha Polakow-Suransky, "Fortress Denmark?," *American Prospect,* May 13, 2002, http://prospect.org/article/fortress-denmark.

3. David Goodhart, *The British Dream: Successes and Failures of Post-War Immigration* (London: Atlantic Books, 2014), 270; Paul Collier, *Exodus: Immigration and Multiculturalism in the 21st Century* (London: Penguin, 2014), 84.

4. Robert D. Putnam, "E Pluribus Unum: Diversity and Community in the Twenty-First Century: The 2006 Johan Skytte Prize Lecture," *Scandinavian Political Studies* 30, no. 2 (June 2007): 137–174.

5. Keith Banting and Will Kymlicka, eds., *Multiculturalism and the Welfare State: Recognition and Redistribution in Contemporary Democracies* (Oxford: Oxford University Press, 2006), 27.

6. Ibid., 80.

7. Ibid., 80, 346–348.

8. Goodhart, *The British Dream,* 273.

9. Robert Anthony Ford and Matthew J. Goodwin, *Revolt on the Right: Explaining Support for the Radical Right in Britain* (New York: Routledge, 2014), 117.

10. Cas Mudde and Cristóbal Rovira Kaltwasser, eds., *Populism in Europe and the Americas: Threat or Corrective for Democracy?* (Cambridge, UK: Cambridge University Press, 2012), 8.

11. Goodhart, *The British Dream,* 269.

12. Ford and Goodwin, *Revolt on the Right,* 134.

13. Catherine Fieschi et al., *Recapturing the Reluctant Radical* (London: Counterpoint, 2012).

14. Herbert Kitschelt and Anthony J. McGann, *The Radical Right in Western Europe: A Comparative Analysis* (Ann Arbor: University of Michigan Press, 2006).

15. Ibid., 261–262.

16. Ibid., 21–23.

17. Ibid., 15.

18. The modern-day DPP grew out of Glistrup's Fremskridtspartiet (Progress Party). Although his platform was primarily antitax in the 1970s, he eventually embraced anti-immigration views in the 1980s, warning of "Mohammedans" coming to Denmark. He was a mentor to Pia Kjærsgaard, who was a prominent member of the Progress Party and later founded the DPP.

19. Maureen A. Eger and Sarah Valdez, "From Radical Right to Neo-Nationalist: Political Party Dynamics in Western Europe, 1970–2015," working paper, Department of Sociology, Umeå University, Sweden, 2017.

20. Ibid. See also Maureen A. Eger and Sarah Valdez, "Neo-Nationalism in Western Europe," *European Sociological Review* 31, no. 1 (2015): 115–130. In this article, Eger and Valdez argue that the "radical right began as the most economically right-wing party

family in Europe, but between 1996 and 2010, they shifted to the left in their economic positions and are no longer right-wing outliers." Further, their voting analyses reveal that welfare chauvinism motivated support for the "far right" between 2002 and 2010. They use the term "neo-nationalist" rather than "right-wing populist."

21. Arne Hardis, interview by author, Copenhagen, April 11, 2016.

22. As mentioned above, there was an earlier successful far-right party, the Progress Party, which gained 16 percent of the vote in 1973; however, it had an antitax platform at the time, not the DPP's current anti-immigration and pro-welfare stance.

23. Thomas Gyldal Petersen, interview by author, Herlev, April 13, 2016.

24. Søren Espersen, interview by author, Copenhagen, April 13, 2016.

25. Lars Trier Mogensen, interview by author, Copenhagen, October 20, 2015.

26. Søren Espersen, interview by author, Copenhagen, April 13, 2016.

27. Arne Hardis, interview by author, Copenhagen, April 11, 2016.

28. Thomas Gyldal Petersen, interview by author, Herlev, April 13, 2016.

29. Polakow-Suransky, "Fortress Denmark?"

30. Thomas Gyldal Petersen, interview by author, Herlev, April 13, 2016.

31. Morten Bødskov, interview by author, Copenhagen, October 20, 2015.

32. Thomas Gammeltoft-Hansen, interview by author, Copenhagen, March 3, 2016.

33. Thomas Gyldal Petersen, interview by author, Herlev, April 13, 2016.

34. Aydin Soei, interview by author, Copenhagen, April 15, 2016.

35. Ibid.

36. Aydin Soei, *Forsoning* (Copenhagen: Tiderne Skifter, 2016).

37. Aydin Soei, interview by author, Copenhagen, April 15, 2016.

38. Bent Melchior, interview by author, Copenhagen, March 7, 2016.

39. Arne Hardis, interview by author, Copenhagen, April 11, 2016.

40. Morten Bødskov, interview by author, Copenhagen, October 20, 2015.

41. Thomas Gyldal Petersen, interview by author, Herlev, April 13, 2016.

Chapter 4: The Danish Cartoon Crisis and the Limits of Free Speech

1. Jytte Klausen, *The Cartoons That Shook the World* (New Haven, CT: Yale University Press, 2009). The imams publicized the cartoons throughout the Middle East and also misrepresented some of what had happened in Denmark by including other offensive drawings unrelated to the cartoons in their dossier.

2. Flemming Rose, *The Tyranny of Silence* (Washington, DC: Cato Institute, 2015), 87–88.

3. Ibid., 190–195, 127–145.

4. Ibid., 190–191.

5. Ibid., 115.

6. Kenan Malik, *From Fatwa to Jihad* (London: Atlantic Books, 2009), 189–190.

7. Klausen, *The Cartoons That Shook the World*, 44.

8. Kenan Malik, *Multiculturalism and Its Discontents: Rethinking Diversity After 9/11* (London: Seagull Books, 2013), 70.

9. Ibid., 60–61.

10. Ibid., 72–73.

11. Nick Cohen, *What's Left?: How the Left Lost Its Way,* updated ed. (London: Harper Perennial, 2007), 9.

12. Ibid., 275.

13. Rose, *The Tyranny of Silence*, 49–50.

14. John F. Burns, "Cartoonist in Denmark Calls Attack 'Really Close,'" *New York Times*, January 2, 2010, http://www.nytimes.com/2010/01/03/world/europe/03denmark.html.

15. This account is drawn from Rose, *The Tyranny of Silence*, 49–51.

16. AFP, "Attacker of Danish 'Mohammed' Cartoonist Sentenced to 10 Years in Prison," *National Post*, May 2, 2012, http://news.nationalpost.com/news/world/attacker -of-danish-mohammed-cartoonist-sentenced-to-10-years-in-prison.

17. Søren Espersen et al., *Danmarks Fremtid: Dit Land, Dit Valg* (Copenhagen: Dansk Folkeparti, 2001). To view the cover photo, see http://www.dba.dk/danmarks-fremtid-dit -land/id-1001114066/.

18. Naser Khader, interview by author, Copenhagen, April 12, 2016.

19. Aydin Soei, *Vrede Unge Mænd* (Copenhagen: Tiderne Skifter, 2011), 264.

20. Ibid., 16.

21. Ibid., 254.

22. Ibid., 202.

23. Ibid., 220–222, 257.

24. Ibid., 16.

25. Ibid., 39.

26. Jakob Scharf (#1), interview by author, Copenhagen, October 20, 2015; Jakob Scharf (#2), interview by author, Copenhagen, April 14, 2016.

27. Søren Espersen, interview by author, Copenhagen, April 13, 2016.

28. TrygFonden, "Ny Rapport: Lokalmiljøet Helt Afgørende I Indsatsen Mod Radikalisering Og Ekstremisme," accessed March 27, 2017, https://www.trygfonden.dk/en /viden-og-materialer/Publikationer/CERTA_rapport.

29. He is echoing an idea most famously articulated in Amartya Sen, *Identity and Violence: The Illusion of Destiny* (New York: W. W. Norton, 2007); Jakob Scharf (#2), interview by author, Copenhagen, April 14, 2016.

30. Jakob Scharf (#2), interview by author, Copenhagen, April 14, 2016.

31. Yildiz Akdogan, interview by author, Copenhagen, April 12, 2016.

32. Jakob Scharf (#2), interview by author, Copenhagen, April 14, 2016.

33. Aydin Soei, interview by author, Copenhagen, April 15, 2016.

34. Soei, *Vrede Unge Mænd*, 352.

35. Ibid., 279.

36. Søren Espersen, interview by author, Copenhagen, April 13, 2016.

37. Pascal Bruckner, *The Tears of the White Man* (New York: Macmillan, 1987), 133, 141–142.

38. Pascal Bruckner, *The Tyranny of Guilt: An Essay on Western Masochism*, trans. Steven Rendall (Princeton, NJ: Princeton University Press, 2012), 164–165.

39. Yildiz Akdogan, interview by author, Copenhagen, April 12, 2016.

40. "Jeg lærte at cykle i Syrien, Bertel Haarder," *Berlingske*, July 3, 2016, www.b.dk /kommentarer/jeg-laerte-at-cykle-i-syrien-bertel-haarder-0; Daud Aron Ahmad, "Bertel Haarder kan ikke definere, om jeg er dansker eller ej," *Politiken*, July 2, 2016, http:// politiken.dk/debat/article5628332.ece.

41. Yildiz Akdogan, interview by author, Copenhagen, April 12, 2016.

42. Soei, *Vrede Unge Mænd*, 140–141.

43. Rasmus Brygger, interview by author, Copenhagen, April 11, 2016.

44. Ibid.

45. Arne Hardis, interview by author, Copenhagen, April 11, 2016.

46. Soei, *Vrede Unge Mænd*, 156.

47. Rasmus Brygger, interview by author, Copenhagen, April 11, 2016.

Chapter 5: Out of Sight, Out of Mind: Europe's Fantasy of Offshoring

1. Thomas Gyldal Petersen, interview by author, Herlev, April 13, 2016.

2. Espersen does offer one solution to the integration problem. He proposes national service—whether military or some other form. "We only enlist five to six thousand a year. When I was in the navy, they enlisted thirty-six thousand, practically everyone." He thinks this would bring young immigrant men into a larger institution and "get them out of their isolation."

3. Søren Espersen, interview by author, Copenhagen, April 13, 2016.

4. Sune Engel Rasmussen, "Tragic Tale of Afghan Brothers Sent Home from Denmark to an Uncertain Fate," *Guardian*, October 6, 2015, https://www.theguardian .com/global-development/2015/oct/06/tragic-tale-afghan-brothers-sent-home-from -denmark-to-an-uncertain-fate.

5. Andreas Kamm, interview by author, Copenhagen, October 20, 2015.

6. Rasmussen, "Tragic Tale of Afghan Brothers Sent Home from Denmark to an Uncertain Fate."

7. Jakob Scharf (#1), interview by author, Copenhagen, October 20, 2015.

8. Anna Meera Gaonkar, "Jeg Føler Mig Provokeret Af Kvinder Med Tørklæde," *Politiken*, July 15, 2014, http://politiken.dk/debat/art5596858/Jeg-f%C3%B8ler-mig -provokeret-af-kvinder-med-t%C3%B8rkl%C3%A6de.

9. Khaterah Parwani, interview by author, Copenhagen, October 19, 2015.

10. Søren Espersen, interview by author, Copenhagen, April 13, 2016.

11. Kenneth Kristensen Berth, interview by author, Copenhagen, March 4, 2016.

12. Michael Gordon, "Revealed: The Cost of Stopping the Boats Put at $9.6 Billion," *Sydney Morning Herald*, September 13, 2016, http://www.smh.com.au/federal-politics /political-news/revealed-the-cost-of-stopping-the-boats-put-at-96-billion-20160912 -grea35.html; Save the Children Australia, "At What Cost? The Human, Economic and Strategic Cost of Australia's Asylum Seeker Policies and the Alternatives," September 2016, http://www.savethechildren.org.au/__data/assets/pdf_file/0009/159345/At-What -Cost-Report-Final.pdf.

13. Michael Bachelard, "Vomitous and Terrifying: The Lifeboats Used to Turn Back Asylum Seekers," *Sydney Morning Herald*, March 2, 2014, http://www.smh.com.au /national/vomitous-and-terrifying-the-lifeboats-used-to-turn-back-asylum-seekers -20140301-33t6s.html. Australia has also flown some boat arrivals from Sri Lanka and Vietnam directly back to their countries.

14. Nick Miller, "Nigel Farage Says Europe Adopting Australia's Refugee Policy Could Have Prevented Tragic Deaths," *Sydney Morning Herald*, September 5, 2015, http://www.smh.com.au/world/nigel-farage-says-australias-refugee-policy-could -have-prevented-tragic-deaths-20150904-gjfpmb.html. The British far right is not a primary focus of this book. This is because the British electoral system's first-past-the-post rules suppress UKIP representation. Though the party received nearly 12.6 percent of the national vote (almost four million votes) it received only one seat in parliament. By contrast, the Scottish National Party received less than 5 percent of the national vote but

gained more than fifty seats in parliament. Although UKIP is undeniably popular and has forced other parties to adopt some of its anti-immigrant rhetoric, it wields very little legislative power when it comes to determining national policies in parliament unlike its xenophobic counterparts in Denmark, Holland, and France.

15. Ibid.

16. Tony Abbott, "Address to the Second Annual Margaret Thatcher Centre Gala Dinner and Banquet," October 27, 2015, http://tonyabbott.com.au/2015/10/address -to-the-second-annual-margaret-thatcher-centre-gala-dinner-and-banquet/.

17. Ibid.

18. "Tories Wince at Abbott Migrant Speech," *Guido Fawkes* blog, October 28, 2015, https://order-order.com/2015/10/28/tories-wince-at-abbott-migrant-speech/.

19. "UKIP's Farage Praises Abbott's Asylum Speech as 'Heroic,'" ABC News, October 28, 2015, http://www.abc.net.au/news/2015-10-28/farage-backs-abbotts-asylum -seeker-call-as-heroic/6891188.

20. Rudy Vercucque and Yohann Faviere, interview by author, Calais, June 14, 2016.

21. Frits Bolkestein, interview by author, Amsterdam, July 4, 2016.

22. Peter Mares, "Ten Years after *Tampa*," *Monthly*, August 1, 2011, https://www .themonthly.com.au/issue/2011/august/1316394350/peter-mares/comment-ten-years -after-tampa.

23. Burnside was trying to force the government to take responsibility for the situation by citing an Australian law requiring the detention—in Australia—of any individual intentionally seeking to arrive illegally in Australia. The goal was to detain the asylum seekers on Australian territory rather than keep them hostage on open seas or remove them to an offshore location.

24. Mares, "Ten Years after *Tampa*."

25. Julian Burnside, interview by author, Melbourne, January 28, 2016.

26. Ben Doherty, interview by author, Sydney, January 13, 2016; Ben Doherty, "Call Me Illegal: The Semantic Struggle over Seeking Asylum in Australia" (Oxford: Oxford Institute for the Study of Journalism, 2015).

27. Ruddock tells the story of the *Tampa* differently. As he explains, the Howard government was adamant no one would get into Australia—neglecting to mention that there was an election just weeks away in which his party faced a threat from the far-right One Nation Party of Pauline Hanson. "We then negotiated to do a deal with Nauru that people could be taken there. And in the end, we transferred the population from their vessel to one of our naval vessels, and by the time that naval vessel took people back to Nauru, they'd been able to build some accommodation there. From then on, we determined that people would be, if they came unauthorized by boat, taken to Nauru."

28. Julian Burnside, interview by author, Melbourne, January 28, 2016.

29. Klaus Neumann, *Across the Seas: Australia's Response to Refugees—A History* (Collingwood, Australia: Black, 2015); Klaus Neumann, interview by author, Melbourne, January 27, 2016.

30. John Menadue, interview by author, Sydney, January 21, 2016. He may have spoken too soon. A few months after I met Menadue, Hanson returned to politics and shocked the country by winning three seats in the senate in the 2016 election after fifteen years in the political wilderness.

31. Doherty, "Call Me Illegal," 32, 44, 48–49.

32. Ibid., 37.

33. Ibid., 65.

34. Philip Ruddock, interview by author, Sydney, January 12, 2016.

35. Mohammad Baqiri, interview by author, Melbourne, January 29, 2016.

36. Tropical diseases remain a problem on the island. In early 2017, there was an outbreak of the deadly dengue fever, and some asylum seekers infected with it had to be transferred to Australia; Paul Ferrell, "Dengue Fever Outbreak on Nauru Threatens Health System," *Guardian*, February 24, 2017, https://www.theguardian.com /world/2017/feb/25/dengue-fever-outbreak-on-nauru-threatens-health-system.

37. Paul Farrell, Nick Evershed, and Helen Davidson, "The Nauru Files: Cache of 2,000 Leaked Reports Reveal Scale of Abuse of Children in Australian Offshore Detention," *Guardian*, August 10, 2016, https://www.theguardian.com/australia-news/2016 /aug/10/the-nauru-files-2000-leaked-reports-reveal-scale-of-abuse-of-children-in -australian-offshore-detention; Mark J. Isaacs, *The Undesirables: Inside Nauru* (Richmond, Australia: Hardie Grant, 2014).

38. Mohammad Baqiri, interview by author, Melbourne, January 29, 2016. The company is Transfield Services (now BroadSpectrum).

39. Philip Ruddock, interview by author, Sydney, January 12, 2016.

40. Klaus Neumann, interview by author, Melbourne, January 27, 2016.

41. Isaacs, *The Undesirables*, 324.

42. Madeline Gleeson, interview by author, Sydney, January 15, 2016.

43. Philip Ruddock, interview by author, Sydney, January 12, 2016.

44. Doherty, "Call Me Illegal: The Semantic Struggle over Seeking Asylum in Australia," 30.

45. Klaus Neumann, interview by author, Melbourne, January 27, 2016.

46. Philip Ruddock, interview by author, Sydney, January 12, 2016.

47. Ibid.

48. Ibid.

49. As quoted in Doherty, "Call Me Illegal: The Semantic Struggle over Seeking Asylum in Australia," 42.

50. Chris Kenny, interview by author, Sydney, February 8, 2016.

51. Ibid.

52. Mohammad Baqiri, interview by author, Melbourne, January 29, 2016.

53. Andrew Bolt, interview by author, Sydney, January 21, 2016.

54. Chris Kenny, interview by author, Sydney, February 8, 2016.

55. Ibid.

56. "$55m Cambodia Deal That Resettled Two Refugees a 'Good Outcome', Says Dutton," *Guardian*, March 8, 2016, https://www.theguardian.com/australia-news/2016 /mar/09/55m-cambodia-deal-that-resettled-two-refugees-a-good-outcome-says -dutton. The latest person sent to Cambodia was a Syrian; four of the seven have since left Cambodia.

57. Andrew Wilkie, interview by author, Canberra, February 2, 2016.

58. Welfare expenditure per year is less than the cost of detention, and if asylum seekers were working, they would be making a contribution to the country's GDP, not just receiving benefits.

59. Chris Kenny, interview by author, Sydney, February 8, 2016.

60. Søren Espersen, interview by author, Copenhagen, April 13, 2016.

61. Philip Ruddock, interview by author, Sydney, January 12, 2016.

62. Søren Espersen, interview by author, Copenhagen, April 13, 2016.

63. Bent Melchior, interview by author, Copenhagen, March 7, 2016.

Chapter 6: Terror and Backlash

1. Ed Payne and Michael Pearson, "A Timeline of the *Charlie Hebdo* Terror Attack," CNN, January 8, 2015, http://www.cnn.com/2015/01/08/europe/charlie-hebdo-attack -timeline/index.html; Angelique Chrisafis, "'It Looked like a Battlefield': The Full Story of What Happened in the Bataclan," *Guardian*, November 20, 2015, https://www .theguardian.com/world/2015/nov/20/bataclan-witnesses-recount-horror-paris-attacks.

2. "Gard: un millier de personnes acclament Marine Le Pen à Beaucaire," *Midi-Libre*, January 11, 2011, http://www.midilibre.fr/2015/01/11/gard-marine-le-pen-acclamee -lors-d-un-rassemblement-citoyen-a-beaucaire,1109297.php.

3. Marine Le Pen, "France Was Attacked by Islamic Fundamentalism," *New York Times*, January 18, 2015, https://www.nytimes.com/2015/01/19/opinion/marine-le-pen -france-was-attacked-by-islamic-fundamentalism.html.

4. Andrea Thomas, "Obscure German Tweet Helped Spur Migrant March From Hungary," *Wall Street Journal*, September 10, 2015, http://www.wsj.com/articles /obscure-german-tweet-help-spur-migrant-march-from-hungary-1441901563.

5. Ibid.

6. Helena Smith and Mark Tran, "Germany Says It Could Take 500,000 Refugees a Year," *Guardian*, September 8, 2015, https://www.theguardian.com/world/2015/sep/08 /germany-500000-refugees-a-year-clashes-lesbos.

7. Robin Alexander, interview by author, Berlin, March 8, 2016.

8. Henryk M. Broder, *A Jew in the New Germany*, trans. Sander L. Gilman and Lilian M. Friedberg (Urbana: University of Illinois Press, 2004), 22–23.

9. "Henryk Broder Kritiserer Tyskland Og Merkel: Befolkningen Har Ikke Stemt for Kulturforandring," YouTube video, 12:18, posted by "Nationalkonservativ," September 27, 2015, https://www.youtube.com/watch?v=QdCSp-jVh3o&app=desktop.

10. Ibid.

11. AFP, "German Politician Stabbed on Campaign Trail Is Elected New Mayor of Cologne," *Telegraph*, October 18, 2015, http://www.telegraph.co.uk/news/worldnews /europe/germany/11939731/German-politician-stabbed-on-campaign-trail-is-elected -new-mayor-of-Cologne.html.

12. Tim Hume, "Outrage as *Charlie Hebdo* Depicts Alan Kurdi as Molester," CNN, January 14, 2016, http://www.cnn.com/2016/01/14/europe/france-charlie-hebdo-aylan -kurdi/index.html.

13. Mariam Lau, interview by author, Berlin, March 9, 2016.

14. The paragraphs above draw on the account in George Packer, "The Astonishing Rise of Angela Merkel," *New Yorker*, December 1, 2014, http://www.newyorker.com /magazine/2014/12/01/quiet-german.

15. Robin Alexander, interview by author, Berlin, March 8, 2016.

16. "Who Is Peter Altmaier and Why Does He Matter?," *Economist*, April 12, 2017, http://www.economist.com/blogs/kaffeeklatsch/2017/04/most-powerful-man-berlin.

17. Robin Alexander, interview by author, Berlin, March 8, 2016.

18. Ibid.

19. Ibid.

20. Melissa Eddy and Eric Schmitt, "Berlin Attack Sets Off Hunt for a Tunisian in Germany," *New York Times,* December 21, 2016, https://www.nytimes.com/2016/12/21 /world/europe/attack-sets-off-hunt-for-tunisian-who-had-slipped-germanys-grasp.html; Stephanie Kirchgaessner, "Police Pore over Polish Truck Driver's Final Hours for Clues to Berlin Attack," *Guardian,* December 20, 2016, https://www.theguardian.com/world/2016 /dec/20/police-pore-over-polish-lorry-driver-lukasz-urban-final-hours-berlin-attack.

21. "How Did We End Up Here?," *Charlie Hebdo,* March 30, 2016, https://charlie hebdo.fr/en/edito/how-did-we-end-up-here/. The quoted portions of the editorial are drawn from my own translation of the French original at the time of publication and differ slightly in word choice from the English translation subsequently posted online by *Charlie Hebdo.*

22. Paul Berman, *The Flight of the Intellectuals* (New York: Melville House, 2011).

23. "How Did We End Up Here?," *Charlie Hebdo.* Riss's views may to some extent be rooted in *Charlie Hebdo*'s tradition of anticlericalism. However, his editorial strays far beyond a critique of clergy and organized religion and displays an overt hostility toward individual citizens and a willingness to scapegoat any Muslim who happens to be religiously observant.

24. Alain Finkielkraut, interview by author, Paris, June 30, 2016.

25. Paul Scheffer, *Immigrant Nations* (Cambridge, UK: Polity Press, 2011), 129. When the historian Geert Mak recalled the roundups and deportations of Jews that tore apart his neighborhood, once largely Jewish, in the 1940s, Scheffer dismissed the analogy.

26. See the Introduction for an in-depth discussion of how a single act of Jewish violence was used as an excuse to mobilize mass anti-Semitic pogroms. Jews were barred from the US, the UK, and Australia on these grounds before and after World War II; see Klaus Neumann, *Across the Seas: Australia's Response to Refugees—A History* (Collingwood, Australia: Black, 2015).

27. Scheffer, *Immigrant Nations,* 129.

28. Leo Lucassen, interview by author, Amsterdam, April 22, 2016.

29. Daniel Lindenberg, interview by author, Paris, May 16, 2016.

30. Daniel Lindenberg, *Le rappel à l'ordre: enquête sur les nouveaux réactionnaires* (Paris: Seuil, 2016).

31. Daniel Lindenberg, interview by author, Paris, May 16, 2016.

32. Olivier Dard, "De quoi Maurras est-il le nom?," *Fragments sur les Temps Présents,* November 29, 2013, https://tempspresents.com/2013/11/29/olivier-dard-de-quoi -maurras-est-il-le-nom/; Olivier Dard, *Charles Maurras* (Paris: Armand Colin, 2013).

33. Alain Finkielkraut, *L'identité malheureuse* (Paris: Gallimard, 2015), 90.

34. Simon Kuper, "Macron, Le Pen and the Battle for the Idea of France," *Financial Times,* May 29, 2017, https://www.ft.com/content/9720e6e2-2f89-11e7-9555-23ef563ecf9a.

35. Lindenberg, *Le rappel à l'ordre,* 96–97.

36. Alain Finkielkraut, interview by author, Paris, June 30, 2016.

37. Lindenberg, *Le rappel à l'ordre,* 92.

38. Ibid., 97–98.

39. Olivier Roy, *La laïcité face à l'islam* (Paris: Fayard, 2013), 169–170. This is my own translation of the French original. There are very slight differences of word choice in the

published English translation. Olivier Roy, *Secularism Confronts Islam*, trans. George Holoch (New York: Columbia University Press, 2009), 101.

40. Lindenberg, *Le rappel à l'ordre*, 97.

41. Daniel Lindenberg, interview by author, Paris, May 16, 2016.

42. Stéphane Charbonnier and Adam Gopnik, *Open Letter: On Blasphemy, Islamophobia, and the True Enemies of Free Expression* (New York: Little, Brown, 2016), 65–67.

43. Ibid., 67–68.

44. Alain Finkielkraut, interview by author, Paris, June 30, 2016.

45. Adam Shatz, "How Did We End Up Here?," *London Review of Books,* April 5, 2016, https://www.lrb.co.uk/blog/2016/04/05/adam-shatz/how-did-we-end-up-here/.

46. Ibid.

47. Thilo Sarrazin, *L'Allemagne disparait: Quand un pays se laisse mourir,* trans. Jean-Baptiste Offenburg (Paris: Editions du Toucan, 2013), 291.

48. James Kirkup, "British Indians: A Remarkable Story of Success," *Telegraph,* November 7, 2015, http://www.telegraph.co.uk/news/worldnews/asia/india/11981677/British-Indians-a-remarkable-story-of-success.html.

49. Emmanuel Todd, *Who Is Charlie?: Xenophobia and the New Middle Class* (Cambridge, UK: Polity, 2015), 68, 6.

50. Ibid., 85, 16. The reference is to the murders of Jewish children, a teacher, and a soldier at a Jewish school in Toulouse.

51. Shatz, "How Did We End Up Here?"

Chapter 7: Nostalgia, Fear, and the Front National's Resurrection

1. Marine Le Pen, *À contre flots* (Paris: Editions Grancher, 2006), 9–11.

2. Ibid., 13.

3. Ibid., 17–18.

4. Ibid., 19–20.

5. Ibid., 20.

6. Marine Le Pen, interview by author, Nanterre, May 18, 2016.

7. A court rejected this move in 2016 and ordered the party to pay damages to the elder Le Pen.

8. Marine Le Pen, interview by author, Nanterre, May 18, 2016.

9. Julien Rochedy, interview by author, Paris, June 29, 2016.

10. Olivier Faye, "Le FN capte l'attention d'une partie de l'électorat gay," *Le Monde,* April 12, 2016, http://www.lemonde.fr/politique/article/2016/04/12/l-attraction-en-hausse-du-front-national-aupres-de-la-communaute-gay_4900269_823448.html.

11. "M.Le Pen persiste: 'il y a occupation,'" *Le Figaro,* December 11, 2010, http://www.lefigaro.fr/flash-actu/2010/12/11/97001-20101211FILWWW00548-mle-pen-persiste-il-y-a-occupation.php.

12. Faye, "Le FN capte l'attention d'une partie de l'électorat gay"; Michel Henry, "Sébastien Chenu. Un gay de la Marine," *Libération,* February 20, 2015, http://www.liberation.fr/france/2015/02/20/sebastien-chenu-un-gay-de-la-marine_1206743; Didier Lestrade, "Philippot, Chenu: les gays au centre du remaniement du FN," *Slate,* December 13, 2014, http://www.slate.fr/story/95745/gays-fn.

13. Michel Henry, "Sébastien Chenu. Un gay de la Marine."

14. Julien Rochedy, interview by author, Paris, June 29, 2016; Abel Mestre, "Sébastien

Chenu, un ralliement précieux pour Marine Le Pen," *Le Monde*, December 13, 2014, http://www.lemonde.fr/politique/article/2014/12/13/sebastien-chenu-un-ralliement -precieux-pour-marine-le-pen_4540027_823448.html.

15. Marie-Pierre Bourgeois, *Rose Marine: enquête sur le FN et l'homosexualité* (Paris: Du Moment, 2016).

16. Marine Le Pen, interview by author, Nanterre, May 18, 2016. Her comments about the Vel d'Hiv roundup of Parisian Jews may have called this into question. Even the government of Israel criticized her.

17. Alain Finkielkraut, *Au nom de l'autre: Réflexions sur l'antisémitisme qui vient* (Paris: Gallimard, 2003), 18–19.

18. Albert Camus, *The Plague* (London: Hamish Hamilton, 1948), 287.

19. Finkielkraut, *Au nom de l'autre,* 20.

20. Alain Finkielkraut, interview by author, Paris, June 30, 2016.

21. "Le Grand Débat du Point: quand Alain Finkielkraut rencontre Alain Juppé," *Le Point,* January 13, 2016, http://www.lepoint.fr/video/le-grand-debat-du-point-quand -alain-finkielkraut-rencontre-alain-juppe-13-01-2016-2009505_738.php.

22. This is a reference to a book by Georges Bensoussan (published under the pseudonym Emmanuel Brenner) *Les Territoires perdus de la République: antisémitisme, racisme et sexisme en milieu scolaire* (Paris: Mille et Une Nuits, 2002).

23. Alain Finkielkraut, interview by author, Paris, June 30, 2016.

24. Ibid.

25. Marine Le Pen, interview by author, Nanterre, May 18, 2016.

26. Jean Baubérot, *La laïcité falsifiée* (Paris: La Découverte, 2014), 8–9, 13–16. For an in-depth discussion of Islam and French secularism, see Soheib Bencheikh, *Marianne et le prophète: l'Islam dans la France laïque* (Paris: Grasset, 1998).

27. Jean Baubérot, *La laïcité falsifiée,* 16.

28. Ibid., 22, 26–27.

29. Marine Le Pen, interview by author, Nanterre, May 18, 2016.

30. Christian Joppke, *Citizenship and Immigration* (Cambridge, UK: Polity, 2011), 136.

31. This is Caldwell's metaphor; see *Reflections on the Revolution in Europe: Immigration, Islam and the West* (London: Penguin, 2010), 255: "Culturally, everyone in a multicultural order is disarmed. . . . Any fervently espoused religion threatens that monopoly, as surely as a private militia threatened the old nation state."

32. She neglects to mention that only 2–3 percent of meat consumed in Île-de-France is actually slaughtered in Île-de-France. In other words, people eating meat in metropolitan Paris are generally eating meat slaughtered elsewhere, where the number of halal-certified slaughterhouses is far lower.

33. Samuel Laurent, "Laïcité à l'école: l'arnaque de Marine Le Pen sur les cantines," *Le Monde,* April 7, 2014, http://www.lemonde.fr/les-decodeurs/article/2014/04/07/porc-a -la-cantine-l-arnaque-de-marine-le-pen_4396864_4355770.html.

34. Marine Le Pen, interview by author, Nanterre, May 18, 2016.

35. Alain Finkielkraut, interview by author, Paris, June 30, 2016.

Chapter 8: The Great Replacement

1. Khan A. and other migrants, series of interviews by author, Calais, April 6–7, 2016.

2. Various migrants, series of interviews by author, Calais, June 13–14, 2016.

3. Khan A. and other migrants, series of interviews by author, Calais, April 6–7, 2016.

4. "Calais: le général Piquemal arrêté," *Le Figaro,* February 6, 2016, http://www
.lefigaro.fr/flash-actu/2016/02/06/97001-20160206FILWWW00110-calais-le-general
-piquemal-arrete.php.

5. Amin Bagdouche, interview by author, Calais, April 8, 2016.

6. Samuel and Pascal (leaders of Reprenons Calais, no surnames given), interview by
author, Calais, June 15, 2016.

7. Renaud Camus, *Le grand remplacement,* 3rd ed. (Plieux, France: Château de Plieux,
2015), Kindle locations 2112–2115, 1172–1180.

8. Ibid., Kindle locations 104–108, 248–254.

9. Ibid., Kindle locations 1102–1104.

10. Samuel and Pascal (leaders of Reprenons Calais, no surnames given), interview by
author, Calais, June 15, 2016.

11. Amin Bagdouche, interview by author, Calais, April 8, 2016.

12. Maryline Baumard, "A Calais, commerçants et habitants au bord de la crise de
nerfs," *Le Monde,* February 3, 2016, http://www.lemonde.fr/immigration-et-diversite
/article/2016/02/03/calais-une-ville-au-bord-de-la-crise-de-nerf_4858300_1654200.html.

13. Rudy Vercucque and Yohann Faviere, interview by author, Calais, June 14, 2016.

14. Macron defeated Le Pen by a 54–46 margin in the town of Grande-Synthe.

15. Damien Carême, interview by author, Grande-Synthe, June 15, 2016.

16. Ibid. All quotes in the preceding paragraphs are drawn from this interview.

17. Marine Le Pen, interview by author, Nanterre, May 18, 2016.

18. Alain Finkielkraut, interview by author, Paris, June 30, 2016.

19. Ibid.

20. Marine Le Pen, interview by author, Nanterre, May 18, 2016.

21. David Rachline, interview by author, Paris, June 28, 2016.

22. Samuel and Pascal (leaders of Reprenons Calais, no surnames given), interview by
author, Calais, June 15, 2016.

23. Marine Le Pen, interview by author, Nanterre, May 18, 2016.

24. Patrick Weil and Nicolas Truong, *Le sens de la République* (Paris: Grasset, 2015), 33.

25. Ibid., 34.

26. Marine Le Pen, interview by author, Nanterre, May 18, 2016.

27. Julien Aubert, "Gagner la guerre de France," *Valeurs Actuelles,* July 21, 2016, http://
www.valeursactuelles.com/politique/gagner-la-guerre-de-france-63751.

28. Julien Aubert, interview by author, Paris, May 17, 2016. Aubert edged out the FN
candidate by one thousand votes in the first round of legislative elections in June 2017,
and in the second round he retained his seat with a margin of just 559 votes.

29. Jean-Yves Camus and Nicolas Lebourg, *Les droites extrêmes en Europe* (Paris: Seuil,
2015), 236.

30. Mabel Berezin, *Illiberal Politics in Neoliberal Times: Culture, Security and Populism
in the New Europe* (Cambridge, UK: Cambridge University Press, 2009), 201.

31. The CRIF went after Le Pen again in April 2017, when she denied France's responsibility for the roundup of Parisian Jews in July 1942 on the grounds that the Vichy government, which deported the Jews, didn't represent France; even the Israeli government,
usually a fan, denounced her.

32. Adam Nossiter, "Marine Le Pen Denies French Guilt for Rounding Up Jews,"
New York Times, April 10, 2017, https://www.nytimes.com/2017/04/10/world/europe

/france-marine-le-pen-jews-national-front.html. Le Pen blamed the roundup on "those who were in power," meaning the Vichy regime, and argued that the true government was De Gaulle's government-in-exile. This argument ignored the fact that it was not Germans but French police, under French command, who carried out the orders to round up and deport Parisian Jews.

33. Marine Le Pen, interview by author, Nanterre, May 18, 2016.

34. Julien Aubert, interview by author, Paris, May 17, 2016.

Chapter 9: Freedom of Religion—for Some

1. Gérard Araud's Twitter feed, posted August 15, 2016, https://twitter.com /gerardaraud/status/765158720728948736.

2. Alissa J. Rubin, "Fighting for the 'Soul of France,' More Towns Ban a Bathing Suit: The Burkini," *New York Times,* August 17, 2016, https://www.nytimes.com/2016/08/18 /world/europe/fighting-for-the-soul-of-france-more-towns-ban-a-bathing-suit-the -burkini.html.

3. "Liberté, Egalité, Burkini?," BBC News, August 24, 2016, http://www.bbc.co.uk /news/blogs-trending-37176299.

4. Angela Charlton, "Are France's Burkini Bans Sexist, or Liberating?," *AP News,* August 17, 2016, https://apnews.com/64e5d4f781a44aec9385ecc7989db672 /french-prime-minister-backs-local-burkini-bans-urges-calm; Remona Aly, "Five Reasons to Wear a Burkini—and Not Just to Annoy the French," *Guardian,* August 15, 2016, https://www.theguardian.com/commentisfree/2016/aug/15/five -reasons-wear-burkini-annoy-french-cannes-mayor-muslim.

5. Gérard Araud's Twitter feed, posted August 17, 2016, https://twitter.com/Gerard Araud/status/765480848472825856.

6. Gérard Araud's Twitter feed, posted August 15, 2016, https://twitter.com/Gerard Araud/status/765110191461466112.

7. The passengers were removed on many occasions; the US government did not defend the removals at the time.

8. Farhad Khosrokhavar, "Jihad and the French Exception," *New York Times,* July 19, 2016, http://www.nytimes.com/2016/07/20/opinion/jihad-and-the-french-exception .html.

9. Iman Amrani, "France's burkini ban exposes the hypocrisy of its secularist state," *Guardian,* August 24, 2016, https://www.theguardian.com/commentisfree/2016/aug/24 /france-burkini-ban-secularist-equality-muslim.

10. Khosrokhavar, "Jihad and the French Exception."

11. "Radicalization, Laïcité, and the Islamic Veil," *Religional,* April 25, 2016, https:// religional.org/2016/04/25/french-connection-part-ii-radicalization-laicite-and-the -islamic-veil/.

12. Ibid.

13. Nick Cohen, *What's Left?: How the Left Lost Its Way,* updated ed. (London: Harper Perennial, 2007); Pascal Bruckner, *The Tears of the White Man,* First Printing ed. (New York: Macmillan, 1987).

14. "Finkielkraut: 'Être français, ce n'est pas une formalité administrative mais une forme de vie,'" Confédération Des Juifs de France et Amis d'Israël, September 10, 2016, http://www.cjfai.com/eventmaster/blog/2016/09/10/finkielkraut-etre -francais-nest-formalite-administrative-forme-de-vie/?print=print.

15. Laura Thouny, "Siam, verbalisée sur une plage de Cannes pour port d'un simple voile," *L'Obs*, August 22, 2016, http://tempsreel.nouvelobs.com/societe/20160822. OBS6680/siam-verbalisee-sur-une-plage-de-cannes-pour-port-d-un-simple-voile.html.

16. Naser Khader, interview by author, Copenhagen, April 12, 2016.

17. Constitution of Denmark, § 78.2, 78.3, http://www.grundloven.dk.

18. Søren Espersen, interview by author, Copenhagen, April 13, 2016.

19. Bent Melchior, interview by author, Copenhagen, March 7, 2016.

20. Johanne Schmidt-Nielsen, interview by author, Copenhagen, April 15, 2016.

21. Jakob Scharf (#1), interview by author, Copenhagen, October 20, 2015.

22. Ahmed Marcouch, interview by author, The Hague, September 14, 2016.

23. This source wishes to remain anonymous.

24. Ahmed Marcouch, interview by author, The Hague, September 14, 2016. Marcouch is echoing the central argument in Amartya Sen, *Identity and Violence: The Illusion of Destiny* (New York: W. W. Norton, 2007).

25. Ahmed Marcouch, interview by author, The Hague, September 14, 2016.

26. Paul Scheffer, *Immigrant Nations* (Cambridge, UK: Polity Press, 2011), 5.

27. Ian Buruma, *Murder in Amsterdam: The Death of Theo van Gogh and the Limits of Tolerance*, (London: Atlantic Books, 2006), 39, 49–50.

28. Scheffer, *Immigrant Nations*, 3.

29. Ibid., 3; Paul Scheffer, interview by author, Amsterdam, March 24, 2016.

30. Scheffer, *Immigrant Nations*, 121, 280.

31. "Pauw & Witteman—24 April 2008," YouTube video, 5:47, posted by "Pauw & Witteman," April 25, 2008, https://www.youtube.com/watch?v=jWx21mY3ZeA.

32. Ahmed Marcouch, interview by author, The Hague, September 14, 2016; Janny Groen, interview by author, Amsterdam, March 22, 2016.

33. Ibid. In Holland, as in Denmark, the concept of free speech has been claimed by the right and in many cases redefined to mean the right to insult Islam.

34. Mattea Battaglia and Benoit Floch, "A Saint-Denis, collégiens et lycéens ne sont pas tous 'Charlie,'" *Le Monde*, January 10, 2015, http://www.lemonde.fr/societe/article /2015/01/10/a-saint-denis-collegiens-et-lyceens-ne-sont-pas-tous-charlie_4553048_3224.html.

35. Ahmed Marcouch, interview by author, The Hague, September 14, 2016.

36. Jakob Scharf (#1), interview by author, Copenhagen, October 20, 2015.

37. Daniel L. Byman, "Do Syrian Refugees Pose a Terrorism Threat?," Brookings Institution blog, October 27, 2015, https://www.brookings.edu/blog/markaz/2015/10/27 /do-syrian-refugees-pose-a-terrorism-threat/.

38. Jakob Scharf (#2), interview by author, Copenhagen, April 14, 2016.

39. Rasmus Brygger, interview by author, Copenhagen, April 11, 2016.

40. Aydin Soei, *Vrede Unge Mænd* (Copenhagen: Tiderne Skifter, 2011), 274–276.

41. Paul Scheffer, interview by author, Amsterdam, March 24, 2016.

42. Ibid.

43. Rasmus Brygger, interview by author, Copenhagen, April 11, 2016.

44. Kenan Malik, *From Fatwa to Jihad* (London: Atlantic Books, 2009), 140.

45. Rasmus Brygger, interview by author, Copenhagen, April 11, 2016.

46. Olivier Roy, *La laïcité face à l'islam* (Paris: Fayard, 2013), 12, 42. This and other translations from the original French version of Roy's book are my own and in some places may differ slightly from the published English translation.

47. Ibid., 63–64.

48. Ibid., 61.

49. Ibid., 148–149.

50. Ibid., 70, 160.

51. Christian Joppke, *Citizenship and Immigration* (Cambridge, UK: Polity, 2011), 123, 139–141.

52. When a supposedly liberal state targets one religion's signs of observance and leaves others alone while celebrating one faith's holidays and ignoring others, it is not neutral; it is effectively funding the arsenal of one faith, to use Caldwell's analogy, in order to defeat another. Whether it is letting nuns wear habits to the beach while banning burkinis or celebrating Christmas in public buildings while claiming to be staunchly secular, "the selective exclusion of Islam and endorsement of Christianity rests on a subtle distinction between religion as faith and religion as culture," a slippery concept that often ends up targeting or marginalizing minority religions. As the Dutch writer Paul Scheffer puts it, "Many countries have regulations that are at odds with the separation of church and state, such as the obligation to pay church taxes in Germany and Denmark." If they purport to be genuinely secular countries, they must address these small hypocrisies, and if they want to fight political Islam, they will have to defend genuine freedom of religion for everyone so that their secularism does not appear selective.

53. "Le Conseil d'Etat met un terme aux arrêtés 'anti-burkini,'" *Le Monde,* August 26, 2016, http://www.lemonde.fr/societe/article/2016/08/26/le-conseil-d-etat-suspend-l -arrete-anti-burkini-de-villeneuve-loubet_4988472_3224.html.

54. Yascha Mounk, "The West Can Have Burkinis or Democracy, but Not Both," *Foreign Policy,* August 27, 2016, http://foreignpolicy.com/2016/08/27/the-west-can-have -burkinis-or-democracy-but-not-both/.

55. Ibid.

Chapter 10: Barbarians at the Gates

1. "Wilders Tells Dutch Parliament Refugee Crisis Is 'Islamic Invasion,'" Reuters, September 10, 2015, http://uk.reuters.com/article/us-europe-migrants-netherlands -idUSKCN0RA0WY20150910.

2. "Inwoners Oranje Blokkeren Toegangswegen En Belagen Staatssecretaris," *NU,* October 6, 2015, http://www.nu.nl/algemeen/4140129/inwoners-oranje-blokkeren -toegangswegen-en-belagen-staatssecretaris.html.

3. "Elf Mannen Opgepakt Na Bestorming Woerden," *NOS,* October 10, 2015, http:// nos.nl/artikel/2062272-elf-mannen-opgepakt-na-bestorming-woerden.html.

4. Amanda Vermeulen, interview by author (phone), October 10, 2015.

5. "Ruzie over PVV Splijt AZC Alert," *NOS,* October 23, 2015, http://nos.nl/artikel /2064646-ruzie-over-pvv-splijt-azc-alert.html. Vermeulen accused the PVV faction of staging a "coup."

6. Tanja Jadnanansing, interview by author, The Hague, April 21, 2016.

7. Anita Hendriks and other AZC-Alert activists, series of interviews by author, Den Bosch, April 18, 2016.

8. "Nieuwsbericht—Bolten en Booij blij met verkiezingsuitslag," *KijkopSteenbergen,* March 21, 2015, https://kijkopsteenbergen.nl/nieuws/bolten-en-booij-blij -met-verkiezingsuitslag.html; Sheila Kamerman and Freek Schravesande,

"Spandoeken Oké, Maar Geweld—Dat Niet," *NRC*, November 9, 2015, https://www
.nrc.nl/nieuws/2015/11/09/spandoeken-oke-maar-geweld-dat-niet-1555251-a1392443.

9. Anita Hendriks and other AZC-Alert activists, series of interviews by author,
Den Bosch, April 18, 2016. There is a pattern of groups denouncing everyone one step
to their right. Holland's PEGIDA leader, Edwin Wagenveld, told me the same thing.
He's proud to lead his own group but insists that if anyone comes near his demonstration
with a swastika he'll kick them out. Edwin Wagenveld, interview by author, The Hague,
April 9, 2016.

10. Anita Hendriks and other AZC-Alert activists, series of interviews by author, Den
Bosch, April 18, 2016.

11. Alexander van Hattem and other provincial officials, series of interviews by author,
Den Bosch, April 18, 2016.

12. Ibid.

13. Geert Wilders, "Let the Dutch Vote on Immigration Policy," *New York Times*, November 19, 2015, https://www.nytimes.com/2015/11/20/opinion/geert-wilders-the-dutch
-deserve-to-vote-on-immigration-policy.html.

14. Alexander van Hattem and other provincial officials, series of interviews by author,
Den Bosch, April 18, 2016.

15. Theodor W. Adorno, *The Authoritarian Personality* (New York: Harper, 1950).

16. Karen Stenner, *The Authoritarian Dynamic* (New York: Cambridge University
Press, 2010), 4.

17. Ibid., 17.

18. Ibid., 20.

19. Jens Rydgren, *The Populist Challenge: Political Protest and Ethno-Nationalist Mobilization in France* (New York: Berghahn Books, 2003).

20. Stenner, *The Authoritarian Dynamic*, 329.

21. Ibid., 327.

22. Ibid., 331.

23. Jonathan Haidt, "When and Why Nationalism Beats Globalism," *American Interest*, July 10, 2016, http://www.the-american-interest.com/2016/07/10/when-and-why
-nationalism-beats-globalism/; David Goodhart, *The Road to Somewhere: The Populist
Revolt and the Future of Politics* (London: C. Hurst, 2017).

24. Paul Scheffer, interview by author, Amsterdam, March 24, 2016.

25. Haidt, "When and Why Nationalism Beats Globalism."

26. Stenner, *The Authoritarian Dynamic*, 136.

27. Emmanuel Todd, *Who Is Charlie?: Xenophobia and the New Middle Class* (Cambridge, UK: Polity, 2015), 127–128, 182.

28. Ibid., 182.

29. Stenner, *The Authoritarian Dynamic*, 136–137; Haidt, "When and Why Nationalism
Beats Globalism."

30. Edwin Wagenveld, interview by author, The Hague, April 9, 2016.

31. Ibid.

32. Ibid.

33. Ibid.

34. Renaud Camus, *Le grand remplacement*, 3rd ed. (Plieux, France: Château de Plieux,
2015), Kindle locations 4162–4181.

35. Edwin Wagenveld, interview by author, The Hague, April 9, 2016.

36. Ibid. For governments who have gone to great lengths to keep these locations secret, it is a telling anecdote.

37. Ibid.

Chapter 11: They're Stealing Our Jobs

1. Tanja Jadnanansing, interview by author, The Hague, April 21, 2016.

2. Liz Alderman, "Guiding Refugees in Europe on a Rocky Path to Assimilation," *New York Times,* October 18, 2016, https://www.nytimes.com/2016/10/19/business/international/guiding-refugees-in-europe-on-a-rocky-path-to-assimilation.html.

3. Paul Schnabel, interview by author, Amsterdam, April 21, 2016.

4. Ibid.

5. Liz Alderman, "Danish Companies Seek to Hire, but Everyone's Already Working," *New York Times,* February 28, 2017, https://www.nytimes.com/2017/02/28/business/economy/denmark-jobs-full-employment.html.

6. Thomas Gyldal Petersen, interview by author, Herlev, April 13, 2016.

7. Kenneth Kristensen Berth, interview by author, Copenhagen, March 4, 2016.

8. Keith Banting and Will Kymlicka, eds., *Multiculturalism and the Welfare State: Recognition and Redistribution in Contemporary Democracies* (Oxford: Oxford University Press, 2006), 26–27.

9. Søren Espersen, interview by author, Copenhagen, April 13, 2016.

10. Kenneth Kristensen Berth, interview by author, Copenhagen, March 4, 2016.

11. Søren Espersen, interview by author, Copenhagen, April 13, 2016.

12. Kenneth Kristensen Berth, interview by author, Copenhagen, March 4, 2016.

13. Thomas Gyldal Petersen, interview by author, Herlev, April 13, 2016.

14. Søren Espersen, interview by author, Copenhagen, April 13, 2016.

15. "Mette Frederiksen: En Åben Udlændingepolitik Ødelægger de Nordiske Velfærdssamfund," *Ugebrevet A4,* January 20, 2016, http://www.ugebreveta4.dk/mette-frederiksen-en-aaben-udlaendingepolitik-oedelae_20352.aspx.

16. Thomas Gyldal Petersen, interview by author, Herlev, April 13, 2016.

17. Yildiz Akdogan, interview by author, Copenhagen, April 12, 2016.

18. Somewhat ironically, their government offices remain in an annex attached to the main parliament building along with those of the far-left Enhedslisten party.

19. Yildiz Akdogan, interview by author, Copenhagen, April 12, 2016.

20. Aydin Soei, interview by author, Copenhagen, April 15, 2016.

21. Johanne Schmidt-Nielsen, interview by author, Copenhagen, April 15, 2016. The party has collective leadership. Schmidt-Nielsen was its most prominent public face until mid-2016, when she announced she'd be stepping back from the spotlight.

22. Aydin Soei, interview by author, Copenhagen, April 15, 2016.

23. Kenneth Kristensen Berth, interview by author, Copenhagen, March 4, 2016.

24. Lars Olsen, interview by author, Humlebæk, April 11, 2016.

25. Thomas Gammeltoft-Hansen, interview by author, Copenhagen, March 3, 2016.

26. "Ikke Så Meget Klynk—Se Så at Komme I Gang," *Berlingske,* February 16, 2016, http://www.b.dk/content/item/307945; "Lad Os Nu Få Indslusningsløn," *Berlingske,* December 14, 2015, http://www.b.dk/content/item/307943.

27. Jakob Hvide Beim, Thomas Flensburg, and Mathias Petersen, "Nu Er Aftale På Plads: Flygtninge Kan Få Ned Til 49 Kroner I Timen," *Politiken,* March 17, 2016, http://politiken.dk/oekonomi/arbejdsmarked/art5615455/Nu-er-aftale-p%C3%A5

-plads-Flygtninge-kan-f%C3%A5-ned-til-49-kroner-i-timen; Nilas Heinskou and Jakob Hvide Beim, "FOA: Kommunerne Tror, at de Kan Slippe Med 49 Kroner I Timen," *Politiken,* March 10, 2016, http://politiken.dk/indland/politik/art5614265 /FOA-Kommunerne-tror-at-de-kan-slippe-med-49-kroner-i-timen; Frederik Hjorth Gernigon, "Under 15 Registrerede: Ny Flygtningeuddannelse Sender Få I Arbejde," *Jyllands-Posten,* October 5, 2016, http://jyllands-posten.dk/indland/ECE9056566/ny -flygtningeuddannelse-sender-faa-i-arbejde/.

28. Leo Lucassen, interview by author, Amsterdam, April 22, 2016.

29. Anders Samuelsen, interview by author, Copenhagen, April 12, 2016.

30. Rasmus Brygger, interview by author, Copenhagen, April 11, 2016.

31. Leo Lucassen, interview by author, Amsterdam, April 22, 2016.

Chapter 12: The Rise of White Identity Politics

1. Andrew Higgins, "Fake News, Fake Ukrainians: How a Group of Russians Tilted a Dutch Vote," *New York Times,* February 16, 2017, https://www.nytimes.com/2017/02/16 /world/europe/russia-ukraine-fake-news-dutch-vote.html.

2. Thierry Baudet, interview by author, Amsterdam, March 21, 2016.

3. "Thierry Baudet, de pianofoto," *Algemeen Dagblad,* March 17, 2017, http://www.ad.nl /nieuws/geen-woord-meer-over-de-piano-van-thierry-baudet~a220b92d/100809956/; Derk Stokmans and Wilmer Heck, "Wie is deze 'belangrijkste intellectueel van Nederland'?," *NRC,* September 28, 2016; https://www.nrc.nl/nieuws/2016/09/28/de -vele-ideeen-en-vrienden-van-baudet-4508787-a1523858.

4. Thierry Baudet, interview by author, Amsterdam, March 21, 2016.

5. Merijn Oudenampsen, interview by author, Amsterdam, April 20, 2016.

6. Roger Scruton, "OIKOPHOBIA," *Journal of Education* 175, no. 2 (1993): 93–98.

7. According to Thijs Kleinpaste, a journalist at the *Groene Amsterdammer,* a left-wing weekly, Baudet is "more Barrès than Burke"—someone who "inhabits a world of books and is not at home among his crowd" of right-wing social media attack dogs. For Kleinpaste, he is someone who "wants to lose the argument with fighting dignity." Thijs Kleinpaste, interview by author, Amsterdam, March 23, 2016.

8. Baudet has elsewhere made it clear that he is partial to patriarchy. For an example of his praise for violence-prone pickup artists and the suggestion that women want to be overpowered, even when they say no, see "Internet Zoekt Al 72 Uur Massaal Naar Dit Jaren Oude Artikel van Thierry Baudet (Fvd)," *Post Online,* March 17, 2017, http://cult .tpo.nl/2017/03/17/julien-blanc-heeft-volkomen-gelijk/.

9. Martin Bosma, *Minderheid in Eigen Land: Hoe Progressieve Strijd Ontaardt in Geno-cide En ANC-Apartheid* (Amsterdam: Bibliotheca Africana Formicae, 2015). In fairness to Bosma, he correctly points out that South Africa's African National Congress, which the Dutch anti-apartheid movement backed in the 1970s and 1980s, committed many crimes of its own during those years and has now transformed itself from a liberation movement into a power-hungry ruling party that has turned the country into a corrupt kleptocracy. Bosma's analysis of current events in South Africa is far more convincing than his discussion of historical ones.

10. Thierry Baudet, interview by author, Amsterdam, March 21, 2016.

11. "Naar Het Veelbelovende Land," *De Groene Amsterdammer,* June 22, 2016, https:// www.groene.nl/artikel/naar-het-veelbelovende-land.

12. Thierry Baudet, interview by author, Amsterdam, March 21, 2016.

13. Christopher Caldwell, *Reflections on the Revolution in Europe: Immigration, Islam and the West* (London: Penguin, 2010), 7.

14. Ibid., 15.

15. Doug Saunders, *The Myth of the Muslim Tide: Do Immigrants Threaten the West?* (New York: Vintage Books, 2012), 59.

16. Theodore Schleifer, "King Doubles Down on Controversial 'Babies' Tweet," CNN, March 14, 2017, http://edition.cnn.com/2017/03/13/politics/steve-king-babies-tweet-cnntv/.

17. Thilo Sarrazin, *L'Allemagne disparait: Quand un pays se laisse mourir,* trans. Jean-Baptiste Offenburg (Paris: Editions du Toucan, 2013), 64–67, 91.

18. Ibid., 268, 369, 331–332.

19. Bent Melchior, interview by author, Copenhagen, March 7, 2016.

20. Saunders, *The Myth of the Muslim Tide,* 51–52.

21. Bent Melchior, interview by author, Copenhagen, March 7, 2016.

22. Sarrazin, *L'Allemagne disparait,* 315.

23. Ibid., 322–323, 404.

24. Jean Raspail, *The Camp of the Saints,* trans. Norman R. Shapiro (Petoskey, MI: Social Contract Press, 2015), 190.

25. Thierry Baudet, interview by author, Amsterdam, March 21, 2016.

26. Merijn Oudenampsen, interview by author, Amsterdam, April 20, 2016.

27. Kustaw Bessems, interview by author, Amsterdam, March 24, 2016.

28. "Wilders Met Spruyt in Nieuwe Rechtse Partij," *NU,* November 4, 2004, http://www.nu.nl/algemeen/436687/wilders-met-spruyt-in-nieuwe-rechtse-partij.html.

29. Merijn Oudenampsen, interview by author, Amsterdam, April 20, 2016. Spruyt has since criticized Wilders and blamed Islamophobic rhetoric for inspiring the Norwegian murderer Breivik.

30. "A Concise History of the Netherlands by James C. Kennedy," Cambridge Core, accessed April 7, 2017, https://www.cambridge.org/core/books/concise-history-of-the-netherlands/F5C341B3BCD9FA3F6846BECBC616A696.

31. Merijn Oudenampsen, interview by author, Amsterdam, April 20, 2016.

32. Ian Buruma, *Murder in Amsterdam: The Death of Theo van Gogh and the Limits of Tolerance* (London: Atlantic Books, 2006), 98–99, 112–113.

33. Zihni Özdil, interview by author, Amsterdam, March 22, 2016.

34. Tanja Jadnanansing, interview by author, The Hague, April 21, 2016.

35. See Paul Scheffer, *Immigrant Nations* (Cambridge, UK: Polity Press, 2011), 280. Here Scheffer calls on Christians to respect Muslims' religious freedoms.

36. Merijn Oudenampsen, interview by author, Amsterdam, April 20, 2016.

37. Buruma, *Murder in Amsterdam,* 19.

38. Scheffer, *Immigrant Nations,* 201–202.

39. Paul Scheffer, interview by author, Amsterdam, March 24, 2016.

40. Kustaw Bessems, interview by author, Amsterdam, March 24, 2016.

41. Nina Siegal, "A Pro-Immigrant Party Rises in the Netherlands," *New York Times,* July 29, 2016, https://www.nytimes.com/2016/07/30/world/europe/dutch-denk-party.html.

42. Kustaw Bessems, interview by author, Amsterdam, March 24, 2016.

43. Willem Schinkel, interview by author, Rotterdam, April 18, 2016.

44. Bas Heijne, interview by author, Paris, March 15, 2016.

45. Kustaw Bessems, interview by author, Amsterdam, March 24, 2016.

46. Ahmed Marcouch, interview by author, The Hague, September 14, 2016.

47. "Dutch PM Rutte: 'If You Don't like It Here, Then Leave,'" BBC News, January 23, 2017, http://www.bbc.co.uk/news/world-europe-38718286.

48. Kustaw Bessems, interview by author, Amsterdam, March 24, 2016.

49. Alain Finkielkraut, *Au nom de l'autre: Réflexions sur l'antisémitisme qui vient* (Paris: Gallimard, 2003), 11.

50. Bram (pseudonym), interview by author, Amsterdam, September 12, 2016.

51. Ibid.

52. Ibid.

53. Ahmed Marcouch, interview by author, The Hague, September 14, 2016.

54. "WATCH: Netanyahu Offers Handshake, Dutch Politician Leaves Him Hanging," *Haaretz*, September 7, 2016, http://www.haaretz.com/world-news/europe/1.740790.

55. Bram (pseudonym), interview by author, Amsterdam, September 12, 2016.

56. Ahmed Marcouch, interview by author, The Hague, September 14, 2016.

57. Bas Heijne, interview by author, Paris, March 15, 2016.

58. "Police Break Up Turkish Consulate Demo, Minister Sent Back to Germany," *DutchNews*, March 12, 2017, http://www.dutchnews.nl/news/archives/2017/03/police-break-up-turkish-consulate-demo-minister-sent-back-to-germany/.

59. Bram (pseudonym), interview by author, Amsterdam, September 12, 2016.

60. "Voyage of the St. Louis," United States Holocaust Memorial Museum, accessed March 27, 2017, https://www.ushmm.org/wlc/en/article.php?ModuleId=10005267. See also Sarah A. Ogilvie and Scott Miller, *Refuge Denied: The St. Louis Passengers and the Holocaust* (Madison: University of Wisconsin Press, 2006).

61. Bram (pseudonym), interview by author, Amsterdam, September 12, 2016.

62. Zihni Özdil, interview by author, Amsterdam, March 22, 2016.

63. Bram (pseudonym), interview by author, Amsterdam, September 12, 2016.

Chapter 13: When the Right Turns Left—and the Left's Voters Go Right

1. Laurent Joffrin, "La mairie FN d'Hayange envoie les huissiers au Secours populaire," *Libération*, September 30, 2016, http://www.liberation.fr/france/2016/09/30/la-mairie-fn-d-hayange-envoie-les-huissiers-au-secours-populaire_1515978.

2. Andrew Hussey, interview by author, Paris, March 14, 2016.

3. Ben Judah, "Islam and the French Republic," *Standpoint*, August 2016, http://standpointmag.co.uk/node/6568/full. In the early 1980s, certain French Communist Party officials voiced anti-immigrant sentiments similar to the FN's positions today.

4. Nuttall ran himself and failed in the Stoke-on-Trent by-election in March. Although Labour won, he came in second and got 25 percent of the vote—a respectable showing for UKIP. Robert Anthony Ford and Matthew J. Goodwin, *Revolt on the Right: Explaining Support for the Radical Right in Britain* (New York: Routledge, 2014), 108.

5. Andrew Hussey, interview by author, Paris, March 14, 2016.

6. James Angelos, "Will France Sound the Death Knell for Social Democracy?," *New York Times*, January 24, 2017, https://www.nytimes.com/2017/01/24/magazine/will-france-sound-the-death-knell-for-social-democracy.html.

7. Marine Le Pen, interview by author, Nanterre, May 18, 2016.

8. Ibid.

9. David Rachline, interview by author, Paris, June 28, 2016; "Livres, boutiques, vidéos . . . enquête sur le business Alain Soral," *L'Obs,* August 26, 2015, http://tempsreel .nouvelobs.com/societe/20150826.OBS4801/livres-boutiques-videos-enquete-sur-le -business-alain-soral.html; "Dieudonné : son lucratif business," *RTL,* November 1, 2014, http://www.rtl.fr/actu/les-lucratives-affaires-de-dieudonne-7768716509.

10. "Alain Soral: 'C'est l'Iran qui a financé la campagne du parti anti-sioniste,'" *AgoraVox,* April 3, 2013, http://www.agoravox.tv/tribune-libre/article/alain-soral-c-est -l-iran-qui-a-38594; Nolwenn Le Blevennec, "Les Iraniens ont-ils financé la liste an-tisioniste de Dieudonné?" *L'Obs,* October 21, 2013, http://tempsreel.nouvelobs.com /rue89/rue89-politique/20131021.RUE9641/les-iraniens-ont-ils-finance-la-liste-antisioniste -de-dieudonne.html. After declaring in the video cited above that Iran had financed the party, Soral later told journalists that it was "local Shiites" in France who provided financing.

11. Mathieu Molard and Robin D'Angelo, "David Rachline, un ancien proche de Soral nommé directeur de campagne de Marine Le Pen," *StreetPress,* September 15, 2016, www .streetpress.com/sujet/1473936987-david-rachline-proche-soral-marine-le-pen.

12. David Rachline, interview by author, Paris, June 28, 2016.

13. Nolwenn Le Blevennec, "David Rachline du FN: 'Je ne suis pas juif selon les codes,'" *L'Obs,* September 11, 2011, http://tempsreel.nouvelobs.com/rue89/rue89-politique /20110911.RUE4255/david-rachline-du-fn-je-ne-suis-pas-juif-selon-les-codes.html.

14. David Rachline, interview by author, Paris, June 28, 2016.

15. Marine Le Pen, interview by author, Nanterre, May 18, 2016.

16. Julien Aubert, interview by author, Paris, May 17, 2016. Indeed, when Aubert's for-mer party boss, Nicolas Sarkozy, attacked the FN in the 2007 campaign, he went after them on economic policy rather than identity issues, trying to tar them with the label "extreme left." It had the effect of shoring up the centrist and economically conservative vote even if the FN was drawing votes from the working class.

17. Mabel Berezin, *Illiberal Politics in Neoliberal Times: Culture, Security and Populism in the New Europe* (Cambridge, UK: Cambridge University Press, 2009), 119, 132, 219–220. In a 2015 article in the *European Sociological Review,* Maureen Eger and Sarah Valdez argue, "Results from our voting analysis confirm that welfare chauvinism—not rightist economic preferences—affects voting behaviour. These findings are consistent with re-cent work that shows voters are not motivated by neo-liberal preferences . . . and other research that identifies particular parties as welfare chauvinist." See also Maureen A. Eger and Nate Breznau, "Immigration and the Welfare State: A Cross-Regional Analy-sis of European Welfare Attitudes," *International Journal of Comparative Sociology* (Feb-ruary 2017).

18. Julien Aubert, interview by author, Paris, May 17, 2016.

19. Marine Le Pen, interview by author, Nanterre, May 18, 2016.

20. Julien Aubert, interview by author, Paris, May 17, 2016.

21. Lars Olsen, interview by author, Humlebæk, April 11, 2016.

22. Johanne Schmidt-Nielsen, interview by author, Copenhagen, April 15, 2016.

23. Søren Espersen, interview by author, Copenhagen, April 13, 2016.

24. Thomas Gyldal Petersen, interview by author, Herlev, April 13, 2016.

25. Søren Espersen, interview by author, Copenhagen, April 13, 2016.

26. Kenneth Kristensen Berth, interview by author, Copenhagen, March 4, 2016.

27. David Goodhart, *The Road to Somewhere: The Populist Revolt and the Future of Politics* (London: C. Hurst, 2017), 79; Ford and Goodwin, *Revolt on the Right*. Jeremy Corbyn's strong showing in the 2017 election may reverse this trend.

28. Michael Collins, *The Likes of Us: A Biography of the White Working Class* (London: Granta Books, 2004), 246–247, 8.

29. Roy Kerridge, "Me and My White Mates," *Spectator*, July 24, 2004, https://www.spectator.co.uk/2004/07/me-and-my-white-mates/; Mike Phillips, "Rivers of Crud," *Guardian*, July 24, 2004, https://www.theguardian.com/books/2004/jul/24/higher education.biography1; Nigel Farndale, "The Salt of the Earth Turns Sour," *Telegraph*, August 2, 2004, http://www.telegraph.co.uk/culture/books/3621549/The-salt-of-the-earth-turns-sour.html.

30. Owen Jones, *Chavs: The Demonization of the Working Class* (London: Verso, 2012), 6–9.

31. Ibid., 116–118.

32. Ibid., 225, 102.

33. "To Their Manor Born," *Independent*, July 24, 2004, http://www.independent.co.uk/arts-entertainment/books/features/to-their-manor-born-49060.html; Mark Simpson, "The Return of the White Working Class," Mark Simpson's blog, April 19, 2006, http://www.marksimpson.com/blog/2006/04/19/to-their-manor-born-mark-simpson-reviews-the-likes-of-us-by-michael-collins/.

34. Daniel Trilling, *Bloody Nasty People: The Rise of Britain's Far Right*, 2nd revised ed. (London: Verso Books, 2013), 137–141.

35. Jones, *Chavs*, 88.

36. Ford and Goodwin, *Revolt on the Right*, 72–73.

37. John Harris, "Britain Is in the Midst of a Working-Class Revolt," *Guardian*, June 17, 2016, https://www.theguardian.com/commentisfree/2016/jun/17/britain-working-class-revolt-eu-referendum.

38. John Harris, "'If You've Got Money, You Vote In . . . If You Haven't Got Money, You Vote Out,'" *Guardian*, June 24, 2016, https://www.theguardian.com/politics/commentisfree/2016/jun/24/divided-britain-brexit-money-class-inequality-westminster.

39. Ford and Goodwin, *Revolt on the Right*, 108, 138, 176.

40. Harris, "'If You've Got Money, You Vote In . . . If You Haven't Got Money, You Vote Out.'"

41. Harris, "Britain Is in the Midst of a Working-Class Revolt."

42. Harris, "'If You've Got Money, You Vote In . . . If You Haven't Got Money, You Vote Out.'"

43. Collins, *The Likes of Us*, 233, 242–246.

44. David Goodhart, "The Outers' Message Resonated with Those Who Feel Left Behind," *Financial Times*, June 24, 2016, https://www.ft.com/content/14eeodd6-39e8-11e6-a780-b48ed7b6126f.

Chapter 14: Xenophobia Beyond Black and White

1. David Goodhart, *The British Dream: Successes and Failures of Post-War Immigration* (London: Atlantic Books, 2014), 247.

2. Louw invited me to join the group in August 2016. I have been privy to the entire group discussion since then, including thousands of messages.

3. Mary Louw, interview by author, Johannesburg, July 28, 2016.

4. Buthelezi is the leader of a Zulu nationalist party that clashed violently with Mandela's ANC during the early 1990s and nearly derailed the transition to democracy.

5. Michael Neocosmos, *From "Foreign Natives" to "Native Foreigners": Explaining Xenophobia in Post-Apartheid South Africa* (Oxford: African Books Collective, 2008), 97.

6. Roni Amit, "Paying for Protection: Corruption in South Africa's Asylum System," Migration Policy Institute, November 5, 2015, http://www.migrationpolicy.org/article /paying-protection-corruption-south-africa%E2%80%99s-asylum-system.

7. Loren Landau, "South Africa's Tough Lessons on Migrant Policy," *Foreign Policy,* October 13, 2015, https://foreignpolicy.com/2015/10/13/south-africas-tough-lessons -on-migrant-policy/.

8. Amit, "Paying for Protection."

9. Richard Stupart, "Is South Africa Home to More than a Million Asylum-Seekers? The Numbers Don't Add up," *Mail & Guardian Online,* August 15, 2016, https://mg.co .za/article/2016-08-15-is-south-africa-home-to-more-than-a-million-asylum-seekers -the-numbers-dont-add-up/.

10. Dominic Frisby, "Zimbabwe's Trillion-Dollar Note: From Worthless Paper to Hot Investment," *Guardian,* May 14, 2016, https://www.theguardian.com/money/2016 /may/14/zimbabwe-trillion-dollar-note-hyerinflation-investment; "Zimbabwe Inflation Leaps to Hyper Level," *VOA,* October 27, 2009, https://www.voanews.com/a/a-13-2007 -05-13-voa20-66555532/554752.html.

11. Jonathan Crush and Sujata Ramachandran, "Xenophobia, International Migration and Development," *Journal of Human Development and Capabilities* 11, no. 2 (May 2010): 6. doi:10.1080/19452821003677327.

12. Ibid., 4–9, 31–37.

13. This does not do justice to Steinberg's book or Abdullahi's story. It is well worth reading in full. Jonny Steinberg, *A Man of Good Hope* (Johannesburg: Jonathan Ball, 2014).

14. The last time a term like that was used was in Zimbabwe in 2005 when President Mugabe declared a vicious attack on opposition supporters known as Operation Murambatsvina—throw out the filth—that left hundreds of thousands homeless.

15. Emmanuel Camillo and Lynsey Chutel, "South African Police Arrest Thousands in Raids Following Attacks on Foreigners," *US News & World Report,* May 15, 2015, https://www.usnews.com/news/world/articles/2015/05/21/south-african-president -apologizes-to-mozambique; Khadija Patel, "Operation Fiela and Our History of Kicking Out 'Illegal' Immigrants," *Daily Vox,* May 28, 2015, http://www.thedailyvox.co.za /operation-fiela-and-our-history-of-kicking-out-illegal-immigrants/.

16. Crush and Ramachandran, "Xenophobia, International Migration and Development," 17–22.

17. Baron Mukeba and Prince Abenge Médard, interview by author, Johannesburg, August 2, 2016.

18. Amanda Khoza, "Zuma's Son Wants Foreigners out of the Country," *News 24,* April 1, 2015, http://www.news24.com/SouthAfrica/News/Zumas-son-wants-foreigners -out-of-the-country-20150331.

19. Marc Gbaffou and Prince Abenge Médard, interview by author, Johannesburg, August 4, 2016.

20. Ingrid Palmary and Jean-Pierre Misago, interview by author, Johannesburg, July 28, 2016.

21. Marc Gbaffou, interview by author, Johannesburg, August 4, 2016.

22. Mary Louw to Proudly SA Citizens group on WhatsApp, various dates August–December 2016.

23. Mary Louw, interview by author, Johannesburg, July 28, 2016. Louw herself tirelessly publicized one such killing; when a young ANC leader in the area killed his girlfriend, she mobilized local women to attend the trial.

24. Ibid.

25. For a broader discussion of this phenomenon, see Jacob Dlamini's excellent book *Native Nostalgia* (Auckland Park, South Africa: Jacana Media, 2009).

26. Ingrid Palmary and Jean-Pierre Misago, interview by author, Johannesburg, July 28, 2016.

27. Ingrid Palmary, *Gender, Sexuality and Migration in South Africa: Governing Morality* (New York: Palgrave Macmillan, 2017), 79–99.

28. Ibid.

29. Ingrid Palmary and Jean-Pierre Misago, interview by author, Johannesburg, July 28, 2016. As Palmary argues, "There had to be a distinction made between what was crime and what was politics" on the grounds that "if it's politics, we have to take it seriously. If it's crime, then . . . we write it off."

30. Palmary, *Gender, Sexuality and Migration in South Africa*, 79–99.

31. Mary Louw, interview by author, Johannesburg, July 28, 2016.

32. Ibid.

33. Samuel and Pascal (leaders of Reprenons Calais, no surnames given), interview by author, Calais, June 15, 2016.

34. Mary Louw, interview by author, Johannesburg, July 28, 2016.

35. Ibid.

36. Ibid.

37. The stridently populist Economic Freedom Front, South Africa's closest thing to an openly populist party, which one might expect to profit from xenophobic sentiments, has actually been the most outspoken defender of immigrants, largely because of its stated commitment to Pan-Africanism, the movement to which it traces its roots.

38. Ngqabutho Mabhena, interview by author, Johannesburg, July 29, 2016.

39. Penelope Mashego and Moipone Malefane, "All Illegal Foreigners, Leave My City—Herman Mashaba," *Sowetan Live*, December 2, 2016, http://www.sowetanlive .co.za/news/2016/12/02/all-illegal-foreigners-leave-my-city---herman-mashaba.

40. Mary Louw to Proudly SA Citizens group on WhatsApp, December 3, 2016.

41. Ibid.

Chapter 15: *Willkommenskultur* vs. Guantánamo

1. For a broader perspective on extralegal violence and extralegal spaces, see, for example, Mateo Taussig-Rubbo, "Outsourcing Sacrifice: The Labor of Private Military Contractors," *Yale Journal of Law & the Humanities* 21, no. 1 (May 8, 2013), http://digital commons.law.yale.edu/yjlh/vol21/iss1/3, and the Israeli film directed by Ra'anan Alexandrowicz, *The Law In These Parts* (New York: Cinema Guild, 2013).

2. Ben Doherty, "Call Me Illegal: The Semantic Struggle over Seeking Asylum in Australia" (Oxford: Oxford Institute for the Study of Journalism, 2015), 43–47.

3. Jeremy Thompson, "Australia, Malaysia Sign Refugee Deal," ABC News, July 25, 2011, http://www.abc.net.au/news/2011-07-25/malaysia-signs-refugee-deal/2809512.

4. John Menadue, interview by author, Sydney, January 21, 2016.

5. Anna Burke, interview by author, Canberra, February 3, 2016.

6. Waleed Aly, interview by author, Melbourne, January 29, 2016.

7. Waleed Aly, "Comment: The Australian Solution," *Monthly*, August 2012, https://www.themonthly.com.au/australian-solution-waleed-aly-5858.

8. Julian Burnside, interview by author, Melbourne, January 28, 2016.

9. Ahmed and Marwan and other detainees (#1), series of interviews by author, Villawood Detention Center, Sydney, January 14, 2016. (These names are pseudonyms; both men prefer not to be identified.) Australia announced in May 2017 that the Manus Island facility will be closed. See Ben Doherty, "Manus Island Detention Centre to Close by Year's End, Inquest Told," *Guardian*, February 15, 2017, https://www.theguardian.com/australia-news/2017/feb/15/manus-island-detention-centre-to-close-by-years-end-inquest-told.

10. Madeline Gleeson, interview by author, Sydney, January 15, 2016.

11. Melissa Parke, interview by author, Canberra, February 3, 2016.

12. Daniel Webb, interview by author, Melbourne, January 27, 2016.

13. Waleed Aly, interview by author, Melbourne, January 29, 2016.

14. Paul Farrell, Nick Evershed, and Helen Davidson, "The Nauru Files: Cache of 2,000 Leaked Reports Reveal Scale of Abuse of Children in Australian Offshore Detention," *Guardian*, August 10, 2016, https://www.theguardian.com/australia-news/2016/aug/10/the-nauru-files-2000-leaked-reports-reveal-scale-of-abuse-of-children-in-australian-offshore-detention; Daniel Webb, interview by author, Melbourne, January 27, 2016. The whistleblower laws have since been softened somewhat.

15. Gillian Triggs, interview by author, Melbourne, January 27, 2016. Triggs is reviled by people like the conservative columnist Chris Kenny for what they regard as partisan favoritism. Triggs kept quiet about detained children under the Labor government and then spoke out when the right came to power in 2013. To Kenny, this is a cardinal sin and a sign of partiality. As Triggs tells it, she didn't hold an inquiry, because the government had pledged to move them out of detention. "Although the numbers were high, the government was actually moving them out in what could be seen as a reasonable space of time. We didn't like it, but they were moving," she told me. When Tony Abbott trounced Kevin Rudd in the September 2013 election and didn't end the detention, Triggs went after the government. The government went on the attack and tried to force her to resign—even offering the incentive of a senior position. "The only way they could get me out was to show that I was bankrupt or that I had committed a criminal offense of some kind," she says. They filed freedom of information requests for all of her phone communications but couldn't find grounds to remove her.

16. See Parliament of Australia, "Migration and Maritime Powers Legislation Amendment (Resolving the Asylum Legacy Caseload) Bill 2014," December 5, 2014.

17. Daniel Webb, interview by author, Melbourne, January 27, 2016. A group of thirty-four babies in this category became the focus of mass protests by citizens and clergy in early 2016, and they were permitted to remain in Australia.

18. David Manne, interview by author, Melbourne, January 28, 2016.

19. Ahmed and Marwan and other detainees (#2), series of interviews by author, Villawood Detention Center, Sydney, February 8, 2016.

20. Ibid.

21. Daniel Webb, interview by author, Melbourne, January 27, 2016.

22. Ibid.

23. This is a pseudonym; he asked that his real name not be used.

24. Mark J. Isaacs, *The Undesirables: Inside Nauru* (Richmond, Australia: Hardie Grant, 2014), 83.

25. Philip Ruddock, interview by author, Sydney, January 12, 2016.

26. Ibid.

27. Steve Cannane and Brigid Andersen, "Federal Government Repatriates Former Military Interpreter to Iraq, Despite Fears His Life Is in Danger," ABC News, November 9, 2015, http://www.abc.net.au/news/2015-11-09/khaled-iraq/6923434; "Australia's '19th Syrian' Injured in Shelling Back Home While His Father Is Killed in the Same Attack," *Lateline*, October 20, 2015, http://www.abc.net.au/lateline/content/2015 /s4335593.htm.

28. Descriptions of these medical conditions are drawn from official medical reports and doctors' notes provided by the detainees.

29. Ahmed and Marwan and other detainees (#2), series of interviews by author, Villawood Detention Center, Sydney, February 8, 2016.

30. Ibid.

31. These declassified government documents were obtained through Human Rights Watch.

32. Ginny Stein, "The Journey of the 19th Syrian—What Happened to the Asylum Seeker the Australian Government Convinced to Return to a War Zone?," *Lateline*, January 10, 2015, http://www.abc.net.au/lateline/content/2015/s4323692.htm; "The 19th Syrian: The Asylum Seeker Convinced to Return to a War Zone," ABC News, October 1, 2015, http://www.abc.net.au/news/2015-10-01/the-asylum-seeker -the-government-convinced-to-return-to-syria/6816336l.

33. "Australia's '19th Syrian' Injured in Shelling Back Home While His Father Is Killed in the Same Attack."

34. Alison Smale and Melissa Eddy, "Angela Merkel Accepts Responsibility for Party's Losses in Berlin Election," *New York Times*, September 19, 2016, https://www.ny times.com/2016/09/20/world/europe/berlin-elections-merkel.html.

35. Ralf Neukirch and Christian Reiermann, "Germany's Divided Conservatives: Merkel Critics Deal a Blow to Chancellor," *Spiegel Online*, December 9, 2016, http:// www.spiegel.de/international/germany/merkel-under-fire-from-critics-within-the -cdu-a-1125213.html.

36. Jens Spahn, interview by author, Berlin, July 7, 2016.

37. Ralf Neukirch, "The Chancellor's Eroding Power: Merkel Adversary Jens Spahn on the Rise," *Spiegel Online*, December 1, 2016, http://www.spiegel.de/international /germany/jens-spahn-emerging-as-conservative-adversary-to-merkel-a-1123652.html.

38. Janosch Delcker, "The Young, Gay, Conservative German Chancellor-in-Waiting," *Politico*, May 12, 2016, http://www.politico.eu/article/jens-spahn-the-young-gay -conservative-german-chancellor-in-waiting-jens-spahn-cdu-csu-angela-merkel-germany/.

39. Neukirch, "The Chancellor's Eroding Power."

40. Jens Spahn, interview by author, Berlin, July 7, 2016.

41. "AfD's Unlikely Duo: Alexander Gauland and Alice Weidel," *Deutsche*

Welle, April 24, 2017, http://www.dw.com/en/afds-unlikely-duo-alexander-gauland
-and-alice-weidel/a-38563247.

42. Philipp Lengsfeld, interview by author, Berlin, July 8, 2016.

43. "Knud Wollenberger: Stasi Agent Who Spied on His Own Family," *Independent*, March 13, 2012, http://www.independent.co.uk/news/obituaries/knud-wollenberger-stasi
-agent-who-spied-on-his-own-family-7563068.html.

44. Philipp Lengsfeld, interview by author, Berlin, July 8, 2016. The source of the final quote wishes to remain anonymous.

45. Philipp Lengsfeld, interview by author, Berlin, July 8, 2016.

46. Ibid.

47. Jens Spahn, interview by author, Berlin, July 7, 2016.

48. Daniel Bax, "Porträt Aydan Özoguz: Hanseatisch, Nüchtern, Erfolgreich," *Die Tageszeitung*, October 20, 2011, http://www.taz.de/!5109453/.

49. "Germany and Europe, World Questions," BBC World Service, http://www.bbc
.co.uk/programmes/p03snhvd.

50. Philipp Lengsfeld, interview by author, Berlin, July 8, 2016.

51. Jens Spahn, interview by author, Berlin, July 7, 2016.

52. Robin Alexander, interview by author, Berlin, March 8, 2016.

53. Philipp Lengsfeld, interview by author, Berlin, July 8, 2016.

54. Christian Schmidt, interview by author, Berlin, May 3, 2016.

55. Ibid. The AfD is considering expelling Höcke. At the time of writing, he is still a member and the state leader in Thuringia.

56. Ibid.

57. Robin Alexander, interview by author, Berlin, March 8, 2016.

58. He ended up founding a new party, ALFA, which has yet to gain much traction.

59. Christian Schmidt, interview by author, Berlin, May 3, 2016.

60. Alexander Gauland, interview by author, Potsdam, May 4, 2016; infographic cited on Philipp Lengsfeld's Twitter feed, posted September 18, 2016, https://twitter.com
/plengsfeld/status/777754695007952896.

61. Alexander Gauland, interview by author, Potsdam, May 4, 2016.

62. "Landtag Brandenburg: Im Boateng-Trikot neben AfD-Fraktionschef Alexander Gauland," *Die Welt*, June 8, 2016, https://www.welt.de/sport/fussball/article156070435
/Im-Boateng-Trikot-neben-AfD-Fraktionschef-Gauland.html.

63. Alexander Gauland, interview by author, Potsdam, May 4, 2016.

64. Ibid.

Chapter 16: *Camp of the Saints* at the White House

1. Robert Ménard, interview by author, Béziers, June 21, 2016. For his views closer to the election, see Anne-Sylvaine Chassany, "The French Town That Shows How Marine Le Pen Could Win," *Financial Times*, April 10, 2017, https://www.ft.com
/content/309292d4-1a28-11e7-a266-12672483791a.

2. Robert Ménard, interview by author, Béziers, June 21, 2016.

3. Martin Thomas, Bob Moore, and L. J. Butler, *Crises of Empire: Decolonization and Europe's Imperial States* (London: Bloomsbury, 2015); Andrew Hussey, *The French Intifada: The Long War Between France and Its Arabs* (London: Granta, 2015).

4. Robert Ménard, interview by author, Béziers, June 21, 2016.

5. Ibid.

6. Bruckner, *The Tyranny of Guilt,* 187.

7. Ibid., 41.

8. Robert Ménard, interview by author, Béziers, June 21, 2016.

9. Julien Rochedy, interview by author, Paris, June 29, 2016.

10. Ibid. All paragraphs above draw on this interview.

11. Zemmour, *Le suicide français,* 15–16.

12. "Éric Zemmour à 'La Synagogue de la Victoire,'" YouTube video, 14:16, posted by "Subversion 2.0," June 11, 2016, https://www.youtube.com/watch?v=JGyJDNSmDNo.

13. Claude Askolovitch, "Zemmour en kippa, ou le prêcheur pétainiste de la synagogue de la Victoire," *Slate,* June 23, 2016, http://www.slate.fr/story/119925/zemmour -kippa-precheur-petainiste.

14. Mark Lilla, *The Shipwrecked Mind: On Political Reaction* (New York: New York Review of Books, 2016), 116.

15. Zemmour, *Le suicide français,* 415–416.

16. Ibid., 430–432.

17. Ibid., 522–523.

18. To his credit, Finkielkraut does not stray into the territory of Vichy apologism.

19. Zemmour, *Le suicide français,* 526–527.

20. Julien Rochedy, interview by author, Paris, June 29, 2016.

21. Paul Blumenthal and J. M. Rieger, "This Stunningly Racist French Novel Is How Steve Bannon Explains the World," *Huffington Post,* March 6, 2017, http:// www.huffingtonpost.com/entry/steve-bannon-camp-of-the-saints-immigration _us_58b75206e4b0284854b3dc03; Ben Mathis-Lilley, "Bannon, Adviser Behind Travel Ban, Is Fan of Novel About Feces-Eating, Dark-Skinned Immigrants Destroying White Society," *Slate,* March 6, 2017, http://www.slate.com/blogs/the_slatest/2017/03/06 /steve_bannon_and_the_camp_of_the_saints.html.

22. Jean Raspail, interview by author, Paris, May 19, 2016.

23. Ibid.

24. Ibid.

25. Raspail, *The Camp of the Saints,* 69 and 80–81.

26. Ibid., 185.

27. Ibid., 112–113, 125, and 159.

28. Ibid., 211.

29. Jean Raspail, interview by author, Paris, May 19, 2016.

30. Ibid.

31. Ibid.

32. Amin Bagdouche, interview by author, Calais, April 8, 2016.

33. Jean Raspail, interview by author, Paris, May 19, 2016.

Epilogue

1. OSF, the philanthropic organization started by George Soros, also generously funded much of the research for this book.

2. Nate Cohn and Toni Monkovic, "How Did Donald Trump Win Over So Many Obama Voters?," *New York Times,* November 14, 2016, https://www.nytimes .com/2016/11/15/upshot/how-did-trump-win-over-so-many-obama-voters.html;

"Just How Many Obama 2012–Trump 2016 Voters Were There?," Rasmussen Reports, November 14, 2016, http://www.rasmussenreports.com/public_content /political_commentary/commentary_by_geoffrey_skelley/just_how_many _obama_2012_trump_2016_voters_were_there; David Weigel, "How Voters Who Heavily Supported Obama Switched over to Trump," *Washington Post,* November 10, 2016, https://www.washingtonpost.com/politics/how-voters-who-heavily-supported-obama -switched-over-to-trump/2016/11/10/65019658-a77a-11e6-ba59-a7d93165c6d4_story.html.

3. Debbie Dingell, "I Said Clinton Was in Trouble with the Voters I Represent. Democrats Didn't Listen," *Washington Post,* November 10, 2016, https://www.washington post.com/opinions/i-said-clinton-was-in-trouble-with-the-voters-i-represent-democrats -didnt-listen/2016/11/10/0e9521a6-a796-11e6-ba59-a7d93165c6d4_story.html?utm_term =.18a427f617a5.

4. Manuela Tobias and Nolan D. McCaskill, "Bernie Sanders Wins Michigan in Stunning Upset," *Politico,* March 8, 2016, http://politi.co/1Px65eS.

5. Jason Russell, "Top Michigan Dem Warned That Trump Would Be Competitive There," *Washington Examiner,* November 11, 2016, http://www.washingtonexaminer.com /top-michigan-dem-warned-that-trump-would-be-competitive-there/article/2607183.

6. The Le Pen percentage is from the city of Calais; the Trump figure is from Monroe County, the epicenter of the Downrivers region Dingell refers to.

7. Nick Cohen, *What's Left?: How the Left Lost Its Way,* updated ed. (London: Harper Perennial, 2007), 196.

8. Robert P. Jones, "Trump Crowds See the Passing of White Christian America," *New York Times,* August 9, 2016, https://www.nytimes.com/roomfordebate /2016/08/09/what-is-with-those-crowds-at-trump-rallies/trump-crowds-see-the -passing-on-white-christian-america.

9. Arjun Appadurai, *Fear of Small Numbers: An Essay on the Geography of Anger* (Durham, NC: Duke University Press, 2006).

10. Robert P. Jones, "The Eclipse of White Christian America," *Atlantic,* July 12, 2016, https://www.theatlantic.com/politics/archive/2016/07/the-eclipse-of-white -christian-america/490724/.

11. J. D. Vance, *Hillbilly Elegy: A Memoir of a Family and Culture in Crisis* (New York: Harper, 2016).

12. Rod Dreher, "Trump: Tribune of Poor White People," *American Conservative,* July 22, 2016, http://www.theamericanconservative.com/dreher/trump-us-politics -poor-whites/.

13. Power transition theory holds that rising great powers and declining hegemons are more likely to go to war at moments of transition either because the declining power preemptively attacks to defend its dominance or the rising power goes to war against a world order it seeks to replace. See A. F. K. Organski, *World Politics* (New York: Knopf, 1968); Graham Allison, *Destined for War* (New York: Houghton Mifflin Harcourt, 2017).

14. Vance, *Hillbilly Elegy,* 191. The appeal is also stylistic. As Vance marvels, "No one seems to understand why conventional blunders do nothing to Trump. But in a lot of ways, what elites see as blunders people back home see as someone who—finally— conducts themselves in a relatable way. He shoots from the hip; he's not constantly afraid of offending someone; he'll get angry about politics; he'll call someone a liar or a fraud. This is how a lot of people in the white working class actually talk about politics."

15. Emma Green, "It Was Cultural Anxiety That Drove White, Working-Class Voters to Trump," *Atlantic*, May 9, 2017, https://www.theatlantic.com/politics/archive/2017/05/white-working-class-trump-cultural-anxiety/525771/; James Fallows, "Despair and Hope in Trump's America," *Atlantic*, February 2017, https://www.theatlantic.com/magazine/archive/2017/01/despair-and-hope-in-the-age-of-trump/508799/.

16. Vance, *Hillbilly Elegy*, 192.

17. Christopher Hayes, *Twilight of the Elites: America after Meritocracy* (New York: Broadway Books, 2013), 21–23.

18. Catherine Fieschi, Marley Morris, and Lila Caballero, *Recapturing the Reluctant Radical* (London: Counterpoint, 2012).

19. Hayes, *Twilight of the Elites*, 23–25.

20. "Résultats de la consultation de Mélenchon: un tiers des militants de la France insoumise choisit Macron," *Le Huffington Post*, May 2, 2017, http://www.huffingtonpost.fr/2017/05/02/resultats-de-la-consultation-de-melenchon-un-tiers-de-la-france_a_22065289/.

21. "Pourquoi faire barrage à Marine Le Pen est une nécessité," *L'Humanité*, May 4, 2017, http://www.humanite.fr/pourquoi-faire-barrage-marine-le-pen-est-une-necessite-635601.

22. "Le vote blanc n'a jamais été aussi élevé," *Le Huffington Post*, May 7, 2017, http://www.huffingtonpost.fr/2017/05/07/vote-blanc-record-aux-resultats-de-lelection-presidentielle-201_a_22074048/.

23. Tristan Quinault Maupoil, "Les jeunes plébiscitent Le Pen et Mélenchon, les cadres votent Macron," *Le Figaro*, April 24, 2017.

24. Ronald Inglehart et al., "How Development Leads to Democracy," *Foreign Affairs*, March 1, 2009, https://www.foreignaffairs.com/articles/2009-03-01/how-development-leads-democracy.

25. Roberto S. Foa and Yascha Mounk, "The Democratic Disconnect," *Journal of Democracy* 27, no. 3 (July 2016): 5–17.

26. Amanda Taub, "How Stable Are Democracies? 'Warning Signs Are Flashing Red,'" *New York Times*, November 29, 2016, https://www.nytimes.com/2016/11/29/world/americas/western-liberal-democracy.html.

27. Ronald Inglehart, "The Danger of Deconsolidation: How Much Should We Worry?," *Journal of Democracy* 27, no. 3 (July 2016): 18–23.

28. For Caldwell, multicultural societies only function if everyone is "disarmed" in a cultural sense. It is a clever reformulation of Max Weber's classic theory of the nation-state—the idea that a state is defined by its monopoly on the legitimate use of violence. A modern state should, Caldwell argues, have a monopoly on the moral order. "Any fervently espoused religion threatens that monopoly, as surely as a private militia threatened the old nation state," he contends, and "Muslims are distinguished by their refusal to submit to this spiritual disarmament." The problem, as we have seen from French beaches to butcher shops, is that the ostensibly secular state has not, in many places, retreated to a neutral stance even if it professes to do so. See Christopher Caldwell, *Reflections on the Revolution in Europe: Immigration, Islam and the West* (London: Penguin, 2010), 255.

29. Ibid.

30. Jon Henley, "How Macron Calmed Whirlpool Workers Whipped Up by Le Pen," *Guardian*, April 27, 2017, https://www.theguardian.com/world/2017/apr/27/how-macron-calmed-whirlpool-workers-whipped-up-by-le-pen.

31. Tristan Quinault Maupoil, "Les jeunes plébiscitent Le Pen et Mélenchon, les cadres votent Macron," *Le Figaro*, April 24, 2017, http://www.lefigaro.fr/elections /presidentielles/2017/04/24/35003-20170424ARTFIG00110-les-jeunes-plebiscitent-le -pen-et-melenchon-les-cadres-votent-macron.php.

32. Paul Guyonnet, "La retraite de Marion Maréchal-Le Pen cacherait un 'calcul démoniaque,'" *Le Huffington Post*, May 10, 2017, http://www.huffingtonpost.fr/2017/05/10 /la-retraite-de-marion-marechal-le-pen-cacherait-un-calcul-demon_a_22079096/.

33. Azar Gat, "The Other N-Word: Well-Meaning Westerners, Including Americans, Should Stop Suggesting That Nationalism Is Imaginary. It's Real, Powerful, and Here to Stay," *Foreign Policy*, April 21, 2017, https://foreignpolicy.com/2017/04/21 /the-other-n-word-nationalism-trump-immigration/.

34. "The Problem of Nationalism," Isaiah Berlin Virtual Library, accessed May 12, 2017, http://berlin.wolf.ox.ac.uk/lists/nachlass/probnati.pdf. Berlin traces the idea to the eighteenth-century German philosopher Johann Gottfried von Herder.

35. "The Problem of Nationalism," 3. See also Isaiah Berlin, "The Bent Twig," *Foreign Affairs*, October 1, 1972, https://www.foreignaffairs.com/articles/1972-10-01/bent-twig.

36. "The Problem of Nationalism," 19.

37. Mabel Berezin, *Illiberal Politics in Neoliberal Times: Culture, Security and Populism in the New Europe* (Cambridge, UK: Cambridge University Press, 2009), 256–257. This is an example of the sociologist Albert Hirschman's classic theory of exit, voice, and loyalty. Those who do not have the luxury of protesting through exit seek other means.

38. Paul Scheffer, interview by author, Amsterdam, March 24, 2016.

39. See chapter 10 and Karen Stenner, *The Authoritarian Dynamic* (New York: Cambridge University Press, 2010).

40. See Paul Collier, *Exodus: Immigration and Multiculturalism in the 21st Century* (London: Penguin, 2014). Collier makes a similar argument citing different countries.

41. Ernst Cassirer, *The Myth of the State* (New Haven, CT: Yale University Press, 2009), 286. Cassirer likened this process in Germany to "a serpent that tries to paralyze its victim before attacking them. . . . They were vanquished and subdued before they had realized what had actually happened."

42. "Les moments marquants du débat entre Emmanuel Macron et Marine Le Pen," *RTBF Info*, May 4, 2017, https://www.rtbf.be/info/monde/detail_les-moments -marquants-du-debat-entre-emmanuel-macron-et-marine-le-pen?id=9597121; "Discours d'Emmanuel Macron au Louvre," *En Marche!*, May 3, 2017, http://en-marche.fr/article /emmanuel-macron-president-louvre-carrousel-discours.

43. Felix Marquardt, "Musulmans de France, les raisons d'un malaise," *Le Journal du Dimanche*, June 28, 2015, http://www.lejdd.fr/Societe/Musulmans-de-France-les-raisons -d-un-malaise-la-tribune-de-Felix-Marquardt-739954. Marquardt argues that to be a law-abiding Muslim in France is to be stuck between the far-right, hard-line secularists and Islamic fundamentalists—attacked from three sides.

44. A (FC) and others (FC) v. Secretary of State for the Home Department, [2004] UKHL 56 (H.L.). As the Dutch academic Cas Mudde warned after the Paris attacks of November 2015, "The real, long-term damage is not done by the terrorists, but by the counter-terrorists." See, for example, Cas Mudde, "European Democracy after Paris," *openDemocracy*, December 1, 2015, https://www.opendemocracy.net/can-europe-make-it /cas-mudde/european-democracy-after-paris.

45. "Katie Hopkins Reported to Police after 'Final Solution' Manchester Attack Tweet," *Guardian*, May 23, 2017, https://www.theguardian.com/uk-news/2017/may/23/manchester-attack-police-investigate-katie-hopkins-final-solution-tweet; Katie Hopkins, "You're Right, Theresa. We Cannot Go On Like This," *Daily Mail*, June 4, 2017, http://www.dailymail.co.uk/~/article-4570622/index.html; Allison Pearson of the *Telegraph* also took to Twitter to call for the "internment of thousands of terror suspects now to protect our children." See Allison Pearson's Twitter feed, posted May 23, 2017, https://twitter.com/allisonpearson/status/866919296919904256?lang=en.

Selected Bibliography

The following list includes books and journal articles consulted during the research for this book. All other references not found here are listed in full in the notes.

Abrahamian, Atossa Araxia. *The Cosmopolites: The Coming of the Global Citizen*. New York: Columbia Global Reports, 2015.

Adorno, Theodor W. *The Authoritarian Personality*. New York: Harper, 1950.

Alesina, Alberto, Edward Glaeser, and Bruce Sacerdote. "Why Doesn't the US Have a European-Style Welfare System?" Working Paper. Cambridge, MA: National Bureau of Economic Research, October 2001.

Appadurai, Arjun. *Fear of Small Numbers: An Essay on the Geography of Anger*. Durham, NC: Duke University Press, 2006.

Arendt, Hannah. *The Origins of Totalitarianism*. New York: Harcourt Brace Jovanovich, 1973.

Banting, Keith, and Will Kymlicka, eds. *Multiculturalism and the Welfare State: Recognition and Redistribution in Contemporary Democracies*. New York: Oxford University Press, 2006.

Baubérot, Jean. *La laïcité falsifiée*. Paris: La Découverte, 2014. Kindle edition.

Bawer, Bruce. *Surrender: Appeasing Islam, Sacrificing Freedom*. New York: Anchor Books, 2010.

———. *The New Quislings: How the International Left Used the Oslo Massacre to Silence Debate About Islam*. New York: Broadside, 2012. Kindle edition.

Bencheikh, Soheib. *Marianne et le prophète: L'Islam dans la France laïque*. Paris: Grasset, 1998.

Berezin, Mabel. *Illiberal Politics in Neoliberal Times: Culture, Security and Populism in the New Europe*. New York: Cambridge University Press, 2009.

Berlin, Isaiah. "The Bent Twig." *Foreign Affairs*, October 1972.

Berman, Paul. *The Flight of the Intellectuals*. New York: Melville House, 2011.

Blanshard, Paul. *American Freedom and Catholic Power*. Westport, CT: Greenwood Press, 1984.

Bolkestein, Frits. *The Intellectual Temptation: Dangerous Ideas in Politics*. Bloomington, IN: AuthorHouse, 2013.

Bosma, Martin. *Minderheid in Eigen Land: Hoe Progressieve Strijd Ontaardt in Genocide en ANC-Apartheid*. Amsterdam: Bibliotheca Africana Formicae, 2015.

Bourgeois, Marie-Pierre. *Rose Marine: Enquête sur le FN et l'homosexualité*. Paris: Du Moment, 2016.

Breivik, Anders B. "Anders Behring Breivik's Complete Manifesto '2083—A European Declaration of Independence.'" *Public Intelligence*. Accessed April 2, 2017. https:// publicintelligence.net/anders-behring-breiviks-complete-manifesto-2083-a-european -declaration-of-independence/.

Brenner, Emmanuel [Georges Bensoussan]. *Les Territoires perdus de la République: Antisémitisme, racisme et sexisme en milieu scolaire*. Paris: Mille et Une Nuits, 2002.

Broder, Henryk M. *A Jew in the New Germany*. Urbana: University of Illinois Press, 2004.

Brubaker, Rogers. *Citizenship and Nationhood in France and Germany*. Cambridge, MA: Harvard University Press, 1996.

Bruckner, Pascal. *The Tears of the White Man*. New York: Macmillan, 1987.

———. *The Tyranny of Guilt: An Essay on Western Masochism*. Translated by Steven Rendall. Princeton, NJ: Princeton University Press, 2012.

Buruma, Ian. *Murder in Amsterdam: The Death of Theo van Gogh and the Limits of Tolerance*. London: Atlantic Books, 2006.

Caldwell, Christopher. *Reflections on the Revolution in Europe: Immigration, Islam and the West*. London: Penguin, 2010.

Camus, Albert. *The Plague*. London: Hamish Hamilton, 1948.

Camus, Jean-Yves, and Nicolas Lebourg. *Les droites extrêmes en Europe*. Paris: Seuil, 2015.

Camus, Renaud. *Le grand remplacement*. 3rd ed. Plieux, France: Château de Plieux, 2015. Kindle edition.

Cassirer, Ernst. *The Myth of the State*. New Haven, CT: Yale University Press, 2009.

Charbonnier, Stéphane. *Open Letter: On Blasphemy, Islamophobia, and the True Enemies of Free Expression*. With a foreword by Adam Gopnik. New York: Little, Brown, 2016.

Cohen, Nick. *What's Left?: How the Left Lost Its Way*. London: Harper Perennial, 2007.

Collier, Paul. *Exodus: Immigration and Multiculturalism in the 21st Century*. London: Penguin, 2014.

Collins, Michael. *The Likes of Us: A Biography of the White Working Class*. London: Granta Books, 2004.

Crepaz, Markus M. L. *Trust Beyond Borders: Immigration, the Welfare State, and Identity in Modern Societies*. Ann Arbor: University of Michigan Press, 2008.

Crush, Jonathan, and Sujata Ramachandran. "Xenophobia, International Migration and Development." *Journal of Human Development and Capabilities* 11, no. 2 (May 2010): 209–228.

Dard, Olivier. *Charles Maurras*. Paris: Armand Colin, 2013.

Dlamini, Jacob. *Native Nostalgia*. Auckland Park, South Africa: Jacana Media, 2009.

Eger, Maureen A., and Nate Breznau. "Immigration and the Welfare State: A Cross-Regional Analysis of European Welfare Attitudes." *International Journal of Comparative Sociology* (February 2017), doi:10.1177/0020715217690796.

Eger, Maureen A., and Sarah Valdez, "Neo-Nationalism in Western Europe," *European Sociological Review* 31, no. 1 (2015): 115–130.

———. "From Radical Right to Neo-Nationalist: Political Party Dynamics in Western Europe, 1970–2015." Working Paper, Department of Sociology, Umeå University, Sweden, 2017.

Espersen, Søren, et al. *Danmarks Fremtid: Dit Land, Dit Valg*. Copenhagen: Dansk
    Folkeparti, 2001.

Fichtner, Paula Sutter. *Terror and Toleration: The Habsburg Empire Confronts Islam, 1526–
    1850*. London: Reaktion Books, 2007.

Fieschi, Catherine, Marley Morris, and Lila Caballero. *Recapturing the Reluctant Radi-
    cal*. London: Counterpoint, 2012.

Finkielkraut, Alain. *Au nom de l'autre: Réflexions sur l'antisémitisme qui vient*. Paris: Gal-
    limard, 2003.

———. *L'identité malheureuse*. Paris: Gallimard, 2015.

Foa, Roberto S., and Yascha Mounk. "The Democratic Disconnect." *Journal of Democ-
    racy* 27, no. 3 (July 2016): 5–17.

Ford, Robert Anthony, and Matthew J. Goodwin. *Revolt on the Right: Explaining Sup-
    port for the Radical Right in Britain*. Abingdon, UK: Routledge, 2014.

Gat, Azar. "The Return of Authoritarian Great Powers." *Foreign Affairs*, July 1, 2007.

Goodhart, David. *The British Dream: Successes and Failures of Post-War Immigration*. Lon-
    don: Atlantic Books, 2014.

———. *The Road to Somewhere: The Populist Revolt and the Future of Politics*. London:
    Hurst, 2017.

Goodwin, Matthew, and Caitlin Milazzo. *UKIP: Inside the Campaign to Redraw the Map
    of British Politics*. Oxford: Oxford University Press, 2015.

Gordon, Peter Eli. *Continental Divide: Heidegger, Cassirer, Davos*. Cambridge, MA:
    Harvard University Press, 2012.

Haidt, Jonathan. "When and Why Nationalism Beats Globalism." *American Interest*,
    July 10, 2016.

Hayes, Christopher. *Twilight of the Elites: America after Meritocracy*. New York: Broadway
    Books, 2013.

Hirsi Ali, Ayaan. *Infidel*. New York: Free Press, 2007.

———. *Nomad: A Personal Journey Through the Clash of Civilizations*. London: Simon &
    Schuster UK, 2011.

Houellebecq, Michel. *Submission*. New York: Picador, 2016.

Hussey, Andrew. *The French Intifada: The Long War Between France and Its Arabs*. Lon-
    don: Granta, 2015.

Ibrahimovic, Zlatan. *I Am Zlatan: My Story On and Off the Field*. New York: Random
    House Trade, 2014.

Isaacs, Mark J. *The Undesirables: Inside Nauru*. Richmond, Australia: Hardie Grant, 2014.

Jones, Owen. *Chavs: The Demonization of the Working Class*. London: Verso, 2012.

Joppke, Christian. *Citizenship and Immigration*. Cambridge, UK: Polity, 2011.

———. *Immigration and the Nation-State: The United States, Germany, and Great Britain*.
    New York: Clarendon Press, 2000.

Kaplan, Leonard V., and Rudy Koshar. *The Weimar Moment: Liberalism, Political Theol-
    ogy, and Law*. Lanham, MD: Lexington Books, 2012.

Kepel, Gilles. *Les banlieues de l'islam: naissance d'une religion en France*. Paris: Points, 2015.

Kirchick, James. *The End of Europe: Dictators, Demagogues, and the Coming Dark Age*.
    New Haven, CT: Yale University Press, 2017.

Kirsch, Jonathan. *The Short, Strange Life of Herschel Grynszpan: A Boy Avenger, a Nazi
    Diplomat, and a Murder in Paris*. New York: Liveright, 2013.

Kitschelt, Herbert, and Anthony J. McGann. *The Radical Right in Western Europe: A Comparative Analysis.* Ann Arbor: University of Michigan Press, 2006.

Klausen, Jytte. *The Cartoons That Shook the World.* New Haven, CT: Yale University Press, 2009.

Kulin, J., M. A. Eger, and M. Hjerm. "Immigration or Welfare? The Progressives Dilemma Revisited." *Socius: Sociological Research for a Dynamic World* 2 (March 2, 2016): 1–15.

Le Pen, Marine. *À contre flots.* Paris: Editions Grancher, 2006.

Lilla, Mark. *The Shipwrecked Mind: On Political Reaction.* New York: New York Review of Books, 2016.

Lind, Michael. *The Next American Nation: The Origins and Future of Our National Identity.* New York: Free Press, 1995.

Lindenberg, Daniel. *Le rappel à l'ordre: enquête sur les nouveaux réactionnaires.* Paris: Seuil, 2016.

Malik, Kenan. *From Fatwa to Jihad.* London: Atlantic Books, 2009.

———. *Multiculturalism and Its Discontents: Rethinking Diversity After 9/11.* London: Seagull Books, 2013.

Maspero, François. *Roissy Express: A Journey through the Paris Suburbs.* London: Verso, 1994.

Morjé Howard, Marc. "The Causes and Consequences of Germany's New Citizenship Law." *German Politics* 17, no. 1 (March 2008): 41–62.

Mudde, Cas. "The Populist Radical Right: A Pathological Normalcy." *West European Politics* 33, no. 6 (November 2010): 1167–86.

Mudde, Cas, and Cristóbal Rovira Kaltwasser, eds. *Populism in Europe and the Americas: Threat or Corrective for Democracy?* Cambridge: Cambridge University Press, 2012.

Nawaz, Maajid. *Radical: My Journey from Islamist Extremism to a Democratic Awakening.* London: W. H. Allen, 2013.

Neumann, Klaus. *Across the Seas: Australia's Response to Refugees: A History.* Collingwood, Australia: Black, 2015.

Organski, A. F. K. *World Politics.* New York: Knopf, 1968.

Palmary, Ingrid. *Gender, Sexuality and Migration in South Africa: Governing Morality.* 2016 ed. New York: Palgrave Macmillan, 2017.

Pryor, William H. Jr. "Moral Duty and the Rule of Law." *Harvard Journal of Law & Public Policy* 31 (2008): 153.

Putnam, Robert D. *Bowling Alone: The Collapse and Revival of American Community.* 1st ed. New York: Simon & Schuster, 2001.

———. "E Pluribus Unum: Diversity and Community in the Twenty-First Century: The 2006 Johan Skytte Prize Lecture." *Scandinavian Political Studies* 30, no. 2 (June 2007).

Raspail, Jean. *Le camp des saints: Précédé de Big Other.* Paris: Robert Laffont, 2011.

———. *The Camp of the Saints.* Translated by Norman R. Shapiro. Petoskey, MI: Social Contract Press, 2015.

Roizen, Ron. "Herschel Grynszpan: The Fate of a Forgotten Assassin." *Holocaust and Genocide Studies* 1, no. 2 (1986): 217–28.

Rose, Flemming. *The Tyranny of Silence.* Washington, DC: Cato Institute, 2015.

Roy, Olivier. *La laïcité face à l'islam.* Paris: Fayard, 2013.

———. *Secularism Confronts Islam.* Translated by George Holoch. New York: Columbia University Press, 2009.

Rydgren, Jens, ed. *Class Politics and the Radical Right.* London: Routledge, 2012.

———. *The Populist Challenge: Political Protest and Ethno-Nationalist Mobilization in France.* New York: Berghahn Books, 2003.

Sarrazin, Thilo. *L'Allemagne disparait: Quand un pays se laisse mourir.* Translated by Jean-Baptiste Offenburg. Paris: Editions du Toucan, 2013.

Saunders, Doug. *The Myth of the Muslim Tide: Do Immigrants Threaten the West?* New York: Vintage Books, 2012.

Scheffer, Paul. *Immigrant Nations.* Cambridge, UK: Polity Press, 2011.

Scruton, Roger. "OIKOPHOBIA." *Journal of Education* 175, no. 2 (1993): 93–98.

Sen, Amartya. *Identity and Violence: The Illusion of Destiny.* New York: W. W. Norton, 2007.

Signer, Michael. *Demagogue: The Fight to Save Democracy from Its Worst Enemies.* New York: Palgrave Macmillan, 2009.

Soei, Aydin. *Forsoning.* Copenhagen: Tiderne Skifter, 2016.

———. *Vrede Unge Mænd.* Copenhagen: Tiderne Skifter, 2011.

Steinberg, Jonny. *A Man of Good Hope.* New York: Vintage, 2015.

Stenner, Karen. *The Authoritarian Dynamic.* New York: Cambridge University Press, 2010.

Taussig-Rubbo, Mateo. "Outsourcing Sacrifice: The Labor of Private Military Contractors." *Yale Journal of Law & the Humanities* 21, no. 1 (May 8, 2013).

Thomas, Martin, Bob Moore, and L. J. Butler. *Crises of Empire: Decolonization and Europe's Imperial States.* London: Bloomsbury, 2015.

Todd, Emmanuel. *Who Is Charlie?: Xenophobia and the New Middle Class.* Cambridge, UK: Polity, 2015.

Trilling, Daniel. *Bloody Nasty People: The Rise of Britain's Far Right.* London: Verso Books, 2013.

Vance, J. D. *Hillbilly Elegy: A Memoir of a Family and Culture in Crisis.* New York: Harper, 2016.

Weil, Patrick, and Nicolas Truong. *Le sens de la République.* Paris: Grasset, 2015.

Ye'or, Bat. *Eurabia: The Euro-Arab Axis.* Madison, NJ: Fairleigh Dickinson, 2005.

Zakaria, Fareed. *The Future of Freedom: Illiberal Democracy at Home and Abroad.* New York: W. W. Norton & Company, 2007.

———. "The Rise of Illiberal Democracy." *Foreign Affairs,* November 1, 1997.

Zemmour, Éric. *Le suicide français.* Paris: Albin Michel, 2015.

Interviews

All the interviews below were conducted by the author. They are listed in chronological order, including some interviews not cited in the book.

Sjoerd Sjoerdsma, The Hague, October 12, 2015.

Sijbolt Noorda, Amsterdam, October 14, 2015.

Khaterah Parwani, Copenhagen, October 19, 2015.

Jakob Scharf (#1), Copenhagen, October 20, 2015.

Morten Bødskov, Copenhagen, October 20, 2015.

Andreas Kamm, Copenhagen, October 20, 2015.

Lars Trier Mogensen, Copenhagen, October 20, 2015.

Deprose Muchena, Johannesburg, November 3, 2015.

Jakob van Garderen, Pretoria,
　　November 4, 2015.
Sipho Malunga, Johannesburg,
　　November 5, 2015.
Fanie du Toit, Cape Town,
　　December 8, 2015.
William Kerfoot, Cape Town,
　　December 9, 2015.
Lynne Minion, Sydney, January 7, 2016.
Ivan O'Mahoney, Sydney, January 8, 2016.
Mark Isaacs, Sydney, January 8, 2016.
Philip Ruddock, Sydney, January 12, 2016.
Ben Doherty, Sydney, January 13, 2016.
Tim O'Connor, Sydney, January 13, 2016.
Ahmed and Marwan (pseudonyms)
　　and other detainees (#1),
　　Villawood Detention Center,
　　Sydney, January 14, 2016.
Claire Hammerton, Sydney,
　　January 15, 2016.
Elaine Pearson, Sydney, January 15, 2016.
Andrew Bolt, Sydney, January 21, 2016.
Sara Whyte, Sydney, January 21, 2016.
John Menadue, Sydney, January 21, 2016.
Daniel Webb, Melbourne,
　　January 27, 2016.
Gillian Triggs, Melbourne,
　　January 27, 2016.
Klaus Neumann, Melbourne,
　　January 27, 2016.
Pamela Curr, Melbourne,
　　January 28, 2016.
David Manne, Melbourne,
　　January 28, 2016.
Julian Burnside, Melbourne,
　　January 28, 2016.
Mohammad Baqiri, Melbourne,
　　January 29, 2016.
Waleed Aly, Melbourne, January 29, 2016.
Andrew Wilkie, Canberra,
　　February 2, 2016.
Melissa Parke, Canberra,
　　February 3, 2016.
Anna Burke, Canberra, February 3, 2016.
Sarah Hanson-Young, Canberra,
　　February 3, 2016.

Neil Pharoah, Sydney, February 6, 2016.
Chris Kenny, Sydney, February 8, 2016.
Ahmed and Marwan (pseudonyms)
　　and other detainees (#2),
　　Villawood Detention Center,
　　Sydney, February 8, 2016.
Thomas Gammeltoft-Hansen,
　　Copenhagen, March 3, 2016.
Kenneth Kristensen Berth,
　　Copenhagen, March 4, 2016.
Bent Melchior, Copenhagen,
　　March 7, 2016.
Thomas Bagger, Berlin, March 8, 2016.
Robin Alexander, Berlin, March 8, 2016.
Mariam Lau, Berlin, March 9, 2016.
Andrew Hussey, Paris, March 14, 2016.
Saïd Mahrane, Paris, March 15, 2016.
Bas Heijne, Paris, March 15, 2016.
Nicolas Baverez, Paris, March 16, 2016.
Gaspard Koenig, Paris, March 16, 2016.
Thierry Baudet, Amsterdam,
　　March 21, 2016.
Rinus Penninx, Gouda, March 21, 2016.
Janny Groen, Amsterdam,
　　March 22, 2016.
Zihni Özdil, Amsterdam, March 22,
　　2016.
Thijs Kleinpaste, Amsterdam,
　　March 23, 2016.
Joris Rijbroek, Amsterdam,
　　March 23, 2016.
Paul Scheffer, Amsterdam,
　　March 24, 2016.
Kustaw Bessems, Amsterdam,
　　March 24, 2016.
Khan Ahmadzai and other migrants,
　　Calais, April 6–7, 2016.
Amin Bagdouche, Calais, April 8, 2016.
Edwin Wagenveld, The Hague,
　　April 9, 2016.
Arne Hardis, Copenhagen, April 11, 2016.
Lars Olsen, Humlebæk, April 11, 2016.
Rasmus Brygger, Copenhagen,
　　April 11, 2016.
Yildiz Akdogan, Copenhagen,
　　April 12, 2016.

Naser Khader, Copenhagen, April 12, 2016.

Anders Samuelsen, Copenhagen, April 12, 2016.

Herbert Pundik, Copenhagen, April 12, 2016.

Thomas Gyldal Petersen, Herlev, April 13, 2016.

Søren Espersen, Copenhagen, April 13, 2016.

Jakob Scharf (#2), Copenhagen, April 14, 2016.

Johanne Schmidt-Nielsen, Copenhagen, April 15, 2016.

Aydin Soei, Copenhagen, April 15, 2016.

Willem Schinkel, Rotterdam, April 18, 2016.

Alexander van Hattem and other provincial legislators, Den Bosch, April 18, 2016.

Merijn Oudenampsen, Amsterdam, April 20, 2016.

Tanja Jadnanansing, The Hague, April 21, 2016.

Peter Rodrigues, Leiden, April 21, 2016.

Paul Schnabel, Amsterdam, April 21, 2016.

Bram (pseudonym, #1), Amsterdam, April 21, 2016.

Leo Lucassen, Amsterdam, April 22, 2016.

Christian Schmidt, Berlin, May 3, 2016.

Alexander Gauland, Potsdam, May 4, 2016.

Daniel Lindenberg, Paris, May 16, 2016.

Patrick Weil, Paris, May 16, 2016.

Julien Aubert, Paris, May 17, 2016.

Marine Le Pen, Nanterre, May 18, 2016.

Caroline Monnot and Olivier Faye, Paris, May 18, 2016.

Jean Raspail, Paris, May 19, 2016.

Fouad Ben Ahmed, Bobigny, May 19, 2016.

Various migrants, Calais, June 13–14, 2016.

Samuel and Pascal (leaders of Reprenons Calais, no surnames given), Calais, June 15, 2016.

Damien Carême, Grande-Synthe, June 15, 2016.

Jean-Yves Camus, Paris, June 16, 2016.

Robert Ménard, Béziers, June 21, 2016.

David Rachline, Paris, June 28, 2016.

Julien Rochedy, Paris, June 29, 2016.

Alain Finkielkraut, Paris, June 30, 2016.

Abdelkader Ben-Ali, Amsterdam, July 2, 2016.

Frits Bolkestein, Amsterdam, July 4, 2016.

Jens Spahn, Berlin, July 7, 2016.

Philipp Lengsfeld, Berlin, July 8, 2016.

Ingrid Palmary and Jean-Pierre Misago, Johannesburg, July 28, 2016.

Mary Louw, Johannesburg, July 28, 2016.

Ngqabutho Mabhena, Johannesburg, July 29, 2016.

Loren Landau, Johannesburg, August 1, 2016.

Baron Mukeba and Prince Abenge Médard, Johannesburg, August 2, 2016.

Marc Gbaffou and Prince Abenge Médard, Johannesburg, August 4, 2016.

Bram (pseudonym, #2), Amsterdam, September 12, 2016.

Ahmed Marcouch, The Hague, September 14, 2016.

Index

Sasha Polakow-Suransky is an Open Society Foundations fellow and was an op-ed editor for the *New York Times* from 2011 to 2015. He was a senior editor at *Foreign Affairs* from 2007 to 2011 and holds a doctorate in modern history from Oxford University, where he was a Rhodes Scholar from 2003 to 2006. His writing has appeared in the *American Prospect, Boston Globe, International Herald Tribune, New Republic, Guardian,* and *Newsweek*. His first book, *The Unspoken Alliance: Israel's Secret Relationship with Apartheid South Africa,* was published by Pantheon in 2010. He divides his time between London and New York.

The Nation Institute

NATION BOOKS

Founded in 2000, **Nation Books** has become a leading voice in American independent publishing. The imprint's mission is to tell stories that inform and empower just as they inspire or entertain readers. We publish award-winning and bestselling journalists, thought leaders, whistle-blowers, and truthtellers, and we are also committed to seeking out a new generation of emerging writers, particularly voices from under-represented communities and writers from diverse backgrounds. As a publisher with a focused list, we work closely with all our authors to ensure that their books have broad and lasting impact. With each of our books we aim to constructively affect and amplify cultural and political discourse and to engender positive social change.

Nation Books is a project of The Nation Institute, a nonprofit media center established to extend the reach of democratic ideals and strengthen the independent press. The Nation Institute is home to a dynamic range of programs: the award-winning Investigative Fund, which supports groundbreaking investigative journalism; the widely read and syndicated website TomDispatch; journalism fellowships that support and cultivate over twenty-five emerging and high-profile reporters each year; and the Victor S. Navasky Internship Program.

For more information on Nation Books and The Nation Institute, please visit:

www.nationbooks.org
www.nationinstitute.org
www.facebook.com/nationbooks.ny
Twitter: @nationbooks